VACATION TOURISTS

AND

NOTES OF TRAVEL

IN

1860.

LONDON:
R. CLAY, SON, AND TAYLOR, PRINTERS,
BREAD STREET HILL.

VACATION TOURISTS

AND

NOTES OF TRAVEL

IN 1860

EDITED BY

FRANCIS GALTON, M.A. F.R.S.

AUTHOR OF "THE ART OF TRAVEL," ETC.

Cambridge

MACMILLAN AND CO

AND 23, HENRIETTA STREET, COVENT GARDEN

London

1861

PREFACE.

THE origin of this volume may be shortly stated. Two of the gentlemen who have contributed papers, consulted with the publishers as to the form in which notes of their respective tours could be placed before the public. In both cases it was felt that some record of their travels ought certainly to appear ; but, while an attempt to compress them into the limits of an ordinary magazine article would plainly diminish their value, the materials did not suffice for separate books. As the difficulty felt in the case of these travellers was far from unusual, it occurred to the publishers that a volume of several tours made in 1860 would supply a palpable want in literature; and, on their applying to me to edit such a book, I fully entered into their views, and agreed to do so.

A little inquiry soon showed a sufficient amount of valuable matter available for our purpose ; and thus, at a comparatively short notice, I have been able to collect what I trust will amply justify the idea from which the book has sprung. Certainly these travels of 1860 will be of no diminished value because they are concisely written, are bound within one cover, and are presented in a readable form.

It depends on the favour of the public, whether or no this volume will be succeeded by others—whether, in fact, "Vacation Tourists" shall become an annual publication. There is abundant space for future writers to occupy: the social and political life of foreign nations offers a wide field and changeful surface for examination; newly discovered objects of interest, and fresh openings for the yearly tide of Vacation travellers, are of constant occurrence; scientific tours offer an endless variety of results; while narratives of adventure never fail to interest.

FRANCIS GALTON.

March 7, 1861.
42, Rutland Gate, S.W.

CONTENTS.

VACATION TOURISTS, &c. IN 1860.

1. *NAPLES AND GARIBALDI.*

BY W. G. CLARK, M.A. F.R.G.S.

Through Turin to Naples.—I left London on the 18th of August, for the tour which has become a matter of annual recurrence. It had been my intention to go to Scotland, but the almost incessant rain which spoilt our last summer drove me to seek for sunshine in some southern land, and the interest attaching to Garibaldi's daring enterprise drew me irresistibly to Italy. The route from England to Naples, travelled every year by thousands of our countrymen and not new to myself, would, in ordinary circumstances, be too hackneyed a topic; and a writer who should suppose that he had anything to say about it which had not been said before—the only justification for writing at all—would show great confidence in his own powers of observation.

But I saw Naples under circumstances the reverse of ordinary—at that critical period when it was the centre of interest to all the nations of Europe; during the occurrence of events so strange and sudden that they resembled incidents of a romantic melodrama rather than real history. The achievements of Rollo and Robert Guiscard were repeated before the eyes of men who are never tired of saying that they live in a prosaic age. The interest of these events is scarcely abated, for they involve momentous consequences yet to come. The great captain who is now playing the part of Cincinnatus at

Caprera has potentially—like another captain who once enjoyed a temporary repose in the neighbouring Elba—an army at his command. He is one of the great powers, who, though not officially represented, makes his presence felt in all the councils of Europe.

I reached Naples two days before the departure of the King. What I saw and heard during the eventful three weeks which followed, will form the main part of my story. I prefer to tell this story (at the risk of occasional repetition) in the words of a journal written on the spot, and at the first leisure hour after the occurrences. In this journal I have corrected nothing but slips of the pen. I have inserted no *ex post facto* prophecies. I have merely added a note here and there by way of correction or explanation.

As the political interest of the time is my only justification for writing at all, I have cut out from my narrative almost all that had not relation to passing events. The excavations at Pompeii and the treasures of the Museo Borbonico have, for the present, lost their interest. Besides, there would be an incongruity in thus mixing contemporary history with antiquarianism and dilettantism; nor would the space at my disposal allow me to do so, in any case. I might have touched in passing many such topics, and given conclusions without arguments; but I remember the warning, "Brevis esse laboro, obscurus fio," and I have reason to think that a love of brevity is liable to be mistaken for an affectation of smartness and a tendency to dogmatism.

I crossed from Folkestone to Boulogne in a storm of wind and rain. The rain accompanied me to Paris, scarcely abated during the two days of my stay there, chased me in flying showers to Macon; then, withdrawing for a while, hung in masses of threatening cloud in front and flank as we crossed the plains and wound along the valleys, guarded with bastions of limestone crag on either hand, the first approaches to the great fortress of the Alps, to Culoz, now, alas! a frontier place no more, thence by the lake of Bourget and Chambéry, where we saw skeletons of triumphal arches destined for the reception of the new master, to St. Jean de Maurienne, where we exchanged the railway for the diligence. The route of the Mont Cenis is, to my mind, the least picturesque of all the Alpine passes. But what it lacks in scenic beauty it makes up in historical interest, as being the route of Hannibal.* At Lanslebourg the clouds, which I had been comparing to hovering bodies of barbarians hanging on the line of the Carthaginians' march, burst upon us in a torrent of rain which lasted to Susa. When at length we reached Turin, at one A.M. (about thirty hours after leaving Paris), there was a cloudless sky overhead, and the soft sweet air of summer Italy to breathe and move in.

I had been much entertained by one of my companions in the banquette of the diligence—an Englishman going to join Garibaldi. Evidently a gentleman, he had "roughed it" through life with the strangest comrades. He had dug for gold in Australia, had driven an omnibus for six months in Melbourne, &c. &c., and now was about to seek his fortune in Italy. "Not," he said, "that he cared a button for one side or the other; he wanted if possible to get a commission in the Sardinian army, and meanwhile, at all events, to have a lark."

* This is conclusively established in a work entitled, "A Treatise on Hannibal's Passage of the Alps," by Robert Ellis, B.D. Fellow of St. John's College, Cambridge, 1853. The subsidiary arguments derived from the Peutingerian table, the names of places, &c., however ingenious and probable, are less convincing than the main arguments, and tend, on a first reading, rather to invalidate the conclusions. I am disposed to think that Mr. Ellis lays rather too much stress on the fact that the plains of Italy are visible from a point near the summit of the pass. Polybius, from his language, seems to suppose that the plains would be visible, as a matter of course, from the summit of any pass, and he himself probably crossed the Alps only once in the way of business; and if he had such weather as has always been my fortune in crossing the Mont Cenis, he could not verify the fact. The story of Hannibal's encouraging his men by showing them Italy is, perhaps, after all only a rhetorical figment. Everybody not familiar with Alpine travel would take it for granted that Italy was visible from the summit (not having a clear understanding of the distinction between "peaks" and "passes"), and the situation, "Hannibal pointing out Italy to his soldiers," is too striking not to be accepted as true: "ut pueris placeat et declamatio fiat." I doubt, too, whether we have got at the true signification of λευκόπετρον. However this may be, Mr. Ellis seems to me to have proved his point abundantly.

I fancy that a good many of the volunteers, if they would confess it, were actuated by similar feelings.

I stayed nearly a week at Turin, where I found several old friends and acquaintances, several of them Neapolitan exiles, who gave me letters to their friends at home. Among them was Baron Charles Poerio, the gentlest and most innocent victim that was ever tortured by tyrant. I observed in him, as well as in others of his fellow-prisoners whom I saw at Naples afterwards, a subdued manner that was infinitely touching. It was as if long imprisonment had crushed their spirit and robbed life of its vitality. Poerio said that, during his short tenure of office, the king affected to treat him as a confidential friend, would offer him a cigar when he went for an audience, and so forth. On the anniversary of the day of his accepting office, he had the chains put on in the court of one of the prisons, the benevolent monarch looking on from a window.

I went one day to a charming villa on the "Collina," near Moncalieri, to visit an exile of a different race. I found him playing with his children, as youthful at heart as any of them. No prison had bowed his spirit down, and even eleven years of exile had not sickened his hope of triumphant return. He had not a shadow of doubt that the sword of Garibaldi would open through Venice a road to Hungary. "Shall we meet next year in London?" I said at parting. "We shall meet next year, if anywhere, at Pesth," was the reply.

On the 28th of August I went to Genoa, on the chance of finding a steamer for Livorno or Naples, there being no trustworthy information to be had in Turin. When I arrived there, I found that I had no choice but to wait till the 31st for the French boat. Three days soon passed among the varied sights of Genoa, the most beautiful as well as one of the busiest of the cities of the world. Garibaldi's portrait was in every window, ballad-singers were chanting his praises, and as you passed a group standing in the street or seated at the *café*, you were sure to hear the magic name. I was made all the more eager to get to Naples, fearing that he might get there before me.

I here insert some leaves of my journal, omitting, as I said, almost all that related merely to the regular "sights" on the way.

Aug. 23.—Turin is the most regularly built city in the world. It would have delighted an ancient Greek. Hippodamus himself might have planned it. Pausanias would have been in ecstasies if he had seen it, all its lines straight and all its angles right-angles. And in his eyes the beauty of the regular city would have been enhanced by contrast with the rough shapeless mountains, glimpses of which you get at the end of the streets that run towards the north and west. Only the Contrada del Po deviates somewhat from the due direction, but this is scarcely appreciable by the eye. The spacious porticoes are thronged with people, notwithstanding that this is the season of the *Villegiatura,* and there is "nobody in town."

I went this morning to call upon a friend at the Ministry of Foreign Affairs, which is modestly lodged in a corner of the Piazza Castello. I was surprised with the quietness of the whole establishment. The porter was dozing at the door; my friend the *employé* was not at home, nobody was waiting for an audience, and M. de Cavour was "disengaged" in the inner room. "Did I want to see him?" asked the porter. Having no pretext for an interview with the great man, and having neither invention, nor impudence sufficient to extemporize one, I was obliged to decline the honour, and I went away wondering at the stillness which reigned at what may be called the central point of European diplomacy. It reminded me of the brain, which, though the source of all sensation, has no sensation itself.

Aug. 24.—This morning I had a call from Signor ——, a ministerial deputy, and an able as well as honest man. He takes a gloomy view of the state of things in Italy. "The

Ministry is excessively embarrassed by the exigencies of France, on the one hand; by the remonstrances of the great Powers, on the other; and by the popular enthusiasm for Garibaldi, on the third. (We may suppose an Executive to have *three* hands, at least: in this case all of them are tied.) Garibaldi is a brave man, but 'a fool' (*sic*); he is easily led by the people about him, and he is surrounded by the most worthless advisers—as, for example, Crespi. The Mazzini party are taking advantage of the discontent excited by the late measures of the Ministry against the volunteers, and of Garibaldi's easy temper, and hope to proclaim first the Dictatorship of Garibaldi, and then the Republic in Southern Italy. The ultra-liberals are blind to facts and consequences; they will not take account of the difficulties in their way; they menace Rome in spite of France and Venetia, in spite of Germany (for it is certain that Prussia has agreed to make common cause with Austria).

"Things are going from bad to worse, and we may lose all we have gained. Old animosities—*la politica di campanile*—are reviving again, and are fanned by the ultra-liberals for their own purposes. The people were humiliated at the loss of Savoy and Nice, but all reasonable men felt that the Government had no choice. The citizens of Turin cared much more for Savoy than Nice, because the change brought the French frontier within sight of their walls. Turin is now a defenceless frontier town, and can never be the capital of Italy."

Aug. 25.—I met another gentleman, neither deputy nor ministerial. He was enthusiastic for Garibaldi, "the honest man and great captain." "Cavour," he said, "has lost all his popularity, not so much from the cession of Savoy and Nice—for there was no resisting the armed brigand who took them—but from the way in which it was done. Cavour did it jauntily and unconcernedly, when, in decency, he ought to have worn an air of dejection. To parody what Jean Jacques said of a bishop: 'Quelque véridique qu'on soit, il faut bien mentir quelques fois quand on est diplomate;' but Cavour lied gratuitously. People have lost all confidence in him since he has sold himself to the devil.

"Garibaldi is true as steel; he will conquer Naples and proclaim the Rè Galantuomo King of Italy, who will then find some honester man than Cavour to be his prime minister."

Aug 26.—*Notes of a Conversation with* ——. "The franchise in Piedmont is given to all who pay forty francs per annum in direct taxes, which, in a country divided into small holdings, is almost equivalent to universal suffrage. But all landholders are conservative, and those of Piedmont Proper exercise it admirably; they are the mainstay of the constitution.

"The so-called Tuscan autonomy is not an autonomy in fact; the word is misapplied. It means in this case that, for the present, the judicial system of Tuscany is maintained intact. For instance, if a dispute arises in Tuscany, it cannot be tried at Turin till they send it for trial.

"Ten years ago, I foresaw that the idea of Italian unity was mounting like a flood, and would sweep all before it. The existence of this idea is a great fact which people at home would not see; I mean, secretaries of state. Naples might have been saved to the king, if he had joined Piedmont. In March, 1859, Lord Malmesbury wanted Sir James Hudson to go to Naples and advise the king to grant a constitution. He said, 'It is no use unless you allow me to advise his sending twenty thousand troops or so, to make a demonstration to the Italian side; a very small demonstration will suffice.' Lord Malmesbury refused; 'he did not wish Naples to be mixed up in the quarrel between Austria and France.' Now the quarrel between Austria and France was 'in the second plan.' The battle of Italian unity was uppermost in men's minds. The great Powers urged the Piedmontese Government to stop the departure of the volunteers as soon as Garibaldi turned his designs on the mainland. Legally, there is no distinction between Sicily and Naples, but morally there is a distinction, because the Sicilians had been deluded by the Bourbons. The promise of a constitution, made in 1812, was never fulfilled. And, as you remind me, Lord Palmerston said in parliament, apropos of non-intervention, that there was no point of international law which is not liable to exceptions in practice. Farini's circular was the result of this diplomatic pressure. If after that he had not prevented the departure of the volunteers, the power of Minister of the Interior would have been at an end. He could not act otherwise than he did. The papers cry out, but their influence is almost *nil*, since Parliament has begun to perform its functions regularly. Ten years ago, the press was very powerful. Cavour himself used to write articles. Now each paper is the organ of some little knot of politicians. Like a volcano (as you say) where there are at first a number of little outlets which all cease when a great crater is formed. If Garibaldi is beaten, the Piedmontese Government will see that it must bide its time; it will still represent the idea of unity, which sooner or later will be realized in fact. The more moderate papers are beginning to see the necessity of waiting for an opportunity of getting Venetia.

"If Piedmont receives any further accession of territory, there is a notion afloat that France will demand the island of Sardinia as the price of her assent. The plains are enormously fertile, yielding, they say, forty-fold. A large outlay would be required for draining, &c. to bring land now idle under cultivation. The volcanic rocks and the high mountains which prevent a free current of wind from west to east, are the cause of the unhealthiness of the place. All the island is unhealthy part of the year, and part is unhealthy all the year round. Sardinia is the most retrograde portion of the kingdom, and disaffected because the high taxation has been most felt there. There is an English party and a French party eager for annexation to one or other country, which is rich, and, as they think, would spend money there, but it would not strengthen either. The Bay of La Maddalena was of service to England in the former war, when they were blockading Toulon; but now that steam-vessels have taken the place of sailing-vessels and can keep the sea in any wind, it will no longer be of service even in war. But politicians at home are governed by traditional views about British interests. That is why we stick to the Ionian Islands, which are no use to us. If we could only get rid of the notion that France is our natural enemy, and that we are bound to keep up posts of possible annoyance to her! The Ionian Islands are a perpetual sore between England and Greece. With Malta it is different. It is an island-fortress—prize of war—and I am for keeping it as long as we can. It would be ridiculous at Malta, or Gibraltar, to submit the question of ownership to universal suffrage.

"The notion prevalent in Germany that the line of the Mincio, or at all events that of the Adige, is necessary to their security in a strategical point of view, is quite unfounded. It has not even the excuse of tradition. Read Metternich's letters, written at the time of the Congress of Vienna, and you will see that he was unwilling to accept the fatal gift of Northern Italy. But now that they have got the four fortresses, and that the Germans conceive their honour as well as their safety involved in the Austrian retention of Venetia, they will keep it as long as they can.

"After all, we must submit all questions at last to the inexorable logic of facts (as the French say)."

GENOA. *Aug.* 29.—Walked for an hour after sunset with a French gentleman, whose acquaintance I had made at dinner, up and down the delightful promenade of the Acqua Sola. It occupies an elevated platform on the eastern side of the city, flanked externally by the walls of the inner circle of fortification, and looking over a valley set thick with painted houses and gardens, the sea to the right, and on the left the hills crowned with fortresses. It is planted with rows of ilex, acacia and plane, and in the centre is an oval pond with a fountain, set round with weeping willows. It is well provided with stone seats. As we sat upon one of these, looking towards the sea, still lighted with reflected splendour from the west—"It is a shame," said the Frenchman, "to talk politics in so lovely a place, and at such a time. We ought to talk poetry."

"It is your restless Emperor," said I, "who forces everybody to think and to talk politics at all places and times."

"Maybe so," he replied; "but his view is the true view, namely, that there will be no secure and lasting peace for Europe until its political system is based upon the principle of nationalities. It may cost us years of disturbance to establish this principle, but it will be the best for peace in the long run. Europe will then be in a position of stable equilibrium (as the mathematicians say). This is the object of French policy. Surely it is nobler and wiser than the hand-to-mouth purblind policy of your Government, which huddles up all quarrels, and has for its object only the adjournment of war in the interest of merchants and fundholders."

He spoke as volubly and rapidly as an actor in a Greek comedy delivering the πνῖγος. When at last he paused for breath, I interposed: "Stop! what do you mean by 'the principle of nationalities?'"

"What do I mean! Surely it is clear enough. It is a phrase universally used. Everybody knows it."

"But if it has a definite meaning, it is capable of definition."

"Well, I suppose we may express it thus: Every nation has a right to belong to itself, and to choose its own form of government, and its own governors."

"What do you mean by a nation?"

"Diable! mon cher Monsieur, comme vous vous posez en Socrate! The words of which one knows the meaning best are precisely those which one feels it most difficult to define. Of such words no one asks for a definition in good faith, but only for the sake of puzzling you, and in order to divert a question of facts into a question of words."

"Don't be angry! In all good faith, I do not know in what sense you use the word 'nation.' Its etymology—"

"Oh, confound etymology—je m'en soucie guère. I use the

word in its modern sense, meaning a people of the same race, speaking the same language, inhabiting the same country."

"As for instance?"

"The French, the English, the Italians—"

"Stay a moment. I doubt whether your instances are to the point. Are the people in Brittany, Lorraine, Alsace, and Gascony, of the same race as the people in the centre of France, and do they speak the same language? Yet they are integral parts of the French nation. So it is with the Welsh, the Scotch Highlanders, the people in the Channel Islands—they are not of the same race, nor do they speak the same language as the bulk of the English nation, yet they belong to it, inseparably attached. Of Ireland I do not speak—"

"No, you would find a difficulty there."

"I may find a difficulty in combating the rooted prejudices existing on the Continent with respect to Ireland, but you must admit—without prejudice to the future rights of King Macmahon—that it forms at present a part of the united kingdom, while two-thirds of the people are of Celtic blood: and a small portion still speak a Celtic tongue. As for Italy, it is inhabited by a multitude of races: Celts and Lombards in the north, Greeks in the south, and a fusion of old Italic tribes in the centre. As to language, a Lombard peasant and a Neapolitan peasant are as mutually unintelligible as an Englishman and a German."

"But there is one language for the educated classes. They understand each other."

"Yes, but that was not what you meant when you mentioned 'a people of the same race speaking the same language.' Look at Hungary again. I suppose you would help in the establishment of a separate Hungarian nationality if you could?"

"Oh, certainly."

"Well, in Hungary there are, I believe, at least four separate races, and four distinct languages, yet all these are united against the Austrian Government, and desire to form one independent nation. We read in the papers how cordially they fraternized at Pesth on the feast of St. Stephen, the other day."

"I admit, my definition will scarcely apply to actual facts; it is rather a definition of the beau ideal of a nation. Let me see if I can modify it so as to make it practical. You English can only comprehend what is practical. As the Emperor said, *you* will never go to war for an idea."

"For my part, I don't see that the annexation of Savoy is a whit more ideal than the annexation of Scinde, unless the combination of fraud with force in the case of Savoy—"

"Ah!" (with a prolonged sneer), "quant à la fraude un fils d'Albion a beau parler."

"Allons! let us not quarrel like a couple of commis-voyageurs, but revenons à nos moutons. By the way, where does that phrase come from? Is it somewhere in Molière?"

"No; it is in the *Avocat-Patelin*, where you will find the source of a great many popular sayings." He mentioned several; and, restored to good humour by this display of erudition, he said with a smile, "Ah oui, nos moutons; où en étions-nous?"

"You were proposing, I said, to modify your definition of a nation. If you had stuck to it, I would have asked you further what you meant by 'race,' and then what you meant by 'language;' and each of these words seems to me to be as difficult to define, practically, as 'nation' itself; that is to say, to lay down any rule capable of practical application as to what constitutes identity and what diversity in race and language."

"Well," said the Frenchman, "let us not quibble any more about words, let us come to things. I say then that a people, of whatever race or language, wishing to separate itself from, or join itself to, another people, has a right to do so."

"Pardon me, I don't wish to quibble about words; but in using the term 'people,' you are in fact begging the question as much as if you had said 'nation.'"

"You are hard to satisfy. I will say, if you like, instead of 'a people,' 'a number of persons living together.'"

"Therefore, if the city of Bordeaux, for example, thinking its material interests more closely connected with England than with France, were to vote for annexing itself to the former country, the French Government would acquiesce?"

"To say the truth, I don't think it would."

"That is to say, that when it found its interest opposed to its principle, it would follow its interest."

"No; your *reductio ad absurdum* is itself absurd. When I said 'a number of persons,' I meant, of course, such a number as might reasonably claim to form a separate nation."

"But in the case I put, it was not proposed that Bordeaux should form a separate nation."

"It would be ridiculous for Bordeaux to pretend to have a will of its own distinct from that of France, of which it forms perhaps in population the three-hundredth part. We punished, if you remember, a similar insolence on the part of Toulon."

"Yes, and you punished a similar insolence on the part of La Vendée, without any particular reference to the numbers of the revolted population."

"That was in time of war, and the necessity of self-preservation imperiously demanded the reconquest of Toulon and La Vendée."

"If you assist the Hungarians to revolt, will it not be 'time of war' then, and will not the necessity of self-preservation, from an Austrian point of view, demand the reconquest of Hungary?"

"Have you then no sympathy with an oppressed people? (You will permit me to use the word in this case.) Do you not think that it is the duty of a great and free nation to protect the weak against the strong?"

"Certainly, but then independent states, represented by their respective governments existing for the time being, have their rights. These may be respected, and yet much good done in behalf of what you call oppressed nationalities, by peaceful diplomacy, friendly advice, grave remonstrance, or even formal protest. I doubt whether the principles of international law (which, I imagine, knows nothing of your 'nationalities'), would sanction a declaration of war in any case."

"There are extreme cases in which necessity knows no law, international or other. The state of Italy could not have been remedied last year without war."

"I doubt that. In a general congress, Austria, by the threat of war, might have been induced to erect Lombardo-Venetia into an independent kingdom, with free institutions, under the Archduke Maximilian, who was personally popular. I believe that the state of Italy would have been better than it is now. At all events a congress ought to have been tried. France would have saved 50,000 men and 500,000,000 of francs, but then Louis Napoleon would have missed the glory of commanding in a real battle, and Nice and Savoy would have still belonged to Sardinia. When once you unchain the demon of war, you know not where the end will be. Over and over again peace has been made at last without any reference to the original objects of the war. No evils are comparable to those of war. The English policy to adjourn war as long as possible, seems to me to be the really noble and humane policy. Induce oppressive governments to adopt gentler means of keeping public order, and time may soften down the fiercest antipathies. Alsace and Lorraine, which detested the yoke of France at first, have now become French at heart; but if Germany had been constantly inciting them to revolt by promises of military support, successive insurrections would have been quenched in blood, and mutual hatred perpetuated for centuries. The policy of your Government towards other nations seems to me the most mischievous possible; it keeps up discontent among the people, who are perpetually told how much they are oppressed, and it piques the pride of the rulers, who will not relax their system lest it should be said that they do so from fear of France."

Surprised that I had not been interrupted during this long speech, and receiving no reply when I paused of my own accord, I turned towards my companion. He was, or feigned to be, asleep.

Aug. 31.—I sailed from Genoa by one of the French steamers "making the scala," as the coasting voyage from Marseilles to Naples is termed. There was a great crowd of passengers—the Neapolitan and Sardinian boats having been taken up for purposes of war.

Next morning we stopped at Leghorn, and the morning after at Civita Vecchia, and remained there six or seven hours, enough to enable a party of American gentlemen to pay their visit to Rome, by aid of the new railway. They returned in triumph, having effected their purpose, and spent, as they said, "fifty minutes, sir, in the E-ternal City!"

A moist scirocco, the prevailing wind during last autumn, brought languor and discomfort to all. We were right glad when about six next morning, September 2, we found ourselves sailing by Capo Miseno, and entering the Bay of Naples. Everything, however, was shrouded in a fog more worthy of England than of Italy.

As soon as we came to anchor, we were boarded by large parties of Neapolitans, chiefly in the new uniform of the National Guard, coming to meet their friends.

After a very cursory examination of passports and luggage, we drove off to the Hotel Vittoria, where I established myself for the next three weeks, in an upper room, looking over the ilex, acacias, palms, and pepper-trees of the Villa Reale.

I kept my eyes and ears open, went diligently wherever there was anything to be seen and heard; taking copious notes day by day, and occasionally writing long letters to friends in England. The tomb of Virgil, Cumæ, Avernus, Pompeii, the statues and frescoes of the Museum, occupy a considerable space in my note-books. All this I suppress for the reasons before mentioned.

Extract of a Letter from Naples, dated Tuesday, Sept. 4.

Naples is officially *in a state of siege;* practically, there is no Government at all. Every man does that which is right in his own eyes, says what he pleases, writes and prints what he pleases, and acts entirely irrespective of all law, military or civil. For instance, three officers of Garibaldi's army on their way to England, charged with the duty of bringing out the 800 volunteers from Liverpool, landed this morning. Their passports bore no Neapolitan *visé*, so the police at the custom-house refused them permission to enter the city, whereupon they pushed the said police aside, and walked on in spite of them.

A crowd of papers has sprung into existence during the last few weeks. They are all openly for Garibaldi. They record triumphantly the progress of the insurrection, and exhort the citizens of Naples to be ready for action at the right moment. They are sold everywhere in the streets, and as the price is generally one *grano* (something less than a halfpenny sterling), everybody buys them.

At the theatres the audience demand "Garibaldi's hymn," a patriotic composition, which is to the Italians of to-day what "Yankee Doodle" and the "Marseillaise" were respectively to the Americans and French in their time. The hymn is sung; the audience stand up, join in the chorus, and, at the conclusion, cry out tumultuously, "Viva Garibaldi," "Viva Vittorio Emmanuele," "Viva l'Italia Unita." I see portraits of Garibaldi and of Victor Emmanuel in every shop; I have not seen one of Francesco II.

The universal opinion here is, that the reign of the Bourbons is over, and that Garibaldi will enter Naples without the faintest show of resistance. If the King had had, as was supposed, any party among his subjects, whether nobles or lazzaroni,* some manifestation would be made in his favour;

* *Lazzaroni.* There is great doubt even among well-informed Neapolitans as to the existence of an organized body to which this term is specially appro-

but there are no signs of the existence of a Royalist party. When the King drives out—as he did daily up to the end of last week—no notice is taken of him. Here and there a spectator, out of pity and courtesy, lifts his hat; but the majority ostentatiously keep theirs on.

Numbers of officers in uniform are driving about in hackney cabs, chatting and smoking, evidently in high spirits at the thought that they can turn their backs on the enemy as soon as he appears, and this time without dishonour. All accounts agree, that neither officers nor soldiers mean fighting. There is not one regiment upon whose fidelity the King can rely. There is one man in the army who is said to be faithful, viz. Bosco, who commanded at Melazzo: but Bosco is a Neapolitan. The National Guard, just organized, and very conspicuous in their uniform of blue coats and red caps, mount guard at various places in the city. They are to a man in favour of Garibaldi. I am informed, on good authority, that the King has given a promise in writing to the British Minister, and probably to all the foreign Ministers, that he will not in any case order his troops in Sant Elmo and the Castelli to bombard the city. A better security than the promise, written or otherwise, of a Bourbon, is the assurance that the troops would not obey such an order. The bombardment of Naples would not save the dynasty, and would eventually entail upon the bombarders certain destruction from popular vengeance. Wherever on the mainland the Neapolitan troops have encountered the Garibaldians, they have fired a few shots, for form's sake, and then surrendered. If such was their conduct when the ultimate result of the

priate. In general it is used vaguely to designate the poorest classes. A species of tax called "gamorra" is levied upon cabmen, small greengrocers, fishmongers, and other tradesmen, by the authority, and for the benefit, of a body of bravoes, called thence *gamorristi*, who co-opt into their body those who, by strength of arm and skill in the use of the stiletto, may have shown themselves worthy of the distinction. One of Garibaldi's earliest decrees declared this tax to be illegal. The account I have just given was told to me by a secretary of legation, long resident at Naples. This he believed to be the only organization among what are called "lazzaroni."

war was doubtful, how can we expect that they will act otherwise when the Bourbon cause is evidently desperate?

If the 14,000 Swiss who served Ferdinand had been still here, they might have made a last stand for his son. Hated as they were by the people, their best security would have been a desperate defence; but they are disbanded, and, as I before said, the unhappy Francesco has not a regiment upon which he can count. The very soldiers on guard at the gates of the palace seem to be under no discipline and no restraint. I saw them last night lounging in all attitudes, laughing, smoking, and playing at mora, with shouts that rang through the courts and must have reached the ears of the King.

As to where Garibaldi is, and when he may be expected here, perhaps you in England know as much as we know. All sorts of reports are circulated. The Café d'Europa is crowded all the evening with people circulating the bulletins issued every hour by this or that committee, and telling and hearing news the authenticity of which cannot be tested, and of which one half contradicts the other. "Garibaldi is at Vallo"—"Garibaldi is at Sorrento"—"Garibaldi is at Salerno"—"The King embarked last night"—"The King is going to-morrow"—"The King declares he will stay at Naples"—"The Ministry has resigned"—"The Ministry has fled in a body"—"The King wants to go, but the Ministry will not let him"—and so forth.

This much we know for certain, that the insurrection has spread from province to province and from town to town. Even Salerno * has established a Provisional Government and proclaimed Victor Emmanuel; and Salerno is under the very eyes of the commander-in-chief of the royal army.

The least sanguine expect that, within a week at farthest, Victor Emmanuel will be proclaimed at Naples. Meanwhile, the city itself, with the exceptions I have mentioned, wears its ordinary aspect. Business goes on as usual; all the shops are open, the streets are crowded with carts and carriages of all sorts. (By the way, Naples is the only Continental capital

* This anticipated the truth by two days.

which is liable to "blocks" such as occur in the thoroughfares of London.) Life and property are just as safe under the new police and the Guardia Nazionale as ever they were; indeed safer, because there are no *sbirri* to inform against honest men. Almost all the exiles have already returned without permission from Government, but certain that it dares not, and cannot, molest them. I have talked during the last two days with many persons of all ranks—I was about to say, of all opinions—but, in reality, I find only one opinion. All agree that the Bourbon rule is practically at an end—and the sooner it is nominally at an end also, the better. All look forward with joyful hope to the impending change, but there are some who fear that, between the fall of one Government and the installation of another, there may be an interval of anarchy, during which the lowest class may take an opportunity for acts of pillage and private vengeance. In case of this fear being realized, I am told that preparations are made for landing sailors and marines to guard the embassies and consulates, where, if necessary, strangers of the various nations may find refuge. But in this fear I do not share. Naples can never have a weaker Government than it has at this moment, when it is not governed at all; and yet, as I have said, the thieves and assassins are no busier than at ordinary times. In fact, the lazzaroni are a bugbear, which has long frightened the shopkeepers, and led them to suppose that a rigorous police was necessary to the protection of their goods and chattels. It is a generic term, including all the very ragged men and boys of the city—a class which, in times of revolution, may be terrible enough, but which is no more organized for mischief than the mob of London. The upper and middle classes, including in the latter class all labouring men with regular employment, are in this instance of one accord. Therefore I believe that the change of Government will be made without any disturbance and without any interruption in the ordinary business and social relations of the place.

In all likelihood, however, the conquest of Naples will

only be regarded by Garibaldi as a starting point for fresh enterprises much more uncertain and much more arduous. "The end is not yet."

Sept. 6.—After spending a long morning at Pompeii, I went with a young English officer by the train at one o'clock, towards Salerno.

As soon as the railroad turns away from the Bay of Naples, it traverses a valley which at the farther end narrows into a ravine. Castles crown each peak, towns and villages stretch in white lines along the slopes. The mountains are covered to the top with trees, ilex, elm, chestnut, the lower slopes with vines in festoons, olives, mulberries, maize yellowing to the harvest, cotton with pink and white blossoms, tomatoes golden among the green. At Nocera we saw the Neapolitan soldiers* in their light blue dresses, crowding the staircase and galleries of the great palace which serves for barracks.

There was a citizen of Salerno in the train, who made polite offers of his services there. We got to Vietri in about an hour, and taking a carriage, drove at a furious pace from that village to Salerno, perhaps two miles distant.

There we found the place all excitement. That morning a Provisional Government had been installed. Four officers of the national guard had taken the place of the Intendente nominated by the King. The Intendenza itself was decorated with Italian colours, and the arms of the Bourbon dynasty over the door were similarly concealed.

A few of Garibaldi's men in red shirts, the only article of dress which is *de rigueur*† in his army, were walking about the town. One of them told me that he had just received a telegraphic despatch, announcing that the general had left Eboli and would be at Salerno by six. Inquiring of another for General Türr, to whom I had an introduction, he took me

* They were part of the force which had just evacuated the lines in front of the capital, and were retreating to Capua—the fatal move which cost Francesco his crown.

† Even the red shirt, as I afterwards observed, was not indispensable. There was nothing *de rigueur* in that army.

into the Intendenza, and presented me to a white-haired, white bearded old gentleman, who, as I understood, was the general's secretary. He was very civil, but could not or would not give me any information.

We then strolled about the town, and went to the cathedral, which has an atrium in front, with columns and capitals taken from some Roman temple. There are a number of sarcophagi under the arches, which had been appropriated by Normans. You may see a knight in armour sculptured rudely, reposing above; and on the side, a group of Cupids and Bacchantes. Two pulpits and the screen of the choir are beautifully preserved specimens of glass mosaic work, such as the tomb of Henry III. at Westminster, long ago defaced.* In the crypt below, rich in marbles, is the body of St. Matthew.

Returning to the beach, we passed one of the King's "Bavarians," very drunk, wearing a kind of cockade of the Italian colours, crying, as well as he could, "Viva Garibaldi," and supported by sympathizing natives. A bystander informed us with an air of triumph, that two hundred of these Bavarians had the previous night mutinied at Nocera, killed (*ammazato*) one of their generals, and one of their captains, and then fled in various directions, several having come to Salerno to offer their services to Garibaldi. This story was, we found, true in the main, only "the general" was an addition. They *had* murdered a captain. My companion, as a military man, took a very different view of the feat, which our Italian friends seemed to think meritorious on the whole.

As the day declined, the crowd gathered more thickly on the terrace which runs along the shore in front of Salerno. New detachments of tumultuary national guards poured in from the neighbourhood, armed with guns of all sorts and sizes, and without any pretence to uniformity in dress. A strong wind was blowing from the west, and clouds of dust

* Is it our damp climate, or our mischievous nature, which mutilates every monument in England? The mosaics at Salerno look as if they had been wrought last year.

swept along the terrace, so that I thought if the General delayed his entry much longer, we should have no sight left to see him withal. The sun went down, and left the hills purple against the clear orange and rose of the sky.

Still he came not. By-and-by, men set out to meet him with bundles of torches ready for lighting, and the householders prepared to illuminate their windows. Bands of music paraded the town, and the crowd kept up a running fire of *vivas* to pass the time. At last, about half-past seven, a louder and more continuous cheer was heard; two or three carriages drove in, surrounded with people waving torches. It was he at last. As he stopped at the door of the Intendenza, the national guard closed in to keep off the crowd, and escorted him up the staircase. A few minutes after, he appeared at the balcony, while some one next him held a moderator lamp so as to throw the light full on his face. He stood bareheaded, fanning himself with his black wide-awake, and looking like anything but the daring freebooter that he is. He has the most benign expression of countenance, and his partial baldness and long beard give him even a venerable look. He might serve as model for the portrait of the most benevolent of ancient philosophers, whoever that may have been.* Long after he had retired, the crowd continued to cheer, "disturbedly," as the old stage direction says. In a little while all the town was lighted up. Nothing could be more beautiful than the lines of light spreading along the steep slopes of the hills and flashing in the sea below. By-and-by the moon rose, and touched with cold greenish light the rocky summits of the hills, convents, and castles, and white villas in the slope, bright enough to distinguish the grey rows of olives above from the thicket of lemon and fig trees below, and at last blending with the ruddy splendour that shone upon town and beach and sea.

We retired at last to sup and sleep at the Hotel Vittoria (almost the last house on the road to Vietri).

* The busts of Euripides, in the Vatican, have a striking resemblance to Garibaldi.

Sept. 7.—About half-past nine, we heard the roar of *vivas* in the street, and coming to the window, saw Garibaldi himself, passing in the direction of Vietri. One of the crowd, while cheering in the most frantic manner, suddenly fell in a kind of convulsive fit. I asked our landlady, a vivacious, black-eyed Calabrese damsel, whether he had not been *drinking* the General's health. "No," she said; "it is joy. Ah," in a tone of reproach, "you English, who have been always free, cannot imagine the delight of deliverance." And she made a gesture as if she were about to fly.

Beside Garibaldi sat a person with gold lace round his cape, who we were told was General de Suget, commander of the national guard. The question for us was, Whither were they bound? Our landlord assured us that they were going no farther than La Cava: he had it from the best authority—it was *certo, certissimo.* So we forthwith engaged a carriage to take us to La Cava. Just as we were setting off, came our acquaintance of the railway, in the uniform of a national guard, who told us that Garibaldi was going straight to Naples, and that we might still be in time to catch the special train that was to take him.

We drove with all speed to the station at Vietri, which was crowded with carriages outside and people inside. There was no chance of getting through in the regular way; so climbing up a somewhat steep bank, and getting over a low wall, we gained the railway. The train was not gone. Without asking any one's leave, we got into a third-class carriage, containing already about thirty people, like ourselves, a self-invited escort for the Dictator. We were welcomed with cries of "Viva l'Inghilterra." It seems that the Neapolitan authorities, after the departure of the King, had sent a telegraphic message to General Garibaldi, asking when and where it would be his pleasure to receive a deputation. The answer was: "Immediately, at Salerno." Accordingly, the deputation came early on Friday morning. To their question, when would the General honour Naples with his presence, he answered, "At once," saying that he preferred a spontaneous to a prepared welcome. So every one was taken by surprise. We congratulated ourselves upon our good luck in being there to see. During the whole of our journey, the thirty or forty occupants of the carriage where we were did not cease shouting and singing. Some were in the uniform of the national guard, and almost all were armed in one way or other. The most conspicuous figure was a priest on the podgy side of forty, in the usual long black gown and broad-brimmed hat, with a musket and wide tricolor scarf. His bass voice was loudest of all in the choruses, and in the cheers as we passed each successive station. In the intervals he was smoking regalias, which he brandished with the left hand, as he brandished the musket with the right. The songs were interminable. Rather, as it was always the same tune and the same chorus, I should call it one song of which the verses were extemporized by one or other of the company. I managed to remember two of these verses, which I give by way of specimen.

"Siamo Italiani,
Giovani freschi,
Contro ai Tedeschi,
Vogliamo pugnar.

(*Chorus.*) Viva l'Italia!
Viva l'unione!
Viva Garibaldi!
E la libertà!

Morte a Francesco,
Del nome secondo,
Piu belva nel mondo,
Trovar non si può.

(*Chorus.*) Viva l'Italia, &c.

The tune resembled the ordinary chant of the saints' litany, "Sancte ——, ora pro nobis," *allegro* instead of *adagio.*

At every station a mob of curious people were gathered, who exchanged cheers with the occupants of the train, but it was evident that they scarcely believed Garibaldi himself to be present. Events had hastened to their *dénouement* so rapidly, that people could hardly credit the evidence of their senses. We stopped at Nocera, Torre dell' Annuziata, and Portici, for a few minutes. The demonstrations of welcome came from all classes; from the fishermen who left their boats on the beach, from the swarthy fellows, naked to the waist, who were winnowing their corn on the flat house-roofs, as well as from the national guards who crowded round the carriage to see the famous chief.

At Naples there was a little delay while the Minister of the Interior, who has transferred his services directly to the Dictator, made a complimentary speech, not a word of which was audible to us. Then Garibaldi got into the carriage which was waiting for him, and drove slowly by the Strada Nuova, the Strada di Porto, and the Largo del Castel Nuovo to the Foresteria. A few carriages followed containing the deputation, and perhaps a dozen of his officers in their red shirts. He himself wore his ordinary costume, red shirt, black wide-awake, black neckcloth, and a coloured silk handkerchief knotted and hanging down his back, to serve, I suppose, on occasion for protection against the sun. A detachment of national guards went before and behind. We elbowed our way among the shouting crowd, and kept close by his carriage all the time. The excitement and enthusiasm were great, but the crowd was an extemporary crowd, composed of persons who had suddenly left their work at the news. Naples had been taken by surprise. The windows were not filled with expectant faces, the houses were not decorated with flags, because no one knew that he was coming. This robbed the event of its beauty as a spectacle, but it threw no doubt on the heartiness of the welcome.

Garibaldi sat for the most part apparently unmoved, but from time to time he lifted his hat, and smiled, as it were, with the eyes rather than the lips. One of his men, with red shirt and plaid scarf and plumed hat, well armed, stood behind the carriage at his back, keeping, as I thought, a sharp eye upon all who came near, as if looking for the handle of a dagger, or the butt end of a pistol. As we passed the Castel del Carmine, a number of the King's troops, still in garrison there, were looking on. The mob in passing called to them, and, with menacing gestures, demanded that they should cry, "Viva Garibaldi." Some few obeyed, but the majority stood with folded arms and closed lips, notwithstanding the imprecations of the crowd below. The procession at last reached the great open place (its shape forbids me to call it a square), in front of the palace. Then Garibaldi left his carriage and entered the Foresteria, a large house intended for the reception of foreign guests of distinction. A few minutes afterwards he appeared at an open window on the first floor, and walked along the balcony to the centre of the building. Loud cries, not like the rolling cheers of an English crowd, but confused and inarticulate, greeted his appearance. He leaned with his left arm on the iron framework of the balcony, and waited patiently hat in hand. At last the crowd began to understand that he wanted to speak to them, and gradually the cries and shouts died away into silence, obedient to reiterated "Zitti, zitti," from the quieter spirits. It was to the following effect:—

"You have a right to exult in this day, which is the commencement of a new epoch not only for you but for all Italy, of which Naples forms the fairest portion. It is, indeed, a glorious day and a holy—that on which a people passes from the yoke of servitude to the rank of a free nation. I thank you for this welcome, not only for myself individually, but in the name of all Italy, which your aid will render free and united."*

He spoke with a clear and loud voice, which was heard by all. The phrase "Italia intiera" occurred twice in his speech, and was pronounced with unusual distinctness and emphasis, eliciting cheers of especial meaning.

Wearied with dust, heat, and excitement, I went home to bathe and rest, and found that some patriot had picked my pocket.

* No newspaper, that I saw, contained a perfectly accurate report of this speech.

Meanwhile the Dictator went to the cathedral, where a service of some kind was performed, and thence to the Palazzo d'Angri, where he has taken up his abode for the present.

About three o'clock I drove up the Toledo, and found the street in front of the Palazzo blocked up by a dense mass of carriages and people on foot, crying "Viva Garibaldi!" at the top of their voices, to bring him to the window. At last one of his men appeared and laid his cheek upon his hand, implying that the general had gone to lie down—"his custom always of an afternoon" (as I am told). He gets up about three in the morning and transacts a vast amount of business before the rest of the world is out of bed. Before the day was over, every house, almost every window in the Toledo and Chiaia and main streets of Naples had its flag. There seemed to be considerable difference of opinion as to what the Italian tricolor was. All were agreed as to the colours, green, white, red; but whether they should be placed like the French, parallel to the staff, or like the Dutch, at right angles; and whether the green should come first, or the red, seemed to be a moot point which each householder decided according to his fancy. The white portion of the flag was adorned either with a portrait of Garibaldi, or with a red shield and the white cross of Savoy. At sunset the town was illuminated, as the Italians say, *à giorno;* crowds of pedestrians and a multitude of carriages paraded the main streets. The noise was indescribable. The hero's name was repeated in all manner of forms, as if it was a declinable noun—Garibaldi, Garibaldo, Garibalda—nay, it was metamorphosed into Gallibar and Gallipot, and Galliboard; at last the two first syllables were suppressed, and "Viva *'Board*" was the favourite cry, the sound of the last syllable being prolonged to the utmost. You heard too, "Viva Vittorio Emmanuele," and still more frequently, "Viva l'Italia unita," which at length was shortened into *una,* and when people got so hoarse that they could not articulate any longer, they held out the forefinger and shook it as they passed, indicative of their desire for unity. Men, women, and boys, crowded the carriages and clung to them like swarming bees—I counted thirteen persons in a small vehicle drawn by one horse. Some waved flags, some brandished daggers, holding them occasionally in unpleasant proximity to one's throat, and shrieking with menacing scowls, "Viva Garibaldi!" others danced frantically along, waving torches over their heads. I have never seen such a sight as the Strada di Toledo presented as you looked up it, the long lines of stationary lights converging in the distance, and the flags drooping from the windows, and down below the mad movements of the torches, and the waved banners and gleaming arms. Here and there an excited orator addressed the crowd about him in wild declamation; little bands of enthusiasts, headed sometimes by a priest and sometimes by a woman, went dancing through the streets and burst into the *cafés*, compelling all present to join in the popular cry. I was forcibly reminded of the scenes of the French Revolution and Mademoiselle Louise Theroigne. When I was in the Café d'Europa a priest rushed in with frantic gestures, with eyes starting from his head, with a banner in one hand and a knife in the other, uttering horrible and inarticulate howlings. Having seen him, I can understand the frenzy of the ancient Bacchantes.

A friend of mine saw a young and beautiful girl, belonging apparently to the upper class, who, standing up in a carriage, began to address the crowd quietly at first, but warming gradually into a fury of enthusiasm, the veins in face and neck swollen, and ending with "Morte ai Borboni," shrieked out with the accents and gestures of a Rachel.

Sept. 8.—The diversion was repeated on this night (and again on Sunday, the 9th), with more vigour and violence and extravagance than ever.

An unfortunate man who did not cry "Viva Garibaldi" when he was bidden, was ripped open by one who carried a dagger, and died on the spot. An English officer saw him lying dead. A proclamation next morning from the new minister of police entreated the people to leave their arms at home, but it did not appear to have much effect. These people have not been accustomed to official entreaties.

On the afternoon, Garibaldi went to the Church of the Piedigrotta, seeing (as the paper informed us) that it had been the ancient custom of the Neapolitan Sovereigns to pay their devotions to the Madonna of that ilk on the 8th of September.

There used to be a great parade of troops on this day, and country people came in from far and near; but this year it had lost all its usual characteristics. There were no troops and few visitors, and a heavy fall of rain completed the failure. This I heard from others, as I spent the day at Puzzuoli Cumæ and Baiæ. I returned in time for the performance at the San Carlo, which the Dictator was present at. The performance was listened to with impatience; people seemed to care for nothing but shouting "Viva" between the acts. Some English midshipmen, from boxes in the third tier, made themselves very conspicuous, by the energy with which they waved their tricolor. The spectacle was spoilt by the avarice of the managers, who had doubled the prices and consequently halved the audience. The thousand or fifteen hundred who were present did their best to compensate for the beggarly account of empty boxes. "Viva Venezia" seemed to be the favourite cry. I saw the Dictator smile grimly when he heard it. Among the persons who came to pay their respects to him was, as I was told, the very Admiral who had commanded the Neapolitan fleet at Palermo, and also Liborio Romano, who bowed in the humblest manner, "con illimitato rispetto."

The ballet was brought to an untimely end by some one in a shooting-coat rushing on the stage and crying out, "Viva," &c. in which the whole *corps de ballet* joined, crowding round the box where the General was and lifting their arms in the theatrical fashion of supplication. A body of national guards, with drawn swords, escorted Garibaldi through the thronged corridors to his carriage. Some one, in loud voice, cried "Silenzio nel nome de Garibaldi!" which was answered by a prolonged shout.

Sept. 9.—About ten o'clock, as I was walking by Sta. Lucia, I saw a great crowd gathered round a brightly blazing pile—a curious sight on a summer's morning. Asking a bystander the meaning of it, I was informed that the pile consisted of the furniture, books, and papers of an obnoxious agent of police. He was about to make his escape. Some of the mob being informed of it were on the watch, and as soon as the cart containing his chattels emerged from the door of the fortified place where he lived, they pounced upon it, made a heap of its contents, and set fire to them. They were dancing round the fire in wild excitement. Old women threw up their skinny arms and shrieked, and the children were mad with delight. I saw one man seize a loose sheet of manuscript, which had been blown away from the pile, crumple it in his hand, throw it down, and stamp on it, then fold his arms and "stare with his foot on the prey," in the attitude of Clytemnestra stamping on the corpse of Agamemnon. The Neapolitans, generally speaking, are not handsome in feature nor picturesque in dress—they are common-place when in repose, but when excited with passion their countenances and gestures are a study for an actor or a painter. While they were thus engaged, a rumour spread that the owner of the furniture was making his escape by sea. Instantly the crowd dispersed. Some put off in boats, others clambered round the rocky point and along the sea-wall—all animated with a desire of vengeance. They were, however, disappointed. The obnoxious functionary either was already gone, or else he prudently waited for a more favourable opportunity.

It is probably because the officials of the King have been for the most part as prudent as their master, and made their escape in time, that so few acts of violence have been committed during these revolutionary days. It is not for want of will on the part of the people. To-day I read in the paper that as Garibaldi was returning from a drive, some one followed him, crying, "Viva Francesco II.," when a "Guardiano della Dogana" came up and shot him dead! The mob wanted to inflict indignities on the corpse (as their wont is), but the Dictator interfered, and ordered that it should be decently buried. It does not appear that he blamed the slayer for excess of zeal.

This afternoon I saw at the Castel Nuovo the King's troops with bag and baggage and arms evacuating the place, and the national guards marching in. A considerable crowd assembled, but there was no manifestation of feeling against the soldiers. About 150 of them waited for an hour or more in the street outside. Passers-by talked to them in friendly terms. As far as I could judge from the countenances of the men, they were quite indifferent, and did not seem to care where they went. They were well armed and clothed, and evidently had been well fed. Had they been well led too, things would have taken a very different turn. While they were still waiting for orders, a regiment of Garibaldians came by, marching, it was said, under General Türr, to repress a reactionary movement at Ariano. The contrast which these filibusters presented to the royal troops was exceedingly striking. Of the Garibaldians, no two men were armed or clothed alike: some had only one shoe, some no shoes at all; there were boys of twelve and thirteen years old in the ranks, side by side with grey-bearded veterans; there were the most *bizarre* contrasts as to personal stature, such as one has only seen in the army of Bombastes Furioso, and they made no pretence of keeping line or keeping step. Many of them carried loaves stuck on the end of their muskets or bayonets. Yet these are the men before whom a well-appointed army of 150,000 men, with a king's name for a tower of strength, have broken, and fled, and melted into nothing.

Apropos of the boys, I was told by one who had seen the battle of Melazzo, that they did excellent service, and showed no sign of fear—laughing and singing, when exposed to a murderous fire, as if their young lives were of no account.

"If such things be done in the green tree," the kingdom of Italy may in reality be formidable to her neighbours a few years hence, and justify the alarm which led Louis Napoleon to appropriate Nice and Savoy for the protection of France.

Sept. 11.—Now that the shouting is over, we have some leisure for thinking what it means, what realities lie under this surface of triumph.

On Wednesday night, Sept. 5th, or rather, early in the morning of Thursday, the King left his palace, committing the town to the care of the general commanding the national guard. The official paper, *Constitutional Journal*, as it was called, contained on Thursday a proclamation from the King in dignified terms, promising that when it should please the Divine Justice to restore him to his throne, he would still preserve the constitution which he had granted. To this was added a protest, countersigned by the prime minister De Martino, in which Garibaldi is called "un ardito condottiere."

The same journal of Friday, changing the title of constitutional to that of official, and substituting Naples for the Two Sicilies, contains a proclamation of Garibaldi to the people, dated that morning at Salerno, and a letter from Liborio Romano to "the most invincible Dictator," announcing the impatience of Naples for the arrival of its "Redeemer," and professing "to await his further orders with unbounded respect." This man had two days before countersigned the deeds of Francis the Second in his capacity of Minister of the Interior. His ostentatious treason has offended even the Neapolitans.

The mode in which the title now borne by Garibaldi was conferred, is singular. Some half-dozen persons, including Liborio, announced that on the invitation of the General they had formed themselves into a provisional Government, and in virtue of the authority so derived they declared General Garibaldi dictator.. A curious *ruse* this for investing the transaction with a semblance of legality. It can only impose upon those who do not see that arguing in a circle proves nothing. By what authority, we may ask, did Garibaldi invite the said half-dozen to form a provisional Government?

The gazettes of Saturday and the two following days are filled with decrees nominating ministers, confirming all subordinate *employés*, except pluralists, in their posts, recognising the national debt, &c.

The ministers named are not in general (as I am told) men of commanding ability, but they are all moderate men, and, as such, give satisfaction to the party represented by the Comitato Unitario, the Cavour party. The party which calls itself the Partito d'Azione, of which Crespi, De Pretis and Bertani (perhaps I should now include Mazzini) are the leaders, is, however, believed to have the Dictator's affections, and in reality to guide his councils. Garibaldi has already alarmed the moderates by the violence of his language more than once. On Friday, in answer to an address, he called Lamoricière "a renegade head of a set of ragamuffins without country and without faith."

The King of Sardinia (I am told) sent an aide-de-camp to consult about the mode of annexation, to which he replied, "It is not even to be thought of till I get to Rome;" and this story is confirmed by the proclamation of this morning, September 11th, to the Sicilians, in which he declares his intention of proclaiming Italian unity from the summit of the Quirinal. This audacious boast has dismayed the moderate party exceedingly. In a constitutional *régime* the ministers would all have resigned.

In the midst of all these political agitations I have found time to visit many of the permanent "sights" of Naples, and especially the Museo Borbonico, which, like the British, contains several museums in one. The picture gallery may, I suppose, be ranked as the sixth in combined excellence and size, after those of the Louvre, Dresden, Madrid, and the two at Florence. It has not so many great pictures as the Vatican, or even perhaps our National Gallery, but they are small galleries. In sculpture, it ranks next to the Vatican and before the Louvre; in ancient bronzes and mosaics it is *facile princeps;* in ancient frescoes it is unique. The frescoes, taken all from Herculaneum and Pompeii, are exceedingly interesting. In point of art, their quality is very various. Some figures are drawn and coloured with a breadth and boldness that reminds one of the Venetian school. There is, for example, a brown stalwart Bacchante which Titian might have painted. But in general they recall the style of the earlier naturalists of Florence more than any other modern school The "house-sign-and-ornamental painters" of a country town in the first century had attained a mastery over pencil and brush which, till Masaccio came, the greatest artists of modern times failed to equal. But then the devotional feeling, the divine calm that charms us in Giotto and Fra Beato, is altogether wanting. Their conceptions are of the earth, earthy. I suppose, however, that we should have found this devotional element in the works of the best painters contemporary with Phidias. He, at least, believed in the gods he moulded, Zeus and Athene.

In these frescoes, even when the drawing is bad, the conception is often good, and now and then we meet with a dash of humour, which, coming to us from a long-buried world, is infinitely charming. The idea we derive from our schooldays of the old Romans is that of a grim, savage, earnest people, who were always fighting, marching, sacrificing, making military roads, innumerable laws, and interminable orations, growing by-and-by foully and desperately wicked Nothing brings us so near to them as a glimpse of their capacity for fun such as we get in the dramatists now and then, in Cicero's letters, or in Suetonius, or in these frescoes from Pompeii. For instance, there is a series of small pictures (absurdly described in the catalogue as signs of shops) representing fat winged Cupids hard at work at various trades. In one they are making boots, very like the modern "Bluchers." I cannot tell why they are comical, but I defy any one to look at them without laughing—which I take to be the best proof that they are comical.

In the centre of the room is a recent addition, quite the reverse of comical—a wax mask found in a tomb at Cumæ along with a headless skeleton, from which it is inferred that the person interred had been decapitated. It is, I believe, the only relic of the kind in existence. The chances are immensely against the preservation of so fragile an object. In the tomb were found some coins of Diocletian. A few years ago the remains would have been at once assumed to be those of a Christian martyr, and a new saint added to the calendar.

I have been to-day, Sept. 12th, with a party of English and Italians to visit the prisons of Naples, in virtue of an order given by I know not what minister. First we saw some dungeons at the Prefecture of Police, behind the Largo del Castello—places without light or air, or bed or seat, where we were assured people were kept for a fortnight, or even a month, without trial. One of these, built for a common latrina, had been used, as one of the new officials told us, for a prison, and a man was confined for eight days there, at the end of which time his toes were found to be gnawed to the bone by rats. The sight and smell of the place made two of our party ill for the whole day.

Then we went, by steep, narrow, filthy bye-streets, to Sta. Maria Apparente. There the cells had been newly cleansed and whitewashed, so that there was nothing disgusting in their appearance; but the prison system in vogue under Ferdinand was such as to convert the most spacious and airy room into a place of torture. There is also a winding passage cut in the rock, which seems formerly to have been divided into cells. Several unfortunates had carved their names, with the date of their imprisonment. One recorded that he had been buried (*sepolto*) for four years, 1856—1860; another added to his name the words, "Reo senza delitto."

After that we climbed up to Sant Elmo, saw its vast subterranean galleries tier above tier, with sloping staircase (if that may be so called which has no steps), like the passages in the Mausoleum of Hadrian. There are prisons also in St.

Elmo, though they have been chiefly used to punish military offenders.* We walked round the ramparts, now sentinelled by Piedmontese troops and by the national guard, and soon, it is said, to be demolished. As a fortress, St. Elmo is formidable to the town, but of little use against an enemy from without, at all events, if he approached by land, as it is completely commanded by the hill on which the Camaldoli stands.

If we may trust the story told us by the officer who was in command of the fortress, the gunners wished to bombard the town on Sunday, and when their officers refused, they shut them up in a guard-room, all but the commandant, who, as he informed us, pretended to be with them in feeling in order to prevent their design. According to his account, he, with the aid of a few soldiers, got a gun in such a position as to command the mutineers, who, not being able to point the guns themselves, at last desisted from their purpose, and went away to their homes or elsewhere. So the officer in question retains his command under the Dictator. When I told this story to an eminent Garibaldian colonel, he said that he did not believe a word of it. The story is, indeed, palpably inconsistent. Why should sixty gunners (for that was their number) not be able to point a gun without their officers? and how could he get a gun to bear upon all the soldiers within the fortress? Fancy a man, wearing epaulettes and a sword, telling such a lie with unblushing face!

* A long account of what we saw that day in the prisons was given in a letter published in the *Times* early in October, by Lord Llanover, who was one of the party. The facts there stated are, of course, strictly correct, but I hesitate to accept some of the inferences drawn or implied. We must remember that the prison at the Prefecture of Police, far the foulest of all, had been recently devoted to the purpose for which it was originally intended, and we had no proof beyond the word of an *employé* of a few days' standing that it had ever been used for a prison at all. And in the other cases our informants were all men who had just been appointed to their offices by the new Government, who knew nothing of the former system of their own knowledge, but were anxious to blacken the late reign, and could not fail to see that each atrocious detail communicated a thrill of sensation, rather agreeable than otherwise, to their auditors. We have evidence enough, from more trustworthy sources, of the cruelties practised by Ferdinand. But I do not think there is any proof that the prison system at Naples under Francesco II. was at all worse than it was in England under George the Third.

Sept. 13.—The same party which had visited the prisons of Naples went to that of Ischia in a despatch-boat, commanded by Captain Marryatt, a son of the novelist, and kindly placed at our disposal by Admiral Mundy. On our landing we were assailed by a crowd of natives offering donkeys and figs, three donkeys at least to each man, and more figs than one could eat in a month, clamouring in all tones from howls of exultation to whines of distress, till the poor stranger became so bewildered that he did not know whether he was expected to mount the figs and eat the donkeys or *vice versâ*.

The prison we were to see is in the Castle of Ischia, which Stanfield's picture has made familiar to English eyes. Only as we saw it the sea was rippling quietly about the base of the breakwater in the foreground, not tumbling in wild billows over it.

Some difficulty was made about our admission; but the combined authority and eloquence of Lord Ll—— and Mr. Edwin J——, aided by the fact that we had come in a ship of war, triumphed over all obstacles.

The prisons here were tenanted only by fleas. They were not particularly dark or dirty, or in any way horrible. We asked in vain for the torture-chamber and the thumb-screws, and on the whole could not but feel disappointed at the result of our inquiry. We were shown the room where Poerio was confined during some of his ten years of durance. There were four rooms *en suite* so arranged that an inspector could look on from a window in his chamber above, and see what was doing in any of them. The wooden tressels on which the prisoners slept and some fragments of their clothing still remained. They had the liberty of walking in a small walled courtyard.

The Ischian prisons were under the charge of the same keepers as before, old soldiers chiefly, who were very much alarmed at our visit and our questions, and as anxious to dissemble the rigours of the former Government as the new keepers of the Neapolitan prisons had been to exaggerate them.

Sept. 15.—I went by railway to Castellamare, and thence, with a carriage, in an hour and a quarter to Sorrento. The Neapolitan coachmen drive like Jehu the son of Nimshi. Even when one takes them by the hour they scarcely abate their ordinary pace, which is very different from the snail-like motion of a London or Paris cabman under similar conditions. One of Dr. Johnson's immortal truths was communicated to Mr. Boswell in these words: "Sir, there is something very exhilarating in the rapid motion of a post-chaise;" and I fancy that the Neapolitan driver feels the pleasure so intensely that he cannot forego it for the sake of sparing his cattle or spinning out the time, even when to him time is money.

The drive to Sorrento is one of the most beautiful in the world. The road at first follows the coast-line, winding into each cove and rounding each headland, then strikes across the valley where Vico is situated, crossing the gorge by a noble viaduct, doubles the next promontory, and, by a gradual descent, comes to the comparatively level plain of Sorrento. This plain is composed of a *couche* of tufa perhaps three hundred feet deep at the base of the hills, and sloping gently down to the water's edge, where it breaks away in an abrupt precipice, varying from one hundred to one hundred and fifty feet in height. This tufa has been deposited in the hollows of the limestone hills by some pre-historic volcano. It has been cut into deep gorges by mountain torrents many ages ago by slow degrees, for the channel is not sensibly deeper than it was two thousand years since, as may be seen by the substructions of Roman bridges, cellars, &c. still apparent. The plain is of wonderful fertility, and, except where there is a street, a house, or a lane sunk between high walls, it is like a continuous garden, "a contiguity of shade," fruit trees of all kinds oranges, lemons, figs, pomegranates, and trellised vines, where you may walk under a roof of matted leaves and pendent clusters. On the amphitheatre of hills which shelters the plain on east, south, and west, you see terrace above terrace, partly artificial and partly the natural formation of the white limestone rock, sprinkled with grey olives, relieved by the brighter green of carob-tree, or fig, or vine, up to the foot of the steep crag, or the verge of the native forest.

No wonder that the Romans were fond of such a place. The beauty of Baiæ must have been in great part artificial, even before its neighbourhood was altered and spoiled by the eruptions of the Solfatara and the Monte Nuovo, and now it presents a somewhat bare hill-side cumbered with shapeless ruins. Baiæ, too, must always have been much hotter than Sorrento, for the former looks towards the south-east, the latter due north.* When the poet said, " Nullus in orbe sinus Baiis prælucet amœnis," he meant an especial stress to be laid on " amœnis," and referred not to the natural beauty only, but to the society and various artificial *agrémens* of the place. If people ever read Statius now-a-days, they would find that even among the Romans there were some who preferred Sorrento. Perhaps the eruption of Vesuvius in '79, which half-suffocated the people at Baiæ, but so far as we know did not affect Surrentum, may have contributed to establish the latter in popular favour. Certain it is, that the ground there was so valuable they they built villas below the cliff on foundations laid in the sea itself. Large blocks of lava in a regular line may be seen below the water from the Hotel della Sirena, and to reach the shore you descend through galleries still covered with stucco, and showing traces of colour. The face of the rock is filled with artificial niches and caves, evidently belonging to Roman houses. On either side of the city is a deep ravine, offering at every step the most lovely combinations of tufa rock and ruins and luxuriant creepers. Round the city is a mediæval wall of great strength once, but now crumbling and ruinous. In the centre is the Cathedral, an ancient church with an open atrium like that of Salerno, but thoroughly modernized. Outside there are some columns

* The modern Sorrentines maintain the superiority of their town to Naples in amenity and healthiness. They have a couplet, the produce of a native genius, which they quote with as much pride as if he had succeeded in making it rhyme :—

> " Napoli bella, Sorrento civile ;
> Chi venga ammalato a Sorrento si sana."

of costly marble fitted with capitals not originally belonging to them, the spoils probably of one or more ancient temples. Near the Cathedral is a remarkable loggia, open on two sides, like the Portico of Orcagna, only on a smaller scale. The arches are round, and the capitals are carved in the flat manner characteristic of Italian Gothic. It is called the "Settina dei cavalieri," but I was not fortunate enough to find any one who could give me an intelligible account of its destination.

I rode in the afternoon of Saturday to the Deserto, a convent now abandoned, and situated on the crest of a hill south-west of Sorrento, commanding a view of the bay of Salerno as well as the bay of Naples. The place was tenanted only by a peasant (a "colon" they call him, still retaining the Latin word,) and his family. The cells were fast going to ruin, and so was the wall which had inclosed round the convent an irregular space of perhaps a hundred acres. Though the wind was "proprio scirocco," there was a delicious coolness about it as I stood on the convent roof. My guide, a good-humoured and in his way intelligent fellow, had been employed with others by the Count of Syracuse to excavate an ancient cemetery close by, which, from his mention of the gold ornaments and other relics found, I suppose may have been the burying-place of Theorica, a Greek city, supposed to have occupied the site of the neighbouring village of Torca.

"This campo santo," said my guide, "was two centuries (due secoli) old; before the world."

"Before the world?" I asked. "How could that be?"

"I mean," he said, "before *this* world; in the time of another world, which was destroyed by a deluge."

"And that," I asked, "was two secoli ago?"

"Precisamente, eccelenza."

"And how many years are there in a secolo?"

"A hundred, or thereabouts."

"Well," said I, with the air of an inquirer thirsting for information, "what happened about the deluge?"

"The flood was sent, eccelenza, because the world was full of bad people; but there was a signore called Noë, who was good. Dunque," he proceeded, putting his finger alongside of his nose, as their manner is when coming to the point of a story, "Jesus Christ, made a great ship, and put Noë in it;" and so he went on with the narrative.

I have given the man's exact words. I tell the incident, as it seems to me characteristic of the amount of education of an ordinary Neapolitan of that class. There is no point in the story except this—that it is a fact.

I have always noticed that genuine tradition has a tendency to diminish the interval of time which has elapsed since the event of which it preserves the memory. I remember asking a farmer, who lived on the field of battle near Nördlingen, whether he had ever heard of such a battle. "O! yes," he said, "he had often heard his father speak of it, and *his* father, who had seen it, told *him*." The remotest event is always supposed to be "in my grandfather's time." This is characteristic of genuine tradition. Forgery, on the other hand, has a tendency to magnify a nation's antiquity, and may sometimes be detected and distinguished by this mark.

Sept. 16.—I learn that, last night, a commissary of police, accompanied by some gens d'armes, arrested the Archbishop of Sorrento and carried him off to Naples. He had been the King's tutor, and so, I suppose, was suspected very naturally of favouring the Royal cause. He is much respected, they say, by the people, and is a good man. Surely it is a mistake for a Government which has just proclaimed liberty to tread in the steps of the old tyranny. What harm could an aged priest do if left alone?

Though the Palermitan monks, and Father Gavazzi, and a few priests have declared loudly for Garibaldi, and though some have even joined the Neapolitan volunteers, the great majority are evidently for the King. The spirit of Garibaldi's movement is thoroughly anti-Papal.

Attempts are being made by the clergy to enlist the superstitious feelings of the people in favour of the King. It was reported that, on the day of the King's departure, the Virgin of Santa Lucia wept tears of blood. The church was crowded with persons who went to see next day. My informant saw the streaks which the tears had left. Last Sunday, too, I have heard vaguely that a friar preaching somewhere appealed suddenly to an image in the church, and asked whose emissary Garibaldi was, and the image answered distinctly "Satan's."

We shall see whether Saint Januarius's displeasure will be shown in the non-liquefaction of the blood next Wednesday. And in that case, will Garibaldi adopt the plan of the French general in command at Naples, who threatened to shoot the officiating minister unless the miracle were immediately performed?

Sept. 17.—In company with an English friend, I took a boat from Sorrento to Capri. A steady scirocco carried us in an hour and a half to the entrance of the Blue Grotto, where a smaller boat from the little port of Capri met us. In this we entered the low mouth of the cave with some difficulty, as there was a swell rolling in. One has a natural aversion to hackneyed sights which you are bound to see because "everybody" sees them, and I went to this grotto prepared to find it unworthy of its fame; but I was compelled to admit the contrary. It is like a scene of enchantment, or the dream of some Eastern tale-teller—a cave with a floor of liquid turquoise and a roof of frosted silver. How is it that the same effect is not repeated in other instances? There are caves enough in other shores. How is it that Capri alone is favoured with two exhibiting this wonderful appearance, and why is one a "blue" and the other a "green" grotto?

The colour of the sea outside the cave was a mixture of dark purple and indigo—such a colour as I have only seen when a strong wind was blowing; and the sky was rather veiled than clouded—as is the case generally during a scirocco. We remembered the *οινοπα ποντον*, "the wine-like sea" of

Homer, but it is not likely that the familiar epithet which is as frequently applied to the sea as "swift-footed" is to Achilles, should have been suggested by a rare and exceptional phenomenon. The phrase probably came down to Homer from earlier and ruder poets, who would observe nature as the author of "Chevy Chase" observed it, but would not scrutinize it like Wordsworth. They saw that gold was red, and woods were green, and they needed no other epithet even for variety's sake. I believe that *οινοψ* simply meant coloured, like wine, as distinguished from the bright transparent water of a fountain (*αγλαον*), and from the dark black water of a well (*μελαν*). In this sense, the epithet is always applicable to the sea, whether it be calm or troubled, whether it be blue, or green or purple.

We landed at Marina, a little village lining the beach ,at the only point where there *is* a beach. Elsewhere a wall of steep rock rises abruptly from the sea. We rode on donkeys through the vineyards and olive-grounds, to the little town of Capri, perched along a ridge, and thence up to what are supposed to be the remains of one of Tiberius' villas. It was a festival at Capri, so we saw all the *belles* of the island, plump brunettes, with dark eyes and hair, tight-laced black bodices, and white muslin handkerchiefs thrown over their shoulders. Capri is famous, we were told, for the industry and morality of its inhabitants, which, we will hope, is the reason why so many of our countrymen have chosen this island for the site of their hermitage.

Or does the gloomy spirit of Tiberius still dwell there as the *genius loci*, attracting kindred spirits? Lest this should offend any one, let me hasten to say that I do not consider the stories told by Suetonius and even Tacitus as worthy of belief. Court scandal is the most easily invented of all scandals, it is the most readily credited, and the most difficult of disproof. The memoirs of hangers-on about a Court are always to be received with suspicion, be they even written by a Duc de Saint Simon, or a Lord Hervey, much more when they are written by some nameless lackey who has no honour to tarnish, and is therefore quite irresponsible for his statements. Suetonius and Tacitus probably derived their Court gossip from a similar source, for it is very rarely that they give authority for their assertions. They only reject a story when it is palpably inconsistent with some other story they have heard. When two memoir-writers had told the same tale, they accept it and endorse it without a suspicion that both may be lying. The medals which are supposed to confirm the worst charges against Tiberius are found, to the disgrace of the ancient world, at many other places besides Capri. The story told by Suetonius about Tiberius throwing criminals down from a precipitous rock for his amusement, is probably a fiction. But it is likely enough that the tremendous precipice shown as the Salto di Tiberio (or Timperio, as the Capriotes call him) may have been in Suetonius' mind when he repeated or made the tale. The peculiarity just alluded to in the Capriote dialect reminded me of a cognate fact—that the modern Greeks express the sound of b by m and p. For instance, they spell tobacco, "tampakko."

One bourgeois, a Corsican, has opened a little restaurant at the Salto di Tiberio. He has bad wine, worse water, and makes exorbitant charges. I am sorry to say this of an old soldier decorated with the St. Helena medal. He has put up an announcement at the Marina in the following terms (I give it *literatim et punctuatim*) :

"Avis au Salto Tiberio onna ovver un restaurant de ce lo calon guii de la vue du golfe de Salerno et Pesto." *

Apropos, I noticed at Pompeii a jocular recommendation of the Hôtel de Diomède, printed by the landlord, beginning, "Je ne suis pas ce terrible Diomède qui faisait tant de peur aux Troyens et Cæsar." The "et Cæsar" is admirable. A name at which the world grew pale is always good for rounding a sentence.

* The interpretation is this :—"Avis : au Salto de Tiberio on a ouvert un restaurant. De ce local on jouit de la vue," &c.

Extract of a Letter, dated Naples, Sept. 18th.

Naples has passed from the government of the King to that of the Dictator with more ease and with less disturbance of public order than any one could have anticipated. Business has not been suspended for a single day, and, but for the noisy demonstrations of delight which continued for three days after the entry of Garibaldi, a stranger might have lived in Naples without knowing that there had been a change of masters. The newspapers will have given you fully detailed accounts of Garibaldi's facile conquest, and of the tumultuous joy with which it was hailed at Naples. I have been throughout an amused and interested looker-on; but I need not tell a tale with which you are already familiar. I will merely mention summarily the successive events in order to add a touch here and there from personal observation. Up to the last moment there were some who believed that the King would not abandon Naples without a struggle. On the afternoon of Wednesday, Sept. 5, it was known that his troops had received orders to fall back from Salerno, and it was supposed that they would occupy La Cava and Nocera, and defend a pass which is so well calculated for defence. But later in the day we heard that they were abandoning all their positions in front of Naples, and were marching by way of Nola to Capua. It was obvious that the King had given up the game for lost, and that he himself must follow his troops and abandon his capital. All that night there was an unusual stir about the Palace; every window was lighted, and hurrying shadows flitted past within; crowds waited round the gates in the vain hope of seeing the departure of the Court, their motive being, as I gathered, not loyalty, but curiosity. Carts loaded with furniture passed out from time to time, the property, I suppose, of Goldsticks, and Chamberlains, and Lords-in-waiting. "The rats are leaving," said one of the crowd. A Council of Ministers was held in the Palace, which did not separate (it is said) till three in the morning. They were engaged in "redacting" the two proclamations which appeared in the Gazette of next day, in the second of which, countersigned by D. Martino, Garibaldi was called "un ardito condottiere." At the breaking up of the Council, the King went on board ship for Gaeta, the Ministers dispersed to their homes, except Liborio Romano, who hastened to offer his services to the Dictator. The conduct of this Romano is universally condemned. While Minister of the King he was in correspondence with Garibaldi, and, instead of defending the interests of the Crown, he did all in his power to thwart them. He wrote, immediately after the retirement of the Sovereign, a letter to Garibaldi, couched in the most fulsome and abject language. A man must be *morbo proditor* to be proud of his treason, as Romano seems to be. On Thursday, September 6th, I went to Salerno, saw Garibaldi's entry there, and returned with him to Naples. In some respects his reception at Salerno was more striking than that at Naples. The people of Salerno had been expecting him for some hours, and had had time to make preparations, the people of Naples were taken by surprise, and the crowds that gathered hastily all along the line of his passage through the city were evidently half-incredulous, and doubted whether it were he or not. There were no flags on the houses. This was all Garibaldi's doing, who said he preferred a spontaneous welcome. The square in front of the Foresteria, from a balcony of which he addressed the people, was not a quarter full. The demonstrations, however, on that and the two following nights were the most noisy and tumultuous scenes that I have ever witnessed. As far as I could judge, the makers of the noise, in very few instances, belonged to the lower classes. The shriekers, the spouters, the torch-bearers, the wavers of flags, and the brandishers of daggers, were persons from the well-fed, well-dressed orders. The lazzaroni are, I believe, quite passive and indifferent; the priests and peasantry Royalist—but the priests are naturally timid, and the peasantry only feel keenly on a question of cheap bread and cheap fruit. A Masaniello must appeal to this sentiment to have success either with peasants or lazzaroni.

The process by which a show of decency and order was given to Garibaldi's nomination as Dictator was curious. First half-a-dozen individuals, with Romano among them, constituted themselves a Provisional Government on the invitation of the Dictator of Sicily, and then, by virtue of their authority as Provisional Government, they nominated him Dictator of the *Two* Sicilies. His first acts gave satisfaction. He chose his Ministers from the Moderate party—the party (that is) which follows the inspirations of Cavour. And for a few days "all was for the best, under the best of all possible" dictatorships. But latterly, the acts and words of the Dictator have given great alarm. In his proclamation to the people of Palermo he spoke of the miserable men who counselled immediate annexation, and declared that he would proclaim Italian unity on the top of the Quirinal. Then, in an order of the day *apropos* of the death of De Flotte, he alluded sarcastically to the Government of Louis Napoleon. Finally, in a letter to one Brusco, he contradicted a rumour that he had been reconciled to Cavour, and said that he could never be friends with "men who had humiliated the national dignity and sold an Italian province"—which seemed even to include Victor Emmanuel. People here are aghast at his imprudence. They ask themselves, Is this a game which he is playing with the secret connivance of the French Emperor, whose heart is with Italy, though he is obliged, as the eldest son of the Church, to keep up a show of opposition? Or is the Emperor bribing Garibaldi's counsellors to urge him on a path that must lead to his ruin? Is Victor Emmanuel consulted, and, if so, does he approve?

The telegraph is, of course, interrupted at Gaeta, and we only heard, yesterday, of Victor Emmanuel's entry into the Roman provinces. Is this step taken in conjunction with Garibaldi, or is it intended to anticipate and in a measure thwart him? These questions may be answered before you receive this letter. At present, every one seems lost in uncertainty. I have spoken of the Moderate party, which includes, I suppose, the vast majority of educated men above twenty-five years old. The other party—the party of action—consists of Bertani, Crespi, and, of course, Mazzini, and boys in general. The latter party seems to have lost its head in the intoxication of success. They talk of marching to Rome as one talks of taking a drive along the Chiaia. Father Gavazzi* is the prophet of the party. His somewhat commonplace declamation has had great success. He preaches every alternate evening in the square of San Francesco di Paola. To hear democracy lauded in the front of a Bourbon palace is a fact sufficiently piquant to give a zest to the most ordinary oratory, just as the mildest jest becomes irresistibly comical in church.

Several other decrees of the Dictator have given great dissatisfaction, as, for instance, that appointing Alexander Dumas† Director of the National Museum, and commissioning him to prepare a great work on the antiquities of Naples and the neighbourhood. The Neapolitans are justly indignant at having a vagabond foreigner, of abandoned character and no knowledge of antiquities or of art, set over the heads of so many persons infinitely his superiors.

The Dictator's weakness is said to be his submission to favourites. Any one may lead him by the nose, if he takes hold the right way. Bertani is, according to the "Moderates," his evil genius. Meanwhile, with the growing discontent of the Moderates, we hear from time to time of reactionary movements at Avellino, and other places. Forty peasants were brought in yesterday, tied together with

* A mistake. I heard the Father once afterwards, and read other discourses, printed from shorthand writers' notes. He always counsels moderation, and disbelieves in unity without monarchy.

† The pranks of this man, while dressed in his brief authority, were incredible. I saw him one night parading Naples in fantastic costume, attended by a score of men waving flags. At each station of the National Guard they stopped, formed a ring round Dumas, and cheered.

He wrote to Admiral Mundy requesting arms and ammunition for his body guard, and when his letter was returned to him by way of answer, he applied to the French Admiral, whose reply was as decided, and still less flattering.

ropes—a sight of ill omen for the new Government. On Saturday, the Archbishop of Sorrento, the King's tutor, was arrested, and brought to Naples. Last night, there was a general alarm and anticipation of reactionary movement among the lazzaroni in Naples itself. The national guard was under arms all night, but nothing happened. My impression is, that things are getting rapidly worse, both here and in Sicily, and that Garibaldi will not be able much longer to govern the country. The sooner the annexation takes place and a regular Government established, the better for all parties.

Sept. 18.—I went with Mr. D—— to Sta. Maria Maggiore, at present the head-quarters of the revolutionary army. Finding that we were too late for the ten o'clock train, we engaged a large-wheeled single-horse vehicle, something like the now extinct English taxed cart, and in little more than two hours reached Sta. Maria. The road passes through Aversa, and lies for the most part over a perfectly flat and exuberantly fertile country, called *par excellence* Terra di Lavoro, for every yard is under cultivation. On the way, we fell inwith a party of Neapolitan soldiers wearing their side-arms. They were making their way across country to join the royal troops at Capua, or where best they could. We had some difficulty in finding our way into Sta. Maria, owing to the barricades which defended the entrance of the principal streets. Happening to ask some question of a portly gentleman whom we saw in the street, he volunteered to show us over the town, escorted us to the amphitheatre, and offered us the shelter of his house, which he said was not magnificent, but entirely at our disposal, such as it was. The last offer we declined for want of time, but it was made in all sincerity. This is one instance of many within my experience of the especial favour with which we English are regarded at the present time by the Liberal party. Our new friend gave us to understand that he was one of the principal legal functionaries of the place, whether as judge or advocate we did not know, and the frequent respectful greetings that he received attested the truth of his pretension. He was an ardent Garibaldian, and anti-Papal to the uttermost. As a boy, he had been educated by the Jesuits at the Collegio Romano, but the oppression under which he had suffered with his countrymen had completely effaced the lessons of the fathers, and had inclined the tree in the opposite direction to that in which the twig had been bent. He told us that Ferdinand, who lived hard by at Caserta, regarded Sta. Maria with peculiar aversion, and kept it under police regulations of extra strictness. He used to say, "Whenever I go through Sta. Maria, I tread on republican stones." The employment of Lamoricière's mercenaries by the Pope had alienated, as our friend said, the firmest of his Holiness's friends. Italy was now virtually a Protestant country.

The amphitheatre is still a magnificent ruin. The two walls which formed the outermost corridors of the ellipse were unluckily built of hewn stone, decorated with marble columns at the entrance. These, therefore, were pulled down to furnish materials for the palace at Caserta, and probably also for earlier buildings. The brick and rubble work remains nearly intact. The amphitheatre of Capua, when entire, was, except the Coliseum, the largest of all. It served as a model for that of Puteoli. The subterranean constructions are on the same plan. The chambers and passages were lighted by a large longitudinal opening along the major axis of the ellipse, and by square openings all round. At the time of the exhibitions, of course, beams were laid over them, and the whole area strewn with a thick covering of sand. One may see the places where the beams rested. The vast space underground did not serve merely, as we are told in the guide-books, for prisons of criminals and dens of wild beasts, but it was the residence of the gladiators. There are plenty of conduits, wells, and drains for carrying off the rain water, so as to keep the place always dry and habitable. The stone seats for spectators have shared the fate of the outer walls, and been carried off. I observed, that in some of the corridors arches of brickwork had been added subsequently to the erection of the building, in order to strengthen the supports of the cavea.

Returning to the town, we took leave of our volunteer cicerone, and went to pay a visit to the General commanding in the absence of Garibaldi, Hieper, or Eber, as his name is variously spelt. I had been acquainted with him when discharging a more peaceful mission at Constantinople some years ago. The palazzo to which we were directed is a charming residence, with large lofty rooms painted somewhat in the Pompeian style, and polished floors deliciously cool, with a garden of lemon and orange-trees behind.

First came a ruddy-bearded aide-de-camp to ask our business. I begged him to aver la bontà, &c. &c.

"Sprechen Sie Deutsch, mein Herr?" he said.

I answered in the affirmative, and said that I supposed he was a Hungarian, like the General.

No, he was "Echt Deutsch aus dem grossherzogthum Baden."

There were many Germans, he told us, in the army, even Bavarians and Austrians, who looked forward to making "*ein* Deutschland," after they had made *Italia una.* Meanwhile they must, I should think, have to exercise all their proverbial national patience, hearing, as they do, perpetually repeated cries of "Morte ai Tedeschi!" We found the General suffering from a fever caught in the marshes of Cosenza, and scarcely able to walk. However, the politeness of a true gentleman never fails. He got up from the sofa, and gave us a kind welcome, though he must have wished us at—the head-quarters of Francesco II. He gave us a written permission to visit the outposts, of which we availed ourselves at once.

In the streets at intervals we found bodies of the Garibaldians with piled arms, sitting or lying on heaps of straw strewn on the shady side; some sleeping, some smoking, some mending their clothes, some cheapening figs—(although, without cheapening, you get for a halfpenny as many as one could eat in a day), all apparently in high spirits and good health, more like "jolly beggars" than a regular army. A barricade of boughs is placed across the brick arch of Roman work which formed the gate of old Capua, and is on the road to the new—distant about two miles. Half a mile beyond is the line of infantry sentries, who stand at irregular intervals, from fifty to one hundred yards apart. They take their work easily, leaning against a vine-clad poplar in any attitude they may fancy. Provided they do their work, Garibaldi and his officers do not seem to care how they do it. A martinet would be sorely out of place here. A quarter of a mile farther in advance, four poplar trees have been felled, and lie across the road. In front of them is a sentry on horseback. We asked him if we could see the Neapolitan outposts. "O yes," he said, "come along with me, and I'll show you them. When we go forward, they always come out to look at us." When we had gone about a hundred yards, they did come out accordingly, two on horseback and four on foot, about a quarter of a mile off. Having satisfied our curiosity, we returned, in obedience to the advice of the General, who had warned us not to go too far, as they were in the habit of picking up stragglers. What earthly good it would have done them to pick us up, I cannot conceive. If they had taken a fancy to pick us *off*, it would not have been so pleasant.

Our expedition terminated without the shadow of an adventure, but it was interesting as the only glimpse I had ever had of a state of war. Evidently it is not in Garibaldi's army that one must look for "pride, pomp, and circumstance."

We returned by railway. As we passed the splendid Palace of Caserta, we saw the great square in front filled with troops. They are under the command of General Türr. At night, I am told, they sleep inside and outside of the palace, as they best may.

This is the result of Ferdinand's policy. His army is scattered, and revolutionary soldiers occupy every corner of his favourite abode. It is reported that he had no misgivings and no remorse, and that almost his last words were that "he died with the consciousness of having done his duty." He sowed the wind, and his son has reaped the whirlwind.

Sept. 19.—I have just returned from San Gennaro, where I have witnessed the far-famed miracle. I went about half-past eight and found the Cathedral partially filled, and a dense crowd in and about the chapel of San Gennaro—a spacious octagon on the south side of the nave. National guards were keeping the door. At a quarter before nine, a loud shout rose from the crowd within. It was a greeting to the saint, whose image in silver gilt had just been placed on the altar. The shout was renewed as the priest adjusted the mitre and cope with which the image was clothed, and again, as an attendant lighted candle after candle beside it. An aged priest, standing within the altar rails, then raised aloft the vessel containing the sacred blood, and at once a forest of waving arms rose above the crowd, and the building rang with frenzied exclamations. Some other priests and assistants now appeared in the organ loft ready to lead the *Te Deum* whenever the miracle should be achieved; meanwhile, the old man continued to hand round the vessel to let all the bystanders see that there was no deception, that the blood was really solid. The vessel in question is a kind of monstrance, round, with glass on each side, and two handles, one above, one below. It is more like a carriage-lamp than anything else I can think of. Inside, are two small phials containing an opaque substance, the blood of the saint. In order to show that it was solid, the priest turned the monstrance upside down, holding a lighted candle behind it, and showed it, round to the spectators just as a conjuror does before commencing his performance. All this time the crowd kept shrieking and screaming—the old women especially were frantic in their cries and gestures, moaning, and sobbing, and stretching out hands in nervous tension. Some men even were affected with this hysterical passion, and wept and moaned like the women. The confusion of endlessly reiterated prayers, uttered in such tones that they resembled imprecations, reminded me of the chorus of the priests of Baal in the *Elijah;* only here the trebles preponderate over the basses. Mendelssohn may have witnessed some such scene; but, so far as I know, the like is only to be seen at Naples, and in the Church of the Holy Sepulchre at Jerusalem on Easter Sunday. For any other parallel, one must go among fetish-worshipping savages.

The priest then turned his back on the audience, and the agitation of the crowd reached a point where it could no longer be expressed in articulate cries, for nothing was heard but sobs and groans. A very few minutes had elapsed, when the priest suddenly turned round and exhibited the blood LIQUID! A wild howl of exultation rose up; flowers were thrown towards the saint, and, strange to say, a number of birds let loose,* which the spectators had brought with them for the purpose. Never had the miracle been performed so soon. All were agreed on this, and eager discussions were going on in all parts of the church as to the exact time it had taken. Was it three minutes or four, or four minutes and a half? The old women were wild with joy. It was clear that San Gennaro was in the best of tempers towards his dear clients, and not at all displeased with them for turning out their king. Two of Garibaldi's red-shirted soldiers, who were making their way out of the chapel, were the objects of tenderly affectionate demonstrations; old women held up their hands to bless them, others patted them on the back and smiled approvingly. As soon as the shout that greeted the miracle had ceased, the men in the organ loft began the *Te Deum*, and the spectators joined in fervent chorus. Above the din we heard the guns of all the forts thundering out their joy. (There must be some means of telegraphic communication with the forts, as very few minutes elapsed before the cannon was heard.) By-and-by the sacred vessel was carried to the high altar, and successive bodies of worshippers were admitted within a railed space to kneel and kiss it, having first assured

* This, I afterwards learned, is the custom at all the great festivals of the Church, and symbolizes the soul's joy when delivered from the sins and sorrows of earth. It is a literal rendering of that passage in the Psalms, "My soul is escaped as a bird out of the snare of the fowler. The snare is broken, and we are delivered."

themselves by means of the candle that the liquefaction had taken place. Some of the crowd near us were very anxious that we should do the like. "Make way," they said, "for the English Signori. Sergeant," to the officer of the national guard who was keeping the wicket, "admit the English Signori." But we declined the honour, and waited till the priest—the same who had officiated in the chapel—brought it round. As there was no candle placed behind it for our benefit, and as the outer glass was dimmed with the kisses it had received, we were not able to ascertain the fact of the liquefaction. But all who have seen it before and after with the aid of the light, agree that the blood, if blood it be, is certainly solid first and liquid afterwards. There is no deception so far. But admitting that, I cannot but remember that I have seen the Wizard of the North and Wiljalba Frikell do as much, and more, with their enchantments. It is certain that the belief of the crowd in the chapel was genuine and profound. This crowd consisted of persons of all ranks, though the poorer classes preponderated. It would scarcely have been prudent for Garibaldi, in presence of this intense and deeply-seated superstition, to forbid the miracle as the *Times* hoped he would. An *émeute* might have been the consequence.

"Paris vaut bien une messe," said Henri Quatre. Garibaldi may say, "Naples vaut bien un miracle."

Some days ago I was expressing to a Neapolitan my wish to see the liquefaction. "Do not mention it," he said; "it fills me with shame." I cannot doubt that this is the general feeling of most educated men, but it is not universal, for among the weepers and the kissers to-day I saw several who, from their dress and bearing, certainly ought to belong to that class. One young priest, of rather attractive countenance, came out of the chapel, his eyes red and his cheeks swollen with weeping, but most of his order seemed impassive and did not attempt even to counterfeit devotion. The venerable old man in rose-coloured robes, who officiated, showed no feeling whatever. Probably perfect self-possession, with a little manual dexterity, is the quality most requisite in the officiating minister.*

Sept. 19.—This evening our dinner was enlivened by animated accounts of a battle which had taken place in the morning, and at which half a dozen of the guests of the hotel had had the luck to be present. They had to tell of hairbreadth escapes, exemplary coolness under first fire, the cowardice of the Garibaldian troops, and their own courage. England had nearly lost an eminent barrister and an eminent artist by a grape-shot, which carried away part of their carriage, a third had arrested the flight of a regiment with his umbrella, a fourth had parried a cannon-ball with his walking-stick.

The real facts, as far as I have been able to gather them by subsequent inquiries, are these : General Hieper and Colonel Roskow, commanding the centre and left, had orders to make a feigned attack upon Capua, while Garibaldi and Türr were to cross the Volturno a few miles up the river and cut off a body of the enemy, occupying a plain on the other bank. Roskow, however, mistaking his instructions, attempted a real attack. As soon as he advanced into an open space in front of the gate of Capua, and within reach of the artillery having no artillery himself, his men were cut down by the fire from the bastions, and refused to advance. As soon as a body of royal cavalry showed itself, they fled precipitately, the officers being the first to set the example. Such was the panic that they rushed through Sta. Maria, and did not stop till they had passed the town, and saw at last that there was no man pursuing. One of my informants saw with his own eyes two of Garibaldi's officers crouching under a haystack to strip off their red shirts, lest they should be recognised. A more disgraceful panic was never seen. The good folks of Sta. Maria, that republican city, made haste to take all the tricolor flags from their windows. Even that which floated

* The secret is known only to the priests of San Gennaro and Mr. R. Monckton Milnes, who tells me that he has not merely witnessed, but once performed the miracle.

from the windows of the house which was General Hieper's head-quarters disappeared. The national guards stripped off their uniforms, and all was prepared for the return of his Majesty. Had the royal army had a leader, they might have marched to Naples unopposed. Meanwhile, Hieper had nothing to do, and did it. Türr and Garibaldi, on the right wing, found their road barred by a fire of artillery which they could not face, and finally retreated to Caserta. The number of killed and wounded in the revolutionary army amounts, according to the best informed statements, to about one hundred and fifty.

The varying accounts of this engagement illustrate the propensity of Italians in general, and Neapolitans in particular, to invention and credulity combined. The *Lampo* for instance, a Garibaldian organ, had the audacity to affirm that the royalist losses amounted to eight thousand in killed and wounded, whereas they could not, by the nature of the case, have exceeded twenty or thirty. But invention is not confined to the Neapolitans. On the authority of one of Garibaldi's generals, it was asserted that the possession of Chaiazzo was the object which the General had in view in making his attack, and that that object had been attained. Military men not connected with either party affirmed that it would be impossible to hold Chaiazzo, being a position quite isolated on the other side of the river, and that no one would have thought of making such an attempt. Up to the day I left Naples, September 22d, it was a matter of doubt whether it had really been taken or not. The last news I heard before leaving was that it been retaken by the royal troops; but it was doubted whether this, too, was not an invention to cover the other lie, and account for the fact that it was in the possession of the Garibaldians no longer.

One lives at Naples in an atmosphere charged with falsehood, and it is impossible to get a breath of native truth. From the evidence of independent witnesses, it is certain that the Garibaldians met with a severe check, the moral effect of which has been very great, and more than counterbalances the manifestation of San Gennaro's favour in the morning.

Sept. 20.—Hearing that it was probable the battle would be renewed this morning, I went, in company with Colonel B—— (who had seen the engagement of the previous day), an English officer, and another friend, to Sta. Maria, whence, finding all tranquil, we proceeded to St. Angelo, a village about three miles off, above which is a hill commanding a wide view of the scene of war. Leaving our carriage at the village, we climbed through oak coppice to the sharp edge of the hill. In ascending, we had a good bird's-eye view of the plain of Capua, and of some 2,500 cavalry occupying it. From the ridge we looked over the winding Volturnus, on the farther bank of which is another plain, divided by a low range of hills from that of Capua, and also occupied by the royal troops. There were two regiments of cavalry and three or four of infantry; double sentries, at short intervals, lining the bank of the river. We were so near that we heard the words of command, and, occasionally, one man calling to another. As we were some time examining them with our glasses, we at last attracted their attention, and a little knot of men gathered on the bank and fired about twenty shots at us, without hitting or coming near us. A tremendous thunderstorm, which had been threatening for some time and at last broke, was much more effectual in dislodging us from our position. We crept behind an overhanging rock, hoping that the rain would cease. From our lair, looking south, we had a prospect of bare, peaked hills, with castles on the top, and agreed, that if we had been transported there in sleep, we should, on waking, have thought ourselves in Rhine-land. But close round us were growing shrubs that never clothe the bleak northern hills—dwarf ilex, and myrtle, and the judas tree. As we descended we were caught in a still more violent shower, and took refuge in the crater of an extinct lime-kiln, where we found a dozen or more peasants and Garibaldini already housed. One was a captain of artillery, who gave us rum and tobacco, and in the course of half an hour communicated, unasked, the story of his life. He told us of his innamorata, showed us her picture and handwriting, and said that he had joined Garibaldi that he might have an opportunity of doing some heroic deed, and might say on his return to the lady of his love (here he threw open his arms), "Ecco-mi! son degno di te!"

Sept. 21.—On going out after breakfast, instead of being assailed by half a dozen cabmen shouting in my ears, cracking their whips in my eyes, and driving across my path, the wheels just missing my toes, I found the stand deserted. It was the same at another stand. There was not a cab to be had. On inquiry, I found that the Government had pressed such carriages, public and private, as they could lay hold off, and sent them to Santa Maria for the conveyance of wounded men. The other cabmen had made off directly, and hid themselves and their horses. Everybody inferred that a great battle was expected, so I immediately walked off to the railway station, where I arrived just as the train was starting. (At these times a ticket is a needless formality—quite an unnecessary expense. You are never asked for your ticket, nor expected to pay anything except a small gratuity to the official who gets you a seat. It is an ill wind that blows nobody good. Even a time of war has its advantages.) When I reached Santa Maria, I found that I had again come on a false alarm. The carriages had been impressed to bring back to Caserta those who had been wounded on the previous Wednesday—such of them, that is, as were capable of removal. I went to see those who remained in one of the hospitals at Santa Maria. The wards were tolerably clean and airy, and the wants of the poor sufferers seemed as well attended to as circumstances permitted; but it was a sad sight. In one case the ball had entered the eye and gone out in the neck—a terrible wound; but the surgeon said he had hopes of saving the man's life. In another case the ball had carried away part of the lower jaw and all the teeth. The saddest case of all was that of a poor child of ten years old, who, with his father, was driving a cart on the day of the battle. They were compelled to come into the field to help in moving the wounded. While so engaged, a grape-shot killed the father and carried off the son's leg. Amputation had been performed, and he was, they said, "doing well." Doing well! When I saw him, he seemed to be asleep. It was piteous to see his sad, pale face, rosy with health but two days ago, now showing sorrow and suffering even in sleep. No one had been to see him or inquire after him. Poor child! I suppose, then, he has no mother, and is an orphan indeed. What a sorrowful beginning of life for him! Perhaps he was the eldest of the family, proud of having in charge his motherless brothers and sisters, and being able to work for them. Think of those little ones in their cottage, waiting and wondering why father and brother do not come home at sunset. How war scatters its miseries, farther and wider than its grape-shot, over the quiet happy fields!

There was one man in hospital the bones of whose hand had been splintered by a bullet. He looked as vivacious as if nothing had happened to him. He was a Venetian, had escaped to Piedmont, entered the service there, was disgusted at not having the medal for the war of '59, and so deserted to join Garibaldi and fight for the liberation of his native town. He said that his only regret was, that he had not had a chance of killing one of the enemy before he was wounded himself, and of washing his hands in his blood. And he said the terrible words, "Lavar mi le mani nel suo sangue," with the sweetest of smiles, as when a gourmet speaks of some favourite dainty. While I was there, Colonel da Porta, a Sicilian commanding his battalion, came in, and filled the man with delight by announcing his nomination as sottotenente (ensign).

The field ambulance of this strange army is under the direction of a Piedmontese lady, the Contessa della T., who attracted great attention in Naples (which, without being uncharitable, one may suppose was not displeasing to her) by the singularity of her manners, language, and costume. She was dressed in a white braided hussar tunic, trousers, and boots outside, with spurs, and a Spanish hat with plumes, and a sword which clanked as she walked in an alarming way. She was attended by three or four Calabrians, dressed like the conventional brigands of the stage, who served as her body-guard. She talked in all languages, and somewhat took off the grace of her charitable deeds by blowing a trumpet so loudly before her.*

In returning, we visited the palace of Caserta. No one was permitted to enter the gardens without an order, which we had some difficulty in procuring. I was referred from one general to another, all royally lodged in the palace; at last General Medici was good enough to let us pass through his apartments on the ground floor.

The arrangement of the gardens resembles that of the gardens at La Granja in Spain, only on a much larger scale. An aqueduct conveys a copious stream of water to the side of a steep ilex-clothed hill about two miles off, at the back of the palace. Thence it descends first in a natural waterfall over rough rocks, and afterwards in small cascades alternating with still pools, to the plain. From the foot of the waterfall to the palace the distance is 3100 yards. Avenues of ilex and other trees bound the terraces on either side, and there is an abundance of statues, gods, men, dolphins, monsters, and grottoes. At the foot of the waterfall are two groups in marble, representing on one side Diana and her nymphs, on the other, Actæon torn by his hounds, all reflected in the dark deep water. The rocks about are clothed with acacia, oleander, and aloe. In the largest pool was a shoal of old carp and one stately swan, which, accustomed to be fed by royal hands, came sailing up to ask for biscuit of the intruders. From the highest terrace is a beautiful and singular view. You look over the palace and the densely wooded level plain in which it lies, like a dark green sea, beyond the rim of which rise the highlands of Capri, and the Punta di Sorrento.

The palace itself is more than 200 yards square,† if my

* When a lady chooses to dress and behave like a man, she forfeits the immunities of her sex, and it is no longer ungallant to criticise her actions.

† Vanvitelli, the architect, published a description of the palace in 1756, from which it appears that the outer sides measure respectively 920 and 720 Neapolitan palms. A copy of this rare work is found—as, indeed, what rare book is not?—in the library at Keir.

rough measurement be right, and is divided into four courts, with an open arcade occupying the ground floor from gate to gate. A broad staircase, lined with costly marbles, leads to a great octagon hall occupying the centre of the pile, with four windows at the angles looking each into a separate court. The octagon is supported by pillars of African marble taken from the temple of Serapis at Puzzuoli. All the palaces I have ever seen yield in magnificence to this; Versailles is *mesquin* in comparison. What would Ferdinand have said had he lived to see it occupied by a rabble of revolutionary troops, lighting camp fires in the centre of his courts, cooking, playing cards, smoking, and singing Garibaldi's hymn? I can easily conceive that the generals who are enjoying royal luxuries, and exercising among them more than royal power, are not anxious for the arrival of Victor Emmanuel, who would relegate them to some less sumptuous abode, and to some inferior position.

When I reached the railway-station, I found a train of empty trucks and cattle waggons just starting. A number of the red-shirted gentry demanded that a carriage should be attached to it for their use. The station-master declared he had none, whereupon they threatened, hustled, and collared him, and finally carried him off to the palace, to answer to some one for his contumacy. This is one instance among many of the insolence which has made the liberators more unpopular at Naples than ever were its former masters.

The train started without waiting for the issue of the dispute. I got upon a truck with a number of common soldiers (Garibaldians), whose behaviour presented a very favourable contrast to that of their officers. One provided me with an inverted basket to sit upon, another compelled me to accept a cigar (very bad, it is true, but the best he had), a third insisted upon my taking a cartridge as a keepsake. One of them had been an artist, he told me, and had abandoned his easel at Milan to carry a musket in Calabria.

Never, surely, was there such a motley army as this. It

contains men of all ranks, and of all characters; there are men of high birth and gentle breeding, there are also outcasts and vagabonds; there are generous and chivalrous enthusiasts, there are also charlatans and impostors, and unhappily it is not always the former who fill the highest places.

I have seldom seen any earthly object arrayed in such glory as was Vesuvius in the splendour of that calm evening. Through vistas of vine-clad poplars we saw the cone all ruddy purple, every furrow in the outer shell of the mountain distinctly marked with blue shadows, which deepened towards its base into the richest ultramarine. The more recent lava-streams were (like the cone) of a bright purple, and looked, to my fancy, like piles of grapes poured out, waiting for the winepress that should extract from them the famous Vesuvian product—Lacryma Christi.

The name Lacryma Christi, by the way, which shocks English ears, at least when translated, is an instance of the familiarity, and, as it seems to us, irreverence with which Italians treat sacred persons and things. I remember to have read a lecture of Dr. Newman's, in which he maintained the thesis, that the profane and blasphemous oaths habitually used by the people in Italy, proved that the objects of devotion were always present to their minds in whatever aspect, and that the state of mind of an Italian was far preferable to the apathy and indifference of the lower orders in England. To this one might reply on behalf of our countrymen, that their favourite expletive, by the same reasoning, proves the thought of eternal salvation to be always present to their minds. Again, Dr. Newman's proposition would lead to the further inference that a man is religious at heart in proportion to the profanity of his language, "which is absurd," as Euclid says. Again, many of the Italian oaths are obscene. Dr. Newman would find it difficult to twist this fact into an argument for their purity of mind. In some, too, which he who has once heard would gladly forget, profanity and obscenity are combined to form a result which outrages every good feeling. Remembering these, one can only think of Dr. Newman's argument with disgust, as something more than disingenuous.

All men of education in Southern Italy disclaim any sympathy with the religion of the lower orders, which is mere paganism disguised under new names, and consists in the worship of a number of local deities. The Madonna of one shrine is, in the popular imagination—for it is not definite enough to be called a creed—quite a different person from the Madonna of another.

The friar who tends the little chapel at the entrance of the Grotto of Puzzuoli begged one day of a passing stranger, "for the Madonna." "La Reina degli Angeli è ricca abbastanza," said the stranger. "Ah! bah!" said the friar, "non à mica la Reina degli Angeli! è la *povera* Madonna della Grotta, che le manca anche per pagare l'olio" (she has not enough to pay for the oil to light the lamps of the tunnel).

A friend among many good stories told me one, *ben trovato*, if not *vero*, which illustrates the primitive simplicity of their faith. A woman at Naples, praying the Madonna to come and heal her son, took care to give her address—"Vieni, Maria, vieni, numero tredici, vicolo della Scrofa, terzo piano, seconda porta a man destra."

Nowhere, probably, in the world is the separation so great between the well-to-do classes and the poor as it is in South Italy. They are quite distinct in religion, thought, and feeling. Between the highest and the lowest there is, indeed, outwardly a familiarity of manner which, at first sight, would point to an opposite conclusion. We see none of the hauteur on the one side, or the servility on the other, which is so common in England; but the familiarity is only superficial and apparent. There is a deep unfathomed gulf fixed between those who have something and those who have nothing to lose. A householder or shopkeeper at Naples speaks of the lazzaroni as a Hindoo living beside a jungle might speak of the tigers. So there is probably no country in the world where the opinion of the middle and upper classes is so fallacious a test of the popular opinion. The newspaper controversies and the theatre-riots of Naples only indicate the division of opinion in the middle and upper ranks—some holding with Victor Emmanuel, some with Mazzini, some with Cavour, some with Garibaldi—but they tell us nothing of the sentiments of the masses. The mob of the towns, the priests and the peasantry, are probably more inclined, by this time, to the old than to the new Government. If you asked a *contadino* his opinion early in September, the answer was always to the same effect: "Rè Vittorio, Rè Giuseppe, Rè Francesco," it is all one provided he gives us "da mangiare à buon mercato." And when they find that prices are enhanced instead of lowered, under the new reign, they will be sure to throw the blame on the Government. I do not doubt that if universal suffrage were honestly applied to test the opinion of Southern Italy, a large majority would be found for Francesco II., at least in the Abruzzi and the provinces adjacent to the capital. Cavour threw a slur on his master's cause, and made a flaw in his claim, by resting it on a successful repetition of that French juggling imposture, which is as discreditable to statesmen as the miracle of San Gennaro is to priests. The intelligence of a country should rule it and determine its destinies; and if all the intelligence be, as in South Italy, centred in one class, that class should alone be called upon to give its suffrage.

Sept. 22.—The last news I heard before leaving Naples was, that Garibaldi's "moderate" Ministry had resigned in a body, and that a set of Red Republicans had succeeded them. People are beginning to fear that in his heart the General wishes for a republic, and that he will play Victor Emmanuel false. After the use he made of the King's name, which has indeed been a tower of strength to him, this would be an act of perfidy without parallel in history. The confidence felt in Garibaldi has, however, been so much shaken, that it is looked upon as a possible contingency. It is reported, that to an aide-de-camp whom the King sent to him two days ago, he said, "Tell your master that if a republic should be necessary, I will do my best to make him Dictator." This doubt of Garibaldi's intentions was evidently felt by the Ministry, who a few days ago insisted upon taking the oath of allegiance to Victor Emmanuel. The Dictator did not take it, probably on the plea that he was already his subject. In three weeks I have seen the extinction of a popularity that seemed boundless. The people who were wild with delight at the arrival of Garibaldi would now be equally delighted to get rid of him. The reasons for this change are obvious. His refusal to declare at once the annexation of Southern Italy to Northern has alienated the moderate party, and generated suspicion of his intentions, which his violent language on several occasions has tended to confirm. In his proclamation to the Palermitans, he said that he would proclaim Italian unity from the top of the Quirinal only—thus menacing even France. In an order of the day lamenting the death of one of his officers, he praised him for being a true democrat; in a letter to one Brusco, published in the official journal, he proclaimed his irreconcileable hostility to the men who had humiliated the national dignity and sold an Italian province. All this has created a feeling that he is dragging Naples on, not towards a peaceful union with the rest of Italy, but towards an abyss of anarchy and war. Again, many of the decrees issued by him far outstep the limits of a confessedly temporary and transitional power. He declares the royal property to be national property—he banishes the Jesuits and confiscates their goods—he does the like to the most eminent prelates—he abolishes State lotteries—he forbids the payment of *gamorra*—he concedes the right of fishing in the ports—all which may be useful measures, but not necessary to be done at once (unless the banishment of the prelates be regarded as a measure of security). These and a number of other measures might be left to the consideration of the regular Government. His nomination of Alexander Dumas to be director of the national museum, offended all men of education. The offence was increased by the summary dismissal, without compensation, of all the *employés* of the museum, and by a paper issued by the new director full of insolence and arrogance, in which he told the Neapolitans that want of education had degraded them to the level of brutes, and that he was about to raise them by showing them all that was great in politics and beautiful in art. If this offended the upper classes, the seizing of the carriages yesterday was a measure which has still more deeply offended the lower—not the owners and drivers alone, but others who see that their rights of property may be any day similarly invaded. Add to these causes of complaint, the bullying and insolent demeanour of many of Garibaldi's officers, and the natural reaction and discouragement which could not but follow such a fever of excitement, and we shall see enough to account for the decline of his popularity. "I'll make you a bet," said a Neapolitan to me, "that his power will not last as long as Masaniello's." "Que venga il Re Vittorio Emmanuele e venga subito, con venti mila soldati per cacciarci da Napoli questa canaglia!" was the fervid exclamation of another who had made himself hoarse with shouting "Viva Garibaldi" on the 7th of September.

Garibaldi's character was thus summed up by a friend of mine at Turin: "He is a brave soldier, but a great fool," using the phrase (I suppose) in the sense of "un grand fou." I thought it harsh at the time, but my Neapolitan friends, chiefly belonging to the "moderate" party, were agreed in thinking it not so far from the truth. He was of course the chief topic of conversation during my stay at Naples. I give, in as few words as I can, the residuum of much talk.

As a soldier, he is of undaunted courage and a master of the "dodges" (passez-moi le mot) which are required in guerilla war, but he has no conception of a general's duties in the field; he is ignorant of the very rudiments of tactics, and incapable of organization on a large scale. He is kind and gentle in his manners, and reluctant to hurt any one's feelings, while he is reckless of their lives. His bravery and gentleness, his generosity and disinterestedness, secure him the personal affection of all around him, and that constitutes his great merit as a commander. He pushes his love of simplicity to a point bordering on affectation, and is almost ostentatious in his dislike of pomp. He is illogical, prejudiced, and obstinate to a degree never before combined. He thinks cavalry useless, and has a profound contempt for cannon. He is perfectly certain that he has only to appear before the walls of Rome, and the French will leave it, taking with them the Holy Father. "What if they don't?" it was urged. "O, but they will!" was the answer, in the tone of a man who admits no further discussion. He thinks that the walls of Mantua and Verona will fall, like those of Jericho, at a shout. He is very easily imposed on, and believes in all those who are about him. Familiarity breeds respect, and no proof will convince him of the dishonesty of any one whom he has once trusted. He has not the moral courage to say "No" to a request of any of these favourites. His ignorance is such that the smallest show of knowledge completely imposes upon him. He thinks Crespi a statesman, and Dumas a scholar. However, in forming an estimate of him, as of other extraordinary characters in history, we ought to be on our guard against the tendency natural to men to reduce eminence to the ordinary level by discovering a number of small failings. And when all abatements are made, there remain the great facts. His achievements are to be accounted for. He alone had gauged correctly the real weakness of the Neapolitan power, and the strength of his own seemingly feeble means, and he had the courage to test practically the truth of his conclusions. His life-long devotion to one great idea, and his strength of will, have made him "a king of men," and distinguish him from the crowd, who are always, on their own showing, victims to "circumstances over which they have no control."

I left Naples for Civita Vecchia on the afternoon of this day. On board the steamer I met General Bosco. He was prevented by illness from following the army to Capua, and was in Naples when Garibaldi arrived. The latter has required or advised him to leave the country for a while: he is therefore going to Paris. He says that all the arrangements for the equipment and feeding of the Neapolitan troops are very good; that, in general, the material order of the army is excellent, but that the late King ruined its *morale* by introducing a system of promotion which has neither the advantages of the Austrian nor of the French system. The officers are not, as in the Austrian army, taken from the upper classes in society, and who therefore command the respect of the soldiers, and have, or ought to have, a nice sense of personal honour; neither are they, as in the French army, chosen in great measure from among the bravest and most intelligent men in the ranks; but they are men without either social rank or individual merit. As far as I could understand, promotion is made by seniority, and is excessively slow. There were some men, he said, still lieutenants at fifty. Most of these old officers are married men and very poor, having little or nothing but their pay to live on, so that their interests and anxieties are with their families and not with the regiment, and thus *ces pères de famille* are capable of any treason or baseness if only they can avoid exposing lives so valuable at home. In the higher grades, of course, exceptions are made. General Bosco's own case is an instance. He was only a major at the accession of the present King—if I may still call Francesco II. "the present King."

Between the police-office, the custom-house, and the railway-station, a traveller's patience is sorely tried at Civita Vecchia, as might be expected, seeing that there is in prescribing formalities a most elaborate system, and in executing them no system at all. One who knows Rome well tells me that utter confusion reigns in all the departments of administration, from the highest to the lowest. In their normal state, the Government offices are like what they were in England, in the days when Samuel Pepys was at the Admiralty; just now they are in the condition which the said offices must have been in after the news of William's landing at Torbay had reached the metropolis. In the best of times every official pilfers quietly, in proportion to his rank; now there is a general scramble.

I was eager to see Rome in this supreme crisis of its fortunes. I find that the crisis is like that of a fever, through which the patient passes in unconsciousness. It is said that there is a committee, or committees, somewhere, in communication with the revolutionists at Genoa and Naples; but no one seems to know or care anything about it. At Naples, in the last days of Francesco, the committees kept issuing, three or four times a day, bulletins of news and inflammatory placards; here I see nothing of the kind. People in the *cafés* talk about the movements of the Piedmontese without fear or restraint; but also, as it seems to me, without interest or sympathy. I see "Viva Garibaldi!" "Viva Vittorio Emmanuele!" scribbled on the walls; but these inscriptions are apparently of old date, and the police have not taken the trouble to efface them—perhaps the most effectual way of neutralising their effect, just as the Irish denunciations of English tyranny are perpetually contradicted by the fact that they are allowed to be expressed. I see no groups, as at Naples, gathered round some one who has the latest news to tell. We are in complete ignorance as to what is going on at Ancona or Capua. We do not even know for certain where the nearest outposts of the Piedmontese army lie. All communications are interrupted, and the latest intelligence is conveyed in private letters from Turin or Paris. If, however, the people here were not indifferent, we should surely hear a great deal of false news and reports, originating in excited imaginations.

The *Giornale di Roma*—the only paper allowed to be printed—gives us news from Shanghai, and a discussion as to whether the Matilda of Dante was an Italian Princess or a German Saint, but contains not a word of news respecting the invading army. It was so with the Government organ at Naples in the last days of Francesco. Meanwhile, every one believes that the days of the Pope's reign, as a temporal sovereign, are numbered. The *dénouement* is certain, in whatever way it may be brought about. We who look on are like the reader of a novel who has peeped at the last page and seen that it ends happily, so that he goes through the book with diminished interest, but with some curiosity nevertheless to see by what ingenious process the author will extricate his characters from their embarrassment.

The conduct of the plot is no doubt all settled between the great *collaborateurs* at Turin and Paris. The Romans, in the meantime, are not at all sorry to let other people play their game, and give effect to their wishes, without being involved in the risk and worry of an insurrection:

> "If fate will have me king, why fate may crown me
> Without my stir."

When a man can lie at his ease while other people climb the tree to shake the ripe fruit down to the ground within his reach, who can wonder at his acquiescence in so comfortable an arrangement?

The Holy Father, it is said, remains at the Vatican, freed from most of the cares of government; eating heartily and sleeping soundly, cheerfully preparing himself for the scaffold or the stake, thus enjoying by anticipation all the glories of martyrdom, together with a comfortable assurance that he will not be called upon to endure the pain thereof.

An ardent Protestant asked the English clergyman the other day, "What arrangements he had made in the event of the fall of the Papacy?" expecting, I suppose, that he would put on his surplice and bands, and, followed by his clerk proceed to read himself in at St. Peter's according to the form prescribed in the Book of Common Prayer.

There is a very general idea prevalent, both among the foes and the friends of the Pope, that the destruction of his temporal will entail the ruin of his spiritual power. Among Protestants the wish is father to the thought, and the impatient interpreters of prophecy find no warrant in their texts for breaking the fall of Antichrist half-wav down.

Among devout Romanists the notion arises from their attachment to the tradition of their Church, which holds the two powers to be inseparable, and which clutches at the substantial patrimony of St. Peter with as much tenacity as his metaphorical keys. In reality, I doubt whether ardent anti-Romanists are wise in advocating the abolition of the temporal power. The notorious scandals of the Papal administration tend to throw a slur upon his spiritual pretensions. If a man know not how to rule his own household, how shall he rule the Church of Christ? How can the worst of temporal sovereigns be the best of spiritual fathers?

I believe that his position as spiritual sovereign would be strengthened by the abolition of the temporal power. It is a reform as urgently needed as the reforms which were brought about within the Roman Church after Luther's secession. From those reforms the Church derived new strength and a fresh lease of existence. That lease is now run out, and can only be renewed on condition of parting with the temporal power. The world is not yet ripe for the destruction of the spiritual domination, and till then the powers of Napoleon, and Victor Emmanuel, and Garibaldi all united will not prevail against it. Not martyr flames nor trenchant swords shall do away that ancient institution.

Sept. 23.—The gardens of the French Academy on the Pincian, open to the public this (Sunday) afternoon, are planted in a manner rather unusual now-a-days. Narrow walks intersect each other at right angles, bordered on each side by tall hedges of box overtopped by ilex and bay (here meriting its name of *laurus nobilis*), with generally at each angle a cypress or pine. Such a garden, delightfully cool and pleasant beneath this Italian sun, would be damp, and chill, and mouldy in England. Nevertheless the lieges of Elizabeth used to love "pleached alleys," and I could fancy that Shakespeare planted for himself some such "trim pleasaunce" at New Place. I wonder if there was more sunshine in England in those days. In Spenser and Shakespeare it is almost always sunshine—a notable storm now and then

—but sunshine as a rule. Is there any truth in the fancy of all old people that the weather used to be warmer and finer when they were young? Or is it that nature has kindly provided for men, whether poets or not, that only the sunny hours of life shall make a lasting impression on the memory, like the dial that says, "Horas non numero nisi serenas?"

In sight of the stone bench where I am sitting are a group of children, from twelve to fifteen years old, playing with a heartiness which we are accustomed to think a special characteristic of English children. It is a sunny hour for them. Their game is called Ladri e Sbirri. The first thing they do is to stand round in a ring. Each holds out three fingers. The biggest boy counts, beginning from his left hand, three, six, nine, &c. up to twenty-one, after which he goes on counting each boy as one till he gets to thirty-one, and number thirty-one is the Capo Sbirro. This elaborate device is to prevent cheating in the choice of a leader. The Capo Ladro is chosen in the same way. The head spy and the head robber then choose their men alternately. The Sbirri tie a handkerchief for distinction round the left arm, and start in chase of the robbers. Some of the stone seats are supposed, "by making believe very much," to be caves, where they are secure. If the robbers succeed in escaping all to the same cave, they win the game. It was curious to observe how, even in the ardour of the game, the slow, *traînant*, distinct enunciation of the Romans was preserved. A strange contrast to the confused gibberish of the Neapolitans.

Sept. 25.—The Pope had ordered solemn prayers for three days—a *triduo* is the name still in use, adopted like so many others from Pagan Rome—to be offered for the success of his arms. These were repeated for three successive evenings at vesper time, in one of the chapels of St. Peter's. Swiss guards lined each side of the chapel, and the Holy Father himself, in scarlet cope, knelt in front of the altar, and once during the ceremony offered incense. The persons present—five or six hundred in number—joined in the chanting with great apparent fervour, but before the service was over, a large part had scurried off, and taken their place in a double line leading to the door, by which his Holiness was to pass on the way to the Vatican. The Pope looked placid and benignant as ever, and showed no trace of care or trouble in face or figure. People dropped on their knees to receive his benediction.

An Englishman, whose Protestantism has been intensified by residence in Rome, to whom I spoke of the effective performance I had just witnessed, said, "Yes, they are consummate actors, but I have long felt that the play has lost its attractiveness by too much repetition, and now it is more dreary to me than ever, for I know that there is no money to renew the dresses and decorations, or to pay the wages of the scene-shifters and candle-snuffers."

Early in October I returned by way of Marseilles and Paris. All the Frenchmen I talked with on the steamer and in the railway carriage showed great irritation against Italians in general, and Garibaldi in particular. They were very sore about Castelfidardo, and the fate of the Pope's French volunteers, who had fought like lions "*un contre cent*," and before succumbing to numbers had annihilated a whole regiment of Piedmontese. If their opinion could be taken as an index of the general feeling of France, the Emperor would be taking a popular course if he were to restore the *status quo* in Italy by force of arms, leaving only Lombardy to Piedmont, as a compensation for Savoy and Nice. It was agreed that the position of Austria in Venice was intolerable. "*Que faire?*" My suggestion that Austria should sell it was ridiculed as "*une idée vraiment Anglaise,*"* they not seeming to remember that the great Napoleon netted a good round sum by a similar transaction with regard to Louisiana.

These same Frenchmen showed, I am sorry to say, no good will towards England. They spoke out their sentiments with

* Now (December, 1860), this very plan is recommended by several journals in France, as the only solution of the difficulty.

that complete disregard of a stranger's feelings which distinguishes them from all other nations, and makes them essentially the rudest nation in Europe. They told me that every one knew the great ultimate purpose of the Emperor's policy was the humiliation of England; that in less than ten years he would take Gibraltar from us, and give it to Spain, he would take the Ionian Islands and give them to Greece, thus making allies for himself everywhere at our expense; that he would seize Egypt, and cut us off from India, &c. &c.

A countryman whom I met at Paris had been the object of similar polite attentions in crossing France. One of his fellow-travellers, rejoicing in the prospect of a speedy war, rubbed his hands and said with a cheerful smile, "Oui, Monsieur, nous vous mangerons les entrailles."

The French say, and by constantly affirming it have half-persuaded themselves, that they are stronger than we, and would, in the event of a war, be certainly victorious, but beneath their boasting lurks a feeling of distrustful fear, which will give them pause, and make them reflect that they may find a cheaper and safer way of gratifying their national vanity by continuing to brag of what they will do than by trying to do it.

2. *A TOUR IN CIVIL AND MILITARY CROATIA, AND PART OF HUNGARY.*

BY GEORGE ANDREW SPOTTISWOODE.

AT the end of October last, our party, consisting of my brother and sister, myself, and the courier, found ourselves at Trieste. A somewhat erratic course had brought us from Innsbruck by Salzburg and Ischl, through Styria to Bruck, where we joined the Vienna and Trieste railway. We had been well rewarded for devoting one day to Adelsberg, where we had spent some hours in exploring the intricacies and beauties of its caves; and were now making preparations for continuing our journey farther south.

Utterly abjuring steamboats, both on general grounds and also on account of a too recent experience of them by some of our party in the Mediterranean, we had intended to proceed by land. The lateness of the season warned us to push on without visiting Pola or the other places of interest in Istria. We accordingly took the direct route to Fiume, which begins to ascend the mountains behind Trieste, immediately after quitting the town; and then striking off from the road to Laibach, continues along a high ridge overlooking, on the left, the desolate region called the Karst. Here the eye ranges over an immense tract of stony country, without catching a trace of vegetation except here and there a wretched stick of a tree, bearing the few twigs which the bitter north-east wind allows to grow.

But though no vegetation meets the eye, there is a peculiarity about this district which considerably modifies its apparent sterility. The surface is honeycombed throughout with circular, funnel-shaped holes, twenty, fifty, or a hundred feet or more in diameter, and at the bottom of these funnels is always a little spot of rich black mould, in every case showing marks of diligent culture. Until these are discovered, the traveller is at a loss to understand whence the population of the large whitewashed villages, scattered at distant intervals over this region, derives its subsistence. A little beyond Castelnuovo, we first catch sight of the country sloping towards Fiume. A steep hill descends at our feet to a sea of tumbled rocks at the bottom, and some miles in front rises a wall of bare stony mountains, gorgeous with the pink and orange hues of sunset. A purple slumber gradually steals over them, followed by the grey twilight, which at last hides them from our eyes.

Fiume is a pretty town of ten or twelve thousand inhabitants. As you look out of the hotel-window over the quay, the mountains of Istria on the right and some islands in front inclose a fine harbour, the great drawback to which is the difficulty of access. Here, as everywhere, the hotel was half occupied by the officers of the garrison, there being in the town nearly as many soldiers as inhabitants.

The intelligence of the new constitutions which were to be granted to the different Austrian states had been received very coldly by the people of Fiume. The studiously vague terms in which the announcement was conveyed, left them in doubt of the point on which their anxiety chiefly centred; namely, whether they were in future to form a part of Hungary or of Croatia. They much preferred the former country; as, being the richer of the two, they thought it would be able to do the most for the encouragement of their free port. But whatever hopes they may have allowed themselves to entertain on the subject have been disappointed; for Fiume has since been declared to belong to the kingdom of Croatia, and Hungary Proper remains without a port of its own. They were also full of complaints of the favour shown by the Government to their rival, Trieste, while they themselves were burdened with duties and taxes which disabled them from entering into a fair competition with that city. The increase in the taxes during the last twelve years is extraordinary: a house which at the former period was rated at eighteen shillings, now pays fifteen pounds.

During the short hour of liberty in 1848, the trade of Fiume showed some signs of vigour, but since the re-establishment of arbitrary government in the Austrian states it has languished. Open spaces along the shore in the neighbourhood of the town, with remains of timber lying about, were once occupied by shipbuilders, but are now deserted and forlorn. A large and profitable trade in staves for beer-barrels has, however, lately been opened with England; and under the freer institutions now promised, Fiume may regain some of her former prosperity.

A remarkable sort of timber used to be a remunerative article of export in former times. It had the appearance of oak, but when sawed up, it was found to be full of circular chambers filled with cigar-shaped preparations of tobacco. The forests where this timber was grown were not indicated to us: our informant, who had evidently made a good deal of money by some trade or other, loudly regretted the disappearance of the good old days, and the prying disposition of the custom-house officials.

The want of communication with the interior is another great drawback to Fiume. The railway from Vienna to the Adriatic was originally intended to pass through part of Hungary, and to reach Trieste by way of Fiume; but it has been constructed along the present line, at great additional expense, in order to punish the Hungarians for their share in the events of 1848. An Englishman, who was in the neighbourhood of Fiume last autumn, has, I understand, since been endeavouring to take steps for the formation of a railway from Sissek to Fiume, in connexion with which a line of steamers is proposed between that port and England. The only communication at present between Fiume and the forests and corn-producing plains of Hungary is the Luisenstrasse—a good road, but the tolls on it are so heavy as to make it in a commercial point of view comparatively useless. The reader will perhaps gain some idea of the disadvantages under which this part of Europe lies from want of means of transport, when he learns that it is cheaper, as well as more certain, as regards time, to import corn to Fiume from Russia by Odessa, than from Hungary.

We received great kindness during our stay at Fiume from Mr. Hill, the English vice-consul, and Mr. Francovich, a timber-merchant, to whom we had a letter of introduction. The former amused us much with stories of persons he had met with in the course of his official residence in the town. The incidents related in the following story, which was told us by Mr. Hill, occurred to a gentleman with whom I am well acquainted, and who, after serving with distinction in the army, had at the period of their occurrence lately taken holy orders.

In the middle of the night, one summer, some three and twenty years ago, Mr. Hill was called up by a messenger, who had ridden in hot haste from a village about eighteen miles inland, and who said that an English gentleman and his son were in trouble, and had been ill-treated and placed in confinement by some peasants, with whom they had had the misfortune to quarrel. It was a matter of a few minutes for Mr. Hill to present himself at the house of the governor, of whom he demanded the services of a surgeon and a lawyer. With these companions he set off for the village indicated, where he found Mr. —— and his son, a boy of about fourteen, in a peasant's cabin, wounded and handcuffed. Leaving the surgeon to administer what relief he could, Mr. Hill and the lawyer hastened to the house where the trial (as it was called) was proceeding. At the centre of a table sat the Giudice dei Nobili, on his right the judge of the peasants, and on his left the Roman Catholic priest of the village.

After some discussion, in which Mr. Hill defended his clients from various accusations, the judge objected that the passport was a forged one; for, having been issued at the commencement of her present Majesty's reign, King William's name had been erased, and that of Queen Victoria substituted. This difficulty was scarcely explained away, when the judge objected again that Mr. —— was described as a lieutenant-colonel.

"And why not?" said Mr. Hill.

"Well," answered the judge, "he may be a lieutenant-colonel, but a little way further on he is described as a gentleman! What can you say to that?"

The idea of a lieutenant-colonel being also a gentleman was beyond the imagination of an Austrian official. Beaten out of this position, however, he renewed the attack; and, taking up a visiting card, showed that Mr. —— was described as the Rev. ——. This did appear rather staggering; but Mr. Hill was equal to the occasion. Knowing nothing of the circumstances of this particular case, he rushed into a general explanation of English manners.

"Oh, that's only your ignorance. In England, livings belong to private persons, and when their sons are not old enough to take them, they put in some one to keep them for a time. Meanwhile, the son goes to college, and then he puts on a red coat and goes into the army (they don't allow him to go into the navy, because sailors swear, and soldiers are not allowed to swear), and then, after a time, he leaves the army and takes orders."

"But," interrupted the priest, "he can't be really a priest, for he has his son with him."

"Are we not in a Greek village?" inquired Mr. Hill; "and has not the Greek priest a wife and children? And though the Greek priest can only marry one wife, an English priest may marry as many as he pleases, in succession."

"But I'm sure he is an impostor," persisted the priest, "for he says he knows Latin, and I can't understand him."

Mr. Hill reminded the Court of the difference in the mode of pronunciation of Latin among different nations, and claimed that Mr. —— should be brought in to answer for himself. The surgeon had by this time produced a great change in his appearance, and Mr. Hill insisted on the irons being taken off before the examination was proceeded with. On a trial in writing, Mr. ——'s Latin was found to be superior to the priest's, so that difficulty was disposed of. But the priest was not beaten yet.

"Well, at any rate, I am sure he is a bad man, for he has got a devil's machine with him."

"A devil's machine! How do you know it is a devil's machine?"

"Oh, I'm sure it is. Look here!"

And he produced, with an air of triumph, a number of rods tied together, and a book containing a collection of the most frightful-looking little imps, with which poor Mr. —— was supposed to make his incantations. Unfortunately for the priest, this horrible apparatus turned out to be nothing but a fishing-rod and fly-book.

Mr. Hill conquered, but was glad to carry off his charge as fast as he could to Fiume. Before starting, however, Mr. —— was taken to a window of the house, from which he was shown the peasants who had maltreated him, being flogged all round. On his arrival at Fiume, he represented his case to the higher authorities, objecting to the punishment being put off on the least guilty parties, and insisting that the judges, and not the peasants, should be punished. The correspondence was kept up in the ordinary official form for a twelvemonth; and the Austrian authorities at last made an end of the matter, by leaving the magistrates in their offices, but flogging the peasants all round a second time.

Bare rocks, and steep mountains, almost destitute of vegetation, were the chief features of the country after leaving Fiume. On the southern slopes of the hills, however, vines are cultivated, and trained over the stones which abound everywhere, in order to catch as many of the sun's rays as possible. At the little village inn of Novi, where we slept, we were warned to beware of the great scourge of this district, the Bora. This wind blows with such violence from the north-east, that it is often impossible for man or beast to stand against it. The whole country lying on the north and north-east of the Adriatic is afflicted with it. Its visits are rare in summer, but increase in frequency towards winter, when it often rages uninterruptedly for three weeks.

It was a bright cold morning when we left Novi for Zengg (or Segna). Our road is on the slope of the bare mountains of the mainland, which sweep upwards to our left, and on our right the equally bare hills of Isola Veglia confine the sea within a narrow channel. A strange-looking streak of foam and spray, which crosses the water at one spot a little before us, attracts our attention. Before long, we know that this is the point where the Bora first strikes the sea. Presently another and another streak appears, and soon the whole surface of the sea is covered with white foam, and clouds of rainbow-coloured spray chasing one another furiously in every direction, the wind meanwhile raging without intermission, bitter and icy. The sun blazing in the cloudless sky seemed to mock at the sea, and the bare motionless rocks looked on helpless as the wind made long furrows on her surface. Without a murmur she suffered, yet neither sun nor mountains were ashamed.

The road, after the fashion of country-roads, runs high or low, now near the sea, now mounting the face of the rock, without any intelligible purpose. With its usual judgment, it chooses the most exposed point of the most exposed mountain for one of these displays of engineering. Mala Draga is the appropriate name of the place.

We had got out of the carriage, and were holding our own with difficulty against the wind, when we suddenly saw seat-cushions, books, and plaids neatly lifted out by the wind, and making their way rapidly up the hill. A general chase ensued, ending in the capture of the greater part of our property, which we prudently packed into the bottom of the carriage, with myself spread out on the top of all to prevent further accident.

Zengg is the head-quarters, or, in the imaginative language of the inhabitants, the birthplace, of the Bora. The town, a seaport, lies at the mouth of a rocky gorge, down which the wind blows in one steady, pitiless storm for nearly six months in the year. It is rather picturesque, half Italian in some of its features; and an old mediæval castle frowns over it. The port shares with Fiume the trade in timber from the interior, and is frequently visited by English vessels, which import the Manchester cotton prints, crockery, and Sheffield ware, which are met with in every town and village along this coast.

An amusing account of the Uscoc pirates, the former inhabitants of Zengg, and of their misdeeds and final removal to the mountains which still bear their name in the neighbourhood of Karlstadt, will be found in Sir Gardiner Wilkinson's work on Dalmatia and Montenegro. It would appear that the climate has not deteriorated since their time, for in 1607, when the Austrian Government, in order to satisfy the Venetians, commanded the Uscocs to desist from all "hostilities against the Turks," as their piracies were called in polite language, they "despatched one of their voivodas to the Imperial Court to represent the impossibility of living at Segna without piracy, and to pray that the taxes levied on certain Morlacchi villages [in Dalmatia] might be assigned for their maintenance."

The delays incident to posting through a country not often visited by tourists, promised to increase as we advanced farther. We decided, therefore, to strike up to the north-east through Croatia into Hungary. There is but one road into and one road out of Zengg, so that our route was not affected by this change of plan till we reached the first post station, Xuta Loqua. As we get away from the neighbourhood of the town some symptoms of vegetation appear, and in one place vines are cultivated. The ascent is tolerably rapid, and in the upper part the road is carried through oak woods, with beautiful views of the Adriatic with its islands, and occasionally Zengg, crowned by its old castle.

At the summit we pass through a new wooden gate, behind which we discover a picquet of Austrian soldiers, with a hastily built guard-house; and above our heads two cannon are planted, commanding the pass. All the hamlets on this side the mountain swarm with soldiers. The fear of Garibaldi and his Hungarian legion has called up these locusts, which, wherever we went, were devouring the land. So great is the alarm his name inspired into the authorities, that not long before our visit, all the Austrian lighthouses in the Adriatic were extinguished for some time. Even the town clock at Fiume was not allowed to shine, lest it should light some Garibaldian vessel to its harbour. The result of this measure was, however, that Austrian and neutral vessels could no more reach Trieste than Garibaldian ships of war. This quite unexpected inconvenience, combined with the raising of the insurance on vessels proceeding to these ports, at last made the Austrian Government rescind this absurd order.

From Xuta Loqua the Dalmatian road turns off to the right, and passing through Ottochacz, crosses the Velebich mountains, and descends thence to Knin, near which place the roads to Zara, Sebenico and Spalato diverge. Travellers visiting Dalmatia almost invariably make use of the steamers which proceed either from Trieste or Fiume, and touch only at the principal towns on the coast. Much of the interest arising from a tour in an unfrequented country is thereby lost. As, however, it is five or six days' land journey from Trieste to Zara, any one whose time is limited would probably do well to profit by the steamer as far as the latter place, and then make his way onwards, either in the light carriages of the country, or, perhaps better, on horseback. We were unable to gain any certain intelligence as to the organization of the post beyond Zara.

The road between Xuta Loqua and Jezerana passes over a wild country, and about a mile beyond the latter place crosses the Kapella mountain, a part of the Julian Alps, from the summit of which there is a fine view, closed by the range of mountains overhanging Zengg. The descent of the Kapella on the north-east side is through a forest of pines, which has suffered much from storms; and the road winds its way round the funnel-shaped holes which here, as in the Karst mentioned above, are the distinguishing feature of the country.

Karlstadt is a town of some seven thousand inhabitants; the older part of it is inclosed by strong fortifications, but beyond the glacis which surrounds them are large suburbs. The young poplars which have just been planted here, replace those removed by order of the military authorities during the Italian war of 1859. The Government were so terrified at the successes of the Franco-Italian army that they did not feel safe even here.

It may be doubted, however, whether the mass of the people in these parts are not still in ignorance of the real character of at least some of the engagements which took place during that campaign; for we frequently saw prints at country inns representing incidents of the battles of Magenta and Solferino, and it was hinted to us that these were circulated by authority, and that innkeepers and others were "invited" to purchase them. The natural conclusion on the part of the people is, of course, that these battles were Austrian victories.

From Karlstadt there is water communication with the Danube by means of the Kulpa and the Save, and good roads lead to the ports of Fiumè and Zengg, and into Dalmatia; but the tolls on the road to Fiume are very heavy, and the navigation of the Kulpa is difficult and tedious, on account of the alternate floods and want of water. Yet, notwithstanding these disadvantages, Karlstadt is the centre of a considerable trade, especially in corn, tobacco, and wood. Sissek, at the junction of the Save and Kulpa, is the great depôt where is collected the timber of Bosnia, and the other neighbouring districts. It is conveyed thence in barges up the Kulpa, to Karlstadt, from which place it is taken to Fiume or Zengg in the little waggons of the country. A peasant, generally accompanied by his wife or son, occupies four or five days in the journey; his cart contains about five pounds' worth of wood, and he receives about thirty shillings for its transport. The wood is principally exported to England in the form of staves; and the forests of Bosnia bid fair to attract to themselves a large portion of the commerce which used to be almost monopolized by Norway. It is hoped, also, that the Admiralty will make use of the timber of this country for ship-building; and the Austrian Government is stated to be willing to facilitate this commercial intercourse with us, as it is at this moment very desirous of cultivating friendly relations with England.

A gentleman, who owns some forests on the other side of the Turkish frontier, and who held contracts from the English Government during the Crimean war, hearing that we were in Karlstadt, offered to take us an excursion of two or three days, to see his forests. We gladly availed ourselves of this opportunity, and Mr. —— having shown our passports to the Commandant at Karlstadt, and obtained permission for us to enter the Military Frontier, we started by daybreak one morning, though the weather looked unpropitious, for the snow was beginning to fall slowly and steadily. When we drove into the back yard of the post-station at Vojnich, about twenty miles from Karlstadt, the carriage was full of snow, and the post-master would give us no horses, as the road by which we were to proceed was not a post-road. The accommodation of the inn did not at that time seem very inviting; but, on our return a few days afterwards, we thought it almost luxurious. A broad entry, with a floor of earth, divided the house into two parts. On one side was the kitchen, and a room for the usual frequenters of the place; drovers, carters, and soldiers. On the other side, two low rooms, with an arch between them, contained two or three beds each. A universal bedroom upstairs completed the establishment.

After some delay we arranged with the peasants for four horses to take us on to Maljevacz, a fort on the border, whence we were to cross, snow permitting, into the Turkish territory. A wild-looking man, with a red Turkish cloak, and something between a cap and an extempore turban, drove the wheelers, while his companion acted as postilion for the leaders. The fare as well as the accommodation of Maljevacz being considered questionable, we packed up some bread, a small cask of wine, and a piece of beef, which we bought of the landlord, who was also a butcher.

It was growing dusk when, after a laborious journey in the snow, we drove through the black and yellow striped gates of Maljevacz. The fort consists of a single two-storied building, from the central portion of which three arms project in different directions; the whole being surrounded by a loopholed wall. The present building occupies the site of one which was burned down by the Turks in 1819. Accommodation is provided on the ground-floor for the soldiers, and on the first-floor for the director or quarantine-officer, the douanier, and the priest. We were received with great hospitality; for each of the three gave up a room, so that at last we were all housed. Having brought provisions to so dreary a spot, we thought it selfish to consume them by ourselves; we therefore invited the commandant and the other officers to supper. The courier, in the meantime, foraged about, and collected chickens and turkeys, the staple food of the country, and by dint of great exertions, a supper, magnificent for such a place, was at last got ready. It is true that the chickens and turkeys were stringy and tough, and that the soup appeared in a wash-hand basin which we had lately used, and which was made available several times during the repast; its last use being to contain a salad, composed principally of cold potatoes and onions with oil and vinegar. But every one took everything in good part, and the priest superintended the succession of the courses, changed the plates, wiped the knives and forks, and was always at hand whenever any attention could be shown to any one. By the help of five languages—English, French, German, Italian, and Slavonic—all of which were talked simultaneously, and of which most of the company understood two, we made ourselves very happy, and interchanged ideas on all sorts of subjects—the snow, the forest, the frontier, the Turks, and even the Volunteers.

The cries of the sentinels every quarter of an hour during the night were anything but cheerful. One of them was stationed just opposite my window, and as I unclosed my shutter in the morning, I saw him open the cloak which he had put over his head, howl for the last time, and then stand, the picture of misery, with the snow deepening round him, till he was relieved. There was no getting away from the place that day, as it was necessary to construct a sledge for the carriage; and even so simple a machine as two logs of wood, hewn moderately square and placed under the wheels, could not be put together in less than a day. Even the wood itself had to be fetched from the Turkish side.

As we are now fairly in Military Croatia, the following outline of the peculiar constitution of this border land may not be uninteresting. The Military Frontier of Austria is a long strip of territory intervening between the Austrian dominions and Turkey, extending from Dalmatia to Transylvania, which latter district, though under a somewhat similar form of government, does not form part of the military frontier strictly so called.

The country is divided into fifteen districts, fourteen of which furnish each a regiment of infantry; the fifteenth maintaining a battalion of river artillery. Commencing from the boundary of Dalmatia, the regiments with their head-quarters are as follow:—

KARLSTADT DISTRICT.

Regiment.	*Head-Quarters.*
Lika	Gospich.
Ottocha	Ottochacz.
Ogulin	Ogulin.
Szluin	Karlstadt.

BANAT DISTRICT.

1st Banat Regt.	Glina.
2nd do.	Petrinia.

WARASDIN DISTRICT.

Warasdin Kreuz	Belovar.
St. George	Belovar.

SLAVONIAN DISTRICT.

Regiment.	*Head-Quarters.*
Gradiska	Neu Gradiska.
Brod	Vincovcze.

SYRMIAN DISTRICT.

Peterwardein	Mitrovicz.
Tschaikist Battalion.	Tittel.

BANAT FRONTIER.

German Banat	Pancsova.
Illyrian Banat	Weisskirchen.
Roman Banat.	Karansebes.

Transylvania furnishes four regiments of infantry, two Szekler and two Wallachian, and one regiment of Szekler hussars.

Scattered military colonies had been formed on the frontiers of Hungary from a very early period, but the present systematic organization of extensive districts dates from the period when Hungary was added to the other dominions of the house of Hapsburg. A bulwark against the Turkish power was desirable and even necessary in days gone by, and a sanitary cordon as a protection from the plague may have mitigated the ravages of this scourge in Eastern Europe; but the rulers of the heterogeneous mass of states swayed by the sceptre of Austria were wise in their own generation when they projected a system which gave them a numerous force of hardy soldiers, sympathising with none of the neighbouring nationalities, untroubled by regret for the loss of or aspirations after political rights, and knowing scarcely any other life than that of the rude camp in which they were nurtured.

It is interesting to watch the slow but steady progress by which this system has been advanced, from its commencement in the west to its present limits eastward. The Karlstadt and Warasdin districts were formed at the end of the sixteenth century, and placed under the immediate authority of the Austrian war-office. The Banat Border District was formed in the seventeenth century, and is so called from its being under the jurisdiction of the Ban of Croatia. The Slavonian District was not formed till the beginning of the eighteenth century, and was at first of much greater extent; but the Hungarians, by this time seeing the true object of these encroachments by the military power, succeeded in effecting a considerable reduction in its extent, for it is now the narrowest part of the military frontier. In the latter half of the eighteenth century, a district at the confluence of the Theiss and the Danube was assigned to the Tschaikist battalion of gunboats, which had been originally raised at Komorn during the wars with Frederic the Great. A little later in the same century the Banat frontier (of Temesvar) was constituted, and the modified military system, which at present obtains in Transylvania, was established.

The whole southern frontier of the Austrian states, from the shores of the Adriatic to the eastern limit ot Transylvania, is thus under military government. The system has not been extended northwards from this point, and it is to be hoped that it never may be. It is a system which, whatever reason may have existed for it in former times, is now of use only to extinguish the efforts of the different provinces to regain the freedom of which they have been stealthily but steadily despoiled by Austria. It is to be hoped that Hungary, of which country these districts are in some degree dependencies, may under the new regime develop some plan for removing at least the most objectionable features of their constitution.

It remains to notice some of the leading characteristics of the system. The districts mentioned above are again parcelled out into smaller portions; the male population from the age of sixteen to sixty within each district forms a regiment; the men of the different smaller portions within that district forming the different companies of the regiment. The boundaries of the regiments and of the companies are indicated on the principal roads by high posts, carrying iron plates, on which may be seen in raised letters either "Boundary of —— and —— Regiments," or "—— Regiment, boundary of —— and —— Companies." The colonel of each regiment resides at the town or village which is its headquarters. The captains and other officers have officers' quarters provided within the limits of their companies. The officer is also the magistrate within the limit of his military jurisdiction, there being no civil government whatever.

Along the whole line of the frontier are placed at intervals forts or stations like that at Maljevacz. Between these forts there is a chain of buildings called chardaks, in each of which a certain number of soldiers are stationed to prevent persons from crossing the border at any unauthorized place or time. These chardaks are square buildings of two floors, the upper one surrounded by a gallery in which the sentinel keeps watch, the whole being covered by a high roof. The garrison is changed on the Monday in each week. For this weekly term of duty, which recurs several times in the year, and which with going and returning sometimes occupies him one-third of the year, the soldier receives no pay, and has to provide his own food. In the event of being called out of the country, to which he is at all times liable, he receives five kreuzers (about 2d.) a day, and half a loaf of black bread.

Each family receives a portion of land to cultivate. The portion allotted to each is sufficient for its support, but the occupants have little time to cultivate it. This land is the property of the State, and inalienable. A glance at the houses and their inhabitants as they swarm out of their dark smoky cabins is sufficient to show the result of this system. Every man (or rather boy,) is compelled by law to marry at seventeen, in order to keep up the supply of soldiers for the State. Although the soil is good, the inhabitants have to purchase many articles of subsistence from the Turks. A market is held at Maljevacz every Monday; at the two markets preceding our visit, no business had been done, as the borderers had no produce to exchange, and what little money they had was useless, for the Turks will not take Austrian paper, except at a ruinous discount. Improvement is impossible under the present system. No manufactures are permitted in the country. No one would be allowed to settle in it, even if disposed to do so; neither may any of the present inhabitants leave it.

From these military districts Austria can raise a force of 140,000 men, ready at any moment to march into a disaffected province, and assist, as they did in Hungary in 1848, in exterminating all symptoms of rebellion.

The last morning of our stay at Maljevacz was occupied in bargaining for some specimens of the work of the Croat women. These consisted of aprons, curiously woven and embroidered with heavy fringe round them, and of girdles and socks of the same kind of work. The news, that we were inquiring about such things, spread rapidly through the village; and we had women of all ages eagerly offering aprons, old and new, and everything else they could think of. Sharp dealing must be an "innate idea" in the human race; for these people, who had no trade in their work, and evidently knew nothing of what it was worth, at once asked a high price, and stuck to it manfully. A sharp skirmish was carried on with each in turn, for we could do nothing when they were all in our room at the same time; and I must confess that we often had the worst of it. One little girl in a Greek costume battled hard, and when we got her to abate one florin in a very long price, retired temporarily from the field; but returned in half an hour to say that her papa would not let the work go for less than the sum originally asked. She would have done honour to New York.

Herr Direktor was a great man, in his own estimation, in this establishment. He was, on the present occasion, the possessor of a sledge, which we coveted greatly. The other officers interceded in turn that we might be allowed to use it, but without effect; so a deputation of us went, and by some means managed to soften him. He was a little man, with a screwed-up face and big spectacles, and would never talk anything but French to us. The power he exercised over that language was extraordinary. Conjugations and terminations of all kinds he dispensed with as unnecessary; and his rather slender vocabulary, which we soon learnt by heart, came out time after time in its well-known order, solemn and stately, with decent intervals between the words.

We were quite sorry to part from the kind, open-hearted old priest, who "gave all that he had from his heart," and who had exerted himself so much for our comfort. Under some pretence or other, we managed to get each one of the officers to accept some recompense for the trouble we had given them. The new silver money which we had with us, and which some of them had never even seen, was very welcome. The incipient thaw delayed our sledge nearly six hours on the nineteen miles of road to Vojnich, and the carriage which followed at a little interval, with a multitude of horses and men, was ten hours on the road.

A good road leads from Vojnich by Glina to Petrinia and Sissek. There is also a pretty road from Maljevacz to Petrinia, down the river Glina, passing through Topusca, where there are remains of Roman baths of Diocletian's time. All such excursions were, however, impossible for us, and we hurried back as soon as we could to Karlstadt and thence to Agram.

This place is the capital of Croatia, but is not an interesting town. The cathedral is a fine gothic building, well cared for, and the Bishop appears to be a botanist. The sights are mentioned in Murray, but are not bewildering, either in number or variety. It being Sunday when we were there, we had a good opportunity of seeing the costumes of the peasants who came into the market in the morning to sell their farm produce. As for the men, some of them wore great white cloaks, like blankets, with quaint devices on them; others, brown felt jackets, embroidered at the sides, and broad-brimmed hats with artificial flowers round the crown; others, again, wore coats or jackets of sheepskin, with the fur inside, some white and some brown, with gorgeous conventional flowers or other patterns on the back and sleeves. All their legs were encased in felt hose, and on their feet they had clumsy low shoes, fastened with long sandals round the ankle. But how shall I describe the costume of the female population? They wear folded handkerchiefs, of a somewhat Roman character, on their heads. Their bodies are encased in sheepskin jackets, or waistcoats, ornamented like those of the men, and, like theirs, apparently worn for life. Under this is a very scanty piece of unbleached drapery, which descends nearly to the knees, with a pretty red stripe near the lower edge; and the costume is completed by a pair of Wellington boots. *Voilà la paysanne Croate.* The town population, however, are quite different in their dress, are well up in the last fashions, and wear crinoline and steel-petticoats of gigantic proportions.

The latter part of the road to Warasdin is through pretty forest scenery. The town itself is in the middle of a marshy plain; the houses are low and irregular, and the streets impassable on account of the mud. The railway from Mahrburg, on the Vienna and Trieste line, along the south side of the Platten See to Stuhlweissenburg, and Buda (Pest), was to be opened on the 1st of January, 1861. At the time of our visit, trains only ran to Gross Kanizsa—a world's end sort of place, with streets deep in mud.

The arrival of an English party excited the liveliest interest in the hotel at Kanizsa. The servants looked through our keyholes to catch a glimpse of the lions; and the daughter of the house, though dressed for a ball, put on an apron and enacted supernumerary housemaid, in order to gain admittance to our rooms. The ball was being given in the hotel in honour of a Jewish wedding. The people goodnaturedly asked us to join them; and after making what preparation we could, we were soon engaged in the waltz or polka, taking first one partner, then another, one turn round the room. Introductions and conversation were equally unnecessary, and, in some cases, equally impossible, for none of our party could speak a word of Hungarian, and several of the natives spoke nothing else. We were by this time in Hungary, and though the country was beginning to be much agitated, and the Hungarians count all Englishmen as friends, the presence of two white-coated Austrian officers effectually checked any allusion to political affairs. The band serenaded us at night, and in the morning we counted sixty people collected at the hotel-door to witness our departure. A general doffing of hats on all sides, with cries of "*glückliche reise*," takes place, and then we drive out into the street. Arrived there, we go bump, bump, into the holes, which lie concealed deep below the surface of the mud. We hope it will be better when we get out of the town; but in vain. For fifteen or sixteen miles we had to tumble out of one hole into another. The road, though marked out with a neat ditch on each side, had never had a stone laid on it, and was left in its native state. A passage wide enough for one, and sometimes two, carriages, had been cleared in the snow, which was, in one place, eight feet deep. At one time we gave up the road and fairly took to the forest, which was a good deal better. Towards the end of this day's journey, some innovating proprietor had conceived the idea of laying down stones, but had not proceeded further than leaving large heaps of them in the centre of the road. But with all these drawbacks, the horses took us at the rate of six miles an hour.

Kesthély is prettily placed on a rising ground, overlooking one end of the Platten See. There is a School of Agriculture here, and the superior style of cultivation adopted as one approaches the town shows the good influence it has had on the neighbourhood. We lionized the gardens of the country house of some noble at the northern end of the town. In one part of the grounds was a summer-theatre, the walls of which were formed of a high beech hedge, cut out into hollows for the boxes. A low hedge screened the orchestra, behind which was a raised stage, backed by a continuation of the beech hedge, which surrounded the theatre. Another curiosity was a sundial, of which the index was a fir-tree, and the hour figures were traced in box.

The country inns in Hungary are usually considered to be almost intolerable; but our experience of them was, on the whole, favourable. Certainly nothing can exceed the dirt of the archway by which you drive in, or of the back yard by which you frequently approach the house. Nor does the appearance of the stairs by which you invariably ascend to the rooms for guests, reassure the doubting traveller. But once arrived at the long passage on the first floor, at one end of which is always the saloon or the billiard-room, the prospect brightens. A row of long, narrow rooms, with one or two windows at one end, the door at the other, a stove in one corner, and generally three beds, is the usual plan of the upper part of the house. It was, of course, often difficult to make the people understand that three gentlemen and a lady could not well sleep in one room; but this point settled, we met with nothing but readiness on the part of every one to do their best for their guests. The floors are, of course, dirty; but the same may be said of those of most continental inns.

The view of a bay of the Platten See, near which the road from Kesthély runs for some distance, with the conical, flat-headed hills in front, is one of the prettiest that we saw in our journey across Hungary. The hills and sloping ground are all covered with vines, and there is an air of neatness and comfort about the neighbourhood which one usually looks for in vain. Two roads lead from Tapolcza to Veszprém : one, direct, inland ; the other, more or less by the shore, passing near the baths of Furëd. We chose the latter, as we were told it was passable ; but we were soon planted in a snow-drift, fifty or sixty yards long, higher than the carriage, through which a narrow winding passage had been cut wide enough for country carts, but scarcely so for a carriage. A pull all together extricated us at last ; and as night closed in we were driving across the fields leading to the baths of Furëd.

The place consists of several large hotels, which looked gaunt enough with their closed, unlighted windows. Hardly expecting to find any one in the place, we were surprised to hear that we could not be accommodated on account of all the rooms being occupied. Summer rooms, without stoves, were out of the question at this season, and the remainder were taken by gentlemen of the neighbourhood, who had come to attend a sort of county meeting about enlarging the baths. Through the kindness of the Director, however, we at last got rooms, and were much interested during dinner, which we had in the *restaurateur's* own apartment, by his graphic account of the sufferings of himself and his family during the bombardment of Pest by the Austrians in 1848. Here, we found, the Hungarians did not think it necessary to conceal their sentiments, and those persons with whom we had an opportunity of conversing, openly avowed their wish to separate from Austria. The arbitrary system of taxation pursued by the Austrian Government appeared to me to be one main cause of the disaffection of their Hungarian and Croat subjects. According to the accounts given to us, each proprietor was assessed arbitrarily, on the principle that, if he was not worth a certain sum, he ought to be ; no explanation from the taxpayer being required or allowed. To take an instance, which occurred just before our visit, and which was mentioned to us at the time. A butcher at Fiume had contracted for a monopoly of the supply of meat to that town for a year. At the end of that time he lost money; but the Austrian authorities considered that he ought to have made a handsome profit, and taxed him accordingly. It was in vain that the poor contractor offered to show his books, or give any explanation. He ought to have made a profit; therefore he did so; therefore he must be taxed proportionably: an example of *à priori* reasoning more satisfactory to the Government than the contractor.

The sights of Furëd itself are soon exhausted. They consist of the pump-room and theatre; a row of baths out in the lake, and a steamboat pier. The steamboat itself is a great resource to the frequenters of the baths in summer, and is perpetually steaming up and down the lake. At the time we saw it, it was under repair in anticipation of next summer, when probably one of its principal occupations will be to convey visitors from the railway-station on the opposite side of the lake. A great increase in the number of visitors is expected next year, as Furëd will then be within a few hours of Pest by the railway.

The great attraction of Furëd, however, in summer must be the never-failing spring of Sauerwasser, which tastes like Selzer water, and is slightly tonic. Add to this, the strains of the gipsy band, excursions among the woods and vineyards of the neighbourhood, on the lake, or to the promontory of Tihany, and you have the means of passing a few summer weeks very agreeably: at least, if you are fond, as all Hungarians are, of life at a watering-place.

Tihany was snowed up, so we could not see it. For the benefit, however, of the British paterfamilias, by whom this part of the world has not been much visited, I may mention that it is a remarkable promontory stretching almost across the lake. A miniature copy of the Platten See, inclosed in a crater-like basin, one of the oldest monasteries in Hungary, with views over the lake, and caves with an echo and unaccountable fossils, are the sights of Tihany, as detailed by Murray, whose account is confirmed by the natives.

Veszprém is about two hours' drive from Furëd; its streets are as dirty as those of other Hungarian towns, but its situation is rather more picturesque than usual. The road between this and Stuhlweissenburg is in very bad order, and as dreary as can well be imagined. Usually flat, it sometimes crosses low ridges, from the summit of which the eye ranges over an expanse of utter monotony. The driver, however, does his best to minimize the dulness of the journey by completing the distance of twenty-eight English miles, without drawing rein, in three hours, through a heavy sea of mud and half-melted snow. Although Stuhlweissenburg was a great city in the old days of the Hungarian monarchy, and is the resting-place of St. Stephen, we did not summon courage to wade through the deep mud which held possession of the streets, but contented ourselves with what we saw of its heavy-looking renaissance buildings on our way to the hotel.

We are glad, at no great distance from Pest, to catch our first sight of the Danube, here rolling its heavy waters southwards through the interminable plain. Before long, we descry the Blocksberg. Passing under its crags, with the river to our right, we have a full view of the Palatine's palace on the heights of Buda. Turning to the right, we cross the suspension-bridge, and are in Pest.

Pest is in a state of ferment. All man-kind is in the national costume. "Pork-pie" hats with streaming ribbons, or perhaps fur caps surmounted by a tall white feather; in either case, with the arms of Hungary in a little medallion in front; long, straight, fur-trimmed coats, with cords and tassels thrown back over the shoulders; tight breeches and Hessian boots: such is the costume in which every Hungarian gentleman now makes a point of appearing.

Grave political events pass, unheard of, over the head of a traveller in most continental countries, and he usually receives the first intelligence of their occurrence through the columns of the English newspapers, which await him from time to time at the post-office of some capital. All that a hasty traveller can hope for, is to watch the little indications which catch his eye as he runs through a country. These, if he is wise, afterwards serve to correct his judgment on, or give him an insight into, events which he would otherwise have misunderstood, or not have comprehended. The sin which so easily besets a tourist, is that of generalizing on the scanty data within his reach. What a man saw, if truly related, is always worth something; what he thought about it, is probably worth very little. I have told the reader as shortly as I can what I saw, and I spare him my reflections thereon.

3. *SLAVONIC RACES.*

BY A FORMER RESIDENT AND RECENT TRAVELLER AMONG THEM.

THE populations of the Slavonic race in Europe comprise about eighty-seven millions of souls, and speak languages differing scarcely more from each other than some of the dialects of the ancient Greek. The large majority belong to a common form of religion; and a considerable proportion look beyond their own frontiers, to the protection of a great foreign power.

Desiring rather to sketch what is common to these nationalities, than to dwell at tedious length on their minute differences, which constitute the charm and delight of ethnological inquiry in the schools of Agram and Prague, I propose in the following pages to make a few general remarks upon the various branches of the Slave family of nations. My summary pretends to be little more than an abridgment of—indeed, is frequently a literal translation from—the researches of Grimm, Vuk, and Schafgarik, yet I hope it may contribute to attract notice towards a subject on which, perhaps, less attention than it merits has hitherto been directed in this country.

Nor is the present moment inopportune for such an inquiry—whether we look to the great social problems in solution in Russia,* or to the efforts which Austria is making to combine the existence of an ancient monarchy with an imperious demand for local franchises, or to the progress of the Turkish

* In addition to the numerous pamphlets on the Serf Question, see "Le Raskol; Essai Historique et Critique sur les Sectes Religieuses en Russie." Paris, 1859. (*Raskol*, from the Russian verb *raskolot*, to separate; raskol, schism; raskolnek, schismatic.)

Government in carrying out the reform of Selim and Mahmoud.

In order to comprehend the affinities and mutual sympathies of the Slave races, it is necessary to touch on their early history, and we must at once go a long way back, even to the sixth and seventh centuries of our era. At that epoch, nearly the whole space between the Adriatic, Black, and Baltic seas was occupied by tribes of Slave race, who filled the space left vacant by successive migrations of the Teutons, southward.

The formation of a Slavonic empire, which might otherwise have been possible, was then prevented by an invasion of Hungarians, who, in the tenth century, after carrying the terror of their ravages from the free marts of Bremen to the "golden gate" of Byzantium, from Rheims in the east to Rome on the south, were finally driven back by a coalition of Germany under Otho, and effected a lasting lodgment in the very centre of the Slavonic tribes.

It is not, however, Vienna, it is hardly Pest or Presburg, but it is Debreczin, with its houses scattered like the tents of the first Tartar encampment, which is now the characteristic home of the Magyar. To this day the great plains of Central Hungary are occupied by a population who live in the saddle;* who speak a language differing completely from the Slave or the German, but akin to that of their old opponents, the Osmanlis. They had driven them across the Balkan, at Nissa (1443), but had succumbed to their terrible artillery at Mohacs (1526), "funestum clade Ludovici Regis Hungariæ locum." They were a race who engrafted on an Eastern stock the institutions of chivalry with much of the haughty freedom of Western feudalism, and who despised the "misera contribuens plebs"—the Slave, the Wallach, and the Saxon, as "captives of the bow† and the spear."

* "Lora termett a Magyar"—Hungarian proverb, "The Hungarian is born a horseman;" literally, "on horseback."

† "Oh, save and deliver us from the arrows of the Hungarians!"—Litany of the middle ages. "Misera contribuens plebs."—Statutes of the Hung. Diet.

The central plains of Hungary, namely, those which are watered by the Maros, the Szamos, and the Theiss, are surrounded by people of Slavonic race. To the north-west are the Slovaks, the Moravians and the Bohemians: to the north-east are the Russians: to the south-west the Slovenes, the Croats, the Dalmatians and the Bosnians; while to the south are the Servians.

However, this circle of Slave nationalities is not completely unbroken. To the south-west a German offshoot separates Moravia from Illyria; while to the east, in Transylvania, Wallachia and Moldavia, are the Rumans, half Latin and half Slave.

These Slave populations are subjects, respectively, of Russia, Austria, Turkey, Prussia, and Saxony.

As to Russia; the Slave element constitutes a great majority of the population of Russia in Europe; and apparently nearly eleven-thirteenths * of the whole population of the empire. In Prussia and Saxony, the Slave element is weak; being, in the former kingdom, about one-eighth of the population, and in the latter about one per cent. In the Austrian Empire, since the cession of Lombardy, the Slaves probably form a numerical majority. Lastly, in Turkey in Europe, they nearly equal the aggregate of all the other populations, including the Ottoman Turks.

But the importance of the Slave element in each state does not depend wholly upon its numerical proportion. It depends largely upon its unity and cohesion. In Russia, the Slave population forms a compact mass; but in Austria it is split into six or seven distinct nationalities, the most numerous of which, the Chechians, amount to above 6,000,000; while the German element in the empire is represented by nearly 8,000,000; and the Magyar by about 5,000,000. In Turkey, the Slave element is weakened, relatively to its numbers, by its division into Mussulman and Christian.

* See, for Russia, the statistics of M. de Koeppen; for Austria, von Czörnig; and for Turkey, Van Reden; also Heuschling's "Empire de Turquie." Brussels, 1860.

Let us, at the risk of some tedium, trace the ramifications * of their two great stems, the Eastern and the Western.

I. The Eastern Slaves comprehend the *Russians*, the *Servo-Illyrians*, and the *Bulgarians*.

1. The *Russian branch* is divided into—

(*a*) The Russians proper, who form the bulk of the population of the middle provinces of Russia in Europe; numerous Slaves scattered throughout Asiatic Russia are of the same race: they all belong to the Greek Church, and their numbers are about 37,000,000.

(*b*) The Russniaks, Ruthenians, Russinians, or Malo†-Russians, who are found in Southern Russia, the South of Poland, Galicia, Lodomeria or Red Russia, in the north-eastern part of Hungary, and are scattered over Moldavia and Wallachia. The Zaporoyne Cossacks belong chiefly to this race, the Cossacks of the Don are more mixed with pure Russians; their numbers are given at 15,000,000; they principally belong to the Greek Church, but a portion of them are United Greek Catholics, acknowledging the Pope of Rome as head of their Church.

2. The *Illyrico-Servian branch* comprises—

(*a*) The Illyrico-Servians proper, with five subdivisions: (*α*) the Servians lying between the rivers Timok, Drina, Save, Danube, and the Balkan; their numbers are about 1,500,000. In earlier times, and especially towards the end of the seventeenth century, many of their race emigrated to Hungary, where they now number about 750,000, exclusive of their relatives, the Slavonians in the so-called kingdom of Slavonia: they belong almost entirely to the Greek Church. (*β*) The Bosnians; between the Balkan mountains and the rivers Drina, Verbas, and Save. Their numbers are about 1,200,000; they belong to the Greek Church, except about 100,000, who are Moslems. (*γ*) The Montenegrins (Czerno-

* This is principally taken from "The Languages and Literature of the Slavic Nations." New York, 1850; following Schafgarik.

† "Malo (Russian), "little:" the southern provinces, of which Kiew was the capital, were called "Little Russia."—See Gibbon, chap. xxx.

Gortzi). These have spread themselves from Bosnia to Antiorri, on the sea-coast, and have never been thoroughly subjugated by the Turks; they enjoy a sort of military republican freedom: their chief was, till lately, the Vladika, or military Bishop, and they are at this moment governed by a prince of the same family. They amount to nearly 120,000 souls, and belong to the Greek Church. (δ) The Slavonians. These are the inhabitants of the Austrian kingdom of Slavonia, and the duchy of Syrmia, between Hungary on the north, and Bosnia on the south. Their numbers are about 300,000, and they belong, except a small minority, to the Greek Church. (ε) The strip of country along the Adriatic, between Croatia and Albania, which, together with the adjacent islands, is called the kingdom of Dalmatia, and belongs to the Austrians; it has about 400,000 inhabitants, all of whom, except 15,000 Italians, belong to the Slave race; they are all Roman Catholics, with the exception of about 80,000, who belong to the Greek Church.

(*b*) The Austrian kingdom of Croatia of our time, with the Croatians in Hungary, Carniola, and Istria, and the inhabitants of the Turkish Sandjak Banialouka, contains about 1,500,000 souls; of these, very few belong to the Greek Church; some are Moslems, the rest are Roman Catholics. The Croats are divided, in respect to their language, into two parts; one of them bearing affinity to the Servians and Dalmatians; the other, to the Slovenes of Carniola and Carinthia.

(*c*) The Slovenes comprise the Slavic inhabitants of the duchies of Styria, Carinthia, and Gorz, with parts of Carniola, Istria, and Venetia; they also extend to the banks of the rivers Raab and Muhr in Hungary: they number above 1,000,000, and, with the exception of a few Protestants, they are all Roman Catholics; they call themselves Slovenes, but are known locally as Wendes, in Styria, Carinthia, and Venetia; as Krainer, in Carniola; as Vandals, in Western Hungary, &c.

3. The *Bulgarian* branch:* the Bulgarians occupy Bulgaria,

* Some ethnologists have thrown doubt on the Slavonic origin of the Bul-

large portions of Rumelia and Macedonia, with small part of S. Servia, Albania, and even Thessaly. They are about 5,000,000 in number, and are the remnant of a great nation: about 80,000 more are scattered throughout Bessarabia, and 25,000 live in the Banat and Transylvania. Most of them belong to the Greek Church, but 1,500,000 of those in Turkey are Mussulmen.

II. The Western Slaves comprise the *Chechians*, the *Polish* or *Leckian*, and the *Sorbian Wendish* branches.

1. The *Chechians* are divided into—

(*a*) The Bohemians and Moravians. These are the Slavic inhabitants of the kingdom of Bohemia and the Margravate of Moravia, both belonging to the Austrian Empire. They are about 4,000,000 in number, of whom about 100,000 are Protestants, the rest Catholics. Schafgarick includes also 44,000 of the Slavic inhabitants of Prussian Silesia in this race.

(*b*) The Slovaks. Almost all the northern part of Hungary is inhabited by Slovaks; besides this, they are scattered through the rest of that country, and speak different dialects. They are reckoned at about two millions.

2. The *Polish-Lekhian branch:* this comprises the inhabitants of the present kingdom of Poland; of what, since 1772, are called the Russo-Polish provinces of the duchy of Posen; and of Galicia and Lodomeria: the bulk of the people in this latter country are Russniaks, or Ruthenians. The peasantry are Russians and Russniaks, in the provinces which were formerly called White Russia, Black Russia, and Red Russia, and which were conquered by the Poles in former times; in Lithuania, the peasantry are Lithuanians or Lettones—a race of a different family of nations. In all these countries, only the inhabitants of the cities are Poles, or Slaves of the Lekhian race. To the same race belongs also the Polish population of Silesia, and an isolated tribe in the

garians; but as it is admitted that, even if of the same family of nations as the Finns and the Magyars, their distinctive nationality became early lost, they are here considered as a Slave people.—See Karamsin, Klaproth, Ritter.

Russian province of Pomerania called Cassubes or Slovines. The Slaves of the Lekhian race hardly amount to the number of 10,500,000 ; in Russia, 6,500,000 ; in Austria, 2,000,000 ; in Prussia, 2,000,000 : all are Catholics, with the exception of 500,000 Protestants.

3. The *Sorabian* (*Wendish*) *branch.* These are remnants of the old Sorabæ, and several other Slavic races in Lusatia. Their number is about 150,000, and they are chiefly Protestants.

There is no doubt that, besides the races here enumerated, other Slavic tribes—inconsiderable in numbers—are scattered through Germany, Transylvania, Moldavia, and Wallachia, and even through the whole of Turkey and Greece : thus, for instance, the Tchachonic dialect, spoken in the eastern part of Ancient Sparta, and the dialects of some of the Greek islands, have been proved to be of Slavic origin.*

As to their history. That of the eastern slaves is partly the history of Russia and Poland ; too extensive a subject, and too well known, to dwell on here. The Illyrian slaves were early divided into small states, amongst which the trading Republic of Ragusa deserves mention. The local situation of most of these western states made them dependent on Hungary ; thus, Croatia, Slavonia, Dalmatia, sometimes under the title of kingdoms and sometimes as dukedoms, became at length provinces of the larger kingdom, and ultimately of the Austrian Empire. Bosnia and the Herzegovine are, to this day, divided in religion and language.

The early history of Servia—which country has always been considered by the southern Slaves as the centre of their nationality—requires a few words of further explanation. Materials, perhaps, exist in national sources † as yet imperfectly examined ; but, amidst a maze of confusion, little has yet been discerned beyond a qualified acknowledgment of the supremacy of the Eastern Empire, with a government under chiefs elected by the people, accounts of encroachments on

* See Leake's "Morea."

† See Ranke's "Servia," chap. i. note.

the part of Constantinople, and of successful resistance on that of the Servians. At a very early period, numerous dukes, princes, and bans, separate, and almost independent of monarchical authority, exercised sway in the country now called Servia, and in the adjoining provinces: Bosnia and the Herzegovine being frequently detached from, and as frequently united to, Servia Proper. The authority of the provincial chiefs, then called Grand Shupans,* was consolidated by the defeat of the army of Monomachus in 1043. The power of Servia next became consolidated under a single ruler, and reached its acme in the fourteenth century under Duschan; for then the sway of the "Macedonian Christ-loving Tzar"—such being the proud title assumed by the Servian monarch—extended from the Danube to the Adriatic, and seemed likely to dispute with the rising power of the Ottoman the possession of Constantinople itself.

A mythical period follows, in which the adventures of Kral Marco fill almost the same position, with a curious resemblance in some of the details of the legend to those of King Arthur, of our own story; for Kral Marco casts his good sword into an enchanted mere, and awaits, in an enchanted cave, the independence of the Servian nation. Marco is, however, taken in bondage, and serves the Sultan. The Ottoman power now gains ground; then follows the fatal defeat of Kossova (1389); a momentary hope from the victories of Hunyad (1443): further on, we hear of religious dissensions; then, of a Servian princess offering the country as a fief to Rome: next, the Servians throw open their fortresses to the Ottomans; then, the great Hungarian and Turkish wars, and the yearly passage of Ottoman hosts. For a few years Servia becomes subject to Austria (1718–39); then, the Servians join Austria, allied with Russia, against the Porte (1788). It is not worth while to extend these

* Shupans, "Lords of the Sunny South:" "shupa," terra aprica, the coast of the Adriatic. (Vuk's Servian Dictionary. Vienna, 1852.) In that curious mixture of Slave and Latin, the modern Rouman, *jupan* is now the term employed in addressing a respectable servant or mechanic.

fragmentary notes, nor to continue them to the present time, by describing, at length, the details of the Servian war of independence; nor how, under her two chieftains, Kara-George and Milosch, she has succeeded in establishing for herself a position of quasi-independence. Reference has been already made to the semi-independent existence of Montenegro.

The language of these various populations divides itself into two principal idioms: each of these into three where the difference is less.* Of the Southern dialect are the Slovaks, the Serfs, and Bulgarians; of the northern, the Bohemians, Poles, and Russians. The northern had a wider expanse; the southern was "shut in between the sea, the Hungarians and the Turks." †

The Slaves who came over the Danube into Moesia, Macedonia, Thessaly, and Epirus, and subsequently formed alliances with the still powerful Greek Empire, adopted the faith of the Eastern Church: so, too, the Southern Slaves; and, later, the Bulgarians and Servians. Croatia and Bulgaria were converted to Christianity in the seventh century, by Italian priests, and Carinthia in the ninth, if not the eighth century. About the same time the southern portion of the Moravian Pannonian slaves were baptized. Under Swatopulk, during whose reign Moravia flourished, the Pannonians sent a Christian Embassy to Constantinople: in 862, the Emperor Michael sent them Methodius and Constantine (Cyril), Greeks by birth, from Thessalonia, but skilled in the Slavonic tongues, and they began a translation of the Scriptures into the Slavonic idiom. The Bohemians were converted about the end of the ninth century, their rulers made open profession of Christianity in the tenth: the North-Western Slaves were the last converted. The Greek rite made considerable progress among the Moravians and Poles, and Russia completely adopted the faith of the Greek Church about the end of the tenth century.

This difference of ritual has facilitated foreign influence and produced enmities between peoples of the same race.

* Grimm. † Ibid.

The populations of the Greek rite suffered the hardest lot: the Northern through the invasions of the Mongols; the Southern, as the fortunes of Byzantium waned and fell, through the Ottomans, against whom the Servians had valiantly striven. Soon followed the apostasy of the Southern Slaves.* The Russian Church gradually withdrew itself from the no longer independent Patriarch of Constantinople, and another portion acknowledged the Archbishop of Carlowitz.

Various institutions and forms of life have fallen under our observation in Slave countries, the traces of which might, perhaps, by a broader inquiry, be detected as existing in all.

A difference in the tenure of land is observable in Eastern and Western Europe. In most of the countries which we have been considering, the relation of proprietor and cultivator is very different from that to which we ourselves are accustomed. In Russia the serf seems to possess a sort of right to his cottage and plot of ground; in Moldavia and Wallachia (where it will be remembered there is a strong Slavonic element in the population), much the same state of things exists. Turnbull and Paget mention the prevalence of somewhat similar customary rights, in the zone of the Austrian Empire occupied by Slave populations: and although in Servia the division of the land, formerly held by the Turkish conquerors, has rendered almost every peasant a proprietor, the recognition of a sort of lien of the cultivator on the soil may be traced in the circumstance that, when a family becomes too numerous to subsist on the portion of ground belonging to it, its members are considered entitled to receive unoccupied land belonging to the commune.

The communal organization in Slave countries is strong, and, it may be added, has many good points. This is the case

* An interesting account of the apostasy of the Albanians and Bosnians (derived from reports of Roman Ecclesiastics to the Pope and Propaganda) is to be found at the end of Ranke's "Letzen Unruhen in Bosmien, 1820–32." A similar apostasy took place in Georgia.—See "Chardin," vol. ii. p. 44.

in Russia.* In Servia the commune existed throughout the Turkish times, for it was ever the principle of the Ottoman conquerors to interfere as little as might be with the internal affairs of the Christian races subjected to their sway. Its present condition is curious; whether in regard to problems of self-government or to those of national prosperity. A commune in Servia is composed of two or three neighbouring villages, or a single village if sufficiently large may be of itself a commune. At the principal village reside the kmet (mayor) and the priest; the church of the commune and the school are usually situated there; each commune has a communal chest; the land belonging to the commune is cultivated each year for the communal account. The rent of the inn (mehana), where one exists, and that from pasture-ground and oak-woods, are the principal sources of the communal funds: moreover, the communal capital, being lent at a moderate interest to the members of the commune, increases yearly. The building and repairs of the church, school, residence of the kmet, and mehana are defrayed from the communal funds, and the commune has the sole control of its property; but must render a yearly statement of its employment to the Government. The members of the commune elect their chief (kmet), who is removable in a few specified cases. In each commune there is a petty court, composed of the kmet, as president, and two assessors: in civil matters, its decision is final in claims not exceeding two hundred Turkish piastres (about 1*l.* 14*s.*); in criminal matters it can inflict three days' imprisonment or ten blows. A tax, proportionate to the number of adult males, is payable yearly by the commune to the Government, but the commune subdivides the amount among families, according to their means; similarly as to other Government charges. The proportion of taxes paid by each adult male to the Government,

* "Et d'abord il faut conserver le mode d'administration des communes russes par les assemblées communales (mirskie skhody). Tout le monde en Russie est d'accord là dessus."—Tourgueneff, "Emancipation des Serfs," p. 44. Paris, 1860.

and including a yearly payment of six shillings to the priest, one shilling and fourpence to the schoolmaster, and eightpence to the kmet, amounts to from twenty-four shillings to twenty-seven shillings yearly. The communes have lately established a pension fund for widows of priests and schoolmasters. The prefect of the district, head of the arrondissement, and Government engineer receive rations and forage for their horses when they visit the commune on public business.

In the mountain districts, taking a general average, a commune consists of from seventy-five to eighty-five houses, containing each one or more families (see the next paragraph, upon the *Sadruga*), and amounting, in the whole, to about 500 to 560 souls; among whom there may be from ninety to ninety-six taxpayers. Each household possesses, on an average, about twenty head of cattle, sixty sheep, two or three horses, fifty goats, twenty-five pigs. In the plain, a commune comprises about 120 houses, 900 to 1000 souls, and 140 taxpayers. Here, each household possesses four or six oxen (few are so poor as to have only two), twenty to twenty-five sheep, sixty pigs, scarcely any goats, and about the same number of horses as on the mountain.

Another remarkable institution, peculiar* perhaps to the southern Slaves, is the Sadruga: curious, as a practical illustration of theories which have, of late years, much occupied a certain school of political economists. It consists of an association of persons, occupying either one or adjoining dwellings; taking their meals together; holding and managing their property in common. In the larger towns, the Sadruga is now scarcely met with; but in the country districts, and especially on the frontier, it still subsists. Each of these communities has a head-man (Starjeschina), who directs its affairs, and distributes the household duties. All property acquired by a member belongs to the community, except a

* Haxthausen, "Transcaucasia," mentions a somewhat similar institution as existing among the "Ossetes."

few articles, as clothes, the embroidered dresses of the women, arms, &c., which are considered personal property. At the death of the father, the children remain members of the Sadruga; and, as they reach the age of fifteen, acquire a participation in the profits: the Starjeschina is the natural guardian of children left orphans. The widow of a member continues to enjoy the same benefits as her husband, but must take her share in the household duties of the community. Till of late years, the law opposed great difficulties to the dissolution of such a partnership; but these provisions have been relaxed, and the institution is gradually disappearing. In Servia, the members of a Sadruga must be relations by blood, or according to the church canons (as godfather and godson); but the original idea of the institution—common to the Austrian and Turkish Slavonic races—is to be probably sought in the facilities it afforded for defence in an unsettled state of society.*

Extract from "Civil Code of the Principality of Servia."
Part II. chap. xv.

"§ 507. Zadrouga est la communauté de la vie et des biens, basée sur la parenté ou l'adoption. Zadrouga s'appelle aussi la maison commune pour différence de la vie séparée.

"§ 508. Les biens et les possessions de la Zadrouga appartiennent à tous ceux qui participent à la communauté; les acquisitions des Zadrougas sont communes.

"§ 509. Les effets exclusivement appartenant à quelqu'un des Zadrougas, sont sa propriété, comme par exemple: les habits, l'argent, servant comme décoration (nakit) des femmes, le lit, les chemises, &c. &c.

"§ 510. On ne peut pas disposer de la propriété commune sans l'accord de toutes les personnes du sexe mâle qui sont majeurs et mariés. Le Starjechina (le commandant de la Zadrouga) dirige la maison commune, mais il ne peut pas aliéner quelque chose sans le consentement préalable des Zadrougas; neánmoins les dispositions du Starjechina sont valables si les Zadrougas ne protestent pas pendant une année contre ses arrangements.

"§ 512. Qui se sépare et prend son partage, quoique restant dans la maison, est regardé comme éloigné de la Zadrouga.

"§ 523. Les veuves de la Zadrouga restent dans la communauté et jouissent du partage de leurs maris; mais elles doivent travailler."

* See also Vuk's German Dictionary, *Sadruga*.

The General Assembly of the nation occurs in the early history of nearly all the Slaves. When those of the eastern branch were, as has been above described, under the sway of a number of independent rulers, the Shupan, or chief of each province, seems to have governed with the assistance of a permanent assembly called the Sabor. Nor does this state of things appear to have been substantially altered, even when the government of these petty states was concentrated in a single hand; for we find the Tsar Duschan, though limiting the attributions of the Sabor considerably, in the laws which bear his name, yet established those laws in "An Assembly of our Orthodox Council, composed of the Patriarch Joaniki, and of all the Arch-priests and Ecclesiastics, small and great, of myself the pious Stephen, and all the notables of the empire, small and great." In Servia, even throughout the Turkish times, the Turks were in the habit of assembling the rayahs, to fix amongst themselves the incidence of taxation, and other questions of administration; and the elders of those assemblies held a sort of conference with the Turkish governors. As the people threw off the Turkish yoke, such assemblies claimed wider attributions; and this is the germ of the Skouptschina (or National Assembly), which, though not mentioned in, or implicitly recognised by, the Fundamental Statute (Ustaw) of 1838, has continued to be convoked from time to time in the country.

The third chapter of Ranke's History of Servia contains a curious account (principally drawn from Vuk) of the Servian national superstitions, showing the extent to which pagan rites have become intermingled with Christian ceremonies among the southern Slaves. Such are the immediate references of every act in life to the Deity: the belief in supernatural agencies; the Vampyre; the Veda, who bears the plague; and the Vili, who watches over the heroes of the nation.

Ranke mentions the great Servian festival in honour of the dead; while the "new Code of Montenegro"—for even Montenegro has now its Code—refers (Art. 87) to the "barbarous custom prevailing among men and women, of, when any one dies, cutting the hair," &c., and prohibits this under pain of a "fine of two ducats of gold, whether the offender be a man or a woman." As to the "Otescha," or forcible abduction of the bride, it existed till very late years, and was only put an end to by Prince Milosch.

The Slave element is almost exclusively to be sought among the classes attached to the cultivation of the soil. In making this broad statement, we speak of Christian Europe, for it is otherwise in Bosnia, and we also put out of the question Russia and Poland, where the state of things is different, and Servia and Montenegro, where only one class, that of a small proprietary, can be said to exist. In Bohemia, in Moravia, in Galicia, Hungary, and Croatia, the bourgeoisie are of German, Italian, or Jewish origin; and, if it be objected that in the Banat and Wallachia a considerable retail trade is in the hands of the Servians, these, we may reply, are all Austrian Slaves, of the south of Hungary, who form an exception to the general rule. Accordingly, the literati of the southern Slaves are not to be found among a higher class than the village clergy, and masters of village-schools. Dobrowsky, and Kollar, Schaffgarik, Schour Vuk Karadjoitch, all belong to this, or even a lower class. With the exception of their beautiful ballads,* and an attempt to note down and dwell on what is peculiar to the Slave peoples, there is little of originality in their literature. "Toutes les productions littéraires des Slaves occidentaux sont des imitations des modèles étrangers; ou si elles visent à l'originalité, ce n'est qu'une originalité de forme qu'ils empruntent à la poésie ou à la langue populaire, sans que la conception ou les idées y portent le cachet de la liberté et de la puissance créatrice." † Not only is this the case with the western Slaves, but to a certain degree with the northern Slaves also; for, with the exception in Poland of the brilliant but fanciful Mickievicz and his

* A list of the principal collections of Slave ballads (Russian, Servian, and Illyrian) will be found at p. 61 of the "Essai sur la Philologie Slave," mentioned above.

† "Les Slaves Occidentaux," p. 61.

school, and some well-known authors of repute in Russia, their literature contains little that is remarkable. But from their national songs, and periodical publications, and almanacks, much out-of-the-way information as to the traditions, superstitions, customs, and aspirations of the Slaves is to be gleaned. We would especially call attention to the Servian Dictionary of Vuk, so often referred to in this paper; many of the articles of which would well repay translation.

When I use the word "aspirations," I do not wish to convey an exaggerated idea of future danger and disturbance, such as is occasionally apprehended. Among a comparatively educated population, as the Austrian Slaves and the Bulgarians, ideas of a Slave nationality may have some existence; while it would be a matter of reasonable doubt how far these ideas could ever be conceived or shared by (for example) the Servian swineherd or the rayah of Bosnia, however much the former may prize, and the latter envy, the concessions which two generations of freemen have extorted from the reluctant but politic Sultans.

4. *A GOSSIP ON A SUTHERLAND HILL-SIDE.*

HALF-PAST FIVE ! The rain pattering against the window-panes, and the birches outside swishing and rasping against the walls, with a vehemence that tells of a rattling south-wester. Dark grey mist driving past, only permitting us to see some fifty yards of the lake—lead-coloured, flecked with foam, and long white waving streaks like a tideway. To dress or not to dress? To turn out and drive seven miles in the teeth of the storm, and find our horizon capable of being touched with the point of a ramrod when we reach the stalking-ground, or to turn in under the warm bedclothes again, to wake at nine o'clock, with a guilty conscience, to the reality of a glorious morning, so clear and bright after the rain that I can almost count the stones on the top of Ben-Clebric—to be told that the household is aweary of mutton and languishes for venison—to find the river in full spate and salmon impossibilities—to have one's health tenderly inquired after by Donald?——Never! Tub—sleep-dispeller, welcome! and to breakfast at six with a Sutherland appetite.

Before the terminal gooseberry jam is attained, the sharp sound of wheels on the wet gravel announces the arrival of Donald, kindest-hearted and keenest of stalkers, and his cheery inquiries as to my state of preparation are promptly answered by my appearance at the door.

We are going to go whatever the weather may be, but we go through the ceremony of discussing whether there is a chance of its being worth the while, and after an interchange of prophecies, believed in by neither of the prophets, we climb into the dog-cart, and turn down sharp by that wonderful post-office, whose master is a "Mairchaunt," and where you can buy, or at least order, everything, from a red hackle to a reaping-machine.

How deliciously the fresh breeze sweeps round the corner, inflating our lungs to their innermost cell, and how the waves lap and jump under it! A wild night last night, judging from those piles of foam along the shore, but those great straggling rifts are beginning to show patches of the cold blue northern sky beyond. Nothing, after all, but a sea-fog! Whether the weather be wet or dry, wet *we* shall be on the hill, and those rifts will let light enough through to show us deer, if the worst comes to the worst.

Trundle along powney, through the stone-inclosed patches of oats, trying to look ripe and failing most dismally in the attempt; past little fields, half arable, half pasture, where the cow feeds tended by the bit, bareleggit lassie, wet through already, but caring nothing for wet now, whatever she may do when she finds herself a wrinkled crone at forty, bent double with rheumatism. Then through the fresh sweet birch coppice, where the "Ladies of the wood" are tossing their lithe arms, and sprinkling sweet odours and sparkling raindrop gems on every side; where the blackcock whirrs up and sails away on his strong-beating wings, and the daintily tripping roe crosses the road shyly, seeking her cozy lair, amongst the sweet bog myrtle and warm tussock grass, after her night's marauding amongst the oats.—Then a moment's pause to pick up Jeemie the gillie, and Clebric the muckle deer hound, and out on to the great brown moor.

Something like the character of the people, serious and cheerful at once; quiet and reserved in general tone, but with bright patches of vivid green and bits of rarely-scented shrub here and there; lighted up with little eyes of water moist and gleaming as those of a girl who has been crying for sheer happiness, and breaks into a smile amidst her tears. Light and shade, rigid fanaticism and wild poetical fervour alternating in fitful gleams: the light at any rate predominating amongst those slim well-grown lasses and lither lads rattling on before us at a hand gallop, going to gather in their marsh hay. Pass them we cannot, nor does Donald seem particularly anxious to do so. We would we "had our Gaelic" to understand the chaff that passes! It must have some fun in it to cause bright eyes to sparkle brighter, and some wit to produce such a severe struggle for instant rejoinder! Poor down-trodden Sutherland highlanders! who to see you galloping along in that fashion would ever suppose that you had all been transported to the uttermost parts of the earth years ago? We are told so in "prent buiks," and so it must be true, but still it is rather puzzling to make out why there are so many more of you now than there were before you were deported in thousands. Verily, if all is true that is said about you, you must be a wonderfully prolific people! Expound unto me, Donald, how it happens that there are so many more people in Sutherland now than there used to be?

"'Deed Sir, I cannot say, except because the old Duchess-Countess moved the people down from the hills, where they were starving, to the sea, where they get the fishing, and a chance of getting in their crops oftener than once in three years, which is about the average in the higher glens."

"Ah! well. I should not wonder either; but another cause is the discontinuance of your good old custom of cutting each other's throats. When you left off that, you became too numerous for the land, as it used to be. If old Sir Robert Gordon is to be trusted, there never were such a set of people for sticking dirks into each other's weams, as you Sutherlanders used to be in the old time, friend Donald."

"Hoot toot! 'Deed Sir, no! It was not the Sutherland folks, it was thae fallows from Assynt, and Edderachillies and Strathnaver, who were aye coming over the marches, and lifting cows and raising blood-feuds that were hard to quell. The Sutherland lads were aye decent people—except some of the clans, maybe."

"Well, I believe that you really were, as you are, better than your neighbours, but there is many a broad blood-spot in your country—even in the fair gardens of Dunrobin.

But we won't quarrel about that now: what is that heap of stones by the loch-side? it looks like a Pictish tower."

"Aye, 'deed is it; and there is another on the Island, and another, and another on the other side. Do you know what they were made for, sir? The old wives say, some that they were built by the Pechts, and some by the Feen: they must have been gay small folk that lived inside them."

"Not I, Donald! I used to think that the Pechts got into the chambers, and put a big stone at the entrance to keep the enemy out, and built them hour-glass fashion to prevent the said enemy scrambling into them; but when I considered that an able-bodied man, with a bit of burnt stick, could pick the whole affair down in no very long time, the Pechts inside being as utterly unable to prevent it as a rabbit is being dug out of his burrow, I doubted. As they seem always to have been built within sight of each other, some people have supposed that they were watch-towers, and those on the coast may have answered the purpose well enough. Most of the inland ones do not, however, seem situated on very good look-out points, and in old times, when the country was covered with wood, must have been useless for that purpose; unless, indeed, they were there before the woods. When the minister of Reay amused himself by pulling them to pieces, about a hundred years ago, he found nothing in them but wee querns, and deers' bones and antlers. He gives drawings of them, with rude stone roofs, with a small hole in the top; but I suspect that he confounded those mysterious slab-built *Uags* with the real hour-glass tower. The Bishop of Ossory, who was antiquity-hunting in Sutherland about the same time, found many of them entire: I wish I could now."

"Weel, sir, some do say that they kept their corn in them, and the old folks say that the good people are very fond of being about them, but I cannot say much about *that*. If you want to see a good one you must go to Dun-Dornadilla, on the road to Loch Hope."

"Aye! that's the best of them now. The one built by King Cole in Strath-dhu is, I hear, very tumble-down. I have seen very perfect chambers in the one in Golspie Glen, and have wormed my way from one to the other in great wonderment; but the quaintest of them all for situation is that at Store Point, which is connected with the mainland by a natural arch, and where Thorkill, the Orkney chief, concealed his lady-love."

Clattering on past curious mounds of gravel, which look very like glacial moraines, our attendant carts suddenly diverge across the moss and plunge into the swollen stream, the very ponies seeming to enjoy the fun, and, half swimming, half scrambling, with shouts and screams, and ringing laughter from the haymakers, they gain the wet fields on the other side, where the coarse marsh-grass, rich mottled brown, like the hair on an old stag's neck, is piled up in vast cocks.

" Farewell, lassies ! "

" Gude day, and a muckle hart for you, sir ! "

We must confess that we are not very well off for houses along the road, and that the gaps between them are considerably longer than those between the Villas of Highgate Hill, but we can see three at once, and that is three more than one can see in the same distance on many a better frequented highland road. The shepherds are scattered about in their bothies, and make but a small show. You must go to the richer straths and the borders of the sea, if you want society in Sutherland. There is some comfort, however, in thinking that the inns are placed with judicious care, and that there is no fear of your being unable to get from one to the other in an easy day's march ; and when you reach them, can you not take your ease in them ?—most comfortable of hostelries !

It is hardly fair to blame the proprietor for not building more, or enlarging those already built. Those already existing are absolutely empty two-thirds of the year, and are let at the magnificent rent of ten pounds a year. As every one of them has been built at the expense of the present duke and his father, the tourist owes, I think, a considerable debt of gratitude to the family ; had their erection depended on private speculation, they would never have existed at all. They would doubtless hold more tourists if they were larger, but whether if they were larger they would have more people in them is another matter. One great comfort is, that express care is taken to prevent their being occupied exclusively by resident sportsmen, a common nuisance in the Highlands, but often the only means by which the host can make money. If the Sutherland inn is full—and, with the exception of the one at Lairg, I never found one so—you can always get a bed somewhere, often at the manse, as you do in the Tyrol. Anybody who wishes to speculate in the innkeeping line would be received with open arms by the duke's agents, I am pretty sure; but unless he is actuated by the purest philanthropy, and is prepared to wait till the "Anti-condensation of Atlantic mist" Company is in full play, he must not expect a quick return for his outlay. The Reay family, to the end of their reign, always stopped and dined at a green knoll near the Crask still called Lord Reay's Table: *now* you have a good inn.

By-the-bye, I remember an anecdote of this same road before it was made, worth the recording. When the father of the last Lord Reay who possessed the estate changed his residence from Skibo to Tongue, his son was put into a creel on one side of a pony, and counterbalanced by his younger brother, the admiral, in another; the old lord being a great lord, and not easily counterbalanced, had *his* opposite creel filled with big stones. Remember, this is not so very many years ago.

The only house we need trouble ourselves about just now stands clear and white on the brown moor, like a target, with a black window for a bull's-eye, the habitation of shepherd Rory. Trundle on, powney, you shall soon be up to your hocks in the warm heather in his stable.

At last, the last bridge, and the last torrent, and the house we have seen so long is reached. A real two-storied house, well built, and warm, and if not comfortable and clean, the fault is the holder's; for a head shepherd is no unimportant personage, and must be well treated. In many cases, he is the real money-winner of the concern, and in all a most important agent in increasing the balance at the Golspri bank.

"How are ye the day, Rory?"

"Brawly, thank you. How's yersel'? Will ye na come ben the hoose, and tak a drink o' milk, or ye tak the hill?"

"Aye, deed will I; for though I cannot say that it is a potation I am much addicted to, I know that you will be hurt if I refuse your hospitality, and I also know that the sma' still whiskey-days have departed from Sutherland, thank heaven!"

The pony is unharnessed, the dog-cart drawn to the side of the road, and Donald disappears with Rory to hold a solemn confabulation on things in general, and deer in particular; and escaping from Mrs. Rory's hot room, that makes one steam like a Geyser, I will go and sit on the parapet of the bridge and moralize.

The hills I am going to stalk are under sheep, like the greatest part of Sutherland, and the shepherds wandering about the hills see a good deal of deer life, and can give most valuable information concerning them. More, indeed, than one desires, as if he has seen the deer, the chances are that the deer have seen him. Oh, happy, black cattle times, when the forester had the right and the power of impounding every beast that strayed beyond its appointed limits, and when two-thirds of Sutherland was one wild unmolested deer forest, well watched and well tenanted! Only sixty years ago! Blessed times! when the foresters had a legal amount of judicial and executive power which would make the Anti-preservation-of-anything Society of our own days open their eyes very wide indeed. All swept away by those wretched cheviots, who, indeed, do clothe the naked and feed the hungry, but give no sport, unless the double system of manœuvring which has to be practised to keep clear of them, and get near the deer, may be considered in that light. Now that the greater part of Sutherland is disforested (though the map-makers persist in scrawling Dirrie-more * and Dirrie-chat † over the country to tantalize us), there are but few peaks left clear, where the scattered remnants of the great deer herds can repose in security. The deer, indeed, rather like the sheep than not, as they save the hinds a great deal of look-out duty, and a flock scampering about three or four miles off is instantly seen and commentated on by them. But the shepherds and the collies! I must give the shepherd the credit of trying to prevent himself spoiling a sport which he loves in his heart of hearts (and I suspect takes a turn at himself, whiles) as much as he can, more particularly when he is treated with consideration, and a tip; but still *he* cannot help the hinds sniffing him out a mile off and retreating into the distance with their antlered lords. Of course, three tourists *per diem* blundering across the moss would put off every deer for miles, and the grand sport of deerstalking would soon become a mere matter of tradition; a consummation which would not very much please even the non-deerstalking population of Sutherland. Independently of the number of men employed as gillies and keepers, the renters of these shootings spend large sums of money every year in parts of the country where no reasonable being would willingly pass four-and-twenty hours without a stronger inducement than looking at scenery, which he very probably might not see the whole of the season after all. Remember, O tourist! that many a barren mountain top, which under no other circumstances could produce a penny a year, either to peasant or proprietor, becomes a valuable source of income to both, if it be but left undisturbed.

From the remotest antiquity this Sutherland has been essentially a country of deer, protected by the sharpest laws. I fancy that it was a conquered country, and that the conquerors imposed forest laws on the conquered, as the Normans did in England. At any rate, never at any period of its history have the deer been less protected than at present. Sir Robert Gordon, who wrote a book in the seven-

* "The great deer-forest." † "The deer-forest of the Clan Chattan."

teenth century, which I think has been prevented from obtaining popularity by being described as "A Genealogical History of the Earls of Sutherland," being in reality the most wonderful collection of legends and stirring highland tales in existence, positively boils over with excitement when he touches on the "vert and venaison" of his native country.

"All these forests and schases are verie profitable for feeding of bestiall, and delectable for hunting. They are full of reid deer and roes, woulffs, foxes, wyld catts, brocks, skuyrells, whittrets, weasels, otters, martrixes, hares, and foumarts. In these fforests, and in all this province, ther is great store of partridges, pluviers, capercaleys, blackwaks, mure-fowls, heth-hens, swanes, bewters, turtledoves, herons, dowes, steares or stairlings, lair-igig or knag (which is a foull like unto a paroket or parret, which makes place for her nest with her beck in the oak tree), duke, draig, widgeon, teale, wildgoose, rin goose, gouls, wharps, shot wharps, woodcock, larkes, sparrowes, snyps, blackbuirds, and all other kinds of wildfowl and birds which are to be had in any pairt of this kingdom."

Well put in, that last, Sir Robert, or we should have had to transcribe the index to Yarrell's birds, for even to this day, Sutherland is a most marvellous country for "fowl;" north enough to be the breeding-place of the wild-goose and the widgeon, and the winter resting-place of innumerable rare Arctic birds, and yet warm enough, thanks to the gulf-stream, to suit the roller and the Bohemian waxwing. Some individuals in Sir Robert's list have disappeared, as, for example, the Capercallzie, probably from the destruction of the woods; and no one, I fancy, who knows him, grieves much at his absence, for two or three birds, the size of turkeys, to the square mile, affording no sport themselves, and not permitting any sport-affording bird to approach their haunts, and, moreover, rather apt to taste like particularly tough old blackcocks, stuffed with blacking-brushes, and a dash of turpentine, can hardly be worth the keeping. If the naturalist wishes to study him, let him go to the "Shramstein" in the Saxon Switzerland, and make the most of him.

That curious fowl, the "Lair-igig, or Knag," has also disappeared with the oaks into which she used to dig her bill—a strange cross between a woodpecker and a puffin ; if, indeed, she be not the latter, who loves to breed in rabbit holes, and might have made herself comfortable enough in a rotten oak-tree. If not a puffin, goodness and Sir Robert only knew what she was—she is gone like the Dinornis, and must remain in abeyance—

"To the Platonic year, and wait her time,
And happy hour to be revived again"—

by Professor Owen.

As far as I can make them out, all the birds named by Sir Robert, with the above-named exceptions, and scores of others, fly, fish, scream, trumpet, and whistle, in Sutherland and the bordering sea, to this day.

True it is, that if you have bad luck, you may drive all round Sutherland without seeing anything more rare than a chance grouse or an accidental blackcock, just as you may do, barring the two named, on a Devonshire or Derbyshire moor. But wander through the wilds, and peer cautiously at the lakes, and above all, paddle off the mouth of the "Little Ferry," in the beginning of November, when the sea is black with birds, and the air resonant with the cry of Haroldus Glacialis and his Arctic friends, and then count the number of strange birds you have seen. Any given day in the year, woodcocks may be flushed in the coverts, and snipes on the moor. Wild geese breed plentifully about some of the lakes, and the young are pinioned and reared by the farmers; so, O tourist! if you find a few swimming on Loch Shin, do not capture them and bring them to Lairg, as did certain young gentlemen last year, or your triumph in your woodcraft will be dashed by the laughter of the gillies, and the blasphemy of the proprietor—as was theirs. The Meganser breeds on Loch Beannach, as I know to my sorrow, for I once slew a whole brood of three at a shot, unwitting what they were; and he who fishes up Loch Shin without hearing the hoarse cry of the black-throated diver, warning her young against his approach, must be unlucky indeed.

The greater number of Sutherland birds belong to classes that love the wild moor, and the silent, rarely visited loch, and when you see them, it is nine times out of ten when you are looking for something else, and seldom do they show themselves to the passing traveller who rattles round the country in the mail cart. The golden eagles were destroyed by the farmers because they killed their lambs, and the foxes more deservingly for the same reason, and the osprey was exterminated to supply the tourist market with herself and eggs, much to the Duke's annoyance. However, the eagles have it all their own way now. It has been found that the destruction of the golden eagle has caused the increase of the blue hare to a formidable extent, and the only way to keep him down will be to let his own adversary have full swing again. I do not regret the coming fate of Lepus variabilis, I like to see him now and then, as he frisks among the stones, or walks about on his hind toes, like a cross between a kangaroo and a dancing dog, but he is an awfu' plague both to the sheep-farmer, the deer-stalker, and the grouse-shooter, when he becomes too numerous—spoiling ten times as much grass as his head is worth, ten times told, putting up the deer in his idiot terror, and seeming to delight in running up hill, and seating himself on the sky-line, so that the whole world may see that he has seen something alarming, and pestering your pointers and setters with his sneaky draws, and foolishly astute meanderings. The Osprey, too, may come back when she likes, and we will gladly pay a tribute of grilse to her ladyship; indeed, she has come back, and was seen last summer floating and peering about, and speculating whether she might trust herself and her family on Loch Assynt again.

What particular kind of weasel a "whittret" (?whitethroat) was, I don't know, but all the other quadrupeds, with the exception of the wolf, may be had now for the seeking. That British tiger—the wild-cat, is now very scarce, but two kittens were seen, and one killed last year. I fancy they will soon follow their old comrade the wolf, and the sooner the better, for of all snarling, ill-conditioned, game-destroying brutes in the world, the wild-cat is the worst, and no one can hear their demoniacal caterwaulings at night, without being seized with an instant and intense desire to extirpate the race there and then. The wolves were the pest of Sutherland down to the end of the seventeenth century, the last one having been destroyed about 1700. One Timothy Pont, who travelled through Sutherland about 1650, speaks of it thus in his MSS. in the Advocate's Library:—

"It is exceedinglie weel stored with fishes, both from the sea and its own rivers, as also dear, roe, and dyvers kinds of wild beasts, *specially heir never lack wolves, more than are expedient;* it is weel stored with wood also."

I am in the habit of taking something readable with me to the hill, to pass away the time when I am waiting for the deer to rise—a habit strongly reprobated by Donald, who assures me that some day a scart of wind will snatch the paper out of my hand, and "birl it o'er the hill like a ghaist," to the terrification of all the deer; but still I do it; and having by chance the account of the destruction of the last wolves in Scotland in my pocket, you shall hear it, though you may have heard it before—mine is, I assure you, taken from the original MSS., and I would not alter a word for the world, for it is evidently taken direct from the Gaelic, by the author.

"There is a solitary moorland lake near the march between the parishes of Farr and Reay, called Loch Soivy,* which has an island reputed, in former ages, as a place of resort and shelter for wolves. At the period referred to, about the close of the seventeenth century, one of the tenants of Trantlemore in Halladale, named Eric-Bain Mackay, is said to have

* *Soivy* is synonymous with *Foick;* both Gaelic words signify the unclean bed or den of a fox, wolf, or similar wild animal. The words, especially *Foick*, are sarcastically applied to a filthy or neglected habitation or apartment.

wandered alone in search of a wolf, which, in consequence of depredations committed on his farm, he believed to be lurking in his neighbourhood. The reputed shelter afforded to animals of prey by the wild grounds around Loch Soivy, induced him to approach the Loch, and in his eagerness to make a complete search in that suspicious neighbourhood, he swam to the island, and contrived to carry his gun along with him; he there discovered marks of a wolf having been recently on the island, and afterwards found its den in which were two young cubs. He instantly killed them, and carried them homewards along with him, as evidence of his success, although the danger of meeting the dam, and being exposed to the well-known desperate fierceness of a she-wolf deprived of her young, occurred to him, and induced him to retreat as speedily as possible. He knew that the old wolf would not be long absent from her den; and during his hurried progress towards the strath in which he lived, he cast many an anxious look towards the loch and along the wide moor over which he was hastening. When about half across the uninhabited hill-grounds, he observed an animal at a distance following his footsteps, and soon discovered, from its peculiar howl, that it was the old wolf he dreaded to meet while carrying off its young, and which, no doubt, had visited her deserted den after he left it. His speed was redoubled; but his exasperated and formidable pursuer was quickly gaining ground on him, and he therefore cast aside the dead whelps, and stood coolly to meet the fierce attack with which he was threatened, and, when within gunshot, he took a deliberate aim, and fortunately succeeded in shooting the advancing wolf. Without awaiting to reload his gun, he continued to run homewards at his fleetest pace, and although one of the best runners in the district, he only succeeded in gaining the descent of the hill, at the foot of which his house was situated, before another, a male or dog wolf, was noticed in full chase after him. Mackay arrived with great difficulty at a rude enclosure near his house, which separated the *infolds* from the *outfolds* of his small farm, before the close approach of this second and equally infuriated wolf; and having managed to reload his gun, and ensured a certain aim by resting it on the wall behind which he stood, he shot this old dog wolf also. After this long-remembered slaughter in one day, by a single individual, of two full grown and two young wolves, there has not been another found in that district of country.

"The death of the last wolf and her cubs in the forests connected with the east coast of Sutherland, was attended with circumstances still more remarkable. For several years before their complete extirpation, the wolves were decreasing in number, and at a time when it was supposed that they had been all destroyed, some nocturnal ravages amongst the flocks in the parish of Loth, gave indication that one or more wolves still survived in the neighbourhood. A great body of the inhabitants met together in order to scour the hilly parts of the parish of any of these ravenous animals that might be lurking in the district; but after a careful and laborious search, no wolf could be found. In a few days afterwards, a person of the name of Polson, who resided at Wester-Helmsdale, followed up the previous more general search by minutely examining one of the wildest recesses in the neighbourhood of Glen Loth, which he thought had not been thoroughly ransacked by the former party. On this occasion he was accompanied by only two young lads—one of them his son, and the other an active herd-boy. Polson was an expert hunter, and had much experience in tracing and destroying wolves, foxes, and other predatory animals; and being well acquainted with the localities, proceeded directly to the wild and rugged ground that surrounds the rocky and nearly inaccessible mountain-gully through which the upper part of the Burn of Sledale runs towards Glen Loth.

"After attentively looking for such marks of the animal he was in search of as his experience had taught him to distinguish as such, Polson discovered a narrow opening or fissure, in the midst of large pieces of fallen rock, which he felt certain led to a larger opening or cavern below, and which it was very probable a wolf or a fox had been in the habit of frequenting. Stones were thrown in, and other means taken to rouse any animal that might be lurking within the opening, and then the two young lads contrived to force themselves through this hole in order to examine the interior parts of it, while Polson remained on the outside. The boys soon discovered that the cavern into which the passage conducted them was a wolf's den, bestrewn with the bones and horns of animals, feathers and eggshells, and enlivened by five or six active wolf-cubs. This intelligence being communicated to Polson, he directed his son to destroy the cubs with all possible haste, and to return up again; but in his anxiety to give these directions, and, if possible, to see the interior of the cavern, he looked down into the passage, and his head thus deprived the persons below of the faint light afforded by the open mouth of the den. They therefore directed him not to obstruct the light, and Polson thereupon stepped a few paces aside. In an instant thereafter he heard the feeble howl of the young whelps as they were attacked below, and, to his great horror, saw at the same time a furious full-grown wolf, evidently the dam, and mad with rage occasioned by the cries of her young, close to the mouth of the cavern, which she approached unobserved among the rocky inequalities of the place, and which she attempted to enter at one bound, from the spot where she was first seen, before Polson could reflect how he should act in this emergency. He instinctively threw himself forward after the wolf, and succeeded in catching a firm hold of the animal's long and bushy tail, just as the fore part of the body was within the narrow entrance to the cavern, and her hind legs still on the outside of it. In the extreme hurry into which Polson was thrown, he omitted to take up his gun, which he had placed against a rock when aiding the boys to enter the opening, and probably he could not have used it with effect at the moment, if it had been in his hands. Without apprising the persons in the cavern of the danger to which they were exposed, Polson kept a firm hold of the wolf's tail, which he rolled round his left arm, and while the animal pulled, and pressed, and scrambled, and twisted, in order to get down to the rescue of her cubs, Polson managed, but with great difficulty, and by pulling the tail towards him with all his strength, to keep her from going forward. This struggle continued for a few moments, Polson, getting the command in his right hand of a large knife or dirk which he carried with him, wounded the wolf with it in the most vital parts he could reach. She made another vigorous effort to move forward, but Polson's strength, and his secure hold of her tail, kept her back. This was succeeded by a desperate struggle to retreat backwards, but the hole in which her head and the fore part of her body were ensconced was too narrow to admit her to turn round in it, and when Polson found her pressing backwards, he squeezed her forwards, and thus kept her stationary in the narrow mouth of the cavern, while he continued to plunge his dirk as rapidly as the struggle would permit of, into the wolf's side. All this occurred in total silence, the wolf being mute notwithstanding the wounds she received, and Polson being also silent, in consequence either of the engrossing nature of his exertions, or of being unwilling to alarm the young persons in the cavern. They, however, although not aware of what was passing at the entrance of the den, were surprised to find it again shut up, and the light excluded from them. This obstruction having continued sufficiently long to annoy the boys, Polson's son complained in a loud voice of the continued darkness; and while the father happened to be pulling the wolf backwards with all his strength, his son asked in an abrupt tone, 'What is keeping the light from us?' and was directly answered by the father, 'If the root of the tail breaks, you will soon know that.' Polson having succeeded in mortally wounding his ferocious prisoner, dragged her out of the hole in which he so fortunately got her secured, and then easily killed her; and she and her dead whelps were brought home by him as trophies of his singular rencounter and victory.

"The anecdote soon became known throughout the whole country, and the singularity of Polson's answer (which tells better in Gaelic, the language in which it was spoken) while uncertain of success in a struggle on which his son's life depended, joined with the fact that the wolf killed under such peculiar circumstances was the last seen in Sutherland, gave great celebrity to this exploit, and has preserved the present traditional account of the occurrence among some of the country people to the present day." *

Mr. Taylor took great pains to make out the time when Mackay and Polson lived, respectively at Helmsdale and Trantlemore, and the time of their deaths, and he decides that these occurrences took place between 1690 and 1700. It gives one a lively hint as to the state of the country —this wolf hunting within ten miles of Dunrobin!

The boar had probably departed long before the wolf; and I know no other mention of him than that contained in the sad and really beautiful tradition of "Dermid the Pure and the Boar with the Poisoned Bristles," of which Mr. Scrope has given an imperfect condensation from the Taylor MSS.

When you are at Tongue, and see the castellated crags of Ben Loyal standing out black and sharp against the sky, you may, if you are sentimentally inclined, croon to yourself:—

"Now were seen in their wounds the son of O'Duin, the excellent, the bloody horseman of Fingal's people, and the lovely branch of the twining lochs (Grana) extended on the hill, beneath the sun at noon. That hill which when we approached we beheld green, red was its hue for one duration of time with the blood of the hero of the musical voice. With the father of the wild sow, they buried on the hill beautiful Grana, the daughter of Cuchullin, and his two white dogs along with Dermid. The hue of blood covers the field. The son of Duin is on the other side. I grieve that thou art laid by the side of the boar under the sloping banks of yonder hillocks, son of O'Duin; great is the misfortune that thou hast fallen by the jealousy of my wife. Her breast

* There is no doubt but that this is the original of Hogg's wild boar story. He most probably obtained it from some Sutherland drover, and, as was his wont, appropriated it.

was fairer than the sun, her lips were redder than crimson blossoms," &c. &c. *ad infinitum.*

This tradition held its own, not improbably by the right of truth, even to our own times. I quote a good authority when I record, that the spot where Dermid and Grana were buried (Ault-na-torc, the burn of the boar), marked by the usual grey cairn, is, or at least was very lately, held in reverence by the neighbouring inhabitants, and to injure or destroy the only remaining tree that shaded Dermid's resting-place, was held to be so extremely unlucky that even cattle were prevented from approaching it. One of the branches was lopped off by a countryman, several years ago, and some misfortunes that subsequently befel him and his family were attributed to the rash act. I quote from the original MSS. of 1837, and old Ross, of Tongue, has whispered the same legends into mine own ears, long since then. But here's Rory.

"Well, what deer are there on the hill, Rory?"

"'Deed ye ken that better than mysel, for I heard ye were after venaison, and no one has been on the hill since I brought the sheep down last week. 'Deed there were deer on Corrie Venchinch, and I heard your shot yestere'en, and heard it tell; and there were fine staigs about the muckle rock. Ye canna' fail o' sport; but 'deed it looks gay moist."

Gay moist, indeed! and the burn, high in spate, not only rattles harshly at our feet, but the swish of the wind brings other murmurs with it that tell of water falling over rocks too rarely covered to be rounded by its action.

"It's moist up there, Rory, no doubt, though the less we say about its gaiety the better."

A wet walk and a weary we shall have amongst the old moss-hags before we gain the spurs of Ben-Clebric; with no excitement to keep us going, nothing but work to be done to gain an end, which, like most of our ends, may turn out worthless when gained. Up along the burn we go, following the narrow sheep-track, deeply indented in the black bank, crossing the sharp, slaty rocks again and again, till it turns out of our course, and we have to take to the splashy moor, too wet to grow heather or to breed grouse, covered with tufts of coarse tussock grass, where the blue hare bounces up and squatters through the plashes like some strange water-work, and where little brown moorland birds spring up every few yards, whistle a few cheery notes, and then settle down into their damp beds again. Then unto the burn again, now grown smaller, running black and quiet in its channel, deeply cut in the gravel, with an edging of bright green turf, and rushes here and there, and walls of black peat, eight or ten feet high, a little wider to the right and left—telling a story of old, old times, and the hard work the little burn has had to make its way in the world. Quite a little sheltered valley, warm and cozy in this stormy day, perfect in itself, with little streams, little meadows, and little black Alps protecting it. It would be a perfect miniature, even to its close little sky of mist, were the effect not injured by the roots and stumps of ancient birch trees sticking out from the boglike bones from a sea-washed churchyard.

"How is it, Donald, that the stumps of these birches show such evident marks of having been *burnt* down?"

"'Deed, sir, I cannot say. They do say that the great witch of Clebric burnt the woods down about some quarrel with a hunter who did not give her venaison; and others do say, that the Danes burnt them down to drive out the Pechts, in the old time; but 'deed I do not know."

You may take which explanation you like, or invent a new one for yourselves; but *burnt* down the trees about here have been, plainly enough. How a wood of growing trees could have been burnt to the stumps, is hard to understand: were the woods old and dead, and hung about with what the Tyrolese call "baum-haar," long, hanging, grey mosses? Had they done their work, and got as much out of the soil as they could, rendering it incapable of supporting them any longer, and so died as they stood, making it fit for new comers, like the Pechts and the Feen? I don't know; there are the burnt stumps, testifying, to this day, of their burning, with three or four feet of turf above them.

Old Sir Robert's list of birds and beasts evidently indicates a country far more wooded than Sutherland is now, as late as the middle of the seventeenth century. Probably the firs came to an end simultaneously, and soon buried themselves in the peat produced by their decay; the stumps being full of turpentine, resisted the process, and remained as they are now. Peat grows fast, and the fathers of young men tell me that they remember groves of pines on the south side of Lairg bridge, where they now dig their winter fuel.

The old birch woods still linger here and there in all their pristine beauty, though diminished in size. On the lower Shin, about Scriberscross, and fringing many a sparkling loch and wild hillside, may the sweet-scented gleaming-leaved birch be found, growing on a soil knee deep in vegetable mould, or perched on the top of a moss-grown boulder, that gives it an uncertain foothold for the time, and then betrays it to the first great blast that sweeps from the sea. It is curious that the great destructive agent of so northern a tree should be *snow;* thousands of birches are destroyed whenever snow falls early enough to find the leaf on the tree; and as far south as Sussex I have seen the tops of innumerable birches snapped off by its weight, even in winter time. Struck down by wind or snow, the birch lies for a time perfect in form and colour, but crumbling to dust internally when touched by the foot; and in the powdery humus the long rich moss finds a fit nidus for its spores, and in a short time all is covered with a green soft carpet, dying at the bottom, growing at the top, the dead part furnishing food for the new generation, and so the peat moss grows: getting gradually dry enough for heather, and maybe even for pasture.

The idea of the first canoe must have been taken from a birch in the state one so often sees it in the north. Long after the interior has crumbled to dust, the silver bark retains its form and colour, and the noble savage who stumbled over it had nothing to do but to stitch the two ends together with a sinew, dab on a bit of gum, and learn to sit steady in it. In Sutherland the birches were too small, and the rivers too wild to induce even the Pechts to take to this form of boat-building; being a pastoral people, an ox's hide stretched over a basket was probably their sea and lake going machine.

The oak in which the Lair-igig delighted to dig her bill has vanished altogether, except about Dunrobin, and I could never hear of or see any in the bogs, so that I expect that even in the old times they were strictly localized. Another old world tree, the alder, is plentiful enough, and I think larger than I have ever seen it elsewhere, but it seldom leaves the river's edge, where the cattle love to shelter themselves under its opaque dark green leaves, and browse on the rich rank grass that springs beneath its shade.

Oh, happy trees! Hieronymus Cardanus, that learned Theban, says that you live longer than animals, because you never stir from your places; and much I wish that I might attain to length of days by remaining in this sheltered burn a little longer, but there is no help for it—scramble up, and out into the storm.

Just as we reach the top of the first low ridge, Donald drops like a stone in the heather, and I drop with him as if we had both been shot with one ball.

"'Deed, sir, there are deer; but I'm thinking they're just the Loch au Fureloch hinds; tak out your glass and see if ye ken them."

Aye, 'deed do I, Donald, as well as I know the pattern of the nails in your shoe soles, and I have studied that often enough as I crawled after you. There are the sixteen of them, walking daintily about, nibbling at the coarse grass, shaking the wet off their hides, with a vehemence which surrounds them with a halo of spray, holding a good deal of communication with each other, and—there—as usual! quarrelling and fighting, rising perfectly upright on their hind legs, ears well laid back, and striking at each other with their sharp fore hoofs. What vixens!

They are an odd little sept, these Loch au Fureloch hinds; always to be seen about the same spot on the lower grounds: so used to the shepherd that they do not move off when they can see him clearly, and watch what he is about; and never by any chance is there a stag in their company, except possibly some effeminate hobbledehoy of a pricket, too weak-minded to take the risks of the hill-side.

It must, however, be understood that these hinds are Amazons, not vestals, as is evident from the number of calves trotting about amongst them; unless, indeed, they are the lady-superintendents of an educational institution for young stags. My own belief is, that they quietly shirk all responsibility as regards the safety and comfort of their lords, and have formed themselves into a society of emancipated and strong-minded hinds; a most detestable state of things, which, were it not for the sake of the calves, I would alter with a rifle-bullet. As it is, we show ourselves just enough to cause them to move off quietly, and avoid giving them the wind, as, if they suspect anything, and have no facts whatever to go upon, they will form a theory of their own, and make as much mischief on the hillside as they possibly can—"like Christians," as Donald would say.

Up across the moss we splash, towards the great outlying buttress of Ben-Clebric, a brown ridge some seven or eight miles long, streaked with meandering strips of bright green, marking where the mountain torrents, cutting deeply into the moss, drain the soil sufficiently to permit the Alpine grasses to flourish. The little valleys in which these patches lie are the corries where the deer love to feed, and about which they are apt to lie after feeding, particularly early in the day, before they draw up to the more prominent points of the hill for their afternoon's siesta. Every corrie—and there are scores of them—has its name; and the forester and shepherd know them as well as a London cabman does the streets.

All this hillside has to be spied most carefully, as, although the wind is in the wrong airt for stags to be on it, there may be a hind or two, who, if disturbed, will go over the ridge and scare the deer on the other side. Before our work is fairly done, the mist rolls down the face of the hill, wave after wave, till not more than a hundred feet of the base is left clear, and that becomes of a strange lurid reddish-purple from the shadow on the heather,—a mighty pleasant prospect for a deer-stalker!

However, it is barely ten o'clock, and no one knows what may happen till the mystic hour of twelve, when it is the established creed of the hill that the great crisis of the weather takes place. Scrambling upwards along the bed of the burn, startling the grousecock from so near our feet that he almost chokes himself with his own crow as he vanishes in the mist, we reach the bothy where one of shepherd Rory's deputies lives, for week after week, in a solitude as complete as ever hermit enjoyed. Indeed, what with the solitude and his enforced temperance, living as he does on oatmeal and water, with an occasional trout, Donald Dhu would be on a par with any anchorite of them all, did he not destroy the virtue of the thing by being a useful man instead of an idle one, counting his sheep instead of his beads. A wild life they live on the hill, these shepherds, but, being for the most part men of reflection and observation, it is by no means without its pleasures. Wondrous combinations of cloud and sunshine, that would be denounced as ravings by a southern connoisseur if faithfully reproduced on canvas, reward his early rising. Not once or twice a year only is he on the higher peaks before sunrise, but day by day for weeks together he sees the marvels of the northern sun sweeping round the horizon, and till evening closes in he is face to face with nature, studying every shift of wind and swirl of vapour, and gaining a practical knowledge of meteorology which would astonish an astronomer from a royal observatory.

Donald Dhu's only companion on the hills is his colly dog, as wise and reflective in his way as his master; understanding his every word and gesture, and executing his commands with a zeal, intelligence, and determination perfectly marvellous. He is not a demonstrative dog; he will hardly give you a wag of his tail for your most insinuating advances; his master loves him next the wife and bairns: but there is no patting and caressing or good-dogging, no trying to wheedle or flatter, or assumption of superiority on his part, or cringing and finger-licking on that of colly, but a real strong male friendship between them. The dog is a good hardworking dog, who knows his business as well as his master, and is perfectly aware of the fact; grave and reserved, perfectly conscious of his own importance, he would scorn to posture for a mouthful of oatmeal were he starving. If you stop and talk to Donald Dhu, colly folds himself up, puts his head between his paws, and watches the sheep intently, evidently saying to himself, "Poor fellow, he must have his crack, I suppose, but somebody must attend to business." A word, a sign, and he is jumping from one woolly back to another, intent on singling out the one which has been indicated to him by a gesture so slight as to be almost imperceptible to a human by-stander, and let woolly-back turn and twist and wedge himself into the huddling mass as he may, out he has to come, and be snipped, or clipped or touched up in some unpleasant way or another, in spite of his teeth. But the sight of sights is to watch two shepherds sorting out their respective sheep when their flocks have become mixed together; and when this takes place on a hillside, where blue hares are numerous, colly-dogs' shrieking struggle between duty and inclination is a study for a moralist!

All books are full of the marvels of colly-dogism, and from what I have myself seen, even Mr. Jesse cannot tell me a story that I will not try to believe.

Colly dog's early training is a rude one, but I think that it is mutual, and that the shepherd picks up a good deal of dog during the process. He is too wise to waste his breath in reproving any little outbreak of juvenile impetuosity; but quietly fills his plaid-neuk full of chucky-stones, with which he peebles the peccant colly, with a force and accuracy that sends him off on three legs, filling the air with penitent howls. Mark, O tourist, when six colly dogs burst out upon you from the shepherd's door; "mak' as if" you were going to pick up a stone, and see how they will extend from the centre, and take cover behind the turf-stack, popping their heads round for an instant to fire a bark at you, and then dodge back like riflemen.

Neither Donald Dhu nor the collies being at home, we take the liberty of inspecting his habitation. The bothy is some twelve or fourteen feet long, and about four feet high in front, strongly built of stone, and nestled well under the bank, which almost touches the heather roof in the rear, making one speculate curiously as to how the summer thunder-storms treat his floor, and whether he goes out and sits on the roof for the sake of comparative dryness when the whole sheet of heather behind is running in a broad stream. There is a padlock on the door; but more for show than use, for the key is rusted tightly into it, and all power of locking has long since departed from the springs; still the thing looks well, and might, probably, prevent a particularly conscientious burglar from breaking in.

Bending low through the doorway, we see the secrets of Donald's domestic economy laid bare. A rude bed on one side, across which lay a pair of well-patched and well-soaked breeks; a table, consisting of a broad flat stone, miraculously balanced on divers bits of bogwood; a shelf, from which depends a worsted stocking with a needle sticking across a vast rent, Donald's last effort at mending himsel' given up in despair, with a stern determination to propose to the pretty lassie at Lairg next Sabbath; a tin plate, a fork, stuck into the shelf to facilitate finding, a basin, with a little dried porridge sticking about it, and a well blacked crock, are all we discover in the semi-darkness until we stumble over something which proves to be a stump of bogwood with the roots whittled off to sufficient evenness to permit of your sitting upon it without being tilted into the fire, that is, if you understand it, and are very careful. Window there is none; the hole in the roof, through which some of the smoke makes its exit when the fire is lighted, does double duty; and as we become accustomed to the twilight which fringes the perpendicular ray passing down it, we become aware of a few cast antlers, well gnawed by the hinds, a brown pan, filled with water, in which lie soaking a couple of dozen split trout, red as salmon, twice as large as I can ever catch—confound that otter! and in a particularly dark corner, a couple of black bottles, which *ought* to contain whisky of the smallest still, but which on examination hold nothing but in the one case a driblet of sour milk, and in the other, some tarry abomination used for doctoring the sheep; that little parcel wrapped up in a pocket-napkin, is Donald's well-thumbed Bible, and many a tough bit of grace and free-will does Donald puzzle over when his work is done, lighted by those splinters of bog-wood in the corner, which burn more brightly than wax—by-the-bye, the best thumbed side of Donald's Bible is the *Old* Testament. If you have imagination enough to double the length of Donald's bothy, without increasing its breadth or height, to turn the addition into a cow-house, of the foulest description—carefully avoid putting up any partition, as that would diminish the warmth, both of yourself and the cow, and make the whole affair ten times more filthy and uncomfortable than it is, and place a sea of liquid manure before the door, just high enough to permit every shower to wash a fair amount of it into the hut—you will get a very tolerable idea of a superior description of that happy home of the western highlander—the black hut—from which he has been so ruthlessly torn. If you doubt it, go and see for yourself, on the west coast, and more particularly on the islands. Suppose a man and his wife, and half-a-dozen children, with, in all probability, one if not two grandfathers and grandmothers, living in such a hovel, depending entirely on the miserable crops of oats or potatoes, without the remotest chance of a paid day's work from one year's end to the other, and you have the sort of existence Donald Dhu would have led in the good old times.

"I suppose he is not very much overpaid now, is he, Donald?"

"'Deed, sir, he's no that ill off; he gets good wages, a

certain number of sheep to himself, lives rent-free, finds himself in oatmeal for two or three shillings a week, and gets plenty of Braxy.

"What *is* Braxy? dead sheep, is it not?"

Well, it *is* dead sheep; but only sheep that die from rapid inflammation at certain times of the year. It is questionable whether it is particularly wholesome, but at any rate the shepherds do pretty well on it. It requires preparation, however; salting and pressing, and other little manipulations, which, when carefully described by an enthusiast in the art, are quite enough to make one certain that it is what Juliana Dame Berners would call "an ill meat for a queasy stomach," and to make one especially shy of pallid salt mutton in highland districts.

Swish! what a drive of cold wind and rain as we put our heads out of the bothy door. Never mind, we will get to the top of the ridge, perch ourselves like a couple of scarts to the leeward of a big stone, and wait for the clearing.

Under this mass of gray gneiss let us sit down, and gossip confidentially in a low voice, for there is no knowing what may hear us. Few sounds do we hear but the whispering of the wind amongst the wet bents. Now and then the croak of the ravens waiting about the stag we killed yesterday, floats down the wind, and the imperative "cr-u-u-u-uck-go-back-go-back" of the old cock grouse, hints that we are not entirely unnoticed in the mist: and there on a stone sits a golden plover, piping out the saddest and wildest of bird music; what has he done to make himself so unutterably miserable? There he sits in the mist, wilfully solitary for the time, giving utterance to a note which has an expression of the most intense broken-heartedness, perfectly indescribable; I know of no inflection of the human voice so unutterably mournful. He must have lived with the Pechts, and be grieving over their downfall. Throw a stone at him, Donald; if I listen to him for five minutes more, I shall begin to believe that highland improvements are a delusion, and that it is never going to stop raining.

To make a small bull, I never heard a complete silence in the open-air world yet. The two most silent situations I know, are an Alp above the snow line, and a gorse common, baking in the summer sun; but even there we have the grinding of ice and the swish of falling snow in the one case, and the crackling of the gorse-buds in the other, to tell us that Nature never sleeps. I wonder, by-the-bye, whether Jeemie is asleep? he ought to be up by this time; and putting the stag on the pony would warm us.

"'Deed, sir, no; it's hard work bringing up the old powney this weather, and all the burns in spate; and he knows that we shall not move till it clears, for fear of doing mischief; and now it wants a quarter of eleven. Hoot! how it rains; it's very hard I can never gae out for a day's pleasure without getting my claes spoiled, as the old wifie said when it rained at her husband's burying. Weel, weel, we must bide where we are till the mist rises, and then, if there are no fit staigs about the head of Brora, we must go over toward Clebric."

"By-the-bye, Donald, Mr. Scrope, who was a great hand at deer-driving in Blair Athol Forest in old times, tells a story about a savage individual of the name of Chisholm, who lived for years in a cave on Ben Clebric; do you know anything about him?"

"Aye, 'deed, sir, I mind the name well enough, but he was not a wild man at all, but a decent body from Rogart, and he only stopped in the cave for a day or two, and glad enough he was to get out o't."

"How?"

"'Deed, sir, there was a great fox-hunting at Lairg, and Chisholm, who lived at Rogart, brought over a dog to run against the Guns of Lairg; they were all Guns in those days. Well! they found a fox up by Loch Craigie, and ran him down to Lairg; and a gran' run they had o't. Well! there was no bridge over the Shin in those days, nor for many a day after: 'deed, I remember when the folks did not cross the water of Shin for months together. So the fox swam the lower end of the Loch where the grilse lie whiles, and where we saw the mouldiwarp swim across, and one of the Guns' dogs and Chisholm's after him, and they foregathered with him on the far side and pit him down, and then, as they wer'n't well acquainted, they girned at each other and fell a fighting over him, and when Chisholm and the Guns had waded and swum across, there was a rare tussle between them. Now whether, in the hurry of pairting the dogs, one of the Guns gave him a blow by chance, or whether from vexation it was given on purpose, I cannot well say, but out came Chisholm's Skean dhu, and three or four of them were lying on the heather in as many blows. When Chisholm saw the red bluid bubbling over the plaids, he jealoused it was time to be off, and he ran up the side of the loch and slipped in, and swam to the little island at the head of the lower loch, and then made as if he were going to swim off to the other side, where the birches are now as they were then; but when he took the water, he made a stroke or two, and then dived back and just kept his nose out of water like a hurt wild duck. The Guns all crossed the water again, thinking to catch him as he made for Rogart, and spread out across the way to Strathfleet, and thought they had him sure. Weel! when he raised his head out of the water and had marked them down well, he slipped down again and swam like an otter up to where the big boat-house is, and up along thae sandy bits by the loch-side where we killed sae many sarpents last year, keeping well under the wood, and when he put his feet on the heather he never stinted or stayed till he got to Clebric, where there was a cave he knew well amongst the craigs by Cairn Vadue. Well, the Guns they swat, and the Guns they swore, and were wud for his heart's bluid, but they could get no guess of him, and all the while he kept the hill, and saw them plowthering about in the moss hags as if they had been looking for a wounded stag; when they came too near he just slipped into his hole like a brock, and waited till they were gone. Well! they went on like this till most of the Guns were tired of looking, and thought that Chisholm had slipped back to Rogart by Stra-na-shalg, till one day two men on the brow yonder, which we cannot see, de'il tak' the mist! saw a man standing on the grey craigs above Loch Furon and jealoused it was Chisholm; so they stepped back and stalked him like a stag. They had no need to mind the wind, for his nose was no' so sharp as an old hind's, and so they got close up to him before he was well aware—so close that he saw it was too late to mak' out, and so he stood steady on the craig. By luck they neither of them knew Chisholm by sight, and so did not like to dirk him at once, and may be they did na' like the chance of a dig of a dirk in their ain weams; so when they got up to him one said, 'It's a fine day!' ''Deed is it,' said Chisholm, 'a nice saft day.' 'Ye have na' seen Chisholm?' said one of the Guns. 'No, indeed I have not!' said Chisholm; and I'm thinking it was nae lie, for there was nae wale o' looking glasses in the cave. 'We are looking after him over the muir, and cannot forgeither with him.' 'What will ye gi'e me if I pit a wrist o' his into each of your hands?' 'All the white silver in our pouches, and as much more as you will from clan Gun, for we hae bluid-feud with him, and his blood we'll ha'e.' 'Weel then, tak' you this wrist and tak' you this y'ane, for I'm Chisholm!' And when they gripped his wrists he kept his arms clenchit, and just made a jerk forward and sent the pair o' them over the craigs towards Loch Furon, but whether they reached it whole I dinna ken. But Chisholm went back to his cave and said to himself—

"'Weel, I hae keepit my promise; but deil burst me, if I didna forget to tak' the siller!'

"Well, it so happened that some other Guns who were out on the moss saw the three together on the craigs, and saw the two men thrown over, and thought sure that Chisholm had a hand in the business, so they followed him so sharp and close, that they saw him enter the cave, and thought, 'Now we have him as safe as a salmon in a cruive.' Just as Chisholm was going into his cave, he turned round and saw the men coming in a straight line towards him, and thought he would break out, but there were over many of them, and so he stepped into the cave, and they followed; and he went further and further toward the end, and heard them aye groping after him, till he got to the bare rock, and couldna get further. Well, he thought it was all over with him, but he stretched out his hands to feel whether there was any way to win further, and he felt the edge of a rock over his head, and he gripped it and drew himself up, and found a shelf where he could lay himself along, about seven feet up the side of the cave. Well, the Guns they came on, stumbling and banning, and breaking their shins in the darkness, for it was as mirk as a wolf's mouth, and stooping down to feel their way, for they didna ken how high the roof was, and they were fearful of breaking their heads. Well, the first Gun ran his head against the end of the cave, and cried out, 'Hoot, lads, I hae him!' for he thought that Chisholm had hit him in the head, and that he had him a' safe, but he hadna, and they groped, and they felt, and they glowered into the darkness, till their eyes shone like wild cats, but deil a thing could they feel, only when one caught the ither by the pow, and gied him a rug: 'tis a wonder they hadna dirked each other in the dark! and all the time Chisholm lay along his shelf, and grinned to himself at the clangamfrey they were keeping below him, and he within reach of their hands. Well, what with ane thing, and what with another, a great fear came on them in the dark cave, and they thought Chisholm must be a warlock, and so they burst out and ran back to Lairg as fast as their feet could carry them. Well, Chisholm waited till they were all gone, and gloaming was come, and then he slipped down to Lairg, where there was an old woman, his foster-sister's aunt's second cousin, who was married on a Gun, and he said, 'Elsie, I'll gie you all the white siller in my pouch'—and they thought more of the white siller then than they do of the red gold now—'if you will do what I wish.' 'Aye, 'deed will I,' said the old carline, blinking her eyes at the siller—''deed will I for ane so near a kin.' 'Well, then, you ken that the Guns are all red-wud at not catching me, and they are all drinking together. Now, when they are fou, slip you down ben the house, and tak' a shoe and a stocking off one, and a shoe and a stocking off another, and put them in a heap in the road just where the sharp stones are, and then come back to me.' So the old body went, and she found that they who were not very fou had put off their clothes before they went to bed, so she wan them easily enough; and they who were blin fou—and that was the maist of them—never fashed their thumbs about her rugging at their shanks, and so brought out the hose and the brogues, and turned them over with a fork, as if she were mixing a midden. Well, when they were all well mixed, Chisholm went before the house where the Guns were lying, and cried with a loud voice, 'Are ye seeking Chisholm? I hae gotten him here.' When they heard that, out they toumelt outright glad, the fou y'anes without their hose and shoon, and the very fou y'anes with a hose and a shoe on the t'ane fit, and nane on t'ither, and they all cried out, 'Whar is he?' and he stood and said, 'Here he is, ye may hae him for the houding;' and when they gat near him, he started up the burn by the blacksmith's smiddy, and made play for Strathfleet like a hunted roe. Weel, the Guns went after him well enough at first, but it was long before the good duke—God bless him!—made the roads, and never a track was there from Lairg into Strathfleet, but the Burn that falls into the Loch by the Post-office, and he with his good brogues sped up it fast enough, but they that had but one brogue, and they that had none, made but a bad race of it: 'deed, the ones that had ane made the worst, for the ane brogue made them bould with the ane fut, and they bounced the ither gay hard against the sclate stones, whilst the ithers went hirpling on tenderly on their ten-taes. Well, they soon saw that it was of no use for men with ane brogue, and men with nane, to tak' the hill against a man with two, so they ran back to Lairg to look for their gear, and they saw the heap in the road, and set to work to fit themselves. 'That's mine, Donald!' 'Gie me my brogue, Rory!' 'What are ye to walk off wi' my hose, Rurich?' and so at last they went wild to think that Chisholm was going over the hill all the time, and they could not suit themselves without breaking the commandment, and taking their neighbour's goods, and the bluid got hot, and the skean-dhus lap out, and sixty and six Guns lay in the white moonlight with the red bluid bubbling out of them. Sair broken was the clan for many a day—and that's the story of the fox-hunt o' Lairg."

"Well, Donald, I can weel believe it, but that is a very different version of the story of Chisholm of Cairn Vaduc, to the one I have generally heard. But the Clan Gun took a deal of breaking; they seem to have fluctuated in the oddest manner between Sutherland and Caithness; when times were tolerably quiet, they put themselves under the protection of the Earl of Caithness, and cultivated their oats and kail in peace; but the moment there was any chance of a row, they went over to the Earl of Sutherland, and fought for him through thick and thin. The consequence of this trimming policy was, that whenever there was a good understanding between the two Earls, which happened about once in a generation, and never lasted much over eight and forty hours, they combined their forces, and offered up as many of the luckless Guns as they could catch, on the altar of reconciliation. Perhaps the cause of their peculiar position may be found in their own tradition, that they were Norwegians, and took the name of Gun, possibly connected with Gunther, from the son of the King of Denmark, who settled in Caithness."

"Well, sir, it may be, but they were sometimes called Clan Cruner, from one Cruner, who was their chief. But, indeed, the earls did not always finish them so easily, for they caught them once on Ben Græm, and shot their arrows too soon, and the Guns took them at short range and beat them off, and then went away south, to Loch Broom, where they were attacked again, and sair harried."

"Well, Donald, to cap your story, I will tell you another, which shows that the Guns were not always as sharp as their neighbours. They had been long at feud with the Kames, and at last a reconciliation was proposed. It was agreed that each party were to send twelve *horse* to the chapel of Saint Tayre, near Girnigo, to arrange the matter. The Guns sent their twelve horse, and when they reached the chapel, the twelve riders, like pious lads, went in to hear mass; whilst they were inside, the Kames arrived with their twelve horse, as agreed, but they had taken the liberty of putting two men on each horse, and they overpowered the Guns, and dirked every man of them. Old Sir Robert says, that he saw the blood on the walls more than a hundred and fifty years afterwards. But hang the Guns! let us think of the rifles; see how the mist is lifting, and how pleasantly the north-wester begins to breathe on our faces."

Gently and gradually our tiny horizon increases in diameter, and light puffs of wind come up from a quarter opposite to that from which the rain has been pattering so unmercifully upon us, sharp as needles, cold as ice; the white fog begins to boil and seethe, and at last is caught up bodily and carried away in the arms of the strong fresh breeze. Stronger and stronger comes the wind, rolling the mist up into great balls, and driving them against the hill-side with a force that scatters them into nothingness. Swell after swell, and peak after peak, stand out bold and clear, the mist hanging round to leeward of them for a moment, cowering under the shelter, till the conqueror brushes off the last trace of the conquered, and the great central basin of Sutherland lies clear at our feet.

"And now for deer—what are you spying down there for, Donald? we must have given the wind to every thing as we came up."

"'Deed, sir, I'm looking for Jeemie and the powney; he cannot get the staig on his back by himself, and I cannot make out the creature."

"What are the sheep galloping for, down there?—there! they wheel round in a mass and face towards the burn. Aye, there is the white powney, and Jeemie, and Clebric, the brute, rugging his arm off to get at the blue hares. They will not be up here this half-hour, so we may as well spread ourselves and our plaids out to dry on the top of the big stone and wait till they *do* come."

If you look at your map, you will find the word "Sutherland" written over across a far larger tract than is encased within the hills that bound our horizon, but for all that a large proportion of Sutherland proper is visible from our station on the shoulder of Ben Clebric. In old times Strathnaver was really independent of Sutherland, though the Earl of that ilk was the feudal chief of the Lords of Reay, and had forest rights in the Reay country. Sutherland was the land south, not only of Caithness but of Strathnaver. Besides Strathnaver, there were the districts of Edderachillies and Assynt, quite distinct from Sutherland, inhabited by different races, and governed by their own chiefs; the latter, indeed, belonged more to the "Lord of the Isles" than to Scotland proper: the great county of Sutherland was only welded into its present form in very recent times. I cannot now, sitting up here on a big stone, with the wind blowing clean through me, giving me the sensation of being clothed in a fishing-net of more than legal mesh, attempt to unravel the tangled web of the ancient history of Caithness and Sutherland; which was first peopled, and why every little province was at eternal war with its neighbours. Even Sir Robert Gordon, who spent his whole life in rummaging out the traditions of the country, becomes puzzled and puzzling on the subject. He believes that Caithness should be read Catti-ness, and yet abuses the Catti of that ilk on every occasion, and exalts the Sutherland Catti beyond all cess. Even the name of the Clan-Chattan is a stumbling-block to him; and he is by no means clear whether they are so called from the name of their original German sept, or from the fact of their chief having literally whipped his weight in wild cats on his first arrival in the country of his adoption. This great fight took place A.D. 91. Don't be afraid, Donald, I will hold it tight.

"The catti and usepii were expelled from Germany for killing of a Roman generall with his legions. At their first arrival at Corry Vale, in the river of Unes (a commanding haven in that country), their captaine went to the shore to recreate himself and spy the land, when he was suddentlie invaded by a company of monstrous big wild catts, that much endomaged and molested the country. The fight between them was cruell, and continued long; yet in the end (very grievouslie wounded in severall places of his bodie) he killed them all, with great danger of his lyff. From thence the Thanes and Erles of Cattey, or Sutherland, even unto this day, do carie on their crest or bage, abowe their armes, a catt sitting with one of his feett upward, readie to catch his prey. Some do think that from this adventure this country was first called cattey, for catt in old Scottish (or Irish language) signifieth a catt. But I do rather incline to their opinion who think that as Murrayland was so called from the Murrays, even so was this people which at this time did arryve ther, called catti." A cat's a cat, Sir Robert, no doubt; and I suspect that, although you are too true a clansman to confess it openly, you sniffed a little taint of "punning heraldry" in your "crest or bage." From the prevalence of the name of Morray, or Murray, in some parts of Sutherland proper, it is not improbable that all the inhabitants of the most north-eastern side of the highlands are of the same original race. In an old charter, even the Earl of Sutherland is called "Moriff comes Sutherlandiæ."

Whether the present inhabitants be the descendants of Scandinavian settlers, or of Celtic tribes driven out of their own country by increasing waves of pure Scandinavianism, the former visited the country often enough, and left their names on many a sculptured stone, and on the more endurable monuments of valleys and rivers. Does not Helms-dale sound like a name in an Edda? and is not Lax-fiord, the bay of the salmon, the paradise of the salmon-fisher to this day?

If Sir Thomas Brown is correct in stating that a brass Jews'-harp, richly gilded, was found in an ancient Norwegian urn, Sutherland may be indebted to the Norwegians for its favourite, I had almost said national, instrument. The bagpipe is no more the national instrument of Scotland than the hurdy-gurdy. Down to the seventeenth century every parish in England had a noise of bagpipes, and every miller could play upon them as certainly as every highland smith now thinks he can. Sir Robert Gordon mentions the Earl of Sutherland's harper in the seventeenth century, and oddly enough records that he died from drinking whiskey, "a fainting liquor in travel," but gives no hint of the pipes. The Jews' or jaws'-harp is but little appreciated by us southerns, except by the youthful population, who find it an excellent accompaniment to the whitey-brown paper and small-tooth comb; but a few years ago it was very popular in Sutherland as a means of producing dance music. It has rather gone out of fashion lately; but last summer I heard a succession of old Gaelic airs played upon it with an amount of tenderness of feeling, clearness of tone, and perfection of time which electrified me. No instrument could have rendered the rapid inflections and changes of the wild old airs more perfectly, and, listening to it, one was inclined to think that it must be older than the pipes, and closely connected with the old metallic stringed chairshoes, so perfectly was it adapted to the spirit of the music. When I leant back, and closed my eyes, it required no very great stretch of the imagination to make believe that I was listening to some strange old-world fairy music, distant yet clear, ringing up from far below some green hillock. It is the oddest sound, soft but metallic, coming and going, as if borne on the fitful waves of the night wind, that ever I heard.

So long did the recollection of the Danes linger in Sutherland, that when the country was being surveyed by the Government engineers, in 1819, the people of the west took it into their heads that they were a detachment sent by the King of Denmark to survey the country, previous to his making an attack on Lord Reay (the then proprietor), in order to avenge an old feud existing between the chief of the Mackays and the crown of Denmark. The foundation for this delicious theory being the fact of the trigonometrical adepts wearing military-looking foraging-caps.

We have no right to be surprised at these old-world fancies having lingered so long in Sutherland, for it was the last part of Great Britain, if not of Western Europe, in which the feudal system had full sway. In the old times, not so very long ago, the tacks-men, who were generally *cadets de famille*—half-pay officers—paid their rent in great part by furnishing men to the family regiment, over which the chief had absolute command, and their sons and relations were promoted according to the number of men they furnished. Of course the chief made it pay in some way or another; his regiment was so much political capital, and the more men he could offer to the Government of the time, the more likely he was to get tolerable pickings out of the public purse. In those days, when the crops failed and the cattle starved, the people were kept alive by the chief, like hounds that must be fed though the frost prevented them hunting.

This system continued, more or less modified, until the highland family regiments were incorporated into the Line and recruited for in the usual way—a woeful change for the men who had been accustomed to return home on half-pay, take a farm, and pay the rent, and support themselves by making bond-slaves of the cotters, forcing them to return meal and eggs and hens, and an indefinite quantity of work, as rent for their miserable crops. I once saw a "rent-roll," if I may call it so, of a farm under the old system, as late as 1811, and it is certainly a most wonderful document! By no means the least curious part of it is the number of *hens* to be furnished to the tacks-man; and that gave me the key to the old story of the highland laird, who gave his guests "ilk a' ane a hen boiled in broth," that we have all heard of. Money there was little or none, a few hundred half-starved stots were sent south every year, and kelp was manufactured to some extent; and at one time a "coal-heugh" was worked at Brora, and salt made; but the coal was a mere small oolitic basin, and soon became exhausted. These were the only sources of revenue of the whole country sixty or seventy years ago. The cattle never did well: they were too heavy-hoofed to cross the deep morasses to gain the best mountain pasturage, and had they succeeded in doing so, would have been impounded by the enraged forester to a dead certainty; there was no winter food for them, and the Sutherland people had as much idea of growing roots or artificial grasses as the Terra del Fuegians; the consequence of which naturally was, that in hard winters the cattle died by hundreds and thousands. The regular practice was to kill every second calf, and even with this restriction of stock, there died in the parish of Kildonan, during the spring of 1807, two hundred cows, five hundred head of cattle, and more than two hundred ponies, of sheer starvation. It is a positive fact that not sixty years ago the wretched people had occasionally to support life by *bleeding* the cattle, and mixing the blood with meal into a loathsome sort of black pudding.

When the military system was changed, the drain of able-bodied men ceased, for no earthly power but the authority of the chief could induce the highlander to enter the army for a lengthened period (his horror of foreign service was intense: the shameful way in which the highland regiments had to be trepanned into going abroad is a matter of history), and the whole system broke hopelessly down. The country became filled with able-bodied men, who looked on manual labour with the most intense scorn, and left all the hard work to the women with an assumption of superiority worthy a Red Indian or a Prussian: in the beginning of the nineteenth century they deserved the reproach which had been cast upon their neighbours in the seventeenth, by their own clansman—

"The people of that country are so far naturally given to idleness that they cannot apply themselves to labour, which they deem a disparagement and derogation unto their gentilitie."

The way in which land was let in townships, instead of to individuals, being afterwards subdivided amongst the small tenants, the community being answerable for the rent, was an admirable arrangement for these gentry, as any individual might loaf about as indolently as he liked, without the slightest necessity of his raising more than was sufficient for his own immediate consumption, his rent being paid for him by the more industrious part of the little community; an admirable encouragement for industry, truly!

On this system the whole country became absolutely useless to the community at large, and a burden on the proprietor; exporting nothing, importing nothing, and starving regularly once in three years in good times, and every other year in bad ones. If a Sutherland man had advertised for a place in those times, he would have expressed his desires somewhat in the following manner:—

"Wanted by a Highland Gentleman, used to habits of idleness, and who can do nothing, a place where there is nothing to do. Salary not so much an object as oatmeal."

It was to remedy this state of things that Sir William Alexander endeavoured to induce his countrymen to emigrate in 1620. The men in those times were principally used up in the Polish service; "they haunt Pole with the extreme of drudgery," he says himself; and complains bitterly of the misery caused in Scotland by an edict of the French king preventing Scotchmen from enlisting in his guards. This sort of system continued longer on the estate of the Sutherland family than in those of the other landowners of the country; as, having other sources of revenue, it was able to spend large sums on the starving population. Lord Reay, and others, saw early that their only chance of doing any permanent good was to move the people from the hills, where the crops were almost certain to be mildewed, down to the good arable land by the seashore, and to devote the hills to sheep; and they did so.

I was rather amused the other day by reading a comparison between Lord Reay and the present Duke of Sutherland, containing a half-concealed laudation of the former for leaving his tenants as they were, and keeping up the family regiment, preferring men to sheep; the real fact being that he moved his people years before anything of the sort was done on the Sutherland estate, and still longer before the Reay country came into the possession of the Duke of Sutherland's father. This lagging behind in the race of improvement caused serious embarrassment when the new system was finally determined on; hundreds of squatters from the neighbouring parts of Sutherland and Ross had eagerly resorted to a country which permitted them to exist in all their beloved laziness and squalor; and every patch of ground that could possibly be cultivated was eagerly seized upon to grow oats and potatoes enough to live on if they did well; if not, the Morfear-chatt would not let them starve. Another cause of the steady demoralization of the country was the enormous quantity of illicit distillation carried on—almost the only means by which money could be obtained.

At length even the purse of the Sutherland family began to show symptoms of exhaustion, and it was very clear that not only must the proprietor be ruined, but that two-thirds of the population must starve unless some change was made; and had it not been made, there is not the slightest doubt that Sutherland would long ere this have suffered the fate of Skibbereen, and from precisely the same causes. Then, though tardily, Sutherland followed the rest of Scotland, and the great Sutherland shifting took place, concerning which such wild and ridiculous statements have been made. One really hardly knows whether to laugh or swear, when one reads how this old matter has been raked up with new and original embellishments, and used as a means of annoyance to the present duke, who had as much to do with it as the great Cham of Tartary, the whole affair having been carried out in his father's time, and indeed before there was a Duke of Sutherland in existence. The measure simply consisted in moving the people from the hills and the wilder straths down to the productive borders of the sea, where they not only had good land, but fish at their doors, enough both for their own support, for sale, and even for manure. Each person who was removed had long warning given ; every one had a plot of ground allotted to him before he removed, and received a sum of money sufficient to start him in his new position, and he was even paid for the miserable sticks which supported his turf roof, and which the highlanders were in the habit of carrying about with them whenever they shifted their bothies, and which, from the difficulty of procuring them, they regarded with a species of veneration. That the poor people, nursed in sloth and idleness, and profoundly ignorant and superstitious, looked with horror at the projected change, and used every art which semi-savage and illiterate cunning could invent, to prevent their removal, is most true ; and wild was the lament and intense the horror at the prospect of being located on the "wild, black Dornoch moors." When you go to Sutherland, just take a look at these "wild, black Dornoch moors" now, and if you can point me out a brighter specimen of cotter prosperity in the north, more luxuriant crops, more productive potatoes and yellow oats, be kind enough to let me know its whereabouts, for I should like to see it. So intense was this terror of the change, that it seemed the same to many of the people whether they went ten miles down the strath, or to America ; and to America some—not many—went. And so strong is the feeling of these emigrants against their old landlord, that a very few years ago, when a relation of the Morfear-chatt visited Nova Scotia, they came sixty miles to see him and were so frightfully excited, that they shook hands with him with the most intense heartiness, and seemed ready to kiss him.

Not one of these people need have gone to America had he not wished it ; every hand that would labour was wanted in the country, and many who went into neighbouring counties soon returned, and eagerly embraced the advantages offered them.

The delicious theory that these changes were undertaken in order that the deer might be undisturbed, is, I am grieved to say, incorrect ; there was as much idea of preserving snapping turtles as deer, when they were made, and many a corrie and wide hillside was disforested to carry them out. Indeed, the old Reay forest and Stack are almost the only remains of the gigantic deer forests which existed at the close of the last century.

But why move all the people at once? Why not let them linger on and die out on the old hillsides they loved so well? Surely a few cotters could not have interfered much with the sheep-farmer? Simply because by so doing you would perpetuate the old mistake, attempting to grow corn crops on land which could only yield a return to the community at large by being kept as a winter feeding. Without the small straths the sheep would fail, as the cattle used to; your whole hillside would be absolutely unproductive, and the landowner would have to keep the people. Moreover, let me whisper in your ear. The sheep used to *go*—goodness knows where—and it was impossible to make the shepherds responsible for the flocks under their care. I believe that there does not exist a more thoroughly honest man than the Sutherland highlander, but his every tradition pointed to cattle-lifting as an honourable pursuit, and the difference between sheep and cattle is not so very great to a starving man, and so they went. *Now*, I believe that sheep-stealing is an unknown crime in the country.

The consequence of the "depopulation" of Sutherland, as it is called, is, that there are more people in it at this present than there ever were at any previous period of its history; and of the turning of arable land into sheep-pastures, that there is now a far greater breadth of land under cultivation than there ever was before, and that not only in the form of large farms, but of cotters' croftings. And the improvement in the art is, I have no hesitation in saying, the most marked that has taken place in any part of Great Britain within the same period.

Previously to 1811, the rents of the estate of Sutherland came into the pocket of the landlord; from 1811 to 1833, all the rents were expended on improvements in the country, and in addition 60,000*l.* was transmitted from England for the same purpose, and with the following results :—

Previously to 1811, there was not a carriage-road in the country, and only one bridge at Brora, and a small one at Dornoch.

Between 1811 and 1845, above 430 miles of road were made, and many more have since been opened. There is not a turnpike-gate in the country.

Previously to 1811, there was scarcely a cart in Sutherland, the property of the people, the carriage of the country being conducted on the backs of ponies.

In 1845, the tenants paying less than 10*l.* a year rent had 890 carts ; the larger farmers, 240.

Previous to 1811, the cultivation in the interior and on the west coast was carried on by means of the crass-crom—a crooked stick shod with iron, with a small projecting bar to rest the foot upon.

In 1845, the smaller tenants owned 569 ploughs; the farmers, 139.

Previous to 1811, there was hardly a shop in Sutherland, except at Dornoch, one in Brora, and one near Helmsdale.

In 1831, there were 46 grocery shops, and, oddly enough, one of the first symptoms of the cotters making money was the demand for *blacking*, a thing unheard of in the good old times.

Previously to 1811, the town of Helmsdale did not exist; in 1840, it exported 37,594 barrels of herrings.

Shall I go on? No, you will fancy that I am talking of America instead of Scotland, though that would be unfair, for no part of America can show a greater advance than Sutherland has made within the last fifty years, and that at the expense of one private family. I do not happen to have any hard figures to throw at you of a later date than 1845, but there is no question whatever that the country has improved immensely in all respects since that time. I am sure that I hope it will continue to do so, as sincerely as I believe it will, for I never met a peasantry in any part of Europe who were more deserving of prosperity than the kind-hearted, warm-hearted, intelligent Sutherland highlanders. Not only have we not lost soldiers, but we have gained sailors, by the great Sutherland changes, from the enormous increase of the fisheries, now of the highest importance. It is true that the people are much too well off to take the sergeant's shilling readily, but that there is plenty of military spirit in the country will be pretty evident to him who watches the Golspie Volunteers in their steady determination to master the difficult problem of knowing their " east legs" from their "wast legs." No reason to cry out against Sutherland sheep-farming for destroying the source from which the defenders of the country may have to be drawn. There they are, soldiers and sailors, ready and willing when wanted, not only in greater numbers than ever they were, but every one of them intrinsically worth three of the old hill men who had to be cheated and bribed into a service they hated.

If the brown moors of Sutherland bore you, go somewhere else, but do not anathematize them as barren and unproductive wastes. They bear sheep to the utmost of their power, and every year shows some improvement in the pasturage. Ask the West Riding folks whether they consider Sutherland a productive country or not? and how much wool they get off those moors? And ask—but no, don't ask the sheep-farmers how many sheep they feed, for they will regard you with a grim and defiant countenance, and shut the portals of their mouth with a snap like a fox-trap; not that they have any Jewish superstition against numbering their woolly folk, but as they are only permitted to keep a certain number by their leases, to prevent overstocking the land, they regard the question as doubt thrown on their honesty.

I wonder the ingenious tourist has never complained that more than 32,000 acres of Sutherland are kept under water for the purpose of producing salmon and trout, but this is a subject I cannot be cross upon, for the glory of Sutherland is her lakes and her rivers; and old Sir Robert says most truly, that "there is not one strype in all these forests that wants trout, and other sorts of fishes." Though the salmon in some of the rivers may not reach the average size of their cousins of the south, their number, beauty, and powers of fighting compensate well for the loss of a pound or two when brought to scale. Of course, the gentle tourist need not expect to have salmon-fishing for the asking for it. A salmon river is far too valuable a piece of property to be left open to the world; and if it were, who is to pay for the preserving? and without water-bailiffs, who must be paid, how many salmon would there be left for anybody? Just the exact number to be found by the said anybody in the open Welsh rivers, a quantity very easily ascertained by any one who tries them. The rivers are let, some for sport, some for profit, many for both, in all cases employing a considerable number of men, and furnishing large quantities of valuable food. If you want salmon-fishing, put money in thy pouch, and having that, you may indeed get fishing worth the paying for; that is to say, if you are content to wait till one of the present renters is gaffed by grim Gilly Death, for nothing but his interference, or a hopeless bankruptcy, would ever make the renter of a Sutherland river give it up to any one else. There are, however, two or three rivers where salmon-fishing may be had by the day; and amongst these is the beautiful lower Shin. This river has one great advantage—you are sure to have a pleasant way of spending your Sunday afternoon, which, if you are neither "free" nor "estaiblished," may chance to hang a little heavy on your hands in a highland inn without books. If you can enjoy a quiet study of natural beauty, you have merely to walk up to the salmon-leap at the Falls of the Shin, one of the prettiest bits of white foam, black swirl, grey rock, and feathery birch, that ever gladdened an artist's eye; and on Sunday afternoon, when the "Slaps" are open, the bright silver bars, springing up at the falling sheet of liquid amber, give a life and spirit to the scene which no mere tumble of water can ever possess. You may sit there musing happily hour after hour, till the red sunbeams stream horizontally through the silver-stemmed birch, and the cold damp reek of the cauldron warns you home; and as you go, you may, if you are romantically given, ponder on the fact, that Ossian began life as a herd-boy in Glen Shin.

In these enlightened days it is perhaps necessary to mention, that salmon do not put their tails in their mouths preparatory to making a leap; they give a series of sharp sculling strokes with their broad helms, which sends them sheer out of the water, four feet and more. If their sharp noses strike the sheet of falling water, they penetrate into it, and, continuing the original sculling motion, force themselves upwards in the most marvellous fashion; but the least turn to either side exposes a slight surface to the rush of water, and then down they go ignominiously into the black swirl again.

If you are very much in want of a fish, you can go and sit close to the edge of the fall, armed with a gaff, and strike the fish that alight on the rock before they wriggle back, but it is not a course I can advise you to pursue, unless you are anxious to inspect the interior of Dornoch gaol. It is true, that that establishment is clean and well kept, but the diet is coarse, and the pursuits monotonous; so, on the whole, you had better go to Mr. Young, take out a ticket, and try a fly.

The Sutherland lakes are beyond all count. I remember being taken to a spot whence I was told I could see a hundred at once (which I did not, for the mist was up to my feet): and their products in the shape of trout are as various in shape, colour, and size, as the lakes themselves. From the little black tarn, twice the size of a blanket, high up on the hill, to the freshwater seas of Loch Shin and Loch Hope, they all are, or rather were, swarming with trout. Up in the tarns you may catch endless dozens of things, which a person of lively imagination might class as trout, but which look more like tadpoles, which have gone on growing as such, lacking the strength of mind or strength of constitution to develop themselves into frogs. The larger lakes used to furnish trout of a size, colour, and flavour not to be surpassed by Hampshire itself. For the last two or three years the trout in some of the lakes have been infested with tapeworm, which, I am told, was first observed about the time the grouse were attacked by a similar parasite. I do not suppose that they are identical, though the brutes have so many different forms, that one hardly knows where to have them; they have both done mischief enough. Of course, the increase of fishermen has had a vast influence on the sport; the very best loch in Sutherland has been entirely destroyed, as far as fishing is concerned, from its having had the misfortune of having a name, and being within reach of an inn, and those who go to Loch-Beannach, on the strength of tradition, will find themselves woefully disappointed. In old times it was a famous loch for trout, they reeled out like salmon, and were the very Apollos of their race. The bottom of the loch is principally composed of clean primary gravel, and, from some cause or other, the Phrygania which were bred in it were twice the size of those which generally flutter over highland waters. Another cause of the excellence of its fish I discovered whilst examining one of them for entomological purposes, and that is the existence of quantities of "stickle-backs;" I cannot say that the prickly one does not exist in other lochs lying as high as Loch-Beannach, but I never saw a trace of him; and it may be worth the while of some Lairg-visiting naturalist to examine whether this sub-alpine form of the Sticklebagulus Choak-perchius of our southern streams may or may not deserve to be elevated into a new species, to be called Sticklebagulus Beannachius.

One cause of the diminution of sport in the Sutherland lochs belongs to bygone times, and is worth mentioning for the sake of the tradition. The old people tell me that in the days of black cattle, they (the cattle) were driven up to the hill in summer, and the lassies used to live in sheilings and tend them—an arrangement which produced a great deal of poetry and feeling, just as it does amongst the "Senn-Huterinn" of the Tyrol to this day. The cattle being teased with midges, took to the lochs, and stamped and plunged in the mud, turning out all kinds of larvæ and affording a fine nidus for the nidification of infinite beetles. Fine living there was for the trout; beetles in abundance, maggots for the taking, and drowned flies in infinity. When the wind was in the right airt and the planetary aspects were in other respects benign, the plough-woman dropped her cras-crom in the scratch that did duty for a furrow, the turf-cutter left her divots unturned, the piper left the last screech to be blown out of his bag by atmospheric pressure, and all rushed to Loch Beannach to catch trout. Unless the old people "romance," which very probably they do, there used to be trouts enough taken in two or three hours to keep the takers in fish for weeks. To keep them, they merely split them and hung them on the cabers of their wigwams, and the creosote distilled from the peat soon rendered the fish as safe from decay as it did the eaters of them. I make this last comparison because certain learned pundits have been lately poking about for a cause for the increase of consumption among the northern highlanders, and they aver that it is the loss of the peat-reek and its creosote, which now goes up the grand stone chimney. However, old authors say, that we English never knew the "quack or pose," those mediæval influenzas, till we started Lums, and we still manage to exist; so let us hope that John Sutherland may take to himself a pocket-napkin and do well yet.

But minished and brought low, as the trout are, the gentle tourist who likes to spend a warm gleamy day, with a rustling south-westerly wind, in a boat, with a big trout spinning over the stern of the boat for *Salmo Ferox*, and the beloved of his heart and a sprinkling of children, well protected against midges, flogging the water right and left, may yet have the chance to bring home a tea-tray full of trout, though, I confess, not often. The trout in the lochs he is likely to frequent have had their noses scratched too often to rise freely; and, I am sorry to say, that certain Philistines have increased the mischief by permitting their gillies to use the otter where their own arts failed, and have returned triumphant with a basket of fish, at the expense of spoiling the bay for the rest of the season. Do not permit it, O tourist, for your own sake; if the gilly otters for you, he will for himself; you will not gain credit long, for in the vanity of his heart he will be certain to peach, and you will have to pay for your short-lived glory by having spoilt your own sport, and made a poacher of a decent laddie. There exist fishes in some lochs that I should like to know more about. So far north are we that char are caught with a fly in lochs but a few feet above the level of the sea; and old Ross of Tongue, who is not given to romance, assures me that he has caught what he calls trout char, weighing from half a pound to a pound and a half, the fly, in the lochs of Ben Hope. What are they?

In Assynt, the lakes are in number infinite, and in variety endless. From noble Loch Assynt, with its islands and woods, down to the little rock-set basin not ten yards across, with its circular wreath of water-lilies, and its smooth, grey, ice-worn, gneiss banks, dashed with strips of purple heather, they meet you at every turn. There you may launch your boat twenty times a day without going far from the road; and if you find the trout in one wee lochie too small or too shy, walk or drive over the bank and find another and another loch, till you come to one that suits you.

I do not care much for loch-fishing, myself; but I am of so fishy and webby a nature, that I take to the water at once, or I should have told you to look at the rocks instead of the lakes; but what should I have profited if I had? for are not the mountain wonders of Assynt and the west coast indescribable, and would you not have looked at them at once on arriving there, without being told to do so, that is if you could see them? Unfortunately for the passing tourist, these western mountains are very coy of discovering their charms, and are much given to the shrouding them for weeks at a time in thick veils of Atlantic mist. But however long you have to wait at Loch Inver, wait patiently, rise early and go to bed late, for any moment may disclose one of the most marvellously strange and beautiful bits of scenery in Europe. That peak of red-sandstone, rising between 1,500 and 1,600 feet in one bold pinnacle, even more precipitous than the form from which it takes its name, standing out clear and distinct from the surrounding mountains, with a boldness and freedom of outline perfectly indescribable, is certainly worth any trouble, waiting, or expense to see. It is hard to say whether the "Sugar-loaf" is grander on a bright day, which brings out its outline clear and sharp, and bathes it in a glorious red glow at sunset; or on a cloudy one, when the summit is shrouded in mist, which throws a deep purple gloom round its base, and removes the background into infinite distance, lurid and mysterious. Alas! I once spent a week at Loch Inver without once seeing it in either state.

If you are an artist in search of a subject, and happen to be at Loch Inver at the time the herring boats are starting for the east coast, I strongly advise you to go to the little fiord, a mile or two to the north, and study what you will see there. That little rocky basin of a bay, the few black huts, with tiny scraps of yellow oats struggling to ripen in the grey gneiss rock—the broad brown boats, sharp fore and aft, with their sturdy crews sorely suffering at the leave-taking, but trying to look stout and cheerful; and the women turning homewards with moist eye and quivering lip, to turn and turn again as the bread-winners disappear round the point—may give you a hint for a picture worth the painting. When the highlanders lived far up in the inland straths, they never dreamt of the riches of the sea; and you might as well have endeavoured to persuade a starving cock-robin that he had nothing to do but to dive into a salmon-pool to procure an abundance of food, as induce any one of them to take to the salt water. Now the case is altered; living by the sea, they have become accustomed to it, and stretch away to the eastward for herrings manfully. Pity it is that they cannot be induced to take to the deep-sea fishing on their own coast, so well protected by the great breakwater of Harris and Lewis.

The only fishing I have seen on the west coast is that

mentioned by an old pamphleteer of 1597, as obtaining in his own time in the opposite island. "People of all sorts and ages sit on the rocks thereof (Harris) with hooke and lyne, taking innumerable quantity of all kinds of fishes." And so they do now in Assynt, and quaint are the figures one sees perched on the projecting rocks fishing for their supper.

Most frequently it is an old woman with her knees drawn up to her chin, with her voluminous mutch flapping about in the wind, fishing for coal-fish with a short rod and half a dozen flies, made of a white duck's feather, which she does not deign to withdraw from the water till each hook has its green and silver victim attached to it. I never saw them catch anything else; but if you, O tourist, will go and spin a butter-fish for Lythe—Merlangus Pollachius—you will there first discover what sport trolling can be. The people are to a certain extent right in keeping to the little Merlangus Carbonarius, for they can be caught to any amount, and are easily dried for winter store. Deep-sea fishing is not an art to be learned in a day; but as soon as Glascow wants more cod and ling, she will certainly get them. If you care neither for painting nor fishing, you may get legend and history enough on the west coast to amuse you well. Of course you will hear how Macleod of Assynt betrayed Montrose; but do not believe them when they tell you that his only reward was a few boles of meal; he got twenty thousand "gude punds Scots," and the captainship of the garrison of Strathnaver for that little piece of business. He was, it is true, sent to Edinboro' as a prisoner at the Restoration, but he made light of it—so light indeed that his levities called down the anathemas of Bishop Burnet, who is indignant that the great entertainments he gave in prison should have made him friends enough amongst the great to permit of his escape, untried and unpunished.

The fact is, that certainly down to the latter part of the seventeenth century, and, I suspect, very much later, there was no such thing as "law" in the west and north of Sutherland.

Every semi-savage who had brutality enough to conceive ingenious plans of murder, and strength enough to carry them out, might do so with impunity, as far as law was concerned, and he would always find men enough to back him. The history of that castle whose ruins you see at the head of Loch Assynt, is but one continuous succession of parricides and fratricides. I have a dim recollection of one Macleod, who possessed it, having died quietly in his bed, after being turned out of it by his relations; and he is specially recorded as having been "impotent of ane leg." Either the impotency of his leg prevented his pressing forward in the fray, or his consciousness that his means of escape were imperfect caused him to beat an early retreat, but he is the only member of the family who was served with a writ of ejectment without having its efficacy secured by a dirk.

When you go to Durness, you will see the tomb of an excellent specimen of the west country highlander of the seventeenth century—one Mac-Murshoo, vic-ean-Mohr., who, determined that posterity should appreciate his character to its full value, composed the following epitaph on himself, which is still to be seen (I quote from memory):—

> "Donald Mak-Murshov Hier lyis lo,
> Vas ill to his Friend, var to his Fo;
> True to his maister, in veird and vo."

I have much matter in my head against this Donald, but you may read the principal traditions of him, taken from the Taylor MSS., in Mr. Scrope's book on Deerstalking. He died in 1623, and was as brutal a ruffian as ever disgraced humanity; he raised murder to the rank of one of the fine arts, and murdered from pure thirst for blood; and yet was permitted to hold his own, unchallenged, probably being useful to his "Maister," who was either the Lord Reay of the time, or the devil. After reading his own epitaph on himself, one has a right to believe anything of him, and so I give willing ear to the legend that he built a house without a door or window, which he entered through a hole in the roof. Certain curious persons who visited this strange den, and asked the reason of its peculiar style of architecture, received a pointed reply in the shape of an arrow; notwithstanding this pretty strong hint, others ventured on a similar visit, and one got killed. "Sarve him right!" should certainly have been the verdict. This chapel at Durness is a most curious old-world place: so old, that the earth has grown high up against the walls from the addition of generations of highlanders, and you go down steps into it. When I saw it a few years ago, it was only partially dismantled; part of the roof and the pews were still standing, and knocking about on the floor was a particularly thick and ill-favoured skull, with a tremendous "blash" across it, from which, however, the recipient had probably recovered, as there was a quantity of new bone thrown out around the cut. It was just such a brain-pan as one would imagine Donald Mac-Corrachy to have possessed, and may, indeed, have held his most abominable brains. He had something to love him, however; for when his tomb was opened many years ago, a female skeleton was found beside the bones of the old freebooter.

Though the innumerable cairns in Sutherland hint pretty strongly at the old value set on human life, they must not all be taken as proofs of actual bloodshed. They were sometimes erected to commemorate the better part of valour, as in the case of Cairn Teaghie, or the cairn of flight, on Ben Gream, which perpetuates the memory of the bolting of the Caithness men from the Sutherland men, and the bloodless recovery of their cows by the latter. Many of these cairns may, I think, fairly be put down to the account of the Danes, and where the groups are very numerous, were probably raised over the victims of their raids by the survivors. The skirmishes amongst the highlanders themselves seldom resulted in the slaughter of any great number on either side, though a great deal of "vaunting" and heroical speechifying, after the manner of the Homeric heroes, took place; but ill words break no bones, and seldom require cairns. The Northmen had a custom of burying their slain heroes hurriedly, and then returning for their remains afterwards, trusting to the good feeling of the people to find them untouched; so the tourist who amuses himself by pulling the cairns to pieces must not be surprised if he find nothing.

I know of three enormous cairns in Sutherland, which have been arranged on a sort of "pea and thimble" principle. Open the right one, and you are a made man; open either of the wrong, and you are a dead one. I decline to point out their exact situation, as I may some day be driven to take the fearful bet myself. "Do you think I should hit the right one, Donald?"

"'Deed, sir, I don't think it's right to meddle with a cairn; it's the same as a grave in a kirkyard, and there may be a bonnie lad lying under it, who wadna wish his bones to be moved till he was called for at the judgment. They tell wild old stories about the evil that fell on men who moved them; but I think they were no that very gude and likely to prosper before they tried it. But, 'deed it's no wonder that the old folks were supersteecious, for there were awfu' things in the forests; things like men, that lived with the deer, and sucked the hinds and eat grass, and went on all fours like the beasts. There was one seen, and there's no doubt aboot it, about a hundred years ago.

"The first time it was seen it came to a shepherd's house in Kildonen, and was naked almost, only a clout or two about it, and it scared the shepherd's wife and bairns out of their wits, as it stood girning and making as if it could not speak. The wife thought it was hunger that moved it, and gave it a cog of milk; and it took it from her, and set it down on the ground, and lapped it like a dog. When the shepherd came home, and saw the awfu' beast on the floor, he went almost off his head for fear, and felt a motion in his heart to attack it, as if it had been a wolf, and the dogs snarled, and yelled, and bristled up their backs, as if they saw something uncanny; and their snarling so startled the thing, that it sprang up and fled over the moor like a stag.

"Another time, a forester met it, or another one, on Morven, and talked to it. The creature told him that it fed on grass, like the deer, and that it had kept the forest since it had killed a herd boy in Dunrobin Glen, and that it believed it would never go to heaven. The last one that was seen gave old John Pope, the forester, a sair fleg.* He and another had gone to sleep on a bit bothy, on Ben Ormin, and were awakened by an awful yell outside, and a screeching voice saying, in Gaelic, 'My bed! my bed!' and then the door opened, and something came in. John Pope was not to be daunted by man nor de'il, and so he grappled with it, and a sair tussle they had, for though John was the strongest man in Sutherland, the thing was as strong as the iron, and as hard as Brora stone under his fingers. The ither forester took up a gun, but could not put out, for it was as mirk as pick, and he only knew where the two were by the noise they made; at last he grappit the thing, and he and John had strength enough to put it out at the door, when it raised a long, long, sad screeching wail, and again called out in Gaelic, 'My bed! my bed!' and then all was silent. They never saw what it was like, either of them, but John Pope said it left a powerfu' smell o' brimstone."

"Donald! Donald! keep out of the regions of Bogledom, and tell me how much longer I am to wait here. What with being wet, and what with being dried, I am getting as stiff as Jack's father."

"I can weel believe it, sir; but how stiff was Jack's father?"

"Listen, and I will tell you."

> "Jacke (quoth his father), how shall I ease take;
> If I stand, my legs ache, and if I kneele,
> My knees ache, and if I goe then my feet ache;
> If I lie, my back acheth, and if I sit, I feel
> My hips ache; and leane I never so weel,
> My elbows ache." "Sir (quoth Jack), pain to exile,
> Since all these ease not, best ye hang awhile!"

"'Deed, did he! and an ill raised laddie he must have been; though it would have been safe advice enough here,

* This took place in 1746.

with no tree nearer than Lairg. But we must be off. There's Jeemie standing and thinking, and Clebric pulling and snuffing, just up the corrie. He's a sharp laddie, Jeemie, and understands what he is told; not like that big donnart we had last year, who came up to corrie Venchnich, and plowthered about all day, and then came back without the deer, and he within twenty yards o't. Aye! he sees the ravens, and is going up. We'll be off and raise the stag, and then see what is on the hill."

Twenty minutes' run brings us up to Jeemie and the white powney, the former staring admiringly, and the latter snuffing complacently at our stag, whilst three pair of ravens croak, and hop, and whet their bills on the stones a few yards off. I should very much like to see how ravens dispose of "Gralloch," particularly when they are tolerably numerous, but that is a business as mysterious as the birds themselves; we left plenty yesterday, and now the heather is clean, and had we not sunk the poch-a-bui (I don't pretend to spell Gaelic, be it clearly understood) with its contained treasures, in the burn, they would have cleared off that too. One pair, evidently young, dance wildly on a stone, under the impression that we are interfering unjustly with their future meals, but the old ones sit solemnly and croak gloomily and reprovingly, as if to say, "Stupid young creatures! don't you know yet, that *they* always get the best of everything." Never mind what they say; let us look at the stag for a moment, and think whether the long curved antlers, springing so boldly out of the purple heather, look as large and have as many points as we fancied last night, when we packed him up. "'Deed it's a bonny staig! and look at his broo antlers, and his dags, and the spread of his cabers." Up with him, Jeemie, though you never killed a stag in your life, you are as keen about them and as much interested in every point as if you stalked every day for your dinner. Like every man, woman, and child, in broad Sutherland.

It is no light business to get our big stag—for he is a big one, a real Sutherland hart—on the deer saddle; and intricate is the combination of knots which keep him there. What a noble beast it is! and how the old poney turns his head round to snuff at him; he has carried them till he has positively become fond of the rich aromatic smell of the deer—that Esau smell, recognised long ago. How well the pair look as they go over the sky-line; and how fondly we watch them till the broad antlers have disappeared!

Now, friend Donald, for another and a bigger!

Why try to describe a "stalk?" Unless the ground is known, the description would be as dull and flat as that of a run with foxhounds to a man who knew not the country: more so, indeed, for even in the reading of a great run some faint echo of the pattering thunder of the hoofs over the turf reaches the heart of the reader, but in the stalk all is silent and patient skill. When one thinks of it, this same stalking is a very wonderful thing: there, two miles off, are lying deer, a score or more, on ground chosen with the hereditary skill and experience of ages; with powers of sight and scent of the most marvellous keenness; all bare around them: apparently not a tuft of rushes high enough to conceal a ramrod within yards of them, pickets of keen eyed and keener scented hinds thrown out in every direction, sentinels who never slumber or sleep, but keep every nerve on the stretch to preserve their great lord from harm. How can we hope to slay him in the very centre of his court?

"They'r as wise as Christians—'deed, they'r wiser! but we'll do it," says Donald, as he softly closes his prospect, and he does it; how, I should like to tell you in this particular case, which was a miracle of stalking, but I cannot. Dream out a stalk for yourself: suppose the wind gained, and every difficulty overcome, and remember the throbbing of your heart when you raised your head, gently—gently—over the heather—what a thicket of antlers! Wait patiently till they rise. What is that clashing, as if a company of Life Guardsmen had simultaneously begun backsword play? The young stags fighting. Venture another peep.—Horror! is that a young six-pointer staring steadily at us? Believe it not, noble youth! We are but two grey stones! Still the antlers of the master-hart are steady above the heather; one after another the younger stags feed down towards the burn; the hinds follow, turning back to invite their great lord to follow. See those two or three determined tossings of the mighty antlers: he is going to rise—he is up! Steady, for a moment, for a broadside—now, whilst he is curving his back, and stretching himself out like a lion. Now!—crack!—slap!—Up into the bauk! There are the hinds and young stags, huddled together. Where is he? Trotting slowly and painfully round the swell. Again—crack!—slap!—what a stumble! He is our own, try as he may, he can never win up the brae. See, how the hinds sniff and start aside as they scent the blood, and how the young stags turn and turn again, to ask his guidance. In vain! one staggering effort to cross the burn, and then down with a crashing stumble—never to rise again!

"Another and a bigger, indeed, Donald. Ten points, and as fat as an ox!"

"Aye, sir! he's none of our deer, he's up from the woods."

"See, if he has a forked tail, Donald. Perhaps he is an Arkle deer."

"Hoot-toot, sir! you don't believe in such old wives' stories, I know!"

"'Deed, I don't know, Donald. I laughed at the fancy till I found an explanation of it worth the recording. The tail of the Arkle deer was not exactly forked, but from its root depended a tuft of coarse hair; and in warm weather, or when the stag was heated in the chase, this tuft became matted together, and produced the semblance of a forked tail, thick and broad at the root, and divided into two parts at its termination, the hair forming one division and the real tail the other."

"I can weel believe it, sir; but we must hurry with the gralloch, or it will be dark before we put up the stag."

Dark, indeed, with sheets of rain and driving mist. Let us race across the wilderness at full trot.

"A dark night, a wearied wight, and a welsome way. God be the guide," as Huntly said, when he was escaping from Morpeth.

A glimpse of Rory's bright turf fire, with the collies lying round it each in his appointed place—and then Lairg-wards, ho!

"Good-night, Rory! Good-night, everybody!"

5. *A VISIT TO PERU.*

BY CHARLES CHRISTOPHER BOWEN.

ON the morning of the 12th of February, 1860, under the sultry heat of a nearly vertical sun, the vessel in which I had taken my passage from New Zealand lay becalmed off the island of San Lorenzo. The summer trade-winds had been light along the coast, and the heavy mist that generally hangs over the mountains and the rainless shores of Peru destroyed all hope of a view of the Cordillera from the sea; but towards noon a breeze sprang up, and the dense curtain rose a little as we rounded the island, and entered the beautiful bay of Callao. Momentary glimpses of the Andes served rather to raise than to satisfy expectation. The harbour was filled with shipping of every size and build, sailing under the flags of all nations. Most of these ships were under charter to carry away cargoes of guano, the great present staple of export from the coast; the Government compelling them to enter inwards at Callao before they proceed to load at the Chincha Islands, and to return to the same port to clear out when their cargoes are on board. If not an enlightened, it is a popular policy to tax foreign shipping for the benefit of the ship-chandlers and crimps of Callao.

As we sailed up the bay, myriads of penguins, divers, and other sea-birds moved lazily along the water out of the way of the ship. The sea was literally alive with them, as they waged their ceaseless war against the fish with which these waters teem. It was nearly six o'clock when we came to anchor; and as there is nothing on first arrival to invite a stay in the post-town of Callao, I determined to get up to Lima at once. The master of the barque accompanied me, and we landed at a wooden pier close to the railway-station,

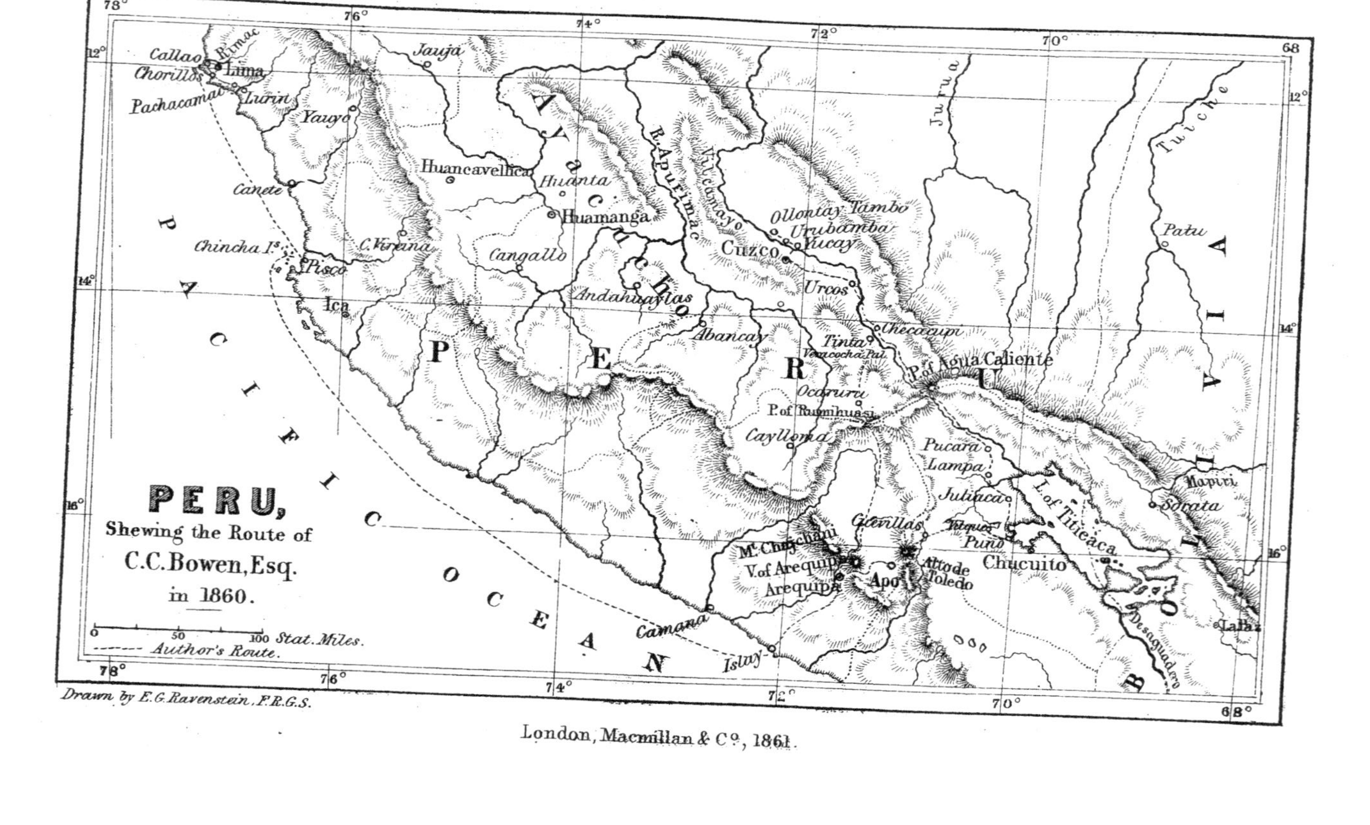

PERU,
Shewing the Route of
C.C. Bowen, Esq.
in 1860.

Drawn by E.G. Ravenstein, F.R.G.S.

London, Macmillan & Co., 1861.

just as the signal was given for the departure of the last train for Lima. My luggage was dragged out of the boat by two or three negroes, and carried off to the station amid the shouts and gesticulations of a very mixed-looking population, with a strong preponderance of negro physiognomy. We hurried after the portmanteaus, and the scene at the station was very characteristic of the manner in which business is done here. An imperturbable clerk declined to give us tickets, on the ground that it was too late; the negroes did not mind him, but rushed through the office, and as the train was moving off, we pitched the portmanteaus into the baggage-waggon, and jumped in on the top of them. There were no porters or other officials to assist or to obstruct us, as the porterage of the station is left to the negroes in a strictly free-trade spirit, and the mulatto guards in the waggon looked on in the helpless and sleepy manner that appeared habitual among the *employés*. When the train had been in motion for about five minutes, one of them roused himself slowly to ask us for our fares, and on receiving the money, relapsed into an apathetic state.

The railway consists of a single line, of rude construction, running alongside of the usual horse-road, through a sandy desert. As you approach Lima, which is situated about seven miles from the sea, you pass between gardens of bananas, oranges, and *chirimoyas*, oases reclaimed from the waste, and enclosed by walls of *adobes*, or large sun-dried bricks. Of this material have been constructed most of the buildings, both of the modern and ancient towns, in the valleys of the coast. The entrance to the city itself by railway is not prepossessing. The line passes through a straggling suburb, and in the large doorways of the houses on each side, crowds of idle, dissipated-looking men, women, and children, of very hybrid breed, stare listlessly at the train as it comes slowly in. No respectable citizen would venture alone on foot and unarmed into that locality at any time of the day or night. On arrival at the terminus, a couple of negroes, who appear to be the self-constituted porters of the station, seized the luggage, and trotted off with it at a rate which made it difficult to keep up with them in the narrow and crowded streets. It was Sunday evening, and every one seemed bent on amusement. Almost all the shops were closed, except those of the very numerous tobacconists, who were driving a large trade all along the principal streets. (Nearly every one you meet in Lima has a cigar or cigarette in his mouth, or is rolling one of the latter in his fingers.) It was so dark when we reached the hotel, that we could not judge of the appearance of the plaza; but it is smaller than I had been led to expect from the importance of the old *Ciudad de los Reyes.* The sound of water from a large fountain in the centre fell gratefully on the ear, and the crowds sauntering about under the *portals* or piazzas that run round two sides of the square, were enjoying the fresh air in this central lung of the metropolis. Morin's hotel is situated in the Plaza, opposite the cathedral, and is one of the best and most conveniently situated: it is as clean as any other in the town; only strangers expect to escape fleas anywhere in Lima. The style of the building is peculiar, and a description of it may answer, with some slight modification, for that of most of the other large hotels. The entrance from the *portal* is by a large gateway, on each side of which shops extend along the frontage of the hotel. Below-stairs, round the open *patio,* or court, are the coffee-room, billiard-rooms, and bar. A broad unroofed staircase leads up to unroofed corridors, on which open the bed-rooms, and the *sala,* or large dining-room. The rooms below-stairs are a sort of lounge for a number of well-dressed inhabitants. This is the club where they meet to talk over the troubled politics of the place, the last scandal, or the last petty war; and to indulge in gambling, the favourite vice of the country.

After dinner we took a lounge through the narrow gas-lit streets; and though it was too late to form a just impression of the place, I could not fail to be struck by the mediæval appearance of one of the oldest European towns on the American Continent. The miserable looking Indian soldiers, that are met constantly marching or rather straggling to relieve guard, told a tale of the absurd and wicked wars for ever raging among these pestilent little South-American republics; and the number of dissolute, ill-looking priests confirmed by their appearance the universal testimony borne to the corruption of the Peruvian clergy. As our eyes were attracted by the varied figures of the passers, the "pacing" horses, and the horsemen in mediæval saddles and bright-coloured ponchos, we wandered farther into the suburbs than we should have ventured unarmed, had we known the present state of the police, and the lawless character of the outlying districts of Lima. On our return to the hotel, we heard enough and to spare on this subject.

In his glowing description of the "Ciudad de los Reyes," I think that Prescott has been rather led away by the exaggerations of the old Spanish chroniclers. Lima cannot be called a beautiful city, and it has as much pretension to beauty now as it ever had. But the thoroughfares were considered wide at the time that Pizarro laid the foundations of his capital, and convenience was far more studied than in most towns of that period. The streets run at right angles to each other, and the water of the Rimac is conducted down the middle of those running parallel with the river, in open *azequias,* or drains, which are a nuisance in the populous neighbourhoods. The authorities are now covering the azequias in some of the main thoroughfares. The inhabitants of a street running out of the plaza, were so proud of having their drain covered in, that they formally opened the new carriage-way with music and flags, and gun-firing, and a procession, in which the government and military figured. The river Rimac (to a corruption of which word the name "Lima" owes its origin) flows through the town, and is spanned by a stone bridge, commonly called after Pizarro. It was really built at great expense in 1613, on the site of the one made by the conqueror, and has resisted the frequent shocks of earthquake that have tried its stability. All the churches and other public buildings which adorn the town, were built in the time of the Viceroys: the Republican

Government has scarcely done anything in the way of improvement. When a public building is wanted now for any purpose, a church or a monastery is taken possession of by the authorities. Part of the extensive monastery of the Franciscans, which once contained one thousand monks, is used as a barrack, and the number of the brotherhood is reduced to about thirty. The college of St. Mark, once the boast of Lima, has been closed, and the chapel appropriated for the sessions of the House of Representatives. The Council of State sits in the once infamous hall of the Inquisition. The Lima terminus of the Callao Railway, was once the convent of San Juan de Dios.

There is, however, a great public building now in course of erection in the Suburb, on the road to Chorillos, which will reflect credit rather on one individual than on the Government of Peru. A wretched and loathsome prison, the *Casas Matas* of Callao, has hitherto been the only place of confinement for prisoners. Here, both in the Spanish and Republican times, many an unfortunate has suffered a long-drawn-out death. Senor Paz Soldan examined and reported upon the prison discipline of the United States, and has persisted in his scheme of ameliorating that of Peru, until he obtained funds for the splendid stone building which he is now erecting on principles suggested by modern experience. Only those who know something of the government and legislature of Peru, will appreciate the enterprise of the man who has succeeded in diverting public money into so philanthropic a channel.

With this single exception, all public and private buildings in Lima are of *adobes*. The churches, of nondescript style of architecture, gaudy, occasionally picturesque, with quaint towers of lath and plaster, and painted façades, are very numerous; but their shrines are not as wealthy as they were in the days of Spanish rule. The necessities of temporary chiefs of the Republic, and the avarice of unscrupulous priests, have gone far to denude the altars, on which, in many cases, ornaments of less value have taken the place of the silver gifts of devotees. No place in Lima is sacred enough to ensure its immunity in these days of anarchy, robbery, and corruption.

The exterior of the private houses gives little promise of the comfort of the interior. A large gateway, with shops on each side, extending along the front of the house, leads into a spacious *patio*, or courtyard ; sometimes the *sala* is immediately opposite the gateway ; sometimes a handsome flight of stone steps leads to a corridor on which the reception rooms open. The principal visiting hour is about eight o'clock in the evening ; after that hour all the drawing-rooms of Lima are open to visitors, and you may meet in the streets ladies in evening-dress, with shawls thrown over their heads, walking from one house to another. The Limenians are most hospitable ;—the ladies have a well-merited reputation for their social qualities and a considerable share of beauty ; but the vice of gambling prevalent among the men is calculated to unhinge society. It pervades all classes ;—the President and the shopkeeper, the soldier and the priest, are alike addicted to it. Business wears a gambling aspect. The Governments and would-be Governments gamble in the issue of paper ; merchants gamble in the purchase of these public *vales*, or bonds, which are often depreciated to an incredible extent ; there is no public confidence or public faith ; and the consequence of all this, together with the abundance of silver, is that ordinary commodities bear a fictitious price. In Lima a dollar goes about as far as a shilling would in England. A man who wins and loses a thousand dollars in a night, does not care what he gives for the necessaries of life. Many of the leading merchants are English and German, and the best shops are kept by Frenchmen and Italians ; each one intent on making all he can in the shortest possible time with a view to returning to his own country.

This is not a place to enter upon a disquisition on the Government, or rather Anarchy, of Peru. But there are some prominent facts which force themselves on the attention of the traveller. In the first place, he must dismiss from his mind any notion he may have formed that the Peruvian independence was won in the same way as that of the United States of America. The intolerable rule of Spain broke down the spirit of the governed and destroyed their self-reliance. Columbian troops and foreign officers* were chiefly instrumental in giving freedom to the Peruvians. As they did not win their independence for themselves, they did not know how to profit by it. They have not yet attained to a thorough national feeling. By blood, the ruling classes are as much Indian as Spanish: few, if any, can boast of the *Sangre Azul* of Gallicia. The Government for the time being is that of the strongest body of brigands in the country; powerful to rob and oppress, but powerless to protect life and property. The rural Indian population, decimated and degraded as it has been by the cruel oppression of the Spaniards, is still peaceable, orderly, and hospitable. But the mongrel population around Lima produces the worst characters. Bands of robbers, chiefly negroes, mulattoes, and men of mixed Indian and negro blood,† infest the neighbourhood and laugh at the police. Of this crew the negroes, and those with negro blood in their veins, are by far the worst. To an Englishman belongs the disgrace of having first introduced negro slaves on

* The world knows now pretty well the return that some of these men have received from the Spanish republics. Lord Dundonald's case will recur to the minds of most readers. But I cannot refrain from noticing that of a distinguished man who has spent the best part of his life in the arduous struggle for South American independence. General Miller (to whom the Peruvians owe more than to any other man, except Lord Cochrane), after the victory was won, and after in vain attempting to maintain the cause of Constitutional government, was obliged to retire into banishment, poor, and crippled by many severe wounds. It is doubtful whether the Peruvians even respected the principle which had kept him poor in commands which had enriched so many others. For twenty years, during which he held the office of British Consul-General in the Sandwich Islands, he was ignored by Peru; and though lately restored by the present Government to his rank as Grand-Marshal, they decline to admit the undoubted claims which he has upon the country. It must be grief enough to those who have spent their lives for the freedom of such a country, to see what a country and what a freedom now exists.

† It is calculated that there are more than twenty different strains of blood in the population of the Lima suburbs, from the intermixture of white men, Indians, and negroes. To these may be added, of late, Chinese.

this coast. The famous John Hawkins of Queen Elizabeth's time began the traffic, and for some time it was an English monopoly. When the Republic was established, a wise and beneficent law was passed, providing for gradual emancipation. It was enacted that all existing slaves should remain so for life; that at the age of fifty their children should be free; and that their grandchildren should be born free. But in the year 1855, the present President suddenly issued a decree, summarily emancipating all slaves. So rash a step cannot even lay claim to the credit of good intention; it was merely one of the many devices illegally adopted by military leaders to secure adherents. Few would be prepared to maintain, that the reparation of a great social evil is to be effected by a *coup-de-main.* And nothing strikes me as much more wicked than to cast loose on society, without warning or preparation, a body of men destitute of training to benefit themselves or to respect the rights of others. What might have been expected has happened in Peru; and the quondam slaves around Lima are now a curse to themselves and to the country. The infamous Chinese Coolie Trade that has sprung up, and is encouraged, exceeds in atrocity the old trade in negro slaves: a tolerably good proof (if any were needed) that the decree of 1855 was not dictated by conscientious scruples.

Almost the first thing I heard on landing, was the news of a sad tragedy which had happened only the week before. Capt. Lambert, Commander of H. M. S. "Vixen," lying in Callao harbour, had gone down alone to bathe in the river below Lima early in the afternoon, and the same evening his body was found on the river bank, half undressed, with marks of violence on his head and arms. A profound sensation was created in the town, owing to the rank of the unfortunate gentleman, and the service to which he belonged, but the authorities were either unable or afraid to make proper inquiries into the matter. The district near which the tragedy occurred, has always had a bad reputation; I certainly never saw a more villanous-looking population than that which I passed through when visiting the spot with a friend of Captain Lambert, who was anxious to make a plan of the localities. This gentleman has at considerable personal risk followed up every clue, to obtain some trace of the murderers, and gives no peace to the apathetic government. It is easy to see that the authorities hope to get rid of an unpleasant topic by procrastination, as the sensation produced at first died rapidly away. When the murder was committed, it was eagerly asked in all the foreign shops, "What will the English Government do?" But soon people said, "The English Government did nothing when their late Minister was shot in this town in broad daylight, and the murderer was allowed to escape; they will do nothing now." This has the very worst effect; and it is to be hoped that the Peruvian Government will not be allowed to pass over this unhappy tragedy so quietly.* As France and America have both serious questions pending with this wretched little republic, it is quite time that these two powers and England should unite, in the interests of humanity, to dictate to the Peruvian Government some necessary steps for the prevention of outrages on foreigners. For one of these powers alone to take vindictive steps against so small a state would be objectionable; but surely it is the duty of great civilized powers to insist on the observance of the common laws of civilization.

The Peruvian Government has now a splendid revenue, chiefly arising from the sale of guano. About 500,000 tons of this valuable manure are exported annually, and it is calculated that even in the wasteful and unbusiness-like manner in which they farm it out to foreign merchants, the

* Some time has elapsed since I wrote the above, and to all appearance the English Government will allow the matter to pass over. In the meantime, no adequate steps have been taken by the Peruvian authorities to discover the murderer. It is pleasant for Englishmen to reflect that on the South American coast the lives and properties of their countrymen are less secure than those of Frenchmen and Americans, whose cruisers make prompt appearance to demand satisfaction for any injury done to French or American citizens. If England is to get any return for the millions she spends to keep her cruisers in every sea, it ought to be in increased security for the lives and properties of her subjects all over the world.

Government net thirty dollars, or about six pounds per ton. No young state ever had such an opportunity of commencing a career of improvement. With this extraordinary revenue (for the ordinary revenue is sufficient to cover all *necessary* expenses of government), a system of great public works, rivalling those of the Incas, might have been initiated, to enlarge incalculably the resources of the country; and public institutions might have been founded to give a permanent character to the civilization of the republic. But the waste and corruption to which this temporary source of wealth has given rise, is almost incredible. The guano islands, which in the days of the Incas were a blessing to the careful agriculturists of the neighbouring coasts, have been the curse of the modern republicans. By means of the income derived from them, ten ships of war have been bought and fitted up, and an army of from 15,000 to 20,000 men is kept on foot, to furnish military tyrants, to depopulate the country by wicked wars, and to take the place of the terrible *mita* of Spanish times. The poor Indian is dragged from his friends and home by a system of irregular impressment that no despotism in the civilized world would tolerate; and leaving his fields untilled, he is forced to fight in quarrels about which he knows nothing, and cares nothing. These little Indian soldiers, wretched as they look, are very brave and enduring, performing incredible marches over deserts and sierras, with a little parched corn for food, and *coca* for stimulant, and fighting stoutly if their officers don't run away. The poor fellows have been known on such occasions to embrace each other, so little heart have they for the quarrels of their superiors. Some of the senior officers of the army are men of ability, though many are stained by gross perfidy; but latterly the officers are drawn from an inferior and often uneducated class, the army has got into disrepute, and the military spirit is not of a high order. As the supreme power depends on the command of the army, and as after a revolution the new President lavishes public money and promotion, a ruler requires a firm hand to hold the reins long. A Peruvian president holds office like the priest of Aricia—

> "The priest who slew the slayer,
> And shall himself be slain,"

that is, he *may* be slain; he certainly will be violently torn from his seat as soon as a large portion of the army have convinced themselves that a successor is able to reward their treason. Echenique, the predecessor of the present president, squandered the revenue on his friends and favourites without stint, and allowed them to rob the public with impunity. This robber fell at last, but "uno avulso non deficit alter *aureus;*" and General Castilla now spends on bayonets as much as his predecessor squandered through ministers and favourites. Castilla, who has a large proportion of Indian blood in his veins, and who can barely write his name, has held power for some time, both before and after Echenique's tenure of office, chiefly because he never runs away in battle; and he is consequently very much feared.* The farce of election, both for President and House of Representatives, is sometimes gone through, but the joke is not countenanced by the respectable classes. In June 1859, after voting supplies, the House of Representatives ventured to ask for accounts, which had not been produced by Government for three years. This was too audacious a proceeding, so Castilla forbade their meeting any more, put a guard at the door of the council chamber, and threw five members who attempted to disobey, into prison. Some persons who are inclined to imagine that representative institutions are the glory of South America, and that Bolivar was to the Spanish South, what Washington was to the Anglo-Saxon States of the North, will be glad to know that a fine equestrian statue of the former hero has, within the last year, been put up opposite the building from which the representatives were so unceremoniously ejected. On the pedestal of the monument is a bas-relief of the battle of Ayacucho, at which Bolivar was *not* present.

* Several attempts have been made on Castilla's life. Two since the date of these notes.

The amiable old President having thus disposed of internal difficulties, proceeded northwards to Guayaquil to prosecute a war with the neighbouring state of Ecuador, where he was when I arrived at Lima. As Ecuador was convulsed by civil feuds, he contented himself with subsidising the chief of one party; and when this worthy appeared to be in a fair way to succeed,* Castilla returned in triumph to Peru, to brood over an expedition against Bolivia, in which republic his predecessor Echenique had taken shelter.

It is scarcely possible to speak or to think of such movements as matter for history; but it is evident that while these republics claim the status of civilized powers, they must learn to respect and to protect the lives and property of foreigners. There is one simple plan of calling Peru to account. If the three great powers I have mentioned unite in taking temporary possession of the Chincha Islands, the Government must attend to their remonstrances; and a step of this sort taken in unison and deliberately, would obviate any suspicion of aggressive or interested motives.

Carnival time is approaching, and a great portion of the fashionable world of Lima is at Chorillos, a favourite bathing place a few miles south of Lima. A railway of the same description as that from Callao, takes you to this little town, with its narrow dirty streets, sandy environs, and bad but expensive accommodations; where the Lima people are fond of spending some portion of the summer months. The occupations of the ladies in this retreat are chiefly visiting and bathing, those of the gentlemen bathing and gambling. I need scarcely add the occupation common to both sexes at watering places all over the world—flirting. It is not to be wondered at that the families who are fortunate enough to obtain the *ranchos* fronting the sea, are glad to exchange the heat of Lima for the cool breezes that sweep through their broad verandahs. It used to be the fashion to live at Chorillos in a very primitive style. But the houses no longer deserve

* The Peruvian President's pet has since been defeated, and turned out of Ecuador.

the name of *ranchos* or huts, as they are still called; and they are improving every day.

The unpleasant old Spanish fashion, by virtue of which people drench each other with water at Carnival time, is in full vogue at Lima. The ladies and the gentlemen wage war in the streets with great vigour. The ladies throw water at the passers-by from the windows and the verandahs; the gentlemen return the compliment by flinging coloured eggs filled with water at the ladies. Sometimes a party of gentlemen attack a house, with the inmates of which they are acquainted, and getting in, carry on the war with scented water, whereon a regular romp ensues. In the evening, parties of gentlemen go about masked, and enter the houses of acquaintances, where the ladies are assembled to dance. Each party of masks elects a captain, and, on entering, this captain steps into a side-room with the master of the house and unmasks; he is responsible for the party he brings with him. The fun, of course, consists in the mistakes made as to the identity of partners. There are people who think the Carnival a nuisance, especially as now and then a great brawny negro woman amuses herself by throwing a bucket of water, clean or unclean, over any well-dressed person who may pass near the window where she is stationed. At Chorillos the "play," as it is called, is chiefly among friends, so those who don't admire Lima "play," prefer being at the former town during the three days of saturnalia. There were two or three Englishmen besides myself at Lima who intended to pay a visit to the ruins of Pachacamac, and we determined to start on the second day of Carnival, as we did not find the watery amusements of the season attractive enough to detain us. I was glad to push on, for I had but a short time to devote to visiting the interesting Indian ruins of the country.

Before the railway was opened, the road to Chorillos was a favourite beat of the robbers of the neighbourhood. Few, but foreigners, or *gringos*, as they are called, resisted them, and the brigands have, it is said, a wholesome dread of Englishmen and Americans (U.S.) The Peruvian gambler, on his way to or from Chorillos with money, was rich and easy prey. The railroad cut up this source of profit; but lately the robbers have become very daring, and three times within the last month large stones have been placed on the line to upset the train; a body of armed ruffians lurking in the neighbourhood, to take advantage of the expected catastrophe. Fortunately the obstruction was seen in time, as the train works very slowly along this treacherous line. Of course nothing was done in the way of apprehending the culprits. As we had to take our horses to Chorillos for the trip to Pachacamac, two of us rode down in the evening—I need not say, well armed; but we were not molested. We stayed on the Sunday at Chorillos, where I met with the same kindness and hospitality which is so pleasant a feature of Lima society; and on Monday morning we set out, a party of four, for the ruins.

On leaving Chorillos, we passed several ruined *huacas*, or ancient burial-places, built up in huge mounds of *adobes*. These *huacas* are generally surrounded by ruins like those of a village; the best conjecture I have met with as to their origin is that of Mr. Markham (one of our present party), who had visited them before. He thinks that "although these were doubtless partly used as burial-places, it is probable that they answered a far more extensive purpose; that they were intended to afford protection against their enemies to the feudal lords of the valley, and to serve as a place of retreat to their retainers."* The whole valley of the Rimac is covered with these artificial hills. On emerging from a little wood of acacias, the road passes near a sandy hill, the northern side of which is white for two or three miles with the skulls and bones of men and women who were buried there, in the days of the Incas. This was a burial-place for the lower classes, and the dryness of the soil has preserved the remains so wonderfully, that the hair is still to be seen on many of the skulls, and the skin clings to the fleshless bones. The extent of this crowded cemetery

* "Cuzco and Lima," by C. R. Markham.

bears witness to the immense population of the coast valleys under the kindly though stern rule of the Incas. If Spain had founded a noble empire in the place of the one she destroyed, we should perhaps have been less inclined to do justice to a ruined dynasty and an injured race; but no one can travel through Peru without a feeling of anger and contempt for the Goths of America, who conquered but to plunder and to destroy; who under the banner of the Cross committed atrocities that would have made all heathendom shudder; and who, from the very commencement of their career, have left a tale of jealousies, and treasons, and barbarities, and lies, unequalled in the history of the so-called civilized world. Tacitus has immortalized a tribe of barbarians in one pregnant sentence; on this desert, populous with the dead, I felt the force of the description:—"Ubi solitudinem faciunt, pacem appellant."

A little beyond this burial-place is a large sugar estate, or *hacienda*, called Villa, formerly worked by negro slaves, but now by free negroes, and Chinese, imported since the Emancipation in 1854. This *hacienda* is separated from the desert of San Juan by a few swampy lakes, the favourite resort of wild ducks.

The whole coast of Peru is of the same character. The traveller does not reach the grassy country till he has penetrated into the Sierra. The coast consists of deserts and dreary, sandy hills, broken at greater or lesser intervals by fertile valleys, which owe their wealth to small rivers, flowing down from the mountains. Under the Incas, large tracts of desert land were reclaimed, by an elaborate system of irrigation, which spread the waters of these streams over a great extent of country. These reclaimed lands have never been extended, and have often fallen back into desert since the time of the Spaniards.

We kept down along the sea-coast for a few miles, where the sand was harder and less trying to our horses, till we reached the farm of Mama-Conas, which in old times belonged to the lady-abbess of a convent of Virgins-of-the-Sun, Mama-

Cona signifying matron, in the Quichua language. This farm is a small oasis just under the ruins of Pachacamac, and surrounding a spring of sweet water. The Indians living here, grow bananas, grapes, and water-melons, the latter of which fruits we saw growing apparently in the sand. While we stopped to rest our horses and search our saddle-bags for eatables, two Indian women from the village of Chilca, many miles to the southward, came in with their donkeys for water-melons, having passed on their way through the fertile valley of Lurin.

On a hill, partly natural and partly artificial, to the seaward of the old town of Pachacamac, rose the great temple of the Deity. Leaving the ruins of the city to our left, we rode up from one broken terrace to another, till we stood upon the summit of the sacred hill. Around us were the gigantic works of a race that had passed away, at our feet lay the city of the dead. To the dryness of a climate in which rain never falls, is attributable the preservation of the sun-dried bricks of which the temple and the town were built, even where the walls have been torn down by the Spanish conquerors. Although the temple itself has been destroyed, enough remains to give an idea of its grandeur in the days preceding the establishment of the Inca empire, when Pachachamac was the Delphi of Peru. The retaining walls of the terraces still stand, built up as they are above the natural height of the hill; and on the western face the paint on the plaster is as fresh as if it had been laid on only a few years back. At an angle from the terraces, walls of *adobes* run down to the plain below, enclosing sandy tracts that once bloomed with the many-coloured fruits and flowers of the temple-gardens. The walls of the terraces were built on foundations of rough stone. A broad inclined terrace on the northern side, which was the approach to the sanctuary, is still almost perfect. Up this approach, the long priestly procession, and the royal cortege ascended to the temple, in sight of the city below. Up this approach marched Hernando Pizarro and his daring followers, when, in sight of the whole population, they tore down the idol and dashed it to pieces; and on this spot the rude soldier preached the tenets of a faith belied by every act of himself and his blood-stained brethren-in-arms.

From the summit of the hill the contrast between the sandy desert and the rich green valley of Lurin is very striking. The ruins are on the northern bank of the river, which is the boundary between sterility and verdure. The towns of the Inca Indians, on the coast, were always built on the edge of the desert immediately adjoining the reclaimed and cultivated districts, but never encroached on them; another proof of the density of the population and the careful economy by which plenty was secured. This economical custom has been particularly pointed out by Mr. Markham.*

We rode down the broad northern terrace to the ruins of the city, passing by the temple of the sun, which was situated on a hill beneath the great temple of the tutelary deity. There is nothing remarkable about this ruin; but the remains of the palace used on the occasion of a royal visit to the great sanctuary of the coast, give some idea of the state in which an Inca Emperor travelled. I stepped the great hall, the walls of which still stand. It is 70 paces in length, by 30 in breadth; that is, about 210 feet by 90. At the end of the hall, and extending beyond the space thus roughly measured, are ruins of what appear to have been rows of seats, one above another. Such an enclosed space near a mediæval ruin, in Europe, might be taken for a tilting-ground. The secret of such great size, of course, is, that there was no roof to support; a sort of awning of thatch, or some very light material, warding off the rays of the sun. There are ruins of an upper story of small rooms at one end of the palace; and in all the apartments, both above and below, there are niches in the wall, at regular intervals. It is thought by some, that in these niches were placed the *canopas*, or household gods. This theory is unsatisfactory, both from the

* "Cuzco and Lima," p. 12.

number and shape of these cavities. They are broader than they are high, and, putting my arm in, I found that some of them were higher inside than they appeared, and that they were regularly roofed.

A narrow street between the palace wall and some other buildings, still exists. It must have been gloomy, as there is no trace of windows in the side walls of the houses on either side. Emerging from this street, we rode through a labyrinth of ruined houses, in many of which skulls, bones, and even clothes used as shrouds, may be seen, preserved in the dry soil. The mortal remains of the upper classes were often buried under their own houses. How little did they think who died and were buried in the holy city, that their bones would lie bleaching in the sun under the ruined walls of the temple of the oracle; that a city of strangers in a neighbouring valley would eclipse the glory of Pachacamac, and that the civilization around them, based apparently on such sure foundations, would ere long be destroyed for ever.

Crossing the suspension bridge that spans the muddy torrent of Lurin, we left the desert behind us, and rode along a narrow road shaded by noble willows, somewhat resembling at a distance, our English weeping-willows, but stronger and less fragile-looking; on either side of the road were fields of sugar-cane and other tropical products growing in rich luxuriance. A little beyond a *hacienda,* called San Pedro, we found the little town or rather village of Lurin, embosomed in trees, and on entering the plaza, saw preparations for Carnival festivities. Around the plaza are the church and the principal houses, built of adobes; the rest of the town consists of narrow lanes of huts built of bamboo and clay, and tenanted by a mixed population, chiefly of negroes and *zambos* (half Indian, half negro). We rode up to the door of one of the principal houses at the corner of the plaza, belonging to the schoolmaster, where, although the house was in great disorder, we were favourably received; the horses were put into the *coral,* or yard, at the back of the house, and having ordered a *chupé** to be made for us, we went off to look for a place to bathe. I regret to say that the lady of the house where we proposed to sleep, and most of the inmates, were more or less under the influence of *pisco* (a white spirit made from the grape). When we returned from our bath, barricades had been put up at the different approaches to the plaza, thereby converting it into a temporary bull-ring. The bull-fight was not to be *à l'outrance;* but the young bulls were to be tried or "played," as they call it. We had scarcely begun to eat our *chupé,* when we heard a scream of delight from the women at the door, who were pushing in to close it. The first bull they said was *muy bravo*, and was coming round towards them. We ran to the door in time to see an unfortunate horse severely gored, and led away, bleeding profusely. The rest of the performance was as mean, cruel, and cowardly an amusement as could have been invented. A number of young bulls were turned into the square one after the other, and excited by red clothes and spear-thrusts; but it would not do, the poor brutes only tried to make their escape, and we were glad that darkness soon obliged the gentle villagers to give up their sport. We then went across the plaza to call on the *cura*, but were told that he had gone out to amuse himself. We had seen his reverence on a balcony with some friends enjoying the bull-fight, and as he probably intended to make a night of it, did not disturb him. Masks and dances at one of the houses were the next amusement, and a good deal of pisco went round, till at last our venerable hostess appeared inclined to return home, to our great delight. This wonderful old woman had certainly drunk more pisco than any one else; she had previously put her son, the schoolmaster, to bed in a helpless state, and she was still brisk, though somewhat tipsy. She

* A *chupé* is a nondescript sort of stew, made of a little meat, and whatever vegetables are within reach (no great variety generally). This dish is flavoured with coarse cheese, and made pungent with *ahi*, the Peruvian pepper. When eggs are put into it, it is tolerably eatable; and even without eggs, and in out-of-the-way places, is not always nasty. But sheer hunger is the only inducement to swallow the chupé made by the Indians in the Sierra.

found us a sheet and a bench each, and then getting hold of our saddle bags, sat down beside us, and proceeded deliberately to eat an enormous supper from their contents. We lay on our benches screaming with laughter, as we saw our ham and cheese vanish, while a stolid little Indian boy stood before her holding a light. It was a ludicrous scene, especially as she came round to each of us in turn to pledge us in pisco, and then wept because she was not allowed to get at the sherry bottle which W—— took possession of, and kept doggedly between his knees, turning a deaf ear to the entreaties and tears of the old lady. At last she went away to bed, on being allowed to take half the cheese with her. Notwithstanding all this, she was the first up in the morning, and got iced-water for her drunken son, and hot water to make our tea. An officer of police from Lima, who was on a visit to the house during Carnival time, informed us that he knew of several brigands who lived in Lurin and robbed travellers to Chilca; but that he could do nothing! He said he was ashamed of the state of lawlessness around Lima, and that if by letting blood out of the veins of his arm he could cease to be a Peruvian, he would do so. After this brave and patriotic sentiment, who could accuse him of neglect of duty? We put fresh caps on our pistols, and gladly rode out of the town of Lurin. It is possibly more inviting at any other time; it certainly does not show to advantage during Carnival.

Following a beautiful road a few miles up the valley, we reached the pretty village of modern Pachacamac. It is almost entirely inhabited by Indians, and the house in the plaza where we got a *chupé* was clean and tidy. The cooking was unusually nice, and the people civil and well-looking. A village belle was just going off, with silver-mounted bridle, and in holiday trim, to "play" carnival at Lurin. We wished her joy. After waiting at this village till the mid-day heat was past, we turned our horses' heads northwards; and, fording the river many miles above the bridge, rode back across the desert to Chorillos.

The sea-bathing at this fashionable watering-place is carried on in the most sociable manner. There are a collection of bamboo ranchos by the sea-side, where you are furnished with a bathing-dress, towels, &c. Ladies and gentlemen make up bathing parties together, and at favourite hours great numbers of people meet in the water. The dress consists of blue serge shirt and trowsers, a straw hat, and a pair of canvas shoes,—not a very convenient costume to swim in. It is rather odd to find yourself in the water, saluting a damp limp-looking nymph, whom you saw but the night before in all the glory of crinoline and flounces. *Quantum mutata!* It is a marvel to me that the ladies of Lima, who are so fond of dress, and so careful of their personal appearance, should venture upon such a metamorphosis; but fashion is all-powerful.

Before we left Chorillos for Pachacamac, we had heard two salutes of twenty guns (the royal salute here) from the direction of Callao; and on our return, we heard that the President, or as he is irreverently called by the English, "Old Boots," had arrived from Ecuador, and had immediately come down to Chorillos, where he bathed with the pomp of the King of the Cannibal Islands. First in procession came the band, then the staff, then the President, and then some sky-rockets. The music subsided into a plaintive air, while His Excellency retired beneath the envious shade of the rancho, but burst out again in triumphant strains as he emerged in his blue bathing-dress, and splashed about in the water among the delighted spectators. The staff looked on respectfully from the beach. After the bath, the virtuous old republican retires to gamble; an amusement which he nominally forbids his subjects to indulge in.

From Lima, M—— was bound for the interior, on a scientific expedition. Mrs. M—— was to go as far as Arequipa, and to remain there while he pursued his journey into the Montaña. M—— and I agreed to travel together to Lake Titicaca, the reputed cradle of Inca civilization. From that point our routes would diverge; he striking into the Caravaya valley, and I turning towards Cuzco, the once famous and now seldom visited city of the Incas.

On Tuesday, the 28th February, we left Callao in one of the fine steamers of the English Company, which has a monopoly of the traffic along the coast from Panama to Valparaiso. There is no greater sign of the debility of the South American race than the fact that almost every enterprise in the country of any moment has been undertaken by foreigners. If the English Steam-packet Company now has a monopoly on the western coast of South-America, it is the fault of the inhabitants of the country; and when they grumble at the very high prices * consequent on monopoly, they should remember that there would be no steam communication at all, if they were left to their own resources. Should competition arise, the Americans (U. S.) will furnish the competing steamers; there is some talk already of an American Company. In the meantime, the Peruvians enjoy punctuality, good accommodation, and cleanliness; and the occasional traveller is glad to pay any price for the only comfortable means of travelling to be met with in that part of the world.

Leaving to the left the now half-dismantled fort of Callao, from under the guns of which Lord Cochrane cut out the "Esmeralda" in 1820, we steamed out of the harbour by what is called the Bucaroon passage, between a reef running out from the main land and the southern end of the Island of San Lorenzo. The evening was very fine, and we had a beautiful view of the Valley of the Rimac, with Lima in the middle distance, and the cloud-capped Cordillera in the background. From this point of view the best idea can be obtained of the valley, and of the natural advantages which induced Pizarro to select it as the site for the Capital town of the new Government. Early the next morning we reached the Chincha Islands, creeping slowly up through the heavy mist that generally hangs along the coast in the mornings. Several times the engines were stopped; then the paddles moved slowly round in the calm water, while captain and officers strained their eyes to get a glimpse of the island. Suddenly the mist rose,

* The fare from Callao to Islay, two and a half days, is sixty dollars, equal, in the depreciated state of the currency, to about 11*l*.

and discovered within about half a mile of the steamer a most wonderful sight. Sixty or seventy vessels, of all sizes, lay at anchor under these barren rocks, from which they were to bear to every part of the civilized world a wealth greater than that of the mines of Potosi. On the shore we could see the deep cuttings in the guano, which lies in depths ranging from thirty to a hundred and twenty feet on the surface of the rock. From these cuttings, which from a distance have the appearance of quarries, a tramway takes the guano down to a pier, at the end of which it is poured through canvas shoots into launches lying alongside. At the cuttings, as well as at the shoots, clouds of dust arise, from which the unfortunate workmen must suffer severely. The ammonia is very penetrating, and although it is said to produce no immediately unhealthy consequences, yet it causes sufficient suffering among the men incessantly employed, to make the labour very unpopular. Some Chinese have been imported lately as labourers, but suicide, by jumping over the cliff, has been common among them. I have already spoken of the large and misused revenue derived from these islands, the prize for which revolutionary parties struggle. We saw a squad of soldiers drilling on one of the points, and the inevitable boat-full of officials boarded us as we lay off the landing-place for half an hour. The great ambition of a Peruvian is to obtain a place under Government, whereby to enrich himself. It was only the second and third in command with their satellites who came off to us from this little rock in the boat of the captain of the port.

About an hour's steaming brought us to the roadstead of Pisco, where the anchor was dropped for a couple of hours. We went ashore in one of the boats which found the steamer out through the heavy mist, and after a pull of about half-a-mile landed on a fine iron pier, built for the Government by an American contractor. I was wondering at and admiring the employment of public money on so useful a work, when we were informed by a gentleman connected with the contractor himself, that the work was a job. The contractor urged the selection of a site about six miles further south, where there is calm water; but local influences prevailed, and the jetty is built where it is comparatively useless for shipping. We had not time to go up as far as the town of Pisco, six or seven miles inland, so we amused ourselves for the time we were on shore, in watching the negro surf-men loading boats with the huge earthen pitchers, in which the spirit called *pisco* is exported to different parts of the coast. The boat lies outside the surf, and each man shouldering a pitcher, and assisted by a strong stick, makes his way through the breakers till he is obliged to turn his back to a wave that breaks almost over him, and then pushes on afresh, till the swell again warns him to turn round.

From Pisco to Islay the country presents few objects of interest. I think it is not generally understood in Europe that a great portion of Peru is a desert—a very dreary desert, studded here and there with rich but slovenly gardens reclaimed from the waste around. Whenever water can be introduced this desert may be made fruitful. During the season in which rain falls on the low hills which run from the sierra towards the coast south of Pisco, they are covered with grass and flowers, and the cattle from the interior are sent down to relieve the upland pastures.

On Friday morning we anchored off Islay, a little wooden town perched on a desert promontory, and serving as a port town for Arequipa, and a large tract of country in the interior. On landing, we had to send up for mules to Arequipa by the *propio*, who was just starting with the mails. The mules did not arrive till Tuesday, so that we were not able to leave Islay till Wednesday morning. Lima is the only town in Peru where there are hotels; elsewhere the stranger is indebted to private hospitality, as we were here. During our stay, droves of mules and asses were constantly arriving from the interior with loads of wool and silver, and returning with foreign merchandise, and guano for the maize crops of the valley of Arequipa. Islay itself is wholly dependent on other places for everything. Not a blade of grass will grow there; and a scanty supply of water for the use of the town was till lately brought down on mules from the gullies of the neighbouring hills. Pipes were laid down about nine years ago, under the direction of an English engineer, and they are now taken care of by an Irishman, who goes by the name of "*Juan de la pila,*" or John of the Fountain. A difficult post he has between the muleteers who break the pipes to water their mules, and the local authorities who try to keep back his pay. However, John is master of the position; as he could cut off the water, he generally manages to obtain justice. During Vivanco's last revolution, Castilla's army was camped a little above the town, and cut off the water; fortunately the British Consul's family, and the foreign merchants got an opportune supply from an English ship of war.

When we arrived, the country was in a very disturbed state, as an attempted revolution had just been summarily put down at Arequipa. There were still rumours of coming troubles, and the little town of Islay was crowded with soldiers; it was thought that the President might be down at any moment to join the army assembled at Puno, near the frontier of Bolivia. It is curious to observe the mixed feelings with which Don Ramon (as Castilla is commonly called) is looked upon. By a large majority of the upper classes he is feared more than liked, though there is an impression that he can rule Peru better than other pretenders. He is fearless, and not cruel; but he is a rough, uncouth soldier, *muy bruto*, with few scruples when his authority is in danger. By the lower classes he is generally liked, and from the ranks of the army he has lately chosen his officers. Under Vivanco and Echenique, who are men of education, the officers were chosen from a higher rank in society; but however much they excelled their successors in polish, they certainly could not be exceeded by the latter in corruption and want of military honour. Yet on the whole, the more I and hear of the country and the people, the more I am inclined to think that "Old Boots" would be a loss at present.

The climate at Islay is delightful for those who are fond of rather hot weather; but it tends more or less to enervate the inhabitants. The mornings and evenings are cool, and M—— and I took advantage of the sea-breeze before breakfast to walk up to the valleys in the neighbouring hills, from which the supply of water is drawn. The season had been unusually wet, so that there was still a little verdure left in the hollows, where a few olives and fig-trees bore evidence to former cultivation. The sources of the water-springs are scanty enough.

Near the shore, a little to the south of Islay, are two large circular chasms, divided from the sea by a narrow ledge of rock. The sea has bored through the hard cliff, and penetrating to a looser soil behind, has gradually torn it away, the retreating tide drawing back the wreck through the holes beneath. This, at least, appeared to us sufficient cause for the formation of the *tinajones*, or "large pans," as they are called; although it certainly is strange that two cavities of similar shape should have been formed close to each other. But as we looked down into these deep caverns, and heard the tide roaring below as if waiting to swallow up the masses that were even then detaching themselves from the cliff, we could see no necessity for attributing the formation to volcanic action. It is, however, the opinion of many that such was their origin.

On Tuesday, our mules arrived, and we had the pleasure of making the acquaintance of one arriero, a man who in any other country would be considered a consummate liar, but who in his native land is looked on as a very respectable man. Indeed, I believe it to be true that he was the best of the arrieros who frequented that route. And here I cannot but observe, that the vice of lying—there is no use in mincing words—is prevalent among all classes of society in this country, from the highest officer to the poorest *peon*. And however much the Peruvian may hate the *Gringo*, he is far more ready to believe him and to trust him than his own countrymen. If I dwell now on our arriero's delinquencies, it is in order to impress on any intending travellers in Peru the lesson I learned early, viz., not to believe anything your muleteer may say; to see his animals put into a corral within your own ken at night; and when en route, to keep him before you, and not to let him fall behind on any pretext.

The route over the desert from Islay to Arequipa is commonly reputed to be about ninety miles in length; while the direct distance from the sea-coast is not more than about sixty miles. As Mrs. M—— was coming as far as Arequipa, some trouble had been taken to make the journey as comfortable as possible. The arriero had made solemn promises to be ready early in the morning, and to push on with the light luggage, so that immediate necessaries should reach Arequipa as soon as we did ourselves. In the morning, however, our gentleman was selling potatoes that he had brought down to Islay on a private speculation, and the heat of the day had already set in when we started with a man whom the muleteer sent with us. When we had gone about nine miles on our way up the long sandy *quebrada* that leads through the hills to the elevated pampas above, the *mozo* wanted us to stop, on the pretext of getting water for the mules. We refused, and proceeded to the *Cruz de Garreros,* where there is a *tambo* or post-house at the top of the ravine. Here we were to halt during the heat of the day. We had, unfortunately, trusted the *mozo* with the saddle-bags containing the eatables, and waited for some time expecting him to come up. At last I rode back in high dudgeon, thinking that the fellow had stopped to get drunk at the tambo, where he had wanted us to stop. As I rode down the hot quebrada again, my wrath increased, and I was rejoicing in the idea of bringing away his mule with the *alforjas,* leaving him to follow on foot, when I met a man who told me he had met our friend posting back towards Islay. It had been preconcerted that we were to be detained at the tambo till it suited the convenience of Senor Muñoz to join us. Soon after my return with this news, Muñoz himself appeared with his mule brutally spurred; and he seemed to consider the state of his steed a sufficient apology for his misdeeds. The sangfroid of these indolent rascals would enrage a saint.

Near this spot, at the entrance of the ravine, a curious incident of the civil war occurred in 1836. General Miller, in his pursuit of the fugitive revolutionary chief Salaverry, found himself here with about fifteen men, when two hundred of the enemy's horse made their appearance on their way to Islay, where a couple of ships were lying in the hands of Salaverry's partisans. General Miller, with a happy audacity, placed his few men behind a hill, with the exception of two or three who were posted like sentinels, and then galloping up to the edge of the ravine called on the cavalry to lay down their arms. His military reputation was such, that the moment he was recognised, the troops were seized with a panic, and they flung their arms at his feet with cries of "*Viva General Miller.*" The next day Salaverry, who had lost himself in the desert with a few followers, came in very much exhausted, and surrendered. A little further on in the desert is buried one of Salaverry's soldiers, who, tradition says, had been flogged to death because he was too much exhausted to march any further. The poor fellow's corpse is scantily covered with sand, a portion of which the passer-by removes to wonder at the perfect preservation of the body in that dry desert soil.

In the centre of the pampa, the tambo of *La Joya*, kept by an Englishman, is a decided improvement on the native post-houses. Here are obtainable clean beds and a good *chupé*. As we left *La Joya* at dawn the next morning the view of the snowy peaks of the Cordillera was magnificent, but they were soon enveloped in mist again. At this season of the year it is only in the early morning that you can get an unclouded view of the highest mountains. In misty weather the desert is very treacherous. Many persons, even arrieros, who are accustomed to the route, have lost their way and perished;—many have been reduced to the last extremity before they were providentially saved. But in this part of the waste there are remarkable guides for those who know how to use them. On the red-coloured surface of the plain are scattered large heaps of the lighter stone-grey sand, raised by the wind. These heaps, called *medanos*, are all of one shape, like a moon in the first quarter; and owing to the prevailing wind, their horns always point to the north-west, thereby affording a natural compass to the traveller. The medanos, which are always travelling in a north-westerly direction, are the most curious phenomena of the desert.

After a few hours' ride, we commenced the hot and weary ascent of the hills that separate the pampas from the valley of Arequipa. The route is by a long sandy quebrada, succeeded by monotonous hills and hollows, rocky and arid, as wearisome to the rider as to the unhappy mules. The bones of their departed brethren greet these poor animals at every step in the toilsome ascent and descent. The fact that no road has been made from Arequipa to the coast, is a disgrace to the Spaniards, who for nearly three hundred years drew so much wealth from the country in this direction. Their miserable policy was *not* to open up Peru for fear of encouraging intercourse with foreigners. And now that the republic has put an end to this policy,—now that foreign houses monopolize the trade of the country,—there is little chance that the Governments that succeed each other in rapid and ignoble succession, will devote public money to so useful a purpose as road-making. It may be asserted that, with the exception of the short bits of railway from Lima to Callao and Chorillos, no such thing as a road exists in Peru at this time. And yet more than four hundred years ago the Incas had made and maintained post-roads throughout the length and breadth of the country. But this was before the introduction of Spanish civilization, and Spanish Christianity.

From the top of the hills the first view of the campiña of Arequipa is a relief to eyes wearied by the glare of the sun on the desert sands. As we approached the valley, the clouds were low on the mountains, hiding the volcano and the peak of Chacani, which rise about 20,000 and 21,000 feet respectively above the level of the sea. These characteristic features of Arequipa are clear from morning till night for the greater part of the year, but during the rainy season (which was just drawing to a close) the clouds descend over them in the afternoon. On emerging from the passes of the hills, the shortest route would have been across the river and through the little village of Tiavaya. But the stream was unfortunately too much swollen to allow us to ford it; we had to cross by a bridge some miles lower down, and to traverse a sandy pampa to the westward of the town;—so it was late before we reached our destination. Our baggage did not arrive till two days after us; during the interval our most respectable arriero quite distinguished himself by his fertility in the art of lying.

Arequipa, the second Spanish city founded by Pizarro, and now the second in importance in Peru, is par excellence the revolutionary city. Here most of the recent revolutions have originated, and the country around has been the scene of many a battle between contending factions. It would be wearisome to a person who knew nothing of the country to wade through an account of these kite and crow wars; it is painful to any one to think of the wicked folly that is the constant cause of bloodshed here. Sometimes the details are sufficiently ludicrous. An officer of the army, perhaps, in consequence of some disgust, determines "to make a revolution." He receives from an exile in a neighbouring state a thousand dollars, to spend in *chicha*, a sort of bad beer made of maize. He distributes this favourite beverage among the turbulent classes, and a revolution breaks out. A few barricades are thrown up, and the populace "descends into the streets," as they say in Paris. Nobody knows when the row commences, whether it will be an émeute put down in a few hours, or whether it will spread over the country till a new "Supreme Chief," or "Liberator of the country," or "Regenerator of Peru" seizes the reins. The revolution that had been put down just before we arrived, was a very slight affair; but three years ago Arequipa was the scene of a bloody struggle, when Vivanco, an old rival of the present ruler, attempted to dispossess Castilla of the supreme power. The majority of the Arequipanians were friends of Vivanco, but this leader, plausible and educated as he is, was no match for the fearless, iron-framed "Old Boots." The latter besieged the town, a long resistance was offered, but in the end Castilla entered in triumph, surprising some of the posts, and carrying others after a vigorous assault. Vivanco fled—indeed Castilla winked at his escape. (It is to be regretted that no punishment now overtakes revolutionary intriguers, who are practically wholesale murderers.) The Arequipanians are very proud of their lengthened stand against so resolute and untiring a foe as Castilla, and it is amusing to hear the names they have given to the different points of defence. A house in the suburbs, which is much battered, goes by the name of the "Malakoff," and the defenders are fully of opinion that they rivalled, if they did not surpass, the deeds of the Crimean war. One of the combatants asked a Frenchman who was in the town whether an equal number of his countrymen would have conducted the assault as well as Castilla's troops. The doughty son of Gaul replied by a vaunt less polite than it was probably truthful. "So many French soldiers," said he, "would have driven Castilla and his troops into the town, and then have driven both parties out at the other side." The Arequipanian naturally put him down as an ignorant rude man. While on the subject of revolutions, it is right to say that old residents bear witness to the good behaviour of the general population in these times of anarchy. The race is very different from the mongrel breed around Lima, as there is no negro element, and Indian blood predominates among the lower classes. The foreign houses are always respected, and money is often brought to the English merchants for safe custody. The population of Arequipa is estimated at about 40,000 souls.

The town is built of a white pumice stone, soft when cut from the quarry, but becoming very hard when exposed to the air. The houses are built with walls of great thickness, and vaulted roofs to withstand the constant shocks of earthquake for which the valley is famous. The streets are at right angles to each other, of tolerable width considering the age of the town, and roughly paved. Open azequias run down the middle of the streets, making them quite impracticable for carts or carriages. Indeed, except in half a dozen streets of Lima, no one dreams of driving a wheeled vehicle of any sort anywhere in Peru. *Portals,* like those at Lima, run round three sides of the plaza, while a large new cathedral occupies the fourth. This building, like all the churches of Peru, is of a nondescript style of architecture, and certainly seems more suited for secular than ecclesiastical purposes. It possesses the great desideratum—strength to resist earthquakes. Some of the churches in Arequipa have very elaborately carved façades ; the softness of the stone when first hewn, affording great facility for this kind of ornament. Over the gateways of many of the best houses are carved the coats of arms of old Spanish families. Some of these old houses are very large, with two or three *patios,* one behind the other, round which the rooms extend over a great deal of ground.

There is something very characteristic about this town of Arequipa. Here you first meet with Peru as it has been since the time of the early Spanish colonist. The view of the Plaza from the top of the cathedral is most striking. Market-women moving about in the gaudy colours, yellow and red, in which Indians delight; droves of mules driven by men mounted in mediæval fashion, and brilliant with many-coloured ponchos; and troops of llamas standing patiently waiting for their loads;—all is new and picturesque. It is here for the first time in Peru that the llama is seen, recalling, with its patient Indian driver, recollections of the days when it was the only beast of burden in the country of the Incas. The animal and his driver are very well suited to each other. The Indian does not value time; and he starts from the interior with his herd of llamas laden with wool, utterly regardless of the number of days he may be on the road. The llama will not allow itself to be overloaded or over-driven, but will travel great distances, slowly, with a fair load, picking up its own food by the way. Every one is familiar, by pictures at least, with the appearance of this animal, with its long graceful neck and patient eye, and broad thick-woolled back,—the link between the camel and the sheep. The wool on the back, which is never cut, serves as a saddle, on which two small bales of wool, weighing altogether about 120 pounds, are secured by a rope. With no further gear, herds of llamas are constantly carrying their loads by easy stages over the Sierra to Arequipa, where the wool is transferred to the backs of asses and mules. An ass's load is the same as that of the llama, but he travels twice the journey; the mule's load is double that of the ass; unfortunately for them the poor mules and donkeys do not understand the passive resistance which the llama opposes to mal-treatment, and the countless bones bleaching on the desert tracks tell how often they are worked till they die under their burdens. But the Indian knows that, if the llama is overloaded or over-driven, he will lie down and refuse to move, and that bullying is of no use, as he will die rather than yield under ill-usage:—coaxing is the Indian's art, and with the Indian the llama is at home. It is curious to observe the love of brilliant colours even in the decoration of these animals. The wool of many of them is stained vermilion, and favourites are often conspicuous by the quaint painting of their finely-pointed ears.

As you approach nearer to the scene that has pleased you from the top of the Cathedral, and walk through the streets of Arequipa, the charm in a great measure vanishes. The dirty habits of the people, the pervading smells in the streets, and the miscellaneous uses to which the azequia water is put, are rather sickening. As in history, so in reality, barbarism has its picturesque side when seen from a distance, but it is barbarism still. It is a relief to escape from the crowded streets into the green Campiña, overlooked by the beautiful cone of the Volcano, and the snowy peak of Chacani.

There are several pleasant rides in the cultivated valley of Arequipa. A favourite one is to the village of Sabandia, where a clear spring runs through large square baths built in the open air: a great resort of the Arequipanians during the bathing season. As water is an element too sparingly used in the usual domestic life of the Peruvians, so strange theories prevail as to its proper application when they go in for a dose during the season. The virtue is believed to exist in a stated number of baths, taken never mind when, or how. For instance, a person goes to Sabandia with the intention of setting him or her self up for the year by means of fifty baths. If time is limited, the patient will take three in the day, and thus get through the prescribed penance rapidly. Of course, there are many who enjoy the fun, and the baths are a sort of lounge for ladies and gentlemen, bathers and non-bathers; some looking on, while others splash about in dresses like those worn at Chorillos.

One day, M—— and I rode over to visit some mineral springs in a valley called Yura, about eighteen or twenty miles to the north-west of Arequipa. The road, or rather the track, is very bad, over a sandy pampa broken by rocky quebradas; of course no attempt has been made to improve it. In a narrow ravine, iron and sulphur springs of different temperatures rise close to each other, and over them a bath-house has been built. Just above the bath-house, quaint stone cells and a little chapel have been erected by a pious Spaniard for the benefit of invalids who might resort to the place for the use of the waters. While our arriero was getting a chupé, we walked down to the little village of Calera, which is picturesquely situated, overlooking the narrow green valley of the Yura. On the opposite side of the valley rise bold stratified mountains, abounding in coal; but the Arequipanians have not availed themselves of it, notwithstanding the scarcity of fuel. On our return to our quarters we dined in the little portal, where we sat till late enjoying the beauty of the evening. In the room behind, a long, dark, stone-vaulted cell, our beds were made of our *pillons* and blankets. When the door was shut, and the cell was lighted by a long dip, which the arriero produced, we could have fancied ourselves in a prison. In the morning, we tried the different springs; the house was in a very dirty state. The bottom of the baths was knee-deep in mud, and the floor of the bath-room at least ankle deep. This mud had been washed in during the late rains, and the *mayor-domo* had been too lazy to have the place cleaned. Two or three dirty invalided soldiers were the only visitors: although the baths are considered very salubrious, the accommodations are not likely to tempt more fastidious patients.

By far the most striking view near Arequipa is from a point about two or three miles up the river. From the quarries near this spot, the stone used in building the town has been conveyed for more than three hundred years on the backs of mules and asses, and will probably be so conveyed for three hundred years more, should the country remain so long in the hands of its present inhabitants. Yet the way to the town from this place is on a gently inclined plane! From the high bank above the river the view is beautiful. Cultivation is carried down to the level of the water by terraces, probably as old as the days of the Incas, and watered by *azequias* fed from the stream above. Looking up the river you see the gorge opening between the volcano and the mountains beyond, while on the other side the white city stands out in beautiful contrast to the background of green.

As Arequipa is upwards of 7,000 feet above the level of the sea, the climate is very different from that on the coast. The mornings and evenings are cool, and the air is peculiarly dry, and sometimes parching. However hot the sun may be, scarcely any amount of exercise will induce perspiration. In March and April, immediately after the rainy season, the weather is most pleasant; but even then strangers sometimes feel the change to an atmosphere considerably rarefied. It is, however, an undoubtedly healthy place, and the people would be healthier still, if they were cleaner.

It is curious to observe the extent to which even in this remote spot English manufactures are to be found, adapted to the wants and tastes of the customers. The yellow and red baize garments on that Indian woman are English; the gaudy poncho on that arriero was made at Halifax, and the huge brass spurs on his heels at Birmingham; but he wears them in happy ignorance of where they came from. A good deal of coarse clothing is still manufactured in the country, as well as some of the fine ponchos of the valuable *Vicuña* wool; but there is no such thing as systematic industry. A plough is not much more than a couple of cross pieces of stick; corn is trodden out by bullocks in a round stone inclosure attached to the farm; and modern improvements are uncared for and unknown. The only energetic attempt to keep up with the civilized world in modern arts is made by the ladies; they devote thought and time ungrudgingly to the subject of dress. Paris fashions find their way here, while European science is at a discount. In few parts of the world, perhaps, would be needed the warning—

> "Let never maiden think, however fair,
> She is not fairer in new clothes than old;"

but nowhere is dress more criticised than in Peru. It is to be hoped that in process of time the necessities of personal adornment may be understood to extend beyond mere show, and that the abominable and most slovenly morning dishabille may be dropped, even at the expense of a little of the evening splendour.

The love of show breaks out in everything Peruvian; in the action of their horses as well as in the style of their dress. To an English eye there is little to admire in the majority of Peruvian horses. Many of the most showy animals are got up to look pretty, especially about the head and tail, but very few excel in the points to which we should look for beauty or utility. At the same time, a high-spirited horse is taught to throw his legs about in a manner perfectly unendurable, knocking them to pieces with a high flashy action, while progressing at the rate of two or three miles an hour. A Peruvian cavallero, riding up the street with cruel bit, cruel spurs, and splendidly useless mediæval trappings, presents an admirable picture of Spanish life; all show and no progress. All the best horses are taught to pace, a style of going which promotes the ease of the rider, but destroys the natural action of the horse. The pleasure of controlling by skill, with a light bit and a light hand, the free vigorous action of a high-mettled horse, would be unappreciated here.

One morning M—— and I sallied out to purchase the accoutrements necessary for our Sierra journey, an occupation that consumed the whole day. If you buy a bit at one shop, you must buy the head-stall at another, and the bridle at another; and it is not at all likely that you will get both saddle and stirrups at the same place. Everything is very dear; and as it is almost impossible to find out the real value of anything, a stranger is sure to pay too much. The custom is to ask an exorbitant sum, and then to request you to make an offer. As an Englishman has seldom the time or patience generally devoted to bargaining by a native, he is looked on as very good prey by the shopkeepers; and if he is not very careful, he is further mulcted by means of the current coin of the State. No Peruvian coinage is now current; as it was purer than that of the neighbouring republics, it was exported rapidly, and the present President won't coin any more. There is little gold in the country, very little small silver, and no copper. If you are going to make any purchases, you must drag about with you a bag of Bolivian half-dollars, or four-real pieces, which are accepted by the Government as legal tender. This Government sanction does not prevent the Minister of Finance from playing strange tricks now and then. The man now in office is a Colonel Salcedo, appointed by Castilla without the slightest regard to his financial knowledge. This worthy issues decrees from time to time, arbitrarily depreciating the current coin without notice. For instance, at the end of the last year, after the introduction into Peru of a large portion of the Bolivian coinage of that year, a decree appeared, suddenly declaring the four-real pieces of 1859 to be only worth three reals. A foreigner who innocently takes the coinage of 1859 in change, is astonished to find that he cannot pass it again without considerable loss. The Brazilian silver coinage is very bad, it is true; but it is not pretended that the issue of 1859 was worse than that of other years, which passes current with the sanction of the Peruvian Government. The notions entertained by the authorities, as to the laws of supply and demand, may be gathered from the fact, that one of the apologies for Castilla's projected war against Bolivia is, that Bolivian money continues to find its way into Peru.

Wherever Spain has ruled, she has left that invincible ignorance that will not be taught. Although the country is now open to foreigners, there still exists the old traditional dislike to learning anything from them. It remains to be seen what effect an increasing love of travel will have on the next generation of Peruvians; it may do something, but a large infusion of foreign blood would do still more. It is wonderful how little is known of the progress of modern civilization in the secondary towns of Peru—what strange ideas of history and geography are held even by men in high positions. A foreign nation is generally respected in proportion to the number of ships and guns that she displays upon the coast. The existence of any lands not thus represented appears very immaterial to the powers that be.

It is not merely with respect to foreign countries that there is a want of inquiry and knowledge. Scarcely any one whom I asked at Arequipa could tell me anything about Cuzco. The antiquities of the country would not tempt a Peruvian across the Sierra. It is only from a native of the place, or from some one who may have been brought there by serious business, military or civil, that a stranger is likely to gather any information as to the ancient capital. As for the rich montaña beyond, comprising more than two-thirds of the finest land in Peru, it is still unexplored, except by some adventurous foreigner who now and then penetrates into the primæval forest. Meanwhile the revenue is gambled away at Lima, and the labour of the country exhausted in disgraceful revolutions, and more disgraceful wars.

On the afternoon of the 22nd March, we left Arequipa accompanied by a gardener who was going into the montaña with M——. As the latter had to take a good deal of extra baggage for his expedition, we had a little troop of mules with us, driven by the arriero and his mozo. As the outfit for a journey in the Sierra is rather old-fashioned, I may as well describe the accoutrements of mule and man. First, as to the mule:—To an enormous bit is attached a heavy plaited bridle, with a thong at the end of it to serve as a whip. The saddle (like a chair, with very high pommel, and round high cantel) is perched upon a heap of saddle-clothes most unscientifically piled one upon another; on the saddle, again, is put a woollen *pillon*, or housing, covered in its turn by a leathern *sobre-pillon;* making, altogether, a tolerably easy seat. A crupper and breeching like those of a pack-horse are the necessary accompaniments of such an erection. Before you mount, you equip yourself in a picturesque, but, to an English eye, a somewhat outrageous fashion. A poncho of many colours; leggings red and green, or yellow; a brilliant woollen comforter; and a pair of brass spurs, with rowels an inch and a half in diameter, gave every man of the party somewhat the appearance of a Peruvian muleteer. W——, a steady Scotch gardener, was gorgeous with a poncho of red, green, and yellow stripes. Warm clothing is very necessary in the lofty passes of the Andes.

With regret we bade farewell to Arequipa, where we had met with great hospitality; and, leaving the volcano to the left, we reached the post-house of Cangallo in the evening. It is situated about twelve miles from Arequipa, in a little valley about 9,650 feet above the level of the sea. The accommodation at all the post-houses in the *Despoblado* is very bad. On this, the most frequented pass to Bolivia, there is not a hut with a decent floor to lay a bed on. I speak from experience when I say that I had rather sleep in the hut of a New Zealand savage, than in most Peruvian post-houses. In the morning we commenced a rapid ascent, winding slowly round the volcano, till we passed over the shoulder of that mountain at an elevation of about 12,600 feet, the beautiful cone rising above us about 6,000 feet higher. It was still covered with snow, for rain and snow were falling in the Sierra, and our journey was, consequently, less easy than it would have been a little later in the year. After losing sight of the volcano, the route lies over a very bleak tract of country. Still ascending, we reached Apo in the evening, not before the rain began to fall heavily. This is a post-house about twenty-four miles from Cangallo, and upwards of 14,000 feet above the level of the sea. The next morning we started at four o'clock, and after crossing several times the feeders of the river of Arequipa, we reached, before midday, the post-house of Pati, on a little green swampy plateau, just below a steep ascent. This place was so disgustingly dirty, that even the arriero suggested our camping outside, which we accordingly did, while a chupé was prepared for us in the house. M——, who was not very well at starting, had been attacked by the *sorochi* at Apo. The symptoms of this illness, which seizes a traveller at great heights, in consequence of the rarefication of the air, are a pressure on the temples, and a feeling somewhat akin to incipient sea-sickness. However, we had a long day's journey before us, and started again at about two o'clock. As we began the ascent, a violent storm of thunder, lightning, and hail overtook us. The effect of the storm, as it rolled over the wild sea of peaks, was more magnificent than pleasant, especially when it settled down into a thick fall of snow, as we reached the pampa which stretches to the foot of the Toledo pass. On this dreary pampa we saw a herd of vicuñas feeding. Although untameable, they did not appear very shy, for we passed them within gunshot.

The *Alto de Toledo* rises gradually out of the pampas; the ground was rotten from the effects of the snow, and sleet was falling thick; the peaks around were bleak and monotonous. Altogether it would be impossible to imagine a more dreary scene. As we reached the summit of the pass (about 15,600 feet above the level of the sea) I felt a slight touch of *sorochi*, and was very glad to descend rapidly on the other side, towards the post-house of Cuevillas. The snow had changed into a drizzling rain, and night had set in, as the sure-footed mules threaded their way along the edge of a torrent, into the valley below. Fortunately the loads on the baggage-mules had been well coated with snow on the heights, and the muleteers were thus able to distinguish them in the darkness. But before long it was found that a spare mule which accompanied them was missing. We insisted on pushing on to the post-house, which we reached late. We had ridden about fifty miles up and down rough and precipitous tracks, having been about seventeen hours in the saddle; and were disgusted to find that the post-house was even worse than usual. The clay floor was wet and dirty; and the only tolerably dry places were two little ledges, one on each side of the room. M—— and I rolled ourselves up on a mattress on one of these ledges, and W—— occupied the other. We got nothing to eat that night; and as we heard something about cows, we waited next morning till they drove in one, and milked it for us. It was after much trouble that the stolid Indians were persuaded to add this luxury to a very nasty chupé, which they gave us for breakfast.

From this place begin the upland grass valleys, stretching down the eastern slopes of the maritime Andes, on which flocks of merinos and alpacas are kept. Cows are to be found in the neighbourhood of some of the post-houses; but if you ask for milk, you are sure to be met with the favourite answer of the indolent people, "*No hai señor, no hai nada.*" By dint of importunity it may be sometimes got at, and M—— who knew the ways of the country, amused me by the pertinacity with which he insisted on its being produced. It rained till late that morning, so it was near ten o'clock when we got away. Before long we began a tedious ascent over swampy and broken ground till we reached the summit of the pass of Laquinillas. Descending, we passed between two sad, silent lakes, and skirting round the eastern one, followed the course of the stream that flows from it as far as the post-house of Compuerta. Here we stopped for the night, as the baggage mules had fallen behind, and it had begun to rain heavily. From La Compuerta the valleys are better grassed, and the sides of the mountains are covered with the ruins of the *Andeneria*, or terraced cultivations of the days of the Incas. These ruined terraces, that may be seen on every available mountain in the Andes, are silent witnesses to the density of the population that was once industriously employed in cultivating every habitable part of the country. Half-way between Compuerta and Vilque we began to meet with slovenly cultivations, and a few miles farther on passed through a poor looking Indian village. From thence, after crossing the low hills, the route to Vilque lies over a swampy plain, difficult to cross at this time of the year. In the middle of this plain stands a large hacienda, very much out of repair, which once belonged to the Jesuits. The energy, both spiritual and temporal, of this untiring but dangerous order, is to be traced in all parts of Peru.

As we approached Vilque, we heard the ominous military band, which warned us that the best accommodations would be pre-occupied. Here was stationed part of the frontier army that threatened Bolivia. Of all the filthy little towns I ever was in, I should unhesitatingly give the palm to Vilque, at least at this time of the year. As we rode up the narrow dirty streets, between the decayed mud and rubble houses, our mules sank to their hocks in the mud-holes. We had not expected good accommodations, but the room we got was worse than we could have imagined. Fancy a den without a window, with a dirty mud floor, damp, crumbling walls, and a filthy smell, the door of which den opened on a muddy, wet yard. It snowed hard in the night. In such a temperature, nearly 13,000 feet above the level of the sea, there was not the alternative of camping out, so we had to make the best of our lodging. The troops appeared to have eaten everything. We got some milk and bad bread by dint of bullying, the answer "*no hai*" being in full vogue at Vilque. This is the town where the great annual fair is held, at which there is a strange gathering of all sorts of people. Merchants from the coast meet the bark-hunters of the Montaña, and the muleteers of the Sierra buy their stock from the breeders of the Argentine provinces. Unfortunately it was too early in the year for us to hope to see this gathering, the only interesting sight about Vilque; and it was with great pleasure that we started for Puno the next morning. The end of the plain we had now to cross, was worse than the beginning. It was wonderful to see the mules drag themselves and their loads through the swampy streams that they had to pass every few yards. After leaving the plain we rode over a series of monotonous hills, where the shy *biscaches* were playing hide and seek among the rocks, till we were suddenly brought to a stand-still by the river Tortorini, at most times an insignificant stream, but now swelled into an impassable torrent. Riding down the river to look for a bridge, we came upon a beautiful waterfall, which the arrieros had never seen. We dismounted to get a better view, and our friends thought that the best way to get out of the present difficulty was to go to sleep, which they accordingly did. We soon roused them up, and from the brow of the hill below the waterfall, M—— discovered a narrow bridge near a *hacienda* in the valley below. Riding down the steep descent over the walls of ruined *Andeneria* to the cultivations beneath, we got a fine view of the waterfall from the little bridge. The first fall can scarcely be less than one hundred feet in depth, and from the ledge against which the water first strikes, the whitened stream rushes in beautiful rapids to the valley. After a rather long ascent over bare hills we came in sight of Lake Titicaca. But a small portion of this magnificent inland sea can be seen from one spot, the shores are so irregular, and the view is so much intercepted by barren islands. The surrounding mountains give it a wild and picturesque appearance, although the want of trees, and almost of vegetation, makes the shores wild and dreary. The softer beauties of a landscape cannot be looked for round a lake whose surface is 12,850 feet above the level of the sea. The bed of a natural watercourse forms the approach to the little town of Puno, and a rough approach it is to a provincial chief town. The rain began to fall heavily as we clattered up the narrow white streets, and we were glad to arrive at the house of a Peruvian gentleman, to whom we had brought letters, and who received us with the usual hospitality of the Sierra of Peru.

The town of Puno, containing about 8,000 inhabitants, rises on the sloping ground that encircles a small bay of the great inland sea of Titicaca. The houses, roofed either with thatch or red tiles, are for the most part poor, when compared with those of Arequipa, but the streets are cleaner and better kept than those of that city. It is a mournful-looking place, with little society, the majority of the population being Indian. A considerable traffic passes through the town both in wool and in the products of the Montaña. No boats of more modern construction than the *balsa* float on these waters. The Indian balsa is the same as that used in the time of the Incas, being made of bundles of reeds tied together; very much like the *moki* used by the New Zealanders for crossing rivers. As we floated on the lake of Titicaca, with a stolid, coca-chewing Indian in the stern, guiltless of Spanish, the ruined Andeneria on the hills above were not needed to remind us that this was the cradle of Inca civilization. From the shores of this lake came the founders of the wise and powerful dynasty who have left such gigantic records of their rule; who, while they studied the interests of the indolent Indian, knew how to make him work for himself and for the state; and whose fall was a death-blow to the progress of a race which has deteriorated under Spanish tyranny, and is deteriorating even more under the misrule of the Peruvian republic. But sailing in a balsa on Lake Titicaca, though pleasant enough while the sun shines, soon becomes cold work. In truth, the climate here, although healthy, is very unpleasant. The air is so highly rarefied that fires are not used; and in the cold houses people sit with hats on always, and cloaks very often. In the middle of the day it is cold in the shade, and out of it, the rays of the tropical sun strike down with unpleasant force.

A gentleman who now superintends the working of the Manto silver mine offered to show us what was to be seen there. Although not a league from the town, no one, except the Indians, ever dreams of walking so far, as the breath is unpleasantly caught in ascending any height; and when riding up the hill to the mouth of the upper mine, we stopped repeatedly to breathe the mules. The mines of Manto have a curious and tragical history. The first man who worked the vein, Salcedo, grew enormously rich; reason enough, in his day, for his being accused of treason on various trumped up charges; and in 1670, he was judicially murdered by the Viceroy, Count of Lemos. A signal instance of retributive justice has been found in the fact, that the vein which had enriched Salcedo was never found again. It was probably worked out. The mines never assumed a prosperous condition again till Mr. Begg, an Englishman, began to work them in 1827. However, in 1840, the men in power made the place too hot for him, and he left it, and died soon afterwards. Since Mr. Begg's death the works have languished year by year; and now the upper mine is worked as of old by Indians carrying up the stone and metal in baskets on their backs. The great works undertaken by the enterprise of Mr. Begg are at a stand-still, and the "English" works are shown rather as a monument of what has been than as a proof of what might be done. Mr. Begg got out a steam-engine, and built all the necessary apparatus for smelting the silver. He converted a subterranean drain into a canal half-a-mile long into the bowels of the hill; from the place where the canal terminates he laid down an iron tramway for another mile into the heart of the mountain, and the ore was carried on foot to the tramway from excavations extending 500 yards farther in. An Indian baled out a fast-decaying iron boat, in which we were conveyed underground to the first loch on the subterranean canal. A dismal navigation it is into the bowels of the earth; by the light of a torch in the bows, we could see when it was necessary to dip our heads low, as the boat was pushed along by the Indian under the vaulted roof of varying height, while the gunwales grated against the rocky sides of the narrow canal. Our Indian guide looked a very Charon, and no poet ever imagined a more doleful Styx. Many a rich freight of silver has been carried down this dark passage, and many a one may yet come down, provided foreigners interfere to inspire renewed enterprise and public confidence.

San Roman, a Grand Marshal of Peru, rather celebrated for treachery and running away in action, commands the army of the frontier, and has his head-quarters at Puno. The absurd pomp of the little military dignitaries of Peru seems to have attractions for the otherwise apathetic population; and whenever San Roman takes it into his head to burn gunpowder in honour of himself or his patron saint, the narrow streets are thronged by admiring spectators. He payed us a ceremonious visit, bringing with him an aide-de-camp, who dared not sit down without express leave from his chief. We heard from him some interesting details of the siege of Puno, in the last great Indian insurrection, previous to the war of independence. Two or three people at Puno talked more of the history of the country than any other people whom I met with in the Sierra. We went down every evening after dinner to take coffee at the house of an old gentleman, where it had become an established custom of our host and three or four other persons to meet at that time; and the conversation often turned on the historical associations of the neighbouring plateaus. I was pleased one night to hear an appreciation of the good qualities of the brave, cruel, faithful old rebel Carbajal, one of the very few Spaniards of the days of the conquest who stood firmly by a falling cause. Wicked and cruel as the old fellow was, this exceptional virtue deserves to be remembered. Señor C—— quoted, with a sort of affectionate regard, the favourite couplet of the ironical old soldier:—

"Estos mis cabellitos, madre
Dos a dos me los llevan en ayre."

This Señor C——, who is one of the most enterprising men in Peru, greatly lamented the want of energy and public faith which prevented the formation of a company to navigate the lake of Titicaca. It is a really wonderful apathy that neglects such a magnificent high-road, in a mountainous region, where every necessary of life is transported on mule-back by long and painful journeys. When steaming, a few months later, across one of the great lakes of North America, I could scarcely help thinking of Titicaca and its Indian balsas as a dream of a previous state of existence.

Very bad accounts reached Puno as to the state of the country between that town and Cuzco, owing to the incessant rains, which were compared, here as at Islay, to those of 1819. The rivers were out, and I was recommended to wait a little time at Puno for finer weather. But time pressed, and I determined to start at once. Unfortunately the weather and the state of the country prevented a visit to the ruins on an island at the southern end of the lake. At this time of the year, such a visit would have detained me too long.

At Puno, M—— and I parted, as he had to take the route for the Caravy valley. It was a dreary place for two Englishmen to part company in a semi-barbarous country.

On the 31st March I left Puno in light marching order, with four mules; one I rode myself, one the arriero rode, the third carried bed and baggage, and a spare mule for change trotted along with the others.

I did not get away till ten o'clock, thanks to my arriero, who made his appearance with different mules from those he had sworn to produce. Our route lay for four days along the high table-lands at the northern extremity of the lake between the two great ranges into which the Andes are here divided. The country was, indeed, as we had been told, frightfully wet, and a great part of the day's work was wading through mud and water, and swamp. There was nothing for it but to harden our hearts and use our spurs. We had not gone far when I discovered that my arriero, Mariano by name, had never been on this route before, although he had declared solemnly that he knew every foot of it, so I was obliged to hire Indians from place to place to run with us as guides. The Indian *postillon* will run all day with no other refreshment than chewing coca leaves, which he carries in a small pouch, tied round his neck. I may say, parenthetically, that I had by this time got over feeling any surprise at a lie more or less in the day's work. Mariano was a highly respected citizen of Arequipa; but he looked on the epithet *mentiroso* as a term of endearment; and, as he constantly deserved it, he was kind enough not to mind it in the least. The only thing he really did mind was a plan I adopted later, of making him get up an hour earlier to saddle the mules, when he had indulged the day before in any lie more mischievous than usual. This plan afforded the double satisfaction of punishing him and of expediting the journey.

It would be but a monotonous repetition to describe the various miserable *pueblos* through which we passed. A grass-grown plaza with a church on one side of it, and houses of adobes more or less ruinous on the other, with dirty streets, or rather lanes, leading from this centre; such are the leading features of a small Peruvian town. The crops in this part of the country looked very cold and wet. There was no attempt at drainage or fencing, and in many places the only thing grown was *quinua*, a small grain something like millet, which grows at an astonishing elevation; but, as the soil got drier, potatoes and barley were to be seen here and there. I slept the first night at Juliaca, where the tambo was a little better than usual, the clay floor being matted; but the people were very dirty and indolent, and I started at seven o'clock the next morning without getting anything to eat. The look of the country improved till we reached a river that we had to cross on balsas, our mules swimming. Many Indians, both men and women, were crossing the river, kneeling one behind the other, in the narrow balsas; and the little boats with their freights looked picturesque enough, as they shot down the stream towards the opposite bank. These Indians appeared to be of a superior race to those nearer the coast; the men were intelligent and well-built, and the clothes of both sexes were warm and comfortable. The men wore long, thick woollen jackets, and strong black breeches open at the knee. The women, coloured bodices, with petticoats of a sort of thick warm baize, reaching below the knee, and stout mantles of the same material. The low cloth hats of both men and women from this to Cuzco, are round and broad-brimmed; whereas at Puno they were square-topped: those of the women are often ornamented with gold and silver lace.

Swampy plains succeed the pretty valley through which the river runs. At the top of one of these plains, on the slope of a hill, lies the town of Lampas. It was full of soldiers, the third division of the army of the frontier being quartered here. The plaza was alive with market-women and soldiers, and sentries were posted at every corner of the square. On inquiry, I heard that the poor Indian lads who composed the rank and file were turned into the plaza under guard for four hours every day; and that they were locked up in barracks for the rest of the twenty-four hours. Desertion had been frequent among these kidnapped recruits, and the severest measures were taken to put a stop to it.

Everywhere there are the same complaints of the roads and the weather. A Spanish merchant, whom M—— and I left at Cangallo, had reached this place without his mules, and he had heard nothing of them for ten days. On the evening I was at Lampas, one of his muleteers appeared to inform him that they had been obliged to leave some of the mules, and to unload others. No wonder foreign luxuries are scarce and dear in the Sierra.

The Government of Peru, such as it is, is a pure centralism. Prefects and sub-prefects exercise a delegated authority in provinces and districts; and under them again the chief man in a village or small town receives a commission as Governor. This dignitary is generally very illiterate, and sometimes tyrannical. He is, perhaps, proud of having a little more "white" blood in his veins than most of the villagers, for nowhere is there a more distinctly organized aristocracy of colour than in the Sierra. A man of very doubtful caste thinks himself quite justified in striking or otherwise mal-treating "un Indio," a mere Indian. There is a second authority in the village, the "alcalde," who is chosen from among the Indians, and acts as a magistrate in Indian affairs. As far as I could judge, he is in most cases a mere tool and servant of the Governor. At Pucara the alcalde waited upon me as a sort of uncivilized "boots," by order of the big man of the village, at whose house I slept one night. The alcalde carries a staff of office, adorned by silver rings, which denote by their number the length of time he has held his appointment.

I must for the rest of the route confine myself to extracts from my notes. The reader will understand from previous details the general style of accommodation and food, and the obstructions occasioned by arrieros and others. To travel fast, a certain amount of coercion is necessary.

Early Start from Pucara.—By dint of perseverance I got Mariano up by three o'clock, and started with an Indian guide to show us the way out. If it had not been for the intense cold, these early rides in the Sierra would have been most enjoyable. At no time is the imagination more excited than when riding up an unknown valley, as the first streak of dawn appears in the eastern sky; when the dark outlines of the mysterious mountains are struggling into light, one by one, out of the darker mass of peaks behind. But the cold at such an altitude, before the sun rises, is very severe, so that the first rays of the tropical sun are gladly welcomed in a scene of almost Arctic desolation.

Pass of Agua Caliente.—It was a delightful prospect, to exchange those dreary uplands, with their ruinous villages and miserable-looking inhabitants, for the traditionally beautiful valley beyond them. By the first streak of dawn we were in the saddle, and reached the summit of the pass by a winding defile, eighteen miles long. The still, snow-capped mountains rose on either hand in wild and desolate beauty. The pass bore that utterly sad and lonely appearance which characterises the heights of the Andes above those of all other mountains I have ever seen. Down by another defile like that by which we ascended,—past a ruined hacienda, near which the hot spring that gives a name to the pass bursts out of the ground, and at last, towards evening, the first cultivations are reached, and the glory of the valley of Vilca-mayu first breaks on the eye.

The Temple and Palace of Viracocha.—The part still standing, consists of a massive wall, with a portion of another at right-angles to it at the upper end. These walls are built of stone, to the height of eight or nine feet, and above that height, of adobes. The main wall is about five feet and a half thick, and must have been at least 300 feet long, and 40 feet high. One pillar of the same construction stands at one side of this wall, at the lower end of the building, and the foundation of another at the other side. It was evidently a magnificent pile that was built by the prophet Inca in his favourite retreat. Standing there, with the history of the unhappy Indian race fresh in my mind,—with one of them beside me, looking depressed and mournful as usual,—I could not but compare the sad prescience that haunted Viracocha, and the subsequent fulfilment of his dreams, to the artistic development of a Greek tragedy. But no legend of an angry Apollo,—no poetical phantoms come between us and the Cassandra-like seer, as he mourned the approaching servitude of his countrymen, with the bitter, hopeless feeling of the Trojan prophetess :—

> "Das Verhängte muss geschehen,
> Das Gefürchtete muss nahn."

Checacupi to Urcos.—The next fifteen miles of the journey is through the same exquisite scenery. Every step in this valley, every turn in the mountain-hemmed river, introduces some fresh beauty. Droves of mules and llamas laden with merchandise for Cuzco, and Indians driving down their cows by precipitous tracks on the mountain-side, give life to the picture. For the first time in Peru, I understood the rapture with which some travellers have spoken of Peruvian scenery. At Quiquihana, the river is crossed by a good stone bridge, and immediately below the village plunges into a narrow gorge which I shall not easily forget. For some distance there is again only room for the narrow track and the foaming river, while as the gorge opens, the *molle* and the willow, interspersed with the fantastic cactus, fringe the path. After following many windings, and passing some small villages, we turned off at Urcos from the main valley. Here the track cuts off a bend of the river, by going over a hill to the little village of Huaruc, about a mile distant from Urcos. In this little town of Urcos, Almagro rested his shattered army on his return from Chili, previous to his seizure of Cuzco. And into the little lake between Urcos and Huaruc, tradition says that the famous Inca chain was thrown, to conceal it from the Spaniards. As I rode by the gloomy tarn, my arriero solemnly told me how, on every Good Friday, at one o'clock in the afternoon, the chain appears to the Indians, though no white man is permitted to see it.

Cuzco.—The traveller approaches Cuzco by a gradual ascent, in the course of which the scene becomes more and more bleak. He first comes in sight of the city at a distance of about five miles, as it stands at the head of the valley, and at the foot of the surrounding mountains. With what different feelings men have reached this spot on their march from the valleys below. Sovereign Incas, or their generals, returning in triumph with their conquering armies from the south and east, home to the royal city; Spaniards eagerly engaged in their manifold intestine feuds, marching upon the capital; and saddest approach of all, Tupac Amaru, the last worthy descendant of a kingly race, borne along, bound hand and foot, to suffer death in the city of his ancestors.

Cuzco is on the whole the most melancholy city that I can conceive to be in the whole world. Numbering, according to the Spanish chronicle, 200,000 inhabitants at the time of the Conquest, it now does not contain more than 20,000: the streets are dirty, the plazas are grass-grown, and the still beautiful cloisters of La Merced are falling into premature decay. Still, to the antiquary, few cities present so many monuments of a state of society wholly passed away. The sad-looking Indian, in his old-fashioned, picturesque dress, stares at a European riding up the street, as though he had dropped from the moon; while the latter gazes just as curiously at the masonry of old Inca palaces and temples that form the foundations of more modern buildings.

Besides the colossal masonry still standing in many of the narrow streets of the city, the principal objects of interest are the church of Santo Domingo, and the ruins on the hill of Sacsahuaman. In the church of Santo Domingo the stones of the old temple of the sun reach about twelve feet from the ground, and above this the Spanish masonry provokes invidious comparisons. Although the European used mortar, and the Indian none, nowhere in Peru can modern masonry bear comparison with the beautifully fitted work of the ancients. To this day the engineer is puzzled to account for the power of the Indians in dealing with immense masses. We know of no machinery adequate to the purpose in use by them; the conquerors have left no hint of such appliances. The Inca historian, Garcilasso de la Vega, is silent on the subject, and yet in many places are seen traces of stonework which might reasonably be supposed too large to have been put together by unassisted human strength. Almost the first work of the Spaniards after the capture of Cuzco, was to convert the temple of the sun into a church, and thus to this day the sacred building of the Incas is still held sacred by their descendants, and those of their conquerors.

But by far the most striking feature of the ancient capital is the hill Sacsahuaman, on which once stood the fortress defended against the assaults of the Spaniards with such devoted courage. The gigantic, closely-fitted stones of the zig-zag defences are still unmoved, and the summit of the hill is crowned by traces of the great stronghold. The hill itself is a very remarkable one, rising as it does precipitously out of the valley, and commanding an excellent bird's-eye view of Cuzco and its neighbourhood. Looking up from the grand plaza, in which the Spaniards were camped during the attack on the fortress, one can easily appreciate the absolute necessity for reducing a citadel that hung so directly over the town.

Wherever you walk through the city, you are reminded of the past; never is there a trace of hope for its future. On one side of the plaza, the Cathedral stands on the site of the palace of Inca Viracocha, on the other side stands the house said to have been inhabited by Almagro; half-way up the hill of the fortress are the ruins of the palace of Huanco Capac, and higher up are seats cut out of the rocks in times immemorial. But Cuzco is situated where no modern ruler would have built a city; war and persecution, and slavery and plague, have reduced the inhabitants from time to time; and if it were not for a few foreigners, and a very few studious men in the venerable cloisters, the memory of its local traditions would pass away for ever. The so-called museum is a disgrace to the authorities. Most of the valuable antiquities have been stolen, and the rooms are filled with rubbish—full-length portraits and other memorials of modern celebrities, robbers more or less successful of the free and independent republic.

Prescott, who, in his description of a country that he never saw, is astonishingly accurate, has, I think, in his account of the former magnificence of Cuzco, been somewhat led away by the first glowing descriptions of the Spaniards. The masonry of the low and gloomy buildings was doubtless very fine, and the interiors blazed with gold; but the low, thatched roofs, the windowless walls, and the narrow streets, or rather lanes, must have destroyed the effect of the massive architecture. Both at Pachacamac, and in Cuzco, wherever any traces of Inca building are found on both sides of the street, it struck me how gloomy the thoroughfares must have been in the most palmy days of old Peruvian cities.

The Sierra rains had not ceased when I arrived at Cuzco, and the climate was cold and comfortless in the extreme. The houses are all built as if for a tropical climate, in a town more than 11,000 feet above the level of the sea, with dark rooms opening on patios or on balconies running round and overlooking them. Fireplaces are unknown, so people sit and shiver in the house with cloaks and hats on, as at Puno, miserable to be seen. There appeared to me to be a positive prejudice against the use of water for purposes of ablution.

The most pleasing feature of society at Cuzco is the great civility shown to a stranger. I brought letters to the Prefect and to one or two of the leading persons in the town, and received from them the greatest hospitality and attention during my visit. But there was another feature of Peruvian life that raised my indignation in Cuzco, as it did elsewhere in this wretchedly governed country. The town swarmed with soldiers: aides-de-camp and officers were perpetually hanging about the Prefect's house, and the ancient cloisters of the Jesuits had been turned into barracks, in which the poor Indian soldiers were confined. When I saw something of the conscription, my indignation was redoubled. I knew that it was arbitrary and illegal, and that the Indian ran and hid himself at the sight of a soldier, as in the old days of the *Mita* he would have fled at the sight of a Spanish official; but I did not realize the whole villany of the system till I saw it put in force. One morning I was talking to the Prefect in the balcony of the prefecture overlooking the court-yard, when a party of wretched-looking creatures in ragged ponchos were marched bound into the patio, and drawn up for inspection. They were recruits, and the Prefect went down to examine them one by one, while the victims eagerly pointed out any infirmity they might be happy enough to suffer from. While this was going on, I asked the aide-de-camp how they were chosen. He explained that the troops surround the houses of the Indians when they are asleep, and bind and carry off those likely to be fit for service.

"Without notice?"

"O yes! without notice; they hate the service so much, that we should never get any soldiers without surprising them."

"Then no Indian when he goes to sleep among his friends knows whether he may be seized or not in the night?"

"Not when we want soldiers."

"Surely this is not in accordance with the laws of the republic?"

"No!" (shrugging his shoulders); "but the Government must have soldiers."

That is to say, that the robber, who for the time being holds supreme power, can use the army as he likes, to oppress the citizens of the republic. And these are the uses to which the independence has been degraded; the independence for which so many brave men died, and for which the eloquence of Canning enlisted the sympathies of the civilized world.

As I was anxious to descend again into the valley of Vilca-mayu to visit Yucay and the remains of the unfinished fortress of Ollantay-tambo, the Prefect furnished me with letters to the governors of the villages through which I was to pass, and allowed one of his aides-de-camp, who was a native of Yucay, to accompany me. Leaving the fortress of Cuzco to the right, we passed over a very wild, bleak country, to the village of Chinchero, where the church is surrounded by the ruined walls of a great Inca palace. The descent from Chinchero, by a precipitous *cuesta*, into the valley of Yucay is surpassingly beautiful; but it was not until we had passed the little village of Urquillos, that I understood the charm that Yucay had for the Inca kings, far beyond that of the royal city, seated in all its splendour on the cold upland. We crossed the river at Huaylabamba by a bridge of *sogas*, or ropes, made of twisted fibres, brought from the forests below in the Montaña, and suspended across the stream: such a bridge as has probably been suspended here since the days of Indian rule. However well calculated for foot-passengers, these bridges are certainly rather dangerous for horses, especially when old and worn as this was. When leading my horse across, he put his foot through the ropes once and stumbled, swinging the crazy bridge most ominously. I let go the rein, and got out of his way, in order to let him go overboard alone; however, he seemed used to it, and recovered himself without being much frightened. A quarter of an hour's ride on the other side of the river brought us to the village of Yucay. Here the Inca sovereigns enjoyed all the beauties and the pleasures of the happy valley of Rasselas. Indeed, the scenery is exactly such as I have always imagined to be described in the most poetic vision of the sober Johnson. The bold and precipitous mountains appear to close in on either side of the luxuriant valley; and yet when the Incas reposed here in state, they received almost hourly communications from the extreme boundaries of the, to them, known world. It was the happy valley without its drawback, and the Rasselas was a Ulysses who had seen the manners of many men and their cities.

Ollantay Tambo.—The Governor at Urubamba had horses ready for us, and we rode on by moonlight to Ollantay Tambo (road by river). At dawn we went to examine the remains of the fortress, which was as unique in conception, as the history of the Peruvian Incas is unique in the records of the world. To this spot in the valley, where the mountains close in on either hand, the rebel Inca, Ollantay, fled, and here determined to make his final stand against the royal house of Cuzco. Ollantay was no mere insurgent, in arms one day, to be put down the next; the massive works begun here, testify to his having been an *ἄναξ ἀνδρῶν* on a large scale. Here, as elsewhere in Peru, the first question that suggests itself is, "How, even with the help of myriads of slaves, could these stones have been hewn out and raised to their present position?" On the right bank of the river, the mountain side is built up into a gigantic flight of *andenes*, or terraces, which serve as the foundation for the fortress destined to frown over the valley. The position, and the massive rocks of which the building is composed, might long bid defiance to modern arms; how utterly impregnable must the proposed stronghold have appeared in the eyes of the Incarian armies! When Ollantay was betrayed into the hands of the Inca Yupanqui, the work ceased, but the remains of "the wall he was raising to last for ever,"* still seem calculated, so far as possible for mortal's work, to defy the ravages of time. The gigantic blocks of granite that are so wonderfully cut out, and fitted together so closely, were brought (let engineers tell us how) from the quarry on the other side of the valley, some five miles down the stream. Two or three similar blocks, called "*piedras cansadas*," lie carved and fashioned, midway between the quarry and the building, as though the works had but lately been brought to a sudden end. Some of the stones in position are more than twelve feet high, while one of the *piedras cansadas* is upwards of twenty feet long by fifteen broad, and nearly four deep. Many half-hewn stones are lying about the building, and one almost expects to find the mason's tools lying beside them. While examining these stones, I found a clue to the manner in which they were patiently wrought into shape. From the bottom of one of them, to the edge of the cliff near which it lies, runs a little stone trough, as though to carry off the water used in rubbing down the surfaces with stone or sand. This must have been slow work, kept up by constant relays of patient slaves; but the direction of these slaves must have been in the hands of enterprising and skilful Engineers.

Remnants of heavy masonry are to be found in the village which is separated from the fortress by the ravine and stream of Marca-cocha. In this ravine are marvellous seats and broad steps cut out in the solid rock: and far above on the mountain side, are remains of what is said to have been a convent of Virgins of the Sun. Near the convent a small tower above a precipice marks the spot whence criminals were hurled in the days of Ollantay. The place is far more suggestive of instant death than the Tarpeian rock of fatal celebrity.

* A sketch of a Peruvian drama on this subject, originally written in the Quichua tongue and apparently contemporaneous with the Incas, is given in Mr. Markham's work. Several extracts translated by him, give a high idea of the dramatic capacity of the author.

On our return, we passed again through Urubamba, the fruit-garden of Cuzco; and, ascending from the valley, we rode on till darkness compelled us to attempt sleep in an Indian hut. After a few hours, we went on by moonlight, and re-entered Cuzco a little after dawn, in torrents of rain.

There were great complaints at Cuzco of the unprecedented continuance of the rainy season. I should certainly advise a traveller to make sure of fine weather in these high regions, by starting a month later than I did. Snow and rain make the mountain travelling unnecessarily severe.

Setting out on my return to Arequipa, I went up the valley of Vilca-mayu, as far as Tinta; and, striking off here, crossed the Despoblado, by the pass of Rumi-huasi. A swampy, dreary country, gradually growing higher and colder, stretches to the foot of the pass. Over these wastes I rode from before dawn till after dark, for two days.

A few miles beyond Ocaruru we got post-mules, after some threats (brutum fulmen) as to what I would get the Prefect to do to the post-master. After many solemn asseverations that there were none, they were produced at last, such as they were. The one my arriero rode nearly died in the ascent. The saddle was transferred to one of our own mules, and the poor beast, thus relieved, managed to stagger to the summit of the pass, 17,700 feet above the level of the sea. If it were not a bore to be always repeating that the Peruvian postas are a disgrace to the country, I would draw special attention to the miserable hut on Rumi-huasi, the highest habitation in the world. On the top of this pass we were half blinded by a heavy fall of snow that drove directly in our faces. The descent is more gradual than the ascent on the other side.

The Volcano of Arequipa again.—Since yesterday the beautiful cone of the volcano of Arequipa and the range of Chacani had been in sight from time to time, appearing and disappearing as I passed from height to hollow. They were like old friends, and certainly no other mountains in that part of the Andes which I had traversed equals in beauty the volcano of Arequipa. From whatever point of view you see it, the cone is perfect, and stands out in fine contrast to the rugged summits of its neighbour, Chacani. As a general rule the mountain scenery in Peru is on too gigantic a scale to enable one to appreciate it. You have to travel over vast wastes before you come upon the lovely spots that nestle in the recesses of the great Sierra. Putting aside such limited scenes as those in the valley of Vilca-mayu, or the campiña of Arequipa, the most striking general view of the mountains that I can recollect, is from the middle of the desert of Islay. But let no one expect in a tropical climate the more varied effects of European mountain scenery. Out of the temperate zones is found no Monte Rosa, "hanging there,"—

> "Faintly flushing, phantom fair,
> A thousand shadowy pencilled valleys
> And snowy dells in a golden air."

The traveller rises so gradually towards what appears to be the base of the gigantic range, that without being aware of it, he has already passed out of the region of the most beautiful vegetation, and the scene has become bare, and cold, and desolate; whereas, among mountains on a smaller scale, you can approach their boldest passes before you have bid farewell to tree, and flower, and grass. But what is lost in beauty is gained in a conception of grandeur and vastness. Never till you have travelled painfully day after day over some small portion of the far-stretching Andes will you understand what a barrier they are; on what a scale the mountain masses are piled together; or that the vast and desolate pampas over which you have been riding, are simply the dreary gradients to mountain tops that roll away as far as you can see. And as you ascend the highest passes, still far above you rise the snow-capped peaks untrodden and perhaps unapproachable for ever.

I spent a couple of days in Arequipa, and enjoyed especially the walk down along the river, through the rich cultivations towards the village of Tingo. An Italian opera in the quaint roofless theatre was an unexpected luxury. The singing was very good, and the strange old theatre, with its temporary roof of canvas, looked wonderfully well, and did wonderful justice to the singers. The inhabitants of Arequipa, as well as of Lima, are very fond of music; and this taste they are prepared to gratify at any cost.

A little after noon, on the 21st of April, I started for Islay, and riding through the night, with a pause of three or four hours at the tambo of La Joya, in the middle of the desert, reached Islay at daybreak the next morning. It was strange enough to be avoiding, as much as possible, the parching heat of a tropical desert, when only a week before, on Rumi-huasi, no clothing would keep out the penetrating cold of rain and snow in a rarefied atmosphere. Now that the journey was over, my arriero Mariano had become wonderfully well pleased with himself and with me. He came on to Islay, and after great professions of friendship, carried off the *alforjas* I forgot to take off the mule, and then asked me to give him as a keepsake my *espuelitas* (little spurs); a curious use, by-the-bye, of the diminutive, seeing that the said spurs had rowels about an inch and a half in diameter. But the use of the diminutive is very frequent, and often very childish. Every lady, never mind her age, is *señorita*, never *señora*, unless, indeed, for a year or two after marriage, as a distinction. No one is ever going to do a thing in a moment, *momentito* is the largest portion of time any one will keep you; and *hasta cada momentito* is an exaggeratedly polite form of leave-taking. If I told Mariano at a village to try to get some *caldo*, or broth (made with eggs, sometimes the food easiest procured), he would make a request for *caldito*, as if that in some way lessened or softened the demand. If a thing was to be done early, they would say *tempranito*, not *temprano;* in order not to shock their lazy nerves, I suppose. And in the same way, when possible, a diminutive is substituted for the vulgar whole. I do not now allude to affectionate diminutives in family life; these are often very pretty; and the flexibility of the Spanish language in forming pet names is very graceful. But it is strange how Peruvians try to take the edge off a downright statement.

On the morning of the 22nd, the fine English mail-steamer, with a punctuality that told of another race, put in at Islay; and after a pleasant passage along the coast on a smooth sea, I reached Callao on the evening of the 25th.

The population of Lima was just beginning to recover from a most desperate fright. Some severe shocks of earthquake had shaken down several houses, and cracked and rendered dangerous many others. A large proportion of the inhabitants had spent two or three nights in the open air, and the days in going in procession to the shrines of all the saints who were expected to interfere in the matter of earthquakes. These processions, I was told, were very efficacious, as the earthquakes had ceased; whereby the reputation of the one or two particular saints was greatly increased.

I spent a couple of days in Lima very pleasantly, and was about to leave for Callao on the 27th, to join the steamer for the north, when I was detained for a while by an event very characteristic of the country. I was talking to a friend at his hotel, when a loud explosion was heard in the street, which in an instant was filled by a curious crowd. We first thought that a revolution had broken out,—this would have been a natural occurrence,—but heard directly afterwards that an attempt had been made to blow up the house of a wealthy citizen with a sort of clumsy infernal machine. The crime of the proposed victim was the possession of wealth, and the immediate cause of this attempt was, that he had not answered threatening letters requiring him to send money to places named. The would-be assassin knew that, if taken, nothing very serious would happen to him. (The republic of Peru is so much in advance of its age, that its legislature abolished capital punishment. This was one of the sentimental steps which has been considered more useful than practical progress. I would invite the attention of English philanthropists to the remarkable success of the Peruvian experiment.) But as it was necessary that a show of zeal should be made by the authorities, and as in a South American republic, the convenience of peaceable citizens need not be consulted, a guard was placed at the door of each of the hotels, with orders to let no one out. Thus a double purpose was served. A fuss was made in the town, and every reasonable chance of escape was given to the criminal, who was not likely to be at any of the hotels. After keeping the inmates of the hotels prisoners during pleasure, the authorities took the guards off, and I was enabled to catch the train to Callao, and the steamer for the north. In the evening we sailed for Guayaquil *en route* for Panama.

THE GRAIAN ALPS,
To illustrate a Paper by J. J. Cowell, Esq[re]

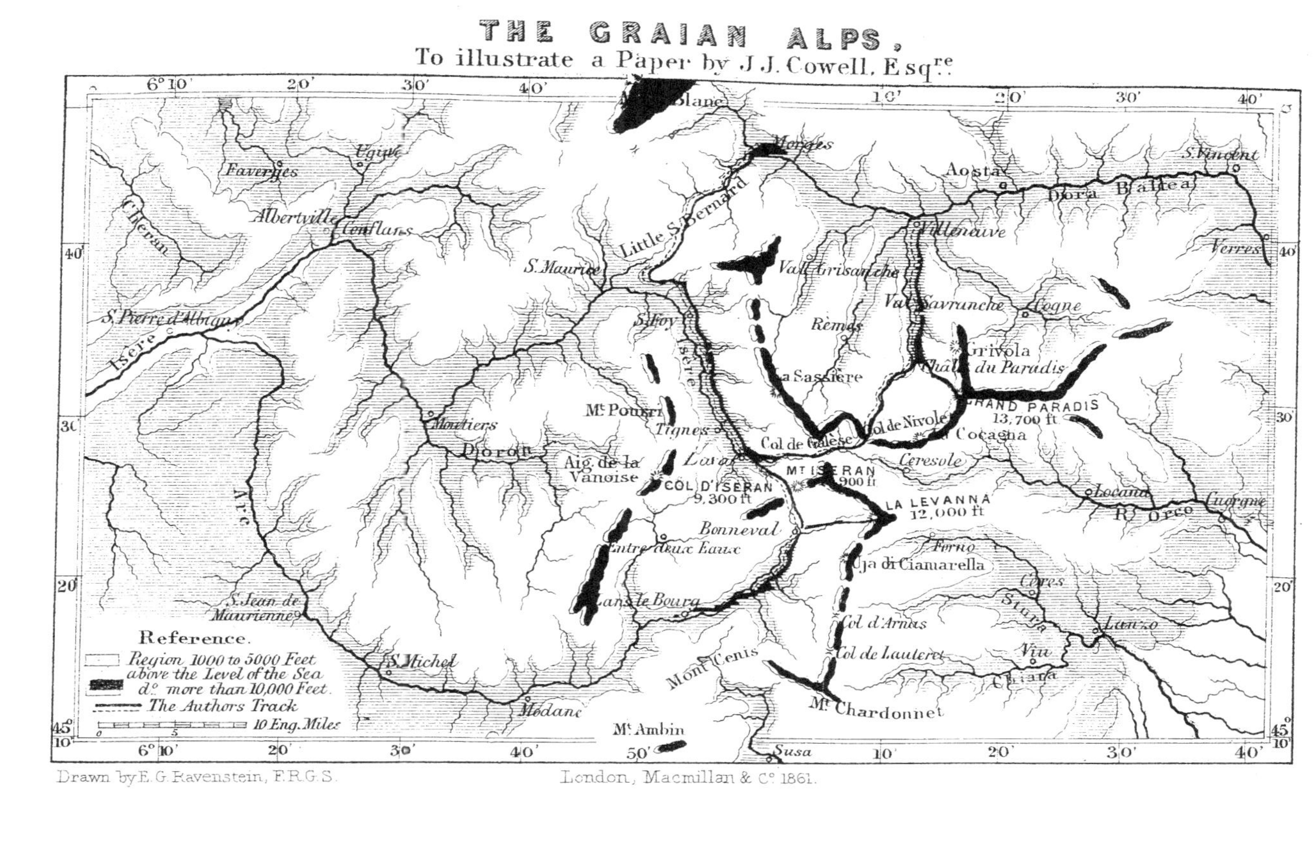

Drawn by E. G. Ravenstein, F.R.G.S.

London, Macmillan & C° 1861.

6. *THE GRAIAN ALPS AND MOUNT ISERAN.*

BY J. J. COWELL, ESQ.

DURING the autumn of 1859, I happened to obtain a very fine and unclouded view of the mountains to the south of Mont Blanc, and finding that little was known about them, determined to visit them in the following summer. Unluckily, however, 1860 proved to be, as everybody knows, a bad year for explorers, and I only half-executed my project, owing to repeated interruptions caused by bad weather.

Before leaving England, I consulted every available map, provided myself with the new Sardinian Ordnance Maps, and took with me my boiling-point thermometer. Finally, I wrote to my trusty guide, Michel Payot, at Chamouni, to tell him to meet me at Cormayeur, on the 26th of August.

It will render the account of our travels more intelligible if I give a general description of the region in which they lay. Its most important feature is, of course, the main range of the Graian Alps, by which the waters are divided; next in order should be placed the two principal valleys, one on each side of the range, in which the greater part of these waters are collected. They are the valley of the Dora Battea, commonly called the Val d'Aosta, on the Italian side; and the Valley of the Isère, on the French side; and they may both be conceived to descend from the Little St. Bernard, which bounds our part of the chain, to the north. On the French side, the tributary valleys are long, and run parallel to the main range, while on the Italian and steepest side of the range they are short, and abut directly against it; these latter are the Val Grisanche, Val de Rhèmes, Val Savranche, all opening into the Val d'Aosta, and the Val de Ceresole, Val Forno, and two others, opening directly into the plain. An important Col, namely, the Col de la Croix de Nivolet, connects the heads of the Val Savranche and the Val de Ceresole. So much for the Italian side.

Now, on the French side, the tributary valleys are only two ; the Val de Tignes, which runs up from the foot of the Little St. Bernard towards the south ; and the Val d'Arc, which runs up from St. Jean de Maurienne, first to the east and then to the north, towards the head of the Val de Tignes, with which it is connected by the Col d'Iseran. The Col d'Iseran is just opposite the Col de la Croix de Nivolet, on the other side of the main range, which is here crossed by the Col de Galèse.

This is a rough description of the country, but it may, perhaps, prove a better guide than most of the ordinary maps, in which these parts are slurred over. My general plan was to cross by the Col de Galèse to Savoy, on which side the slopes of the mountains are more gradual and easy of ascent, and there to climb any high peak that might tempt me, and especially to make trial of the Levanna and Mont Iseran, both of which I had heard were inaccessible ; Mont Iseran being generally described as having a needle-like point that tapers to a height of more than 13,000 feet.

On Monday, Sep. 3, we left Villeneuve, and ascended to the head of the Val Savranche, where we spent the following day. When we started on Sep. 5, we were obliged to take a guide as far as the Châlets de Nivolet, because the first part of the road to them, was not included in my sheet of the Ordnance Map, by help of which we usually found our way. We went a little way down the valley, and then turned to the left, up a very steep zig-zag path which led us to the beginning of a long "plateau," called the Plan de Nivolet. This has an elevation of, I should say, nearly 7,000 feet, and is consequently very bare and barren ; but its aspect is improved by a chain of small picturesque lakes which occupy half of its length.

On that edge of the plateau which overhangs the Val Savranche, stands the cross, or Croix de Nivolet, that gives its name to the Col.

Near here, the guide told us his father had been attacked by a highwayman, and had run for his life all the way down the zigzag path, till he reached a house in the valley below; the robber, he said, was a Piedmontese. Hereupon, both my companions began to revile the Piedmontese in general, and to tell lively stories about their way of murdering, robbing, and so forth. This surprised me; but I found out that by "Piémontais" they meant only the people of the Val de Ceresole, and the three valleys to the south of it, in opposition to the people of the Val d'Aosta and its tributary valleys, whom they eulogized as "Valaisans," a name which I had never heard applied on that side of the Alps. The guide declared that in the territories of these Piémontais solitary travellers were often waylaid; and Payot said that some Chamouni men travelling in the Val de Ceresole had been attacked by a gang in the open day.

No other accident befell us than that we were benighted; nevertheless, being benighted on a mountain path is very unpleasant, as one constantly knocks one's feet against the great stones that are sure to be sticking up, and one takes long steps where one ought to take short ones, and *vice versâ.* We found the path overflowed in several places, and our progress was often interrupted:—at length the guide announced he could find the track no longer. The consequence was, that for nearly an hour we went dabbling on over land and water, leaping the pools by help of our alpenstocks, and trusting to luck for a firm footing beyond; fortunately, I never fell down on any of these occasions, though my knapsack made me feel very top-heavy. By the time we reached the Châlets de Nivolet, we had had enough, and were glad to dry ourselves before a good fire. I was the least sufferer of the party, as my leather leggings had protected me from wet and mud; and all I had to do was to take off boots and leggings, and put on my slippers, while Payot had to dry his legs elaborately before he could make himself comfortable; so I unhandsomely took advantage of the opportunity, and preached to him upon the utility of leggings.

The châlet belonged to a family of brothers, who received us kindly; they all spoke French, and I chatted with some of them, learning all I could about the geography of the surrounding district. Their châlet was distant from Villeneuve, in the Val d'Aosta, seven hours and a half; from Ceresole, four; and from Laval, in the Val de Tignes, seven, by the Col de Galèse, over which one of our hosts agreed to guide us on the following day.

When we came in, they were preparing their supper in an immense copper pot, which we found to contain "polenta." Though this compound must be well known to travellers in Italy, it was new to me, and I shall hazard only one remark upon it; it is not bad when hot, but it is very nasty, and I think unwholesome, when cold. I ate mine with hot milk. Afterwards they took us to a snug-looking stone cottage, close by, where I thought we should sleep—but no! it would not be ready till next year, as unfortunately it had no roof. They only wanted to show it to us: we should have to sleep over the cows this year. So we climbed up a ladder into a hay-loft, under which were not only the cows, but the cows bells, which kept up a steady jingle, as their wearers went on placidly munching, all night. Whether cows in general, or whether only these particular cows, remain awake and munch; or whether they go to sleep and still munch, I do not know; but I am sure that in some way or another the ringing was constantly maintained. In other respects I was comfortable, by help of hay, of my warm plaid, and of a pair of straps, which last articles I consider essential whenever one sleeps in one's clothes. I was agreeably surprised at finding myself exempt from the attacks of certain objectionable insects that are supposed to abound in hay: there were none in any of the châlets.

On Thursday morning, when I started, as usual, in search of the nearest rill, it was snowing, and everything around looked so cold and miserable, that only the practice acquired by tubbing in cold water on frosty mornings, could have enabled me to persevere with my toilet under such discouragement. When this fearful task was over, I considered what was to be done. Should I try to get to Laval over the Col de Galèse? On the one hand, it was entirely contrary to my principles to attempt a glacier pass in bad weather, as such a proceeding is disagreeable, unprofitable, and frequently dangerous. But I was tired of sleeping on hay; we had only one day's provisions left; waiting would be disagreeable; and as our guide declared the glacier to be as easy as possible, and only half a mile across, I determined to try it, though I saw from the account in Murray that we might meet with some difficulties. We made haste to prepare a breakfast of hot wine and bread—a plan taught me by Payot. We usually took it when we expected hard work or cold. The wine is heated with sugar and cinnamon, and forms a most invigorating beverage, of which the good effects continue for several hours.

Soon after eight we started, and came into a small plain, which was the *rendezvous* of the King and his suite when he came on a hunting expedition two years before. It appears that all this part of his dominions is maintained by the King as a royal preserve for bouquetins and chamois; but as for this particular little stony plain—with steep rocks on each side, and accessible only by precipitous paths,—I could not imagine how the King's mounted retinue ever got there, or what they did when they arrived.

We passed the lakes on our left, and descended rapidly from the Col into the Valley of Ceresole, where we found the weather clearer, and caught glimpses through the clouds of a high steep mountain overhanging the valley on the south, which I set down as La Pointe des Trois Becs, or Levanna. At ten A.M. we reached the Châlet de Surie,—the highest in the valley,—from which we learned a flock of sheep had just started for the Col de Galèse; this encouraged us, and we followed them, going nearly due west, and climbing up the rugged cliffs that enclose the head of the valley. On the top of these lay a slope of snow, beyond which rose a high wall of rock, with its jagged summits faintly outlined through the storm.

It was the crest of the Alps, rising two thousand feet above us, and accessible only by a steep narrow gully paved with snow. This gully led us to a deep notch in the ridge, and resembled on a large scale the "Cheminée" of Mont Brevent at Chamouni. Down the gully swept wind and snow, which we had to face as we plodded upwards; but presently, when the slope became steeper, so much loose snow slid upon us that we could hardly make any progress; as one or other of us was frequently swept or blown off his legs. Things did not appear promising, so we held a brief consultation; we had evidently but a choice of evils. I did not like the idea of giving up, and scrambling down those awkward cliffs in order to get back to the hay and to the cows, while Payot pointed out that we were secure against the real danger of losing our way on the glacier on the other side, as we had but to follow the sheep-tracks.

We therefore determined to force our way over the pass if possible; and at once took the necessary precautions. We tied ourselves together, and screwed the axe-head on to Payot's alpenstock; this plan had been invented by himself, to dispense with the necessity of carrying an axe separately. With this heavy, long-handled instrument he could, at one blow, cut a niche deep enough to afford firm footing. We were now fairly between the two walls of the gully, which narrowed from fifty feet at its mouth up to ten at its head, in a length of five hundred yards; but so much snow had accumulated in it that it was constantly swept by avalanches.

Still, we were encouraged by hearing the sound of the sheep far above us, and the incessant barking of the dog, who, poor fellow! was very indignant at finding that the sheep got on much better than he in scaling the slippery rocks. The guide told us he was not prepared for such a state of things, as generally there was no snow whatever on our side of the pass. Presently, there came rolling down a lot of stones, detached by the sheep above, who maintained an intermittent discharge of these small shot till they were clear on the other side. The stones luckily rolled, and did not bound, so they only struck us on the legs (here again, I may say, my leggings did me good service), until, what with being bothered by the stones, and being half-smothered by the avalanches and the driving storm, and being knee-deep in snow, and, in general, cold and uncomfortable, I began to despair of success, especially when Payot expressed his opinion that before long the gully would be swept from end to end by a large avalanche that we should be unable to withstand. These avalanches must have begun to fall but a short time before—perhaps not till after the passage of the sheep—as the first few were small. It seemed as if we had come just at the time, when the gully could no longer contain the constant accumulations of snow.

We had hitherto avoided approaching the sides, because the snow fell over them in regular cascades, collected from the rocks and ledges above; but I now proposed that we should submit to this inconvenience, in order to evade the greater one; I argued that, as the gully widened regularly from the top, no avalanche, however large, could ever completely fill it: this proved a good plan, for we escaped both stones and avalanches. At last we came to where the snow ceased, and we had to climb between two faces of rock that met at the bottom, and were coated with clear ice.

The shepherds had avoided this "couloir," by passing along a ledge to the left, but the flock had climbed straight up it, for in such a place a sheep would climb with comparatively little difficulty. Unluckily we did not discover the shepherds' path, and though we were but one hundred yards from the top, we were occupied more than an hour in reaching it. It was almost impossible to secure a footing anywhere: without the axe, we never could have done it; we had to cut more than a hundred resting-places for the feet, first scratching off the ice from the rocks, and then knocking out a bit of stone here, or chipping off a piece there, or tearing up some loose fragments. Sometimes I hitched my alpenstock across the gully for Payot to stand on; or else we shoved and hustled him up where he could not climb, that he might pull us up after him; and thus we scrambled up to the top at two P.M. having been three hours in doing less than a mile. Here we rested a little, to go through a general rubbing of hands, which were much numbed by constant holding to the frozen rocks. However, we had no time to lose, as the falling snow would soon obliterate the sheep tracks, so we started across the glacier, which was smooth and level. We could see nothing, except that there was a small lake in the ice to our right; it was not a time for taking observations, so I can only guess at the height of the pass, which I should estimate at a little more than 9,000 feet. The tracks were scarcely visible to me, but my companions made them out readily, and we went along at a rapid trot, till we came to where the glacier terminated, breaking abruptly off at the edge of a cliff; this rather startled us, because there was the edge, and there were the tracks going right up to it; it seemed as if they had gone over it. The only explanation was that the flock had returned upon its old track, and then struck off again.

We then immediately turned back, and sought for the junction of the missing track with the old one, but without success; we then extended our sphere of search. The other two were to go each on one side of the track about 300 yards, straight away, and then to walk with their faces to the wind—that was westward. I was to remain where I was, and to blow my large fog-whistle every minute; by this they were to guide themselves until one of them shouted, in which case the other and I were to follow him. We at once untied ourselves, and they both disappeared; I coiled up the rope, and, sitting down upon it, got out the map and the compass in order to decide what course to take should the track be irrecoverably lost.

We had consumed our provisions, we had even eked out our vile supply of brandy by the vile admixture of the contents of my spirit lamps; we had been snowed upon for six hours, and the thermometer marked 248 under the hanging flap of my plaid. It was therefore a great relief to me when, after whistling for about ten minutes, I heard Payot's voice in the north-west; we soon rejoined him, and found that he had lighted upon the track at the point where it quitted the glacier. Here, and throughout the rest of the descent, it could easily be traced, as the snow was only a few inches deep, and was all discoloured with the mud and stones that had been stirred up.

We followed the track down into the valley—the head of the Val de Tignes, where the weather was clearer, and though the valley was in itself of the most chilling, cheerless aspect, without a tree or bush to be seen, yet to us it was truly welcome, and a hospitable shelter from the storm. We hastened on, often congratulating ourselves upon being well out of it. Payot attributed our success to "le vin chaud," which alone, he said, enabled us to hold our own against the cold so long; and no doubt he was right, but I knew that the main element of our success was Payot himself, for without his assistance I never could have got up that most impracticable "couloir." Just before reaching Laval we passed our highly esteemed pioneers, the sheep, who numbered about 250, and we were surprised that the track of so numerous a flock had been so soon effaced. The inn was a most wretched place, but it was comfortable in comparison with a châlet; we reached it at six P.M.

Near Laval three short valleys unite, and form the Val de Tignes; the middle one leads to the Col d'Iseran; the left-hand one to the Col de Galèse. We started the next morning for Bonneval, by the Col d'Iseran; over which we easily found our way by help of the map, and the pyramids which Murray warned us to look for. In respect of Mont Iseran, which I had not yet seen, the hand-book rather confused me, by calling the pass first Col d'Iseran, and then Mont Iseran. The mountain tops were still covered, and we could learn nothing about them at Laval, neither were we the wiser through what we could see in mounting the Col, which, though usually free of snow, was on that day deeply covered for three miles on each side of the top, as snow was still falling.

We found our way at once by help of the pyramids, which are not mere heaps of stones, but regular edifices, some of them twenty-five feet high, with large niches, in which one can conveniently take shelter, as, by some oversight, none of them had been filled with the proper apparatus of dolls, lace, crosses, and pictures.

We met several hundreds of good fat sheep coming from Bonneval. It appeared there was a general movement of sheep and cattle from all parts to Bourg St. Maurice, at the foot of the little St. Bernard, where there was a great fair on the day of Saint Grat—whom I was always tempted to call Saint Gras, since these ample supplies were all to centre in him.

The top of the Col was reached in three hours from Laval, and there, for the first time since leaving Val Savranche, we got a view, though Mont Iseran, the long-sought object of my ambition, was still hidden. Towards the south many high mountains and a vast area of glaciers were visible, all at a great distance. At eleven A.M. a bright circular rainbow formed round the sun on a stratum of dark grey cloud less than two thousand feet above us; it enclosed an immense space having an inner diameter of about 50°, the bow having a breadth of about 5°; it continued till 11·50 A.M., when the clouds were disturbed by a change of the wind from N.W. to S.W. I watched it with great pleasure, till Payot explained to me that it was an infallible sign of bad weather.

We found in descending that a great deal of the winter's snow still lay across the pass; in some places the whole ravine was choked, the road and the torrent disappearing for the time. There were several châlets by the road at which we tried to get some milk; but the inhabitants were shy, and discourteous; they made no objection to their dogs flying at us. In all parts of this valley the same thing took place; the dogs resembled the Scotch shepherd's dog, and were very fierce and spiteful, always flying at passers-by, without interference from their masters. They did not seem to care whether we or the dogs got the better, but, like a mob at a prize-fight, were quite content as long as somebody was being hurt.

We reached Bonneval at two, and soon found the inn of M. Jean Culets; he had not much accommodation, but did his best to make us comfortable. He could supply nothing but eggs, and bread and butter, and wine, which last was most excellent.

After dinner, I had a long conversation with him about the mountains in the neighbourhood, and we soon came to an understanding about the Levanna; it had been ascended once by himself, and he would take us up on the first fine day. But about Mont Iseran, to my astonishment, he knew nothing; declaring positively that there was no mountain at all on the site indicated in the Ordnance Map—he did not care for the map, he had travelled upon these mountains for thirty years, and was ready to swear that the peak existed solely in the imaginations of geographers. This quite confounded me; I was not in the least prepared for it, as I no more doubted the existence of Mont Iseran than I did that of Mont Blanc. Every map marked it: in the Piedmontese Ordnance Map, sheet number thirty-seven was named after it, and gave its height as 4,045 metres, or more than 13,000 feet; the Alpine Club, in their list, marked it 13,271 feet; and Payot said that he had often seen it from the top of Mont Blanc, while I had seen it, or what I thought was it, from the Col du Géant and the Cramont.

Here, then, was a question of fact of the most elementary kind, decided in one way by a remarkable combination of evidence, and, in the contrary way, by the experience of a man who could not possibly be mistaken. I could only suspend my judgment until I should have examined for myself; I would go to the very place, and if Mont Iseran did not stand there, I would stand there instead, and testify against him.

I wanted, of course, to go there the next day, Saturday, September 8th, but was met by two difficulties. In the first place, there was every appearance of bad weather—as foretold by the circular rainbow; and, secondly, Culets could not come with us, because the day was the property of St. Grat, and it would be necessary to go to mass, which ceremony being unfortunately at eleven o'clock, was incompatible with mountaineering. With reference to this feeling about Saints' days, Payot told me the following story:—

The late fatal accident on the Col du Géant had happened on August 15th; now this is a Saint's day, and the coincidence had been much remarked. It appeared, moreover, that the Curé of Chamouni had, at the beginning of the season, reminded the guides that it was likely to prove unusually dangerous, and exhorted them never to travel on Saints' days without going to the five o'clock mass. On this account, poor Tairraz had been very unwilling to try the Col on August 15th, but had yielded to the natural impatience of the three Englishmen. It was also remembered that, when Tairraz's brother was swept away by an avalanche in 1820, that accident also occurred on a Saint's day. So that, on the whole, the impression made at Chamouni had been such, that no guide would, if he could avoid it, try a dangerous pass or mountain on these occasions.

I was interested in the story, and decided that nothing of importance was to be done till the Monday. Hereupon, in order to confirm me in this laudable resolve, old Culets came in with another sad story: a young Sardinian officer of engineers had been killed in a crevasse, while surveying near the Col de Lauteret on the previous Sunday.

The next day was stormy, hail and snow falling frequently; but I succeeded in making some acquaintance with the geography of the neighbourhood in the intervals of fine weather. In the evening some English gentlemen arrived from Forno, over the Col Girard; I had not met a soul for a week, and expected some news about Garibaldi, but they knew none, having been for some time, like myself, in unfrequented regions.

They had had a dreadful passage over the Col Girard, and, in my opinion, had very narrowly escaped a fatal accident; the weather had been dreadful on the pass, and the snow on the steep slopes was in a most dangerous state. Both their guides refused to carry anything for them, or even to give them a helping hand, in difficult places; they would simply show the way and nothing more. One even refused to do that, and followed in the rear, saying he was afraid of crevasses; and it turned out that this fellow was responsible for the accident to the poor surveyor on the Col de Lauteret; having misled him, and then made little effort to save him. On the Col Girard, he used neither axe nor ropes, and one of the party would, in consequence, have disappeared down a couloir, but that his friend behind adroitly caught him by the arm. Other narrow escapes took place among the dangerous crevasses on the Italian side.

This sort of thing constantly happens in the less frequented passes of the High Alps, where no one ought to trust himself to unknown guides unless he be himself an experienced mountaineer. There were six fatal accidents in the Alps this year, and, probably, narrow escapes innumerable—I know the details of half-a-dozen or more—but there need be no cause for surprise, when one sees so many tourists utterly inexperienced, but ready to undertake anything. At Aosta, two gentlemen consulted me as to whether they had better go on the next day over the Col du Géant, or spend a day in going up the Mont Cervin, which they heard was well worth a visit.

On Sunday the weather was rather better, and I walked down to Lanslebourg, for the purpose, *imprimis*, of getting a good dinner, not having dined to any extent for a week. I wanted also some spirits of wine for my lamp, and a supply of provisions to support us at Bonneval, where one could get nothing but eggs, and very large cabbages, which, with hay and onions, appear to be the sole products of the upper part of the valley.

The general character of the mountains near Bonneval is

very decided; there are a great many peaks of nearly the same height (about 12,000 feet), sloping up on the west, from vast table-lands covered with glaciers, and presenting tremendous precipices towards the east. The glaciers are of immense extent, but of no great thickness, because of the inferior size of the mountains; they are in consequence crevassed in almost every part, as their surfaces are affected by every little inequality in the rocks over which they move, while, in the case of a thick glacier, many rents must be made below, which never extend themselves as far as the upper surface. The same cause leads to other important results; owing to its thinness, the glacier breaks and crumbles over the edge of a precipice, where a thick one would bend down and make an ice-fall. Again, owing to its deficiency of volume, it seldom descends below the snow line, even if not interrupted by the precipices which nearly everywhere bound the table-land. Few, therefore, of the glaciers are accessible, and still fewer practicable, unless one can reach their nevés. There is so little bare rock, that moraines are rare, and the summits easy of ascent, if one can but approach them. Although these are not high, yet the general crest of the range much exceeds 10,000 feet, and is nowhere to be crossed without difficulty.

These ice-fields cover so large a space, and are so much exposed to every wind, that they render the climate of the adjoining valleys very rigorous. It was dreadfully cold at Bonneval, snow falling frequently and injuring the vegetation; no grain would ripen there, and no pines would grow even on the lowest grounds. Many of the inhabitants appeared to suffer from rheumatism, and soon after my visit I had myself an attack of that complaint; Culets said he had long been subject to it through sleeping out on the mountains. For the present he gave a good report of the weather, and had no doubt of our being able to ascend the Levanna on the morrow.

Fortunately, the morning proved very fine. We started at six, ascending the valley, and leaving on the left the road to the Col d'Iseran. The Levanna itself was not visible from Bonneval, and it was not until we had been nearly an hour on the march that Payot and I for the first time caught sight of the mountain that we were to climb ; it seemed to be very distant, as only the summit was visible, but our guide assured us we should be at the top in less than six hours. However, it was soon hidden from sight by the steep mountains at the head of the valley, whose sides appeared more bare and bleak than near Bonneval. Even the birches had disappeared, and a great part of the slopes were covered with dark grey stones.

At half-past seven we reached the last inhabited place, a châlet belonging to Culets, and, in a few minutes after, came to the end of the glacier that descends from the Levanna and the Col Girard,—the only one that reaches the valley. We now began to ascend, with the glacier to our right, advancing in a direction parallel to it until we reached the base of the snow-slopes that extended up to the highest ridge, which once more became visible. Here we sat down to breakfast, and I took the opportunity of examining our guide's rifle, which he always carried with him, as he was constantly on the look-out for chamois.

It was an old rifle, but appeared still very serviceable ; its chief peculiarity was that it could be fired twice, though it had but one barrel. This was effected by an arrangement that was quite new to me ; first, the rifle was loaded in the usual way, but with a wad above the bullet ; then, above the wad, a fresh charge of powder and a fresh bullet were placed, so that by the help of a second trigger, hammer, and nipple, this charge could be fired off, without disturbing the charge behind it, which was held in reserve for a second shot. The piece was thus as useful as a double-barrelled rifle ; it had killed, in Culets' hands, about a thousand chamois, of which he said half would have escaped him but for his second shot.

In a few minutes we started again, mounting steep slopes of snow, on which our guide said he usually found game. He now unslung his rifle, carrying it at the long trail, and instructed us, in case of seeing a chamois, to throw ourselves flat on the snow. However, the first game we saw was not chamois, but ptarmigan ; a brood of six rose close to us from some stones, among which they had been concealed, and I expected Culets to fire at them, but he would not do so, as he feared to frighten away the chamois, of which we soon afterwards saw three at some distance above us on the slope. I happened to be first, and the moment we had lain down, I heard him say, "You must excuse my firing over you ;" whereupon he laid the barrel over my shoulder and fired, but without effect. He was prevented from making use of his second charge by a curious incident ; the slope of hard snow was so steep, that when we threw ourselves down, we were obliged to use our hands to avoid slipping, but the marksman of course had both his hands occupied, and as he had not secured himself with his feet, it so happened, that the recoil of the piece was sufficient to dislodge him. He slid down some way, while I felt the barrel being rapidly drawn over my shoulder, and slipping down along my back ; so that at that moment I should have been better satisfied had there been no second charge in the rifle. However, no harm happened, except that before he had recovered himself, the chamois had vanished. We presently reached the spot where the chamois had been standing, and found that the bullet had struck the snow between his feet.

I was struck with thc pcculiarity of tho roport, which resembled that of a drawing-room pistol, and was sharp and short; it was morc reduced in power than I should have expected, considering our moderate elevation (less than 11,000 feet) ; the smoke, too, did not rise into the air, but rolled slowly upwards like a small cloud.

Soon afterwards the rifle was left behind, there being no chance of finding chamois any higher, because all the region beyond was accessible only by the narrow slope up which we were climbing. This fell away to the right and the left, so that we presently found ourselves upon a narrow arête of rocks and soft snow, up which we scrambled unpleasantly till we reached the side of the highest ridge. This ridge is narrow, and bounded by two precipices that do not meet at the top to form an arête, but are connected by a narrow surface of snow. But the precipice on the eastern or Italian side is much the highest, and also the steepest, therefore this surface slopes sharply down to meet the top of the lower precipice on the Savoy side, where it is cut short, as the sloping roof of a house is cut short by the wall. The ridge extends about 300 yards to the right, where it terminates abruptly, after culminating at its very extremity in a small heap of rocks, which formed the summit of the Levanna.

We had to go the whole length along this surface, which required some caution, for it consisted of loose, unfrozen snow, lying upon a hard, smooth slope, which in its steepest part was inclined at an angle of 43°, as measured by my clinometer. We dared not venture near to the higher part, because the surface curled over the precipice below like a cornice, terminating in a thin edge of ice; nor could we safely pass on the lower side, lest our weight should detach the loose snow, and make it slide away from under us. As the rope would have been of no service in such a case, we did not tie ourselves together, but went each by himself at a considerable distance apart, keeping about half-way up the slope, and so we reached the top without difficulty, at a quarter before twelve.

The actual summit is most remarkable; it consists of a large slab resting upon a heap of loose rocks; the slab was not horizontal, but sloped away from us towards the Italian side, overhanging the precipice considerably; its position appeared frightfully insecure to us who proposed mounting on to it, as we half-expected to see it slide off its pinnacle, and sweep down the abyss. We found that it was so coated with clear ice, that we could not stand on it, and that sitting, though possible, would be very unpleasant. But against this, and against any attempt to mount it, both guides protested, and I yielded, half-disappointed, and yet half-pleased at being spared the unnecessary risk and discomfort of so cold and slippery a seat. Perhaps the danger may have been more in appearance than in reality; but I have never quite made up my mind whether our caution was prudent or ridiculous.

However, as we could see over the stone, it was no impediment to the view, and we beheld a magnificent spectacle, including almost every high peak in the main range of the Alps. Part of these we had seen during our ascent, for on our side snow-covered peaks were visible in every direction; to the west and south-west was the knot of high mountains that lie between the Mont Cenis road and the Isère, and whose summits appear to rise from out of a vast table-land of glaciers. Beyond were Mont Tabor, and to the left of it a fine peak that we could not identify, but which Payot remembered to have seen from Mont Blanc; perhaps Mont Pelvoux, if there be such a mountain; and he professed likewise to make out with the telescope the pointed summit of Monte Viso through the haze on the southern horizon; however, the view in that direction was in great part bounded by the peaks near Mont Cenis. But when we turned our eyes from the mountains towards the eastern valleys, hoping to discern Turin, Milan, and the Italian plain—there, alas! neither plain nor city could be seen, for all the lowlands lay hidden by heavy clouds.

In the north, no such disappointment awaited us. The whole of the great chain from where we stood, for more than a hundred miles,—the Graian and the Pennine Alps, lay before us; the range of Mont Blanc appeared to very great advantage, and Monte Rosa, and all the high peaks about it, were brilliantly visible, except the Weisshorn, which was concealed by the Dent Blanche. The Rhætian Alps were mostly hidden by Monte Rosa, but to its right were the Bernina, Monte Della Disgrazia, the bare peak of Monte Legnone beyond the Lake of Como, and last of all, the white cone of the Ortler Spitze.

But the finest and most striking sight of all was that splendid pair—the Grand Paradis and the Grivola, which, standing apart from the chain, alone and unsupported, yet rose in front of us to the height of 13,000 feet; the Grand Paradis especially towering grandly above us,—the highest mountain in Italy, and by far the most imposing object in the whole of that magnificent panorama.

I was obliged to defer till afterwards my full enjoyment of the scene, in order to attend to what I called "business," or, as Payot used to call it, "les machines." He, poor fellow! was at first too uncomfortable to interest himself as usual in my operations, as his feet were so cold that we became very uneasy about him; but he met the difficulty by taking off his dripping shoes and socks, and wrapping his feet tightly up in my plaid. By this means, in about half-an-hour, they were completely revived. It may seem surprising that we should have had the plaid with us, as it was a very decided addition to our "impedimenta;" but the fact was that we had come to the conclusion that our worst enemy, next to bad weather, had been the severe cold upon the high mountains during that inclement season. Glaciers and precipices could be crossed and surmounted, but the cold could not be so easily disposed of; some time before, Payot and I having, after a two days' expedition, reached an elevated summit, had been overpowered by the piercing cold, and driven down, after a stay of only four minutes, which were exclusively employed in deciding by mutual consent that it was impossible to stay there.

In consequence of this misfortune, we made it a rule always to take the plaid wherever cold was to be apprehended, and we considered it as much a part of our necessary equipment as the axe and rope. On this occasion, had it not been at hand we must have returned at once, for we all knew better than to make light of a frost-bite. Curiously enough, I subsequently heard a report that on this very day, Sept. 10, a guide had been incurably frost-bitten in the feet, by delaying on the arête of Monte Rosa, perhaps while I was scrutinizing that very place with the telescope, and while Payot, in his comfortable wrapper, was busying himself with "les machines" under shelter of the rock.

The flat slab sloping down from us formed a sort of roof on our side, just high enough to allow of our sitting under it; here we were sheltered from the north-east wind, and had a clear view to the south and west.

My first task was the determination of the boiling-point of water; and this, after the usual difficulties with my lamp, was ascertained to be 190°·6. Although this measurement could not by itself decide the height, it was sufficient to disappoint my ideas of the grandeur of the Levanna. I almost doubted whether this were the Levanna, as late events had been sufficient to cast suspicion on any mountain, however distinguished; but I was reassured by seeing all the valleys, where I expected, as agreeing with the map, while at our feet was the Col Girard, on which the track of those who had passed on the 8th was discernible for several miles. Besides, I thought, as I held by the stone and looked over on to the Italian side, it is impossible to mistake this astonishing precipice; it must be that which we had seen through the clouds from the Val de Ceresole, and which I had wildly estimated at 3,000 feet in height.

There were two beautiful mountains to the south, both a little higher than we were,—the Uja* di Ciamarella and the Mont Chardonnet; the first appeared practicable, and I determined to try it; but the latter was supported all round on our side by cliffs that seemed to be insurmountable: I believe this mountain to be that which overlooks Susa on the north, but am not quite satisfied about it. At the end of the Val d'Arc we could see the church spire of Lanslebourg, and to the left the first two zigzags by which the road climbs the Mont Cenis. I bore this in mind when I crossed the pass shortly after, and from this short bit of the road obtained a beautiful view of the Levanna, just illuminated at sunrise. We now saw something being drawn up the pass by two horses and eighteen mules; I at last made it out to be a heavy gun, probably from Fort Lesseillon, as the Emperor

* The local corruption of the word Aiguille is Ouille, which, on the Italian side, appears as Uia or Uja.

allowed the Piedmontese to withdraw their own artillery from their own forts.

I had for some time been conscious that the Mont Iseran of my imagination was "conspicuous only by its absence," and upon a closer examination observed that a ridge lower than ourselves hid the place where it ought to be; this was, of course, conclusive evidence on the main question, but still I determined to examine the place in person.

At last the time came for departure, to my great regret, as I had never been better rewarded for climbing than on that day; my hour spent on the top was most interesting, and I only wanted to have had a minimum thermometer to leave behind as a memorial of my visit, as I never saw a high peak so admirably adapted for the reception of that, or any other registering instrument. I took a last look over that most seductive precipice; it was, indeed, the grandest which I ever had the good fortune to look over. There is a great satisfaction in thus looking over; it gives one a feeling of triumph at having surmounted such an obstacle by any means.

The snow was now much softer, and we went along the ridge very gingerly; soon afterwards we picked up the rifle, and descended by a different route, more to the right, which led us down a series of the most delightful glissades. Below them lay two small lakes which Culets was anxious to show me, but before reaching them we met with a most agreeable adventure. On our right was a glacier at a little distance, and near the moraine there suddenly appeared a chamois. He saw us, and bounded off among the rocks so rapidly, that I feared Culets would have no chance at him; but the wary old guide knew better; he counted upon the chamois' fatal habit of stopping every now and then to look back, and did not fire till the incautious animal half turned round on the very top of the moraine to have a last look at us. The moment he had fired, the poor chamois bounded high into the air, and descended the moraine in one leap; he made three other wild leaps, and then disappeared among the rocks. We knew he was hit, because a chamois always runs down hill when he is wounded. Close to where we had lost sight of him he was lying quite dead, shot through the heart; yet his four leaps had carried him more than 40 yards. We complimented Culets on so excellent a shot at 250 yards, the extreme range of his rifle.

I had never seen a chamois killed before, and was very glad to have the opportunity of ascertaining the amount of its vital heat, which I had always believed to be very great, so I wanted to put a thermometer inside his carcase, at once, while it was being cleaned. But no step of this kind could be taken without our having water at hand; so we carried him over the rough ground, and then sent him down the glissades till we came to water, where the necessary operations were performed. I then gave Culets the thermometer, bidding him ensconce it in some warm place. It was left there for five minutes, and the chamois had been dead just half-an-hour when I took it out, and found it standing at 117°. How much heat the body had lost while being pulled about on the snow, with the temperature of the air at 43°, I had not sufficient knowledge to estimate, but I should not be surprised if the amount were considerable. Nothing but a great reserve of vital heat could enable the chamois, with its very thin coat, to withstand the rigours of an Alpine winter.

The old hunter was determined to show us how he carried his game, and would not let us assist him. He tied the legs together with a strong cord, and then hoisted the body on to his shoulders, putting his head partly between the legs, till it was exactly in the position of a porter's knot. Although so heavily loaded, he easily kept up with us, and we reached the lakes about three o'clock.

These were certainly very remarkable; they were each about half-an-acre in extent, and surrounded by snow reaching down to the water's edge, except where a narrow ridge, about ten feet high, divided them. A glacier stream ran into one, in which the water was consequently quite white, like milk-and-water. In the other it was quite black, like peat-water. Both were exposed to the sun, and of course I expected the black one to be the hottest; the white one was partially frozen over, and had some lumps of ice floating in it, while the temperature of the black one was 39°, only 4° colder than the air, though it was above the snow line. I could discover no cause for the black colour; perhaps both lakes might be black but for the glacier water, for when we reached the point where their two little streams united, I saw that the white colour completely effaced the black. Soon after we struck into our old track, and reached Bonneval before six, after a very easy and successful day's work.

On Tuesday the weather was again as bad as ever, with drizzle and sleet all the morning. In the afternoon we went out fishing in the Arc, and caught a fine trout, which made me an excellent dinner. Two dinners in three days! I was evidently in luck. Thus fortified, I felt prepared to abide the final issue of the great question which was to be solved, weather permitting, on the morrow.

The weather—how I hated the word at last—did give a temporary permission, and we made the most of it. All we had to do was to mount the Col d'Iseran, and go up the little peak to its east. Of course, I had left in me but little belief in Mont Iseran, and before we were half-way up the Col, I perceived the absolute necessity of abandoning all faith in it. I was incensed against the mountainous nothing and vacant habitation that had usurped so splendid a name, and excited so vain an ambition. But I would have my revenge; I would go to the place; I would boil water there, and make disparaging observations upon it to the best of my power.

The crag was rugged and steep, and more than an hour's scramble above the Col; there was a good deal of snow on it, and a small glacier at the top. The boiling-point there was 192°·9, and on the Col, 195°·9; the difference in height was therefore 1,580 feet. Towards the east, the peak presented a fine precipice more than 1,000 feet in height, and quite perpendicular. This point, such as it is, stands on the spot usually assigned to Mont Iseran, and so I call it by that name. I may as well mention here the results of some subsequent inquiries. These parts had been visited and the popular error ascertained in the previous year by a member of the Alpine Club, but I am not aware whether any particular point was considered worthy to possess the well-known name. Also, in a work entitled, "Mémoires de la Société Académique de Savoie," Tome XI., there appears the following, as the result of a barometrical measurement by two Canons of Chambery, about the year 1842, I believe:—"Mont Iseran (*point culminant*), 2,481 metres," that is, 8,134 feet; but whether the Col or a peak is meant, there is nothing to show.

I looked in all directions to find a mountain in the neighbourhood of size sufficient to account for the popular error, but I could not perfectly satisfy myself with any one. In fact, there is no mountain south of Mont Blanc of the required height, but the most prominent are these three: Le Rocher de la Sassière, a long ridge, culminating at one end, distant about six miles northwards from our position; La Pointe des Grands Couloirs, an immense mass, quite flat on the top, about eight and a half westwards; and Mont Pourri, a very steep-sided sharp peak, about eleven and a half to the north-west. As seen from where we stood, the two former mountains had neither of them that needle-like apex which has been supposed to be the distinguishing mark of Mont Iseran, and I am therefore inclined to accept Mont Pourri as most likely to be the proper representative. It seems to be the highest of the three, and accessible but with difficulty. It is very conspicuous from the Cramont, bearing S. by W.

On a subsequent day we re-crossed the Col d'Iseran, where I reflected with pleasure that, in spite of my bad luck in regard to weather, I had still been able to satisfy myself that no high mountain existed at the source of the Isère, in the place usurped by Mont Iseran, on the maps.

I append a list of my observations on the temperature of boiling water at different places, in which I do not reject those I made at the well-determined altitudes of the Col de Ferret,

Cramont, and Bonneval, since they will serve as a criterion of the amount of dependence to be placed on those of the Grand Paradis, the Levanna, and Mont Iseran. The water I used was snow-water in every case, except at the Châlet du Paradis, at Bonneval, and at the Petit St. Bernard.

Place.	Date.	Hour, P.M.	Temperature of Boiling Water.	Temperature of Air.	Barometer at Turin.	Temperature at Turin.	Deduced Altitude.
Col de Ferret	Aug. 29	3	197°·6	59°	28·782	89°	8,030
Cramont	Aug. 30	1	195°·7	63°	28·884	88°	9,290
Châlet du Paradis	Sept. 3	8	197°·6	60°	29·055	71°	8,180
Grand Paradis	Sept. 5	1	188°·1	51°	28·977	78°	13,700
Levanna	Sept. 10	1	190°·6	43°	28·932	79°	12,020
Bonneval.	Sept. 11	6	201°·5	60°	28·885	72°	5,760
Mont Iseran.	Sept. 12	noon	192°·9	44°	29·100	78°	10,880
Col d'Iseran	Sept. 12	1	195°·9	63°	29·098	78°	9,300
Petit St. Bernard	Sept. 14	3	199°·3	58°	29·082	69°	7,200

7. THE ALLELEIN-HORN.

BY LESLIE STEPHEN, M.A.

THE season of 1860 was as remarkable in the Alps as elsewhere for a long continuance of bad weather. Rain, snow, and mist, and, worse than all, bitterly cold and violent gales of wind, made summer in the High Alps as severe as an English Christmas. Bad weather, and especially windy weather, is no joke on exposed mountain-ridges; it almost destroys the pleasure even of mountain-climbing, to be assaulted by the fierce gales, under which the snow-covered summits may be seen smoking like volcanoes. You are, perhaps, creeping carefully along a kind of knife-edge between two precipices, your fingers freezing to the rocks to which you must cling. Suddenly, a savage gush dashes down upon you, puffs the frozen snow into your face and up your trousers, and seems to whistle through your very bones.

It is curious to observe how capricious these assaults are both in duration and place. A perfect storm may be raging on one mountain-top, whilst you may be able to light matches on another within half a mile of it. During an ascent of the Wetterhorn this year, we could see heavy clouds lying motionless as wool on all the surrounding summits, whilst just over our heads we could hear the wind screaming, and see the mists flying past, and the snow being torn in clouds from the sharp ridge above us. It suddenly lulled into perfect stillness for an hour, during which we made our ascent, and then began again with its former fury. A good Scotch plaid and a pair of thick woollen mits are the best protection; still the experience of many travellers, and of more guides, can testify to the danger of frost-bites on these occasions.

In July, 1860, I was at Saas, in company with Mr. Short, of New College, Oxford, with whom I had been trying some practical experiments on the varieties of Alpine bad weather. We had just crossed the Weissthor, blindfolded by a thick driving mist, with the thermometer at 22°, and a powerful gale blowing. Next day, in a comparatively agreeable fog, we had hopelessly lost our way on the high snows of the Fée glaciers. "Losing your way" may mean either that you do not know where you are, or that, knowing where you are, you do not know how to get any further. The first of these misfortunes is commoner on a Scotch moor than on the Alps. In the vast snow-fields, however, which lie to the north of Monte Rosa, the small and varying inclination of the slopes in that great moor-like wilderness of snow, and the monotonous forms of the huge mounds of névé, make it as hard to find one's way in a mist as on an actual moor. Under such circumstances, it is a matter of some nicety to hit off the exact point where the "*arête blanche*" joins on to the great range of cliffs above Matmark and Macugnaga. One of our guides had, on a former occasion, walked straight over the edge of these cliffs by mistake, and only saved himself by the obvious but rather difficult expedient of jumping back again. Warned by this, we went carefully forwards, and making a beautiful shot at the pass, we crossed the ridge without difficulty. Next day we were not so fortunate; we were on a glacier where none of us had ever been before. We had a general guess as to where the pass ought to be; and Franz Andermatten, of Saas (one of our guides), said that he should know it if he came to it. Unfortunately, we were surrounded by a light but pertinacious mist, with a bright glare of sunshine through it, which made it perfectly impossible to see anything. Looking upwards or downwards, right or left, exactly the same formless glare seemed to dazzle our eyes. The last man in the line could see the first, but the first could see nothing but diffused light, and found it just as difficult to walk straight as if he had been blindfolded. He enjoyed, in fact, much the same kind of view as a fish would in a thick basin of milk-and-water when the sun was shining. At last, guided by some objects which we fancied to be cliffs, but which afterwards turned out to be crevasses, we left our true course, and suddenly found ourselves on the edge of a long and steep snow-slope. We were in a delightful perplexity. One of the guides stoutly maintained that we had reached the Col we were looking for. The other, Franz Andermatten, whose local knowledge was most to be depended upon, was only certain of one thing, viz., that we were somewhere else. My own observations, aided by a map and a compass, showed distinctly that, by descending the slope before us, we should return to the point from which we started. In our complete ignorance of the geography of the glacier it was hopeless to persevere, and we accordingly turned back; and following our footsteps in the snow as the only clue, soon found ourselves safe on the rocks from which we had started. The highest peaks were still clear, as they had been when we were there before. The valley below was also as clear as at first, but along the ridge we were to pass, a heavy bank of mist lay motionless all day, as impenetrable a barrier as the steepest and most difficult cliffs.

We were resolved, however, to try the ascent again next morning, if the weather improved. The pass which we were endeavouring to make out was one which would evidently be the shortest connecting line between Saas and Zermatt, two of the most inexhaustible centres of interest in the Alps.

The vast ridge which runs due north from Monte Rosa to divide the valleys of Saas and Zermatt, is at first considerably nearer to the Saas side. The huge Görner, Findelen, and Täsch glaciers, all descend from this part of the ridge by a long and slow descent to the head of the Zermatt valley. The glaciers on the other side are much shorter and steeper. Across this part of the ridge lie three passes, the Weissthor, the Adler, and the Allelein (the two last of which have been admirably described by Mr. Wills). The end of this portion of the ridge is marked by the Allelein-horn, where it suddenly turns due west, and runs towards the valley of Zermatt, forming the northern boundary of the Täsch glacier. At the long flat-topped hummock called the Alphubel, it again turns northwards, but is now, of course, nearer to the Zermatt than to the Saas valley, from which it is divided by the vast system of the Fée glaciers, whilst the glaciers on the Zermatt side become comparatively insignificant. Now, it will easily be seen by a map, that a line drawn straight from Saas to Zermatt would cross the long mound-like wall, connecting the Allelein-horn and the Alphubel, and running nearly east and west. We knew that, on the Saas or northern side, it descended by tolerably easy snow-slopes to the higher part of the Fée glaciers. If it should prove practicable to descend on its southern side to the margin of the Täsch glacier, it was evident that we should have made the most direct route from Saas to Zermatt, which would have the additional advantage of leading through the magnificent scenery of the Fée glaciers, and also of avoiding the détour by the cold and smoky inn at the Matmark See.

We were joined in the evening by two gentlemen, Messrs. Jacomb and Fisher, who had just crossed the Allelein pass with old Peter Taugwald and Johann Kroneg of Zermatt. We were glad to join forces, and, as we had already Franz Andermatten of Saas, and Moritz Anthonmatten of Visp, with us, we formed a strong party. In fact, if the nature of our work had not proved to be such as to make a strong party useful, we should have been rather too many for business. One or two travellers and two guides can go up or over any place in the Alps. Any increase in the numbers is certain to cause delay, and can seldom add to safety or comfort. Not only has the pace of the party to be regulated by that of its slowest member, but at any difficult place every one has to wait till every one else has been separately helped, hauled, or hoisted over his troubles. In a large party, there are often one or two with whom this process is rather a long one. Now, in the Alps, getting up a mountain, especially a new mountain, is generally simply a question of time. It is seldom possible or desirable to camp out more than one night. The amount of provisions and coverings necessary to be carried on longer expeditions produces a very severe strain upon men who have to walk a good many miles and do a good deal of hard work in the course of the day. Neither is it pleasant to sleep for many nights together on a bed of rock, with a stream trickling on your nose, nor possible, as a rule, to sleep under any circumstances, within some 1,000 feet of the highest peaks. Consequently, the great object is to get to the nearest habitable place to your mountain, and to make as vigorous a dash at him as one day, or at most two days, will allow. Saving a few minutes, especially a few minutes' fine weather, may easily make the whole difference. A mist may float up at the critical moment, or a slope that has been safe and easy till the sun touched it, may become perilous and difficult to pass an hour afterwards. To save time is the one essential for success; and there are very few cases in which the largeness of a party is not in direct proportion to the time wasted: one is, when heavy snow-work has to be done, which is often too fatiguing for one man to do alone. Even then two guides are generally enough. I say nothing of the increased chance of your having perfect confidence in the last, and skill of every member of the party, when the party consists of one or two, nor of the possibility of an expedition being totally ruined by the failure of one man.

It might, perhaps, be possible, if the size of the party and the quantity of preparations were increased, to spend more nights upon the glaciers. But the practical advantage would be small. All the higher and more enticing peaks are fenced round by walls of rock and snow, and guarded by regions of frost and wind, through which a passage, if made at all, must be made between sunrise and sunset.

Early on the 1st of August, I was awakened by the usual report, "Schlechtes Wetter." I interpreted this to Short in the next room, by telling him that he might go to sleep again. As he had been very unwell for the two days past, on each of which we had had long snow walks, he received this intelligence with a certain complacency. Unfortunately for him, he allowed his satisfaction to appear a little too openly. Thankfulness for bad weather in the Alps is a crime under all circumstances. Accordingly, I watched the clouds with great interest, and at the first gleam of sunlight jumped up, dressed, ran down stairs, and soon succeeded in persuading myself and the guides that it was going to be a fine day. By half-past five, Short having shown the most amiable resignation to his fate, we were already on the march for Fée. The light mists which were driving up the valley hid the mountains, except when the top of the Mittaghorn occasionally looked down upon us through the clouds. Suddenly, some one pointed to what looked like a sheet of silver, gleaming at an almost incredible height through the mists. It is always strange to observe how much the apparent height of a mountain is increased when it is looking over clouds. I should hardly have believed that any mountain in the Alps could rise so high above us as the glaciers, which were now shining down upon us from the mists; and yet I remembered that, in the summer before, I had stood upon the summit of the Dom, and seen these very glaciers lying almost immediately beneath me at the foot of a sheer precipice some ten thousand of feet high. It is true that, at the same time, we had seen on one side the Lago Maggiore, twenty miles off, lying like a deep green pond below us, and unknown lakes and plains stretching far away beyond it. By turning our heads, we looked upon a purple sheet of haze, which concealed the Lake of Geneva. I had scarcely time to remember this, when, in almost one instant, the mists that had surrounded us were swept away, and, as if by magic, the whole glorious semicircle of peaks, from the Allelein-horn to the Mischabel, sprang up before us. All that unrivalled sweep of glaciers, and every rock and cliff that rise from them, shone out instantaneously, without even a shred of mist to conceal their beauties. I have scarcely ever seen a more startling effect even in the Alps. It put every one of the party into the highest spirits, and we pressed on in a confident hope of a fine day at last. I must take the opportunity of recommending all visitors to Saas to take the trouble of climbing a short way up the lower slopes of the Weissmies, *behind* the village. It is impossible, from any other position, to realize fully the unapproachable beauty of the great Fée glaciers. Another most beautiful point of view is gained by taking the path, which we now followed up to the summit of the ridge of rock which divides the glacier into two great tongue-like masses, and terminates in the "Gletscher Alp." There is no difficulty in reaching the summit, where you stand, as it were, in an island surrounded in every direction by the magnificent crevasses of the glacier. At this point we had breakfast No. 2, at about nine o'clock, and then started across the snow-fields for the foot of the Allelein-horn, at first almost in the footsteps of the previous day. I afterwards discovered that the right track would have been to the foot of the Alphubel, on the south side of which there is a very level col, leading by an easy descent to Zermatt.

We soon found ourselves plodding laboriously through a huge snow-field, whose very existence could scarcely have been suspected from below. What looks like a slight wrinkle in the névé below the Alphubel, conceals a level plain of snow, whose apparent size struck me as being about equal to that of Hyde Park. It took us, however, rather longer to get to the end of it, than I hope we should have been in crossing Hyde Park. The snow was exceedingly deep and tiring, and at its farther extremity the inclination became respectable, and the glacier seamed with long and broad crevasses. There is no Alpine work so tiring as this snow-wading, as the guides call it. The deep, half-melting snow above your knees, which will get into your boots and coat-pockets; the glare from sun and snow all above, and below, and around, which you know will deprive your face of every particle of skin; and the steady, monotonous plunge with which you flounder along, like a fly in a honey-pot, become rather tiresome. Moreover, we had for some time very little excitement from crevasses.

The crevasses on a level are, of course, narrow, although sometimes deep—deep enough, at any rate, to be dangerous. I shall never forget, one day, stumbling along down the level snow-trough which leads from the Lôtsch Saltel to the Aletsch glacier. The burning light and the monotonous motion had produced their usual soporific effect, and we were foolish and lazy enough not to have put on the rope. Suddenly, one of the party all but disappeared. A narrow crevasse had opened beneath him like a trap-door. With his feet wedged against one side, his shoulders against the other, and his back resting upon nothing at all, it was well for him that the crevasse had not been a little broader. The man behind caught him by the collar as he went down, and in a moment he was on his feet again, on sound footing. But the view of the two parallel walls of green ice sinking vertically downwards into utter darkness, has often come back to me since. Somehow, no one even then suggested the rope, and we plodded quietly and sleepily along—fortunately without further accident. I hope, however, that I learnt a lesson as to the propriety of using the rope on such occasions. It is true that a man has in general no business to fall down a crevasse. A concealed crevasse is almost always so narrow that it is rather difficult than otherwise to fall down it without touching either side. If you are carrying your alpenstock "at the trail," so as to form a bridge as you fall, or if you throw yourself well backwards or forwards directly you feel your footing give, you must come upon a firm support. Still, no one has a right to presume so far upon his skill and presence of mind as not to adopt a precaution which secures absolute safety. There have, indeed, been warnings enough lately, to impress this upon most people's minds.

We plunged on slowly and laboriously, with one or two half-immersions in crevasses, and I found time gradually passing, whilst the Allelein-horn seemed resolutely to keep its distance. The snow perspective is always exceedingly deceptive; but when I found that we had had three hours' steady plodding, and the pass was still distant, I began to think it was going too far. I boldly informed my companions, and tried to persuade myself, that another half-hour would take us to the top; but I secretly felt that I was a humbug. As the snow-fields rose up against the mountain, and became seamed with broader and deeper crevasses, in which it was necessary to seek carefully for a safe snow-bridge, the slowness of our progress became more than ever wearisome. We were tied together in two parties, and took it in turns to go first. Old Peter Taugwald, who led the other party, is a solid, steady-going old fellow, as broad as he is long, and as firm as a rock. The stolid calmness, from which he never wavers, becomes occasionally tiresome. He annoyed me now by the extreme deliberation with which he halted every few minutes to munch a great lump of sugar, whose good qualities he delights to expatiate upon, as being an excellent thing on the snow.

The day, which had been nearly perfect, was again beginning to look doubtful. A light cloud every now and then touched the top of the pass before us, and I began to fear that we might lose our view, and perhaps lose our way too, when we got there. Franz Andermatten, of Saas, was next to me—one of the merriest, strongest, and most willing little guides I ever met with. He had twice before walked with me, and on one of these occasions had resolutely insisted, notwithstanding our protests, on carrying three knapsacks on his own back for two consecutive days of twelve hours apiece. He is always ready to laugh at the mildest of jokes, and is very fond of quoting and expounding the most elaborate and unintelligible of proverbs, which are probably considered amusing by the natives of Saas. I pathetically remarked to him that, though this was the third season on which we had met, we had never yet had a fine day together. He immediately rushed forwards, declaring that "Herr Stiffs" should, at any rate, see something to-day. Away he went, plunging through the deep snow, like a small but infuriated bull. Spurts do not generally answer on these occasions; but Franz's energy carried us with a rush up to the top of the pass, and not too soon. It was already two o'clock, and we had had five hours of deep snow. But this was not enough for him.

We were now looking down on to the lower reach of the Täsch glacier. It had been my plan to effect a descent straight to this glacier by the rocks below us. Both Herr Imseng and Franz had, as I understood, declared this to be practicable. But now, to my astonishment, Franz resolutely declared that he knew the rocks to be impassable. The other guides mildly remonstrated, and proposed a trial. But Franz was obstinate: he said that our only course was to ascend the Allelein-horn on our left hand, and, from its summit, to descend to the very head of the Täsch glacier, *i. e.* to the col of the Allelein Pass. This, it was obvious, would involve a very long circuit, and would ultimately bring us round to the point immediately below us, only by means of first ascending a high mountain, and then going round over a lofty pass. The fact was, however, that the Allelein-horn was a great pet of Andermatten's, who had made the first ascent (which had never since been repeated) in company with Mr. Ames. When I hinted mildly that he was taking us rather out of the way, he skilfully asked me, with an air of astonishment, whether I did not wish to go to the top of the mountain? Of course, it was impossible exactly to say "No," and before I could expose his sophistry and show the absurdity of calling it a pass to go up a mountain 13,000 feet high on one side and down on the other, I felt the rope tighten round my waist, and Franz was off like a steam-engine, with his small train of travellers and guides panting behind him. The guides do not often study the science of knots, and consequently when the first man in the line is going his best, and the last is disposed to take it easily, the unfortunates in the centre are apt to find their waists growing most unpleasantly small. As Short and I were in this unfortunate predicament, we complained as pitifully as the small amount of breath left in our bodies would allow. It was of no use. One long slope of snow (fortunately in good order) lay between us and the summit, and straight up that slope we were dragged at our best pace, without halt or hesitation. At half-past two, we were sitting at the top round the little cairn which Franz had previously erected, loosing the ropes, and allowing our internal arrangements to return to their natural state. The other party followed us more deliberately, and we were soon all seated together, discussing our position and the view. We had lost the best part of the day, and thick clouds were hanging over the Italian plains and over many of the neighbouring heights. But the huge black ridges of rock which form the backbone and the ribs of the Alps rose up only the more grandly through the threatening masses of clouds. The Oberland mountains, of which we had had distant views for some time, were still visible, and occasionally we had glimpses of the green valley of Zermatt.

People still sometimes ask (though they have often had it explained to them), What is the use of going up a mountain? What more do you see at the top than you would at the bottom? Putting out of the question the glorious exercise and excitement of climbing a mountain, it would be well worth any trouble to see such views as those which can only be seen on the highest peaks. No doubt there are many views downstairs more capable of being made into pictures. The vast cloudy panorama stretched below your feet from an Alpine summit makes an impression upon your mind which can be described neither on canvas nor in writing. It gives a most exhilarating sense of unrivalled sublimity, which could no more be given in a painting than one of the scenes in "Paradise Lost." It is the constant presence before your eyes of such impressive though indescribable scenery, which gives to Alpine exercise such absorbing interest. Most people probably pass as much time in thinking about their dinner as they do about the scenery; but the presence of the scenery, though its beauty may not be so directly a subject of thought or interest during your toils and your hunger, goes for more in producing pleasure than it does even in such pursuits as fishing or shooting, As for the theory that you ought to walk ten miles a day and meditate on the beauties of nature, it may do for poets or painters, but it is hard doctrine for a man with a fair allowance of stomach and legs. A man can no more feel the true mountain spirit without having been into the very heart and up to the very tops of the mountains, than he can know what the sea is like by standing on the shore. It is just as easy to evolve the idea of a mountain-top out of the depths of your moral consciousness as that of a camel. The small patch of glistening white, which you are told is a snow-slope, looks very pretty out of the valley to any one, but it will look very different to a man who has only studied it through an opera-glass, and to one who has had to cut his way up it step by step for hours together. The little knob which your guide-book says is the top of some unpronounceable "Horn" will gain wonderfully in majesty when you have once stood upon it, and felt as if you were alone in the midst of the heavens, with the kingdoms of the earth at your feet; and if you meditate till doomsday on the beautiful lights and shades and the graceful sweeps of the mountain-ridges, you will not be one bit nearer to the sensation of standing on a knife-like ridge, with the toe of your boot over Italy, and the heel over Switzerland.

I make these remarks because I think Alpine travellers are apt to give way too much on this point, and to admit that, because the view from a mountain peak can't be put into a picture, it is not worth looking at. I must admit, however, that, as we sat on a mixture of ice and pebbles round the little stone "man" on the Allelein-horn, our thoughts were irresistibly drawn to the question of getting down again. The prospect which lay close to us was, therefore, decidedly the most interesting. At intervals, in the clouds, we could see the whole of the Täsch glacier, from the col of the Allelein Pass to its foot. Its broad level surface of snow was distinctly marked by the track which our companions had made on the previous day. But near and inviting as it looked, the difficulties which intervened seemed rather formidable.

A huge buttress runs south from the Horn to the top of the Allelein Pass. On its western side it descends in long and steep snow-slopes to the Täsch glacier. On the eastern side, the snow, which slopes steeply from its ridge, soon terminates at the edge of steep rocky cliffs, which sink, I presume, to the higher level of the Allelein glacier; as we saw them, they disappeared in a great lake of mist. These cliffs were covered, apparently, with loose stones mixed with fresh snow—a remarkably disagreeable combination. It was along the face of them, however, that Franz had passed with Mr. Ames on the previous ascent, and he now proposed to follow the same route. All our other guides protested against them, and preferred trying to find a way along the higher snow-slopes of the buttress. As they were in a majority, Franz, much to his annoyance, was compelled to give in. He was very eloquent to me afterwards on our folly in not following his advice, and I am disposed to think he was right. As it was, we came in for some varied practice in snow-work.

The buttress I have mentioned may be compared to the roof of a church tilted up at a steep angle; the tiles on either side representing the snow-slopes, which on one side reached only a short way to the edge of the cliffs, and on the other, or western side, stretched much farther to a level and easy glacier. Now, it is generally pretty good going along an arête, even though inclined at a considerable angle, so long as you can keep, as it were, on the backbone, and have a slope on each side of you. It is like walking along the ridge of the church roof; but when the roof makes a sudden break in its elevation, as at the joining of the nave and chancel, or when spikes suddenly protrude and drive you to circumvent them by making a short excursion on the tiles, the difficulty is very much exaggerated. In our case the spikes were represented by sharp spires of impracticable rock, which at once sent us down on to a snow-slope, decidedly steeper and more treacherous than ordinary roofing-tiles. We crept down towards it over a few firm rocks, and Franz, taking a big stone, dropped it quietly on the snow, to try its condition. The snow was old and hard beneath; but a thick cake of comparatively new snow, a few inches thick, was frozen on to its surface. The stone, as it fell, detached part of this cake from the snow beneath; the part detached slid down, dragging more after it, and, in a moment, a broad sheet of it was pouring down with a low hissing sound over the rocks below, leaving bare a surface of hard névé: where the snow went to I can't say, farther than that it was down a couloir and over a cliff. Of course, if we had rashly trodden upon it, we should have followed its example; as it was, we had cautiously to stick our feet into the firmer snow beneath, as far as we could; then driving our alpenstocks vertically down into it a little above our footsteps, we got a secure anchorage in case of an attempt at an avalanche from the snow above. We moved onwards very cautiously and slowly, and being firmly roped together, there was no danger from this cause; the only thing that annoyed me was produced by our friends' ingenuity in scrambling along close to the foot of the crest of rocks above. The result of this manœuvre was occasionally to send big stones down, rotating with extreme velocity around their minor axes, and taking playful and irregular bounds down the slopes towards us. This danger is one of the most annoying in the Alps; and it is one of the disadvantages of a large party that, by scattering, they may give space for the stones to get up their pace in. I once had a very narrow escape from causing a most serious accident in this way. Climbing up the side of the Bietschhorn, I was scrambling up some rocks, when a huge stone, about the size of a large folio volume, gave way as I laid my hand upon it, flew some twenty feet through the air, and bounded off the side of one of my guides down the cliffs below. It very luckily struck him on a knapsack which he was carrying, and beyond disturbing his balance and damaging the knapsack, did no harm. We managed to avoid the stones which our friends had started, and soon rejoined them on the ridge below the protruding rocks. Here, however, another difficulty met us; the ridge was now cut off by an abrupt descent, like that to which I have referred between the roof of the chancel and nave of a church. It became impossible to follow it, and we determined, after some dispute, to descend straight down the long snow-slopes on the side of the buttress to the Täsch glacier. For some way the descent was tolerably satisfactory. A huge rocky rib ran down the side of the mountain from the point where we stood. A kind of gutter in the ice was formed close to its side. The rock being tolerably sound, gave occasionally good holds for the hands or feet. Cutting a few steps in the gutter, and clinging firmly to the rocks, we were able to make tolerable progress; one or two of the party holding on firmly in favourable positions till the others had lowered themselves, and were able to give assistance in their turn. By this means we crept carefully down to the end of the rock, and then, perched upon a narrow ledge, began to consider what was to be done next. We were looking down a blank wall of ice, inclined, I should guess, at some 45°, and reaching without intermission to the glacier, at a depth of several hundred feet below. I knew, by very disagreeable experience, that it would probably take several hours to cut steps down to it; and yet, near us, the ice showed no snow on its surface to help us. It was already late, the sun was near setting, and the mists were getting thicker every moment. Soon, even the glacier below us was entirely concealed. I was making some hasty reflections as to the comfort of passing the night perched like a jackdaw on the side of a cliff, with dinner and coffee some thousands of feet below us. From certain recollections of a night so spent the summer before, I had no desire to repeat the performance; meanwhile there was no doubt a chance that there might be more snow on the ice farther down, but the question was whether we should be able to get there in time.

After a lively discussion between the guides, we adopted the following plan, suggested by the ancient and many-counselled Peter: By fastening our two ropes together we obtained a length of about a hundred feet. Moritz Anthonmatten then tied one end round his waist and was let down by the rest of the party to the full extent of the rope. The ice along which he slid was so steep and so free from snow, that his weight was borne almost entirely by the rope.

When he was let down as far as possible, there was still no foot-hold to be obtained. He quickly cut a couple of steps in the ice, and then freeing himself from the rope, cut a line of steps in a horizontal direction to a part of the slope where the snow seemed to be deeper. Another guide was let down in the same way, and helped to polish up the steps. Then each of the travellers, in succession, was lowered. We felt ourselves perfectly helpless bundles, sliding along the vast sheet of hard ice which sank into the mists at our feet, and in which it was almost impossible to obtain hold enough with the point of one's alpenstock, to serve as the slightest drag.

On arriving at the steps, I cast off the rope and hurried to the end of the line. I was delighted to find that the snow was there much deeper, and that it seemed probable that we might soon trust to a glissade. Meanwhile, I turned with some curiosity to see how the last guide, old Peter Taugwald, would descend. After letting down Franz, he drew up the rope, and doubled it, and placed the loop round a projecting point of rock; then, hanging on to it, and every now and then using a tremendously heavy axe, which he displayed with great pride, as a kind of ice-anchor, he let himself down to the end of the rope. Meanwhile, Franz had rapidly cut some slight steps (not too slight, however, for men accustomed to hold on by their eyelids) upwards to meet him. He unhitched the rope above, descended this perilous staircase, and they overtook the rest of the party in a few seconds along the laborious pathway, which took us long to cut, and a very short time to follow. We had now managed cautiously to descend the snow a few paces without any more "hacken," and by the time we were all together again, it had become tolerably firm and deep. By this manœuvre we had gained considerably in time in fact, the whole time which would have been necessary to cut a staircase 100 feet long in hard ice, which, as Alpine travellers well know, is something not to be neglected. We had had at intervals one or two looks at what lay below us, and it was fortunate for us that we had; for by this time the mist was growing thick and firm, and our only prospect was a few feet of the snow-slope. We now roped ourselves once more; old Peter sat down in front, with his huge axe held across his knees; I sat down close behind him, placed my boots on his thighs, and sticking my alpenstock into the snow on one side. The rest of the party took up similar positions, and we formed a compact train, well roped together, and with alpenstocks alternately to the right and left. The word "Vorwärts!" was given, and away we shot, with a general yell, down the soft snow into the gloom before us. We were tolerably certain that there was no bergschrund below, but the descent was rather exciting. Once the lumpiness of the snow disconnected the train, and we pulled up all in confusion in a heap of deep snow, with the rope dragging us all kinds of ways. We joined on again, and, with discordant howls of delight, shot away like lightning down the slope. This time we brought up all safe at the foot of the slope, and below the mists, amongst huge lumps of half-melted and half-frozen snow, which had, no doubt, come down the couloir in avalanches. Our boots and pockets were filled with snow; we had been bumped, and bruised, and cut, and had scraped the skin off our hands; but we were all in a state of absurd exhilaration at our sudden escape from our difficulties, and at the smooth plain of snow which now lay before us. We jumped up, gave ourselves a shake, and started across it at the double. It is not exactly usual to cross a glacier at a run, however smooth it may be. We wished, however, to make up for lost time, as it had taken us over four hours from the top of the Allelein-horn, which was still close above us. We were now all in the highest glee, and the pace we went soon brought us to the edge of the snow, on to the Alps, and within sight of châlets, and within sound of the cowbells below.

We had still a long, though, as we flattered ourselves, an easy walk before us. We found it rather worse than we had bargained for. The sun had set some time before we had crossed the Alps, and entered the pine forests on the side of the Zermatt Valley. A kind of small aqueduct leads through the woods from the mouth of the Täsch Valley, to irrigate some of the meadows. Along the side of it lies what in broad daylight is a tolerable footpath. The path, however, is not at all particular about being level or smooth. When it meets a big rock, it turns sharp up hill or down hill, to avoid it. It changes its level every now and then from pure caprice, and thinks nothing of being interrupted by a heap of stones as big as one's head, or having a *chevaux de frise* of fir branches across it, at the level of a man's eyes. This is all very well in daylight; but for tired men in the dark it is distressing, and rather trying for the temper. Sprained ankles and black eyes seemed very probable accidents. After an hour or so, stumbling, hobbling, and reeling about to avoid the various half-seen pitfalls with which it was playfully strewed, we were not a little pleased to run in the dark down a slippery grass slope covered with big stones, and to land ourselves without damage in the Zermatt Road. We reached M. Seiler's most hospitable and pleasant inn at 9.30, ready for supper.

A few days afterwards, after an inspection of our path from that most beautiful point of view, the Mittelhorn, I discovered what our true pass should have been. It lies close, not to the Allelein-horn, but to the Alphubel. I ascended this last with Melchior Anderegg, and we reached a col close to its south-east shoulder, by a secondary glacier which descends from it towards the lower part of the Täsch Valley. There was no difficulty whatever in the ascent to this part, and from it the path down the Fée glaciers to the Gletscher Alp was easily to be traced. It lies very near to that which we in fact took, and from which it is separated by a ridge of rocks.

8. PARTIAL ASCENT OF THE MATTERHORN.

BY F. VAUGHAN HAWKINS, M.A.

THE summer and autumn of 1860 will long be remembered in Switzerland, as the most ungenial and disastrous season, perhaps, on record; certainly without a parallel since 1834. The local papers were filled with lamentations over "der ewiger Süd-wind," which overspread the skies with perpetual cloud, and from time to time brought up tremendous storms, the fiercest of which, in the three first days of September, carried away or blocked up for a time, I believe, every pass into Italy except the Bernina. At Andermatt, on the St. Gothard, we were cut off for two days from all communications whatever by water on every side. The whole of the lower Rhone valley was under water. A few weeks later, I found the Splügen, in the gorge above Chiavenna, altogether gone, remains of the old road being just visible here and there, but no more. In the Valteline, I found the Stelvio road in most imminent danger, gangs of men being posted in the courses of the torrents to divert the boulders, which every moment threatened to overwhelm the bridges on the route. A more unlucky year for glacier expeditions, therefore, could hardly be experienced; and the following pages present in consequence only the narrative of an unfinished campaign, which it is the hope of Tyndall and myself to be able to prosecute to a successful conclusion early next August.

I had fallen in with Professor Tyndall on the Basle railway, and a joint plan of operations had been partly sketched out between us, to combine to some extent the more especial objects of each—scientific observations on his part; on mine, the exploration of new passes and mountain topography; but the weather sadly interfered with these designs. After some glacier measurements had been accomplished at Grindelwald, a short spell of fair weather enabled us to effect a passage I had long desired to try, from Lauterbrunnen direct to the Æggisch-horn by the Roth-thal, a small and unknown but most striking glacier valley, known to Swiss mythology as the supposed resort of condemned spirits. We scaled, by a seven hours' perpendicular climb, the vast amphitheatre of rock which bounds the Aletsch basin on this side, and had the satisfaction of falsifying the predictions of Ulrich Lauener, who bade us farewell at Grindelwald with the discouraging assertion that he should see us back again, as it was quite impossible to get over where we were going. As we descended the long reaches of the Aletsch glacier, rain and mist again gathered over us, giving to the scene the appearance of a vast Polar sea, over the surface of which we were travelling, with no horizon visible anywhere except the distant line of level ice. Arrived at the Æggisch-horn, the weather became worse than ever; a week elapsed before the measurement of the Aletsch glacier could be completed; and we reluctantly determined to dismiss Bennen, who was in waiting, considering the season too bad for high ascents, and to push on with Christian Lauener to the glaciers about Zinal. Bennen was in great distress. He and I had the previous summer reconnoitred the Matterhorn from various quarters, and he had arrived at the conclusion that we could in all probability ("ich beinahe behaupte") reach the top. That year, being only just convalescent from a fever, I had been unable to make the attempt, and thus an opportunity had been lost which may not speedily recur, for the mountain was then (September, 1859) almost free from snow. Bennen had set his heart on our making the attempt in 1860, and great was his disappointment at our proposed departure for Zinal. At the last moment, however, a change of plans occurred. Lauener was unwilling to proceed with us to Zinal: we resolved to give Bennen his chance; the theodolite was packed up and despatched to Geneva, and we set off for Breuil, to try the Matterhorn.

In order to explain the nature of the operations I am about to describe, I must say a few words as to the exact form of this extraordinary mountain, about which a good deal has been written, and some misconception, I venture to think, still prevails. The accompanying figures will, I hope, assist

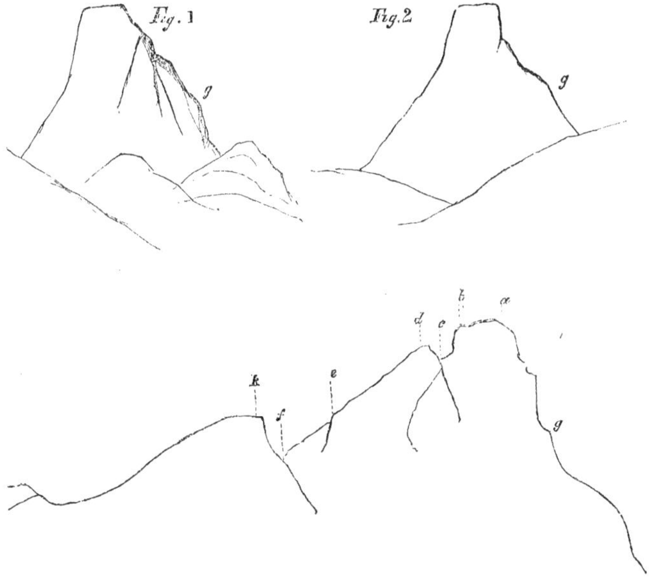

Fig. 3.

my explanations; they are taken from sketches carefully made by my friend the Rev. F. J. A. Hort, to whose kindness I owe them, and their accuracy is to be depended on. Fig. 1 conveys a better idea of the general shape of the mountain than any I have seen: it is taken from the top of Altels, very nearly due north, and about thirty miles distant, through a telescope. Fig. 2 is an outline similarly taken from the upper part of the névé of the Wildstrubel glacier, a little farther to the west than Altels. It will be observed that in both these outlines the right end of the top appears a little, but a very little, higher than the left. Fig. 3 gives the outline as seen nearly from the south, from a point 500 or 600 feet above Breuil. The spectator is here rather too much under the mountain to observe its true proportions. The top, as is always the case, is dwarfed; and the actual form of the west or left-hand side is a good deal obscured by the secondary ridge *d e*. This would have sunk into its proper place, and the top, *a b*, risen to a much greater height above *f*, if the view had been taken from a greater distance; and the outline would then have been very nearly the converse of that from Altels, *i.e.* that which the latter would present if held up against the light and turned the wrong way. I remember the exact converse of the Altels outline, *i.e.* as seen from S. instead of N. from a point in the hills above Anthey, in Val Tournanche. The obtrusion of the secondary ridge *d e*, before adverted to, also produces in great measure the apparent descent from *d* to *c*, preparatory to the final ascent, which does not appear in the Altels and Wildstrubel outlines. An admirable finished sketch of the mountain from the neighbourhood of Breuil, by Mr. George Barnard, is given in "A Lady's Tour round Monte Rosa." Fig. 4 is the well-

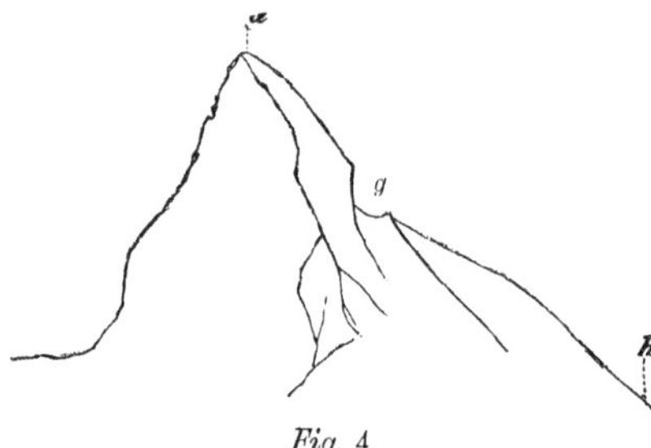

Fig. 4.

known outline seen from the Riffel hotel; the central part of the mountain appears correctly as seen from E., nearly in the form of an obelisk, an appearance which more distant views abundantly confirm; but the part from *g* to *h* is somewhat deceptive; it forms no part of the central mass of the mountain, but is one of several buttresses which radiate out from it in a northerly direction, the ground plan of which, as, indeed, of the whole of the mountain, is very accurately laid down in Studer's map, the study of which I recommend to any who feels a difficulty in reconciling the appearances which the mountain presents from different quar-

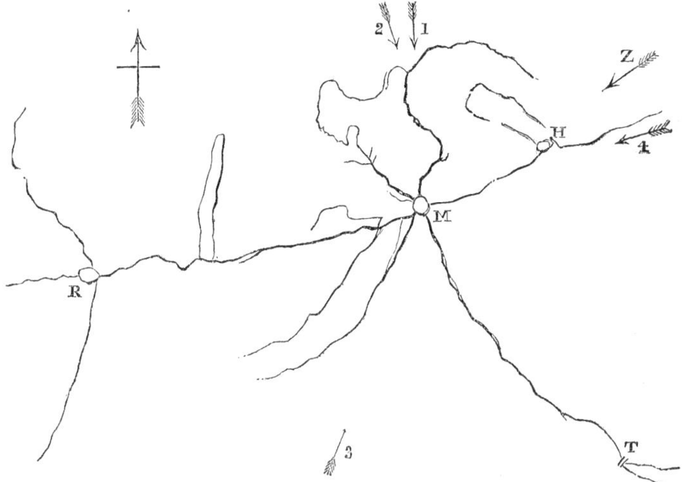

This figure is an outline of Studer's ground plan. M is the Matterhorn; R, the Dent d'Erin; Z, Zermatt; T, the Théodule Pass. The arrow heads show the directions whence the views Figs. 1, 2, 3, and 4, were severally taken.

ters. This somewhat deceptive buttress masks the true form of the peak on one side of it, in all views from Zermatt and its neighbourhood, and gives it the well-known resemblance to a horse or other couching animal.

The reader can now, I hope, form a correct idea of the shape of the actual peak of Mont Cervin, which rises from 4,000 to 5,000 feet on all sides above the elevated plateau or ridge, itself 10,000 feet or more in height, which extends in a semicircle from the Mischabel to the Weisshorn, and forms the base of all the high peaks in the Zermatt district. The Matterhorn, as seen from the north or south, is evidently a tower: the east side is somewhat steeper than the west, but not very greatly so, as may be seen from figs. 1 and 2. The top of the tower is a nearly level space of no great extent, the actually highest point being rather nearer the western than the eastern declivity. The eastern base of the tower rests on the ridge which forms the col of the Théodule: the western on the similar but rather higher ridge which stretches to the Dent d'Erin. If we now move through 90°, and observe the mountain from east or west, we see that the north and south sides of the tower are as steep as the east, but that several buttresses flank the mountain on the north, of which *g h*, in fig. 4, is the principal one: we see, also, that the breadth (from north to south) of the top of the tower is so small, that the sides appear almost to meet at the top in a point, and thus the mountain, when seen edgewise (from east or west, that is), may be not incorrectly styled an obelisk, while from north or south, seen lengthwise, it appears as a blunt and precipitous tower: a tower almost, if not quite, "without a stair."

Forbes's description of the Matterhorn, therefore, as "a stupendous and inaccessible obelisk of rock," is by no means an inaccurate one; and I think that even so accurate and practised an observer as Mr. Ruskin, while objecting to this as exaggerated, has himself fallen into several misconceptions about it of a curious kind. Certainly, I was never more surprised than to find Mr. Ruskin saying, at p. 57 of the first volume of "Stones of Venice," that "the Matterhorn has been *falsely represented as a peak or tower.*" Mr. Ruskin seems, in fact, to have thought that what appeared a peak was only the end of a long wall, extending to the Dent d'Erin, and that the right-hand slope, as seen in the Riffel view down to *g*, or nearly so, was so immensely fore-shortened, as to appear a steep slope, while it was in reality horizontal; and that the actual top of this supposed wall, if top it could be said to have, lay somewhere nearly as low down as *g*, which would have made the optical delusion, indeed, considerable. I confess I was led to doubt whether Mr. Ruskin had ever been at Breuil, or seen the mountain from its south-west side, and to suspect that his observations had been made in too close proximity to the deceptive buttress *g h*. In the fourth volume of "Modern Painters," pp. 183, 199, Mr. Ruskin has entered into an extended discussion on the subject; but I scarcely think he even there has seized, or at least conveyed to his readers, the true idea of its form, as a gigantic tower. So, at least, I interpret his confession of being unable, after all, to determine where the top really is: he raises it from near *g* to a point nearer *a*, but still does not seem to realize what I take to be the fact, that the real top lies somewhere but a little way *behind* the apparent top *a* in the Zermatt outline (certainly it can be no farther than the distance *a b*, in fig. 3), and that *no* part of the right-hand slope in the Zermatt outline is really horizontal, or at all approaching to horizontality. Nor does he, I think, realize the fact, that from the real top, *a b*, the mountain falls almost sheer for thousands of feet before the ridge is reached which stretches towards the Dent d'Erin. The Matterhorn may certainly in one sense be called a continuation of the latter ridge, inasmuch as it rises from it; but Monte Rosa might to the same extent be called a continuation of the (so-called) old Weiss-thor. And though the western slope is less steep than the east, yet so tremendous does it appear from a distance, that I know that a party of first-rate Alpine men, who surveyed it this summer with Melchior Anderegg from a considerable height up the Dent Blanche, came to the conclusion that this, the only supposed accessible side, was altogether impracticable.

Bennen and myself had sketched out a general plan of attack the year before, based on observations, not only from Breuil, but from points farther to the south and west, from whence the peak could be seen in its true proportions. It had been suggested by some to start from the hut on the top of the Théodule pass, and work round to the south; but this appeared impossible, and we decided that the only feasible plan was to start from Breuil, and endeavour to reach the point *f* or *k* in fig. 3. A party from Val Tournanche had succeeded in reaching the ridge at a point to the west of *k*; but we suspected, as the fact turned out to be, that it might be impossible to descend from the ridge at *k* into the gap behind the point *f*, from whence the actual peak rises, the Matterhorn being thus cut off from the ridge which runs from it to the Dent d'Erin, by an impassable gulf, so that all attempts to scale it either from Zermatt or from Breuil, by gaining that ridge anywhere to the westward of *f*, must be unavailing. We therefore decided to make directly for the gap *f*, which Bennen declared to be possible, though even this part of the ascent seemed by no means easy: a narrow line of broken and crevassed glacier fell steeply from it, and the rocks on either side appeared from a distance by no means inviting.

The gap at *f* reached, the ascent from *f* to *c*, behind the ridge *d e*, seemed not impracticable: indeed, though some parts appeared difficult, I confess that in 1859, when the ridge was almost free from snow, I was far from foreseeing the obstacles to be encountered all along this part of the route, the vast and rugged crags all along it being diminished by the great scale of the mountain into mere points and undulations on the sky line, as seen from Breuil. The last part of all, from *c* to *b*, seemed to me, as it does to most observers, the grand problem; but Bennen has always declared that, provided we do the rest, he is tolerably certain that we can find a way up that; and I am inclined to believe he is right. The top of a smaller mountain may be rendered inaccessible by a fosse or vertical wall of no great size, but impossible to be surmounted, as is the case with the Riffelhorn on its western side; but on the Matterhorn everything is on so vast a scale, that such an obstacle can almost always be got round or in some way avoided: while any large perpendicular cleft, defending the whole side of the mountain, if such existed, would probably be visible from a distance.

Accessible or not, however, the Mont Cervin is assuredly a different sort of affair from Mont Blanc or Monte Rosa, or any other of the thousand and one summits which nature has kindly opened to man, by leaving one side of them a sloping plain of snow, easy of ascent, till the brink of the precipice is reached which descends on the other side. The square massive lines of terraced crags which fence the Matterhorn, stand up on all sides nearly destitute of snow, and where the snow lies thinly on the rocks it soon melts and is hardened again into smooth glassy ice, which covers the granite slabs like a coat of varnish, and bids defiance to the axe. Every step of the way lies between two precipices, and under toppling crags, which may at any moment bring down on the climber the most formidable of Alpine dangers—a fire of falling stones. The mountain too has a sort of *prestige* of invincibility which is not without its influence on the mind, and almost leads one to expect to encounter some new and unheard of source of peril upon it: hence I suppose it is, that the dwellers at Zermatt and in Val Tournanche have scarcely been willing to attempt to set foot upon the mountain, and have left the honour of doing so to a native of another district, who, as he has been the first mortal to plant foot on the hitherto untrodden peak, so he will, I hope, have the honour which he deserves, of being the first to reach the top.

John Joseph Bennen, of Laax, in the Upper Rhine Valley, is a man so remarkable, that I cannot resist the desire (especially as he cannot read English) to say a few words about his character. Born within the limits of the German tongue, and living amidst the mountains and glaciers of the Oberland, he belongs by race and character to a class of men of whom the Laueners, Melchior Anderegg, Bortis, Christian Almer, Peter Bohren, are also examples—a type of mountain race, having many of the simple heroic qualities which we associate, whether justly or unjustly, with Teutonic blood, and essentially different from—to my mind, infinitely superior to—the French-speaking, versatile, wily Chamouniard. The names I have mentioned are all those of first-rate men; but Bennen, as (I believe) he surpasses all the rest in the qualities which fit a man for a leader in hazardous expeditions, combining boldness and prudence with an ease and power peculiar to himself, so he has a faculty of conceiving and planning his achievements, a way of concentrating his mind upon an idea, and working out his idea with clearness and decision, which

I never observed in any man of the kind, and which makes him, in his way, a sort of Garibaldi. Tyndall, on the day of our expedition, said to him, "Sie sind der Garibaldi der führer, Bennen;" to which he answered in his simple way, "Nicht wahr?" ("Am I not?") an amusing touch of simple vanity, a dash of pardonable bounce, being one of his not least amiable characteristics. Thoroughly sincere and "einfach" in thought and speech, devoted to his friends, without a trace of underhand self-seeking in his relations to his employers, there is an independence about him, a superiority to most of his own class, which makes him, I always fancy, rather an isolated man; though no one can make more friends where-ever he goes, or be more pleasant and thoroughly cheerful under all circumstances. But he left his native place, Steinen, he told me, the people there not suiting him; and in Laax, where he now dwells, I guess him to be not perhaps altogether at home. Unmarried, he works quietly most of the year at his trade of a carpenter, unless when he is out alone, or with his friend Bortis (a man seemingly of reserved and uncommunicative disposition, but a splendid mountaineer), in the chase after chamois, of which he is passionately fond, and will tell stories, in his simple and emphatic way, with the greatest enthusiasm. Pious he is, and observant of religious duties, but without a particle of the "mountain gloom," respecting the prevalence of which among the dwellers in the High Alps, Mr. Ruskin discourses poetically, but I am myself rather incredulous. A perfect nature's gentleman, he is to me the most delightful of companions; and though no "theory" defines our reciprocal obligations as guide and employer, I am sure that no precipice will ever engulf me so long as Bennen is within reach, unless he goes into it also—an event which seems impossible—and I think I can say I would, according to the measure of my capacity, do the same by him. But any one who has watched Bennen skimming along through the mazes of a crevassed glacier, or running like a chamois along the side of slippery ice-covered crags, axe and foot keeping time together, will think that—

as Lauener said of his brother Johann, who perished on the Jungfrau, *he* could never fall—nothing could bring him to grief but an avalanche.*

Delayed in our walk from the Æggisch-horn by the usual severity of the weather, Tyndall, Bennen, and myself reached Breuil on Saturday, the 18th of August, to make our attempt on the Monday. As we approached the mountain, Bennen's countenance fell visibly, and he became somewhat gloomy; the mountain was almost white with fresh-fallen snow. "Nur die schnee furcht mich," he replied to our inquiries. The change was indeed great from my recollection of the year before; the well-marked, terrace-like lines along the south face, which are so well given in Mr. Barnard's picture, which I have referred to, were now almost covered up; through the telescope could be seen distinctly huge icicles depending from the crags, the lines of melting snow, and the dark patches which we hoped might spread a great deal faster than they were likely to, during the space of twenty-four hours. There was nothing for it, although our prospects of success were materially diminished by the snow, but to do the best we could. As far as I was concerned, I felt that I should be perfectly satisfied with getting part of the way up on a first trial, which would make one acquainted with the nature of the rocks, dispel the prestige which seemed to hang over the untrodden mountain, and probably suggest ways of shortening the route on another occasion.

We wanted some one to carry the knapsack containing our provisions; and on the recommendation of the landlord at Breuil, we sent for a man, named Carrel, who, we were told,

* As Bennen and Tyndall were going up the Finster-dar-horn once upon a time, the work being severe, Bennen turned round and said to Tyndall, "Ich fühle mich jetzt ganz wie der Tyroler Einmal," and went to relate a story of the conversation between a priest and an honest Tyrolese, who complained to his father confessor that religion and an extreme passion for the fair sex struggled within him, and neither could expel the other. "Mein Sohn," said the priest, "Frauen zu lieben und in Himmel zu kommen, das geht nicht." "Herr Pfarrer," sagte der Tyroler, "*es müss gehen.*" "Und so sag' ich jetzt," cried Bennen. "Es müss gehen" is always his motto.

was the best mountaineer in Val Tournanche, and the nephew of M. le Chanoine Carrel, whose acquaintance I once had the honour of making at Aosta. From the latter description I rather expected a young, and perhaps aristocratic-looking personage, and was amused at the entrance of a rough, good-humoured, shaggy-breasted man, between forty and fifty, an ordinary specimen of the peasant class. However, he did his work well, and with great good temper, and seemed ready to go on as long as we chose; though he told me he expected we should end by passing the night somewhere on the mountain, and I don't think his ideas of our success were ever very sanguine.

We were to start before 3 A.M. on Monday morning, August 20th; and the short period for sleep thus left us was somewhat abridged in my own case, not so much by thoughts of the coming expedition, as by the news which had just reached us in a vague, but, unfortunately, only too credible form, of the terrible accident on the Col du Géant a few days before. The account thus reaching us was naturally magnified, and we were as yet ignorant of the names. I could not at night shake off the (totally groundless) idea that a certain dear friend of mine was among them, and that I ought at that moment to be hurrying off to Cormayeur, to mourn and to bury him. In the morning, however, these things are forgotten; we are off, and Carrel pilots us with a lantern across the little stream which runs by Breuil, and up the hills to the left, where in the darkness we seem from the sound to be in the midst of innumerable rills of water, the effects of the late rains. The dark outline of the Matterhorn is just visible against the sky, and measuring with the eye the distance subtended by the site we have to climb, it seems as if success *must* be possible: so hard is it to imagine all the ups and downs which lie in that short sky-line.

Day soon dawns, and the morning rose-light touches the first peak westward of us; the air is wonderfully calm and still, and for to-day, at all events, we have good weather, without that bitter enemy, the north wind; but a certain opaque look in the sky, long streaks of cloud radiating from the south-west horizon up towards the zenith, and the too dark purple of the hills south of Aosta, are signs that the good weather will not be lasting. By five we are crossing the first snow-beds, and now Carrel falls back, and the leader of the day comes to the front: all the day he will be cutting steps, but those compact and powerful limbs of his will show no signs of extra exertion, and to-day he is in particularly good spirits. Carpentering, by the way—not fine turning and planing, but rough out-of-doors work, like Bennen's—must be no bad practice to keep hand and eye in training during the dead season. We ascend a narrow edge of snow, a cliff some way to the right: the snow is frozen and hard as rock, and arms and legs are worked vigorously. Tyndall calls out to me, to know whether I recollect the "conditions:" *i.e.* if your feet slip from the steps, turn in a moment on your face, and dig in hard with alpenstock in both hands under your body; by this means you will stop yourself if it is possible. Once on your back, it is all over, unless others can save you: you have lost all chance of helping yourself. In a few minutes we stop, and rope all together, in which state we continued the whole day. The prudence of this some may possibly doubt, as there were certainly places where the chances were greater, that if one fell, he would drag down the rest, than that they could assist him; but we were only four, all tolerably sure-footed, and in point of fact I do not recollect a slip or stumble of consequence made by any one of us. Soon the slope lessens for a while, but in front a wall of snow stretches steeply upwards to the gap *f*, which we have to reach, in a kind of recess, flanked by crags of formidable appearance. We turn to the rocks on the left hand. As, to one walking along miry ways, the opposite side of the path seems ever the most inviting, and he continually shifting his course from side to side, lengthens his journey with small profit: so in ascending a mountain one is always tempted to diverge from snow to rocks, or *vice versâ.* Bennen had intended to mount straight up towards the gap, and it is best not to interfere with him; he yields, however, to our suggestions, and we assail the rocks. These, however, are ice-bound, steep, and slippery: hands and knees are at work, and progress is slow. At length, we stop upon a ledge where all can stand together, and Carrel proposes to us (for Bennen and he can only communicate by signs, the one knowing only French, the other German) to go on and see whether an easier way can be found still further to the left. Bennen gives an approving nod: he looks with indulgent pity on Carrel, but snubs all remarks of his as to the route. "Er weisst gar nichts," he says. Carrel takes his axe, and mounts warily, but with good courage; presently he returns, shaking his head. The event is fortunate, for had we gone further to the left, we should have reached the top of the ridge from which, as we afterwards found, there is no passage to the gap *f*, and our day's work would probably have ended then and there. Bennen now leads to the right, and moves swiftly up from ledge to ledge. Time is getting on, but at length we emerge over the rocks just in face of the gap, and separated from it by a sort of large snow-crater, overhung on the left by the end of the ridge *k*, from which stones fall which have scarred the sides of the crater. The sides are steep, but we curve quickly and silently round them: no stones fall upon us; and now we have reached the narrow neck of snow which forms the actual gap; it is half-past eight, and the first part of our work is done.

By no means the hardest part, however. We stand upon a broad red granite slab, the lowest step of the actual peak of the Matterhorn: no one has stood there before us. The slab forms one end of the edge of snow, surmounted at the other end by some fifty feet of overhanging rock, the end of the ridge *k*. On one side of us is the snow-crater, round which we had been winding; on the other side a scarped and seamed face of snow, drops sheer on the north, to what we know is the Zmutt glacier. Some hopes I had entertained of making a pass by this gap, from Breuil to Zermatt, vanish immediately. Above us rise the towers and pinnacles of the Matterhorn, certainly a tremendous array. Actual contact immensely increases one's impressions of this, the hardest and strongest of all the mountain masses of the Alps; its form is more remarkable than that of other mountains, not by chance, but because it is built of more massive and durable materials, and more solidly put together: nowhere have I seen such astonishing masonry. The broad gneiss blocks are generally smooth and compact, with little appearance of splintering or weathering. Tons of rock, in the shape of boulders, must fall almost daily down its sides, but the amount of these, even in the course of centuries, is as nothing compared with the mass of the mountain; the ordinary processes of disintegration can have little or no effect on it. If one were to follow Mr. Ruskin, in speculating on the manner in which the Alpine peaks can have assumed their present shape, it seems as if such a mass as this can have been blocked out only while rising from the sea, under the action of waves such as beat against the granite headlands of the Land's End. Once on dry land, it must stand as it does now, apparently for ever.

Two lines of ascent offer, between which we have to choose: one along the middle or dividing ridge, the back-bone of the mountain, at the end of which we stand; the other by an edge some little way to the right (in fact, the northern side of the ridge *d e* in fig. 3): a couloir lies between them. We choose the former, or back-bone ridge; but the other proves to be less serrated, and we shall probably try it on another occasion: both converge near the top about the point *c*. As we step from our halting-place, Bennen turns round and addresses us in a few words of exhortation, like the generals in Thucydides. He knows us well enough to be sure that we shall not feel afraid, but every footstep must be planted with the utmost precaution: no fear, "wohl immer achtung." Soon our difficulties begin; but I despair of relating the incidents of this part of our route, so numerous and bewildering were the obstacles along it; and the details of each have somewhat faded from the memory. We are immersed in a wilderness of blocks, roofed and festooned with huge plates and stalactites of ice, so large that one is half disposed to seize hold and clamber up them. Round, over, and under them we go: often progress seems impossible; but Bennen, ever in advance, and perched like a bird on some projecting crag, contrives to find a way. Now we crawl singly along a narrow ledge of rock, with a wall on one side, and nothing on the other: there is no hold for hands or alpenstock, and the ledge slopes a little, so that if the nails in our boots hold not, down we shall go: in the middle of it a piece of rock juts out, which we ingeniously duck under, and emerge just under a shower of water, which there is no room to escape from. Presently comes a more extraordinary place: a perfect chimney of rock, cased all over with hard black ice, about an inch thick. The bottom leads out into space, and the top is somewhere in the upper regions: there is absolutely nothing to grasp at, and to this day I cannot understand how a human being could get up or down it unassisted. Bennen, however, rolls up it somehow, like a cat; he is at the top, and beckons Tyndall to advance; my turn comes next; I endeavour to mount by squeezing myself against the sides, but near the top friction suddenly gives way, and down comes my weight upon the rope:—a stout haul from above, and now one knee is upon the edge, and I am safe: Carrel is pulled up after me. After a time, we get off the rocks, and mount a slope of ice, which curves rapidly over for about three yards to our left, and then (apparently) drops at once to the Zmutt glacier. We reach the top of this, and proceed along it, till at last a sort of pinnacle is reached, from which we can survey the line of towers and crags before us as far as *c*, the part just below the actual top, and we halt to rest a while. Bennen goes on to see whether it be possible to cross over to the other ridge, which seems an easier one. Left to himself, he treads lightly and almost carelessly along. "Geb 'acht, Bennen" (take care of yourself)! we shout after him, but needlessly; he stops and moves alternately, peering wistfully about, exactly like a chamois; but soon he returns, and says there is no passage, and we must keep to the ridge we are on.

Three hours had not yet elapsed since we left the gap, and from our present station we could survey the route as far as the point *c*, which concealed from us the actual summit, and could see that the difficulties before us were not greater than we had already passed through, and such as time and perseverance would surely conquer. Nevertheless, there is a tide in the affairs of such expeditions, and the impression had been for some time gaining ground with me that the tide on the present occasion had turned against us, and that the time we could prudently allow was not sufficient for us to reach the top that day. Before trial, I had thought it not improbable that the ascent might turn out either impossible, or comparatively easy; it was now tolerably clear that it was neither the one nor the other, but an exceedingly long and hard piece of work, which the unparalleled amount of ice made longer and harder than usual. I asked Bennen if he thought there was time enough to reach the top of all? he was evidently unwilling, however, to give up hopes; and Tyndall said, he would give no opinion either way; so we again moved on.

At length we came to the base of a mighty knob, huger and uglier than its fellows, to which a little arête of snow served as a sort of draw-bridge. I began to fear lest in the ardour of pursuit we might be carried on too long, and Bennen might forget the paramount object of securing our safe retreat. I called out to him, that I thought I should stop somewhere here, that if he could go faster alone, he might do so, but he must turn in good time. Bennen, however, was already climbing with desperate energy up the sides of the kerb; Tyndall would not be behind him; so I loosed the rope and let them go on. Carrel moved back across the little arête, and sat down, and began to smoke: I remained for awhile standing with my back against the knob, and gazed by myself upon the scene around.

As my blood cooled, and the sounds of human footsteps and voices grew fainter, I began to realize the height and the wonderful isolation of our position. The air was preternaturally still; an occasional gust came eddying round the corner of the mountain, but all else seemed strangely rigid and motionless, and out of keeping with the beating heart and moving limbs, the life and activity of man. Those stones and ice have no mercy in them, no sympathy with human adventure; they submit passively to what man can do; but let him go a step too far, let heart or hand fail, mist gather or sun go down, and they will exact the penalty to the uttermost. The feeling of "the sublime" in such cases depends very much, I think, on a certain balance between the forces of nature and man's ability to cope with them: if they are too weak, the scene fails to impress; if they are too strong for him, what was sublime becomes only terrible. Looking at the Dome du Gouté or the Zumstein Spitze full in the evening sun, when they glow with an absolutely unearthly loveliness, like a city in the heavens, I have sometimes thought that,—place but the spectator alone just now upon those shining heights, with escape before night all but impossible, and he will see no glory in the scene:—only the angry eye of the setting sun fixed on dark rocks and dead-white snow.

We had risen seemingly to an immense height above the gap, and the ridge which stretches from the Matterhorn to the Dent d'Erin lay flat below; but the peak still towered behind me, and measuring our position by the eye along the side of our neighbour of equal height, the Weisshorn, I saw that we must be yet a long way beneath the top. The gap itself and all traces of the way by which we had ascended, were invisible; I could see only the stone where Carrel sat, and the tops of one or two crags rising from below. The view was, of course, magnificent, and on three sides wholly unimpeded: with one hand I could drop a stone which would descend to Zmutt, with the other to Breuil. In front lay, as in a map, the as yet unexplored peaks to south and west of the Dent d'Erin, the range which separates Val Tournanche from the Valpelline, and the glacier region beyond, called in Ziegler's map Zardezan, over which a pass, perchance, exists to Zermatt. An illimitable range of blue hills spread far away into Italy.

I walked along the little arête, and sat down; it was only broad enough for the foot, and in perfectly cold blood even this perhaps might have appeared uncomfortable. Turning to look at Tyndall and Bennen, I could not help laughing at the picture of our progress under difficulties. They seemed to have advanced only a few yards. "Have you got no further than that yet?" I called out, for we were all the time within hearing. Their efforts appeared prodigious: scrambling and sprawling among the huge blocks, one fancied they must be moving along some unseen bale of heavy goods, instead of only the weight of their own bodies. As I looked, an ominous visitant appeared: down came a fragment of rock, the size of a man's body, and dashed past me on the couloir, sending the snow flying. For a moment I thought they might have dislodged it; but looking again I saw it had passed over their heads, and come from the crags above. Neither of them, I believe, observed the monster; but Tyndall told me afterwards that a stone, possibly a splinter from it, had hit him in the neck, and nearly choked him. I looked anxiously again, but no more followed. A single shot, as it were, had been fired across our bows; but the ship's course was already on the point of being put about.

Expecting fully that they would not persevere beyond a few minutes longer, I called out to Tyndall to know how soon they meant to be back. "In an hour and a half," he replied, whether in jest or earnest, and they disappeared round a projecting corner. A sudden qualm seized me, and for a few minutes I felt extremely uncomfortable;—what if the ascent should suddenly become easier, and they should go on, and reach the top without me? I thought of summoning Carrel, and pursuing them; but the worthy man sat quietly, and seemed to have had enough of it. My suspense, however, was not long: after two or three minutes the clatter, which had never entirely ceased, became louder, and their forms again appeared: they were evidently descending. In fact, Bennen had at length turned, and said to Tyndall, "Ich denke die Zeit ist zu kurz." I was glad that he had gone on as long as he chose, and not been turned back on my responsibility. They had found one part of this last ascent the worst of any, but the way was open thenceforward to the farthest visible point, which can be no long way below the actual top.

It was now just about mid-day, and ample time for the descent, in all probability, was before us ; but we resolved not to halt for any length of time till we should reach the gap. Descending, unlike ascending, is generally not so bad as it seems ; but in some places here only one can advance at a time, the other carefully holding the rope. "Tenez fortement, Carrel, tenez," is constantly impressed on the man who brings up the rear. "Splendid practice for us, this," exclaims Tyndall exultingly, as each successive difficulty is overcome. At length we reach a place whence no egress is possible ; we look in vain for traces of the way we had come : it is our friend the ice-coated chimney. Bennen gets down first, in the same mysterious fashion as he got up, and assists us down ; presently a shout is heard behind ; Carrel is attempting to get down by himself, and has stuck fast ; Bennen has to extricate him. We are now getting rapidly lower ; soon the difficulties diminish ; our gap appears in sight, and once more we reach the broad granite slab beside the narrow col, and breathe more freely.

Two hours have brought us down thus far ; but if we are to return by the way we came, three or four hours of hard work are still needed, before we arrive at anything like ordinary snow-walking. We hold a consultation. Bennen thinks the rocks, now that the ice is melting in the afternoon sun, will be difficult, and "withal somewhat dangerous" (etwa gefährlich auch). The reader will remark, that Bennen uses the word "dangerous" in its legitimate sense. A place is dangerous where a good climber cannot be secure of his footing ; a place is *not* dangerous where a good climber is in no danger of slipping, although to slip might be fatal. We determine to see if it be possible to descend the sides of the snow-crater, on the brink of which we now stand. The crater is portentously steep, deeply lined with fresh snow, which glistens and melts in the powerful sun. The experiment is slightly hazardous, but we resolve to try. The crater appears to narrow gradually to a sort of funnel far down below, through which we expect to issue into the glacier beneath. At the sides of the funnel are rocks, which some one suggests might serve to break our fall, should the snow go down with us, but their tender mercies seem to me doubtful. Cautiously, with steady, balanced tread, we commit ourselves to the slope, distributing the weight of the body over as large a space of snow as possible, by fixing in the pole high up, and the feet far apart, for a slip or stumble now will probably dissolve the adhesion of the fresh, not yet compacted mass, and we shall go down to the bottom in an avalanche. Six paces to the right, then again to the left; we are at the mercy of those overhanging rocks just now, and the recent tracks of stones look rather suspicious; but all is silent, and soon we gain confidence, and congratulate ourselves on an expedient which has saved us hours of time and toil. Just to our right the snow is sliding by, first slowly, then faster; keep well out of the track of it, for underneath is a hard polished surface, and if your foot chance to light there, off you will probably shoot. The snow travels much faster than we do, or have any desire to do; we are like a coach travelling alongside of an express train; in popular phrase, we are going side by side with a small avalanche, though a real avalanche is a very different matter. Soon we come somewhat under the lee of the rocks, and now all risk is over, we are through the funnel, and floundering waist-deep, heedless of crevasses in the comparatively level slopes beyond. We plunge securely down now in the deep snow, where care and caution had been requisite in crossing the frozen surface in the morning; at length we cast off the rope, and are on terra firma.

We shall be at Breuil in unexpectedly good time, before

five o'clock; but it is well we are off the mountain early, for clouds and mist are already gathering round the peak, and the weather is about to break. Tyndall rushes rapidly down the slopes, and is lost to view; Bennen and I walk slowly, discussing the results of the day. I am glad to see that he is in high spirits, and confident of our future success. He agrees with me to reach the top will be an exceedingly long day's work, and that we must allow ten hours at least for the actual peak, six to ascend, four to descend; we must start next time, he says, "ganz, ganz früh," and manage to reach the gap by seven o'clock. Presently we deviate a little from our downward course; the same thought occupies our minds; we perceive a long low line of roof on the mountain side, and are not mistaken in supposing that our favourite food will at this hour be found there in abundance. The shepherds on the Italian hills are more hospitable and courteous, I think, than their Swiss brethren: twenty cows are moving their tails contentedly in line under the shed, for Breuil is a rich pasture valley, and in an autumn evening I have counted six herds of from ninety to a hundred each, in separate clusters, like ants, along the stream in the distance. The friendly man, in hoarse but hearty tones, urges us on as we drink; Bennen puts into his hand forty centimes for us both (for we have disposed of no small quantity): but he is with difficulty persuaded to accept so large a sum, and calls after us, "C'est trop, c'est trop, messieurs." Long may civilization and half-francs fail of reaching his simple abode; for, alas! the great tourist-world is corrupting the primitive châlet-life of the Alps, and the Alpine man returning to his old haunts, finds a rise in the price even of "niedl" and "mascarpa."

The day after our expedition, Bennen and myself recrossed the Théodule in a heavy snow-storm. Tyndall started for Chamouni, for the weather was too bad to justify an indefinite delay at Breuil in the hope of making another attempt that year, and by waiting till another season, we were sure of obtaining less unfavourable conditions of snow and ice upon the mountain.—We had enjoyed an exciting and adventurous day, and I myself was not sorry to have something still left to do, while we had the satisfaction of being the first to set foot on this, the most imposing and mightiest giant of the Alps—the "inaccessible" Mont Cervin.

9. *FROM LAUTERBRUNNEN TO THE ÆGGISCHHORN BY THE LAUWINEN-THOR.*

BY JOHN TYNDALL, F.R.S.

LET me be excused if I commence this brief article by a few personal references, intended to show why, apart from all scientific considerations, men like myself should highly value a periodic visit to the Alps.

For several weeks previous to my release from London, last August, the state of my health had been a frequent source of uneasiness, if not of alarm. Mental exertion, unwisely persisted in, had brought on a curious kind of giddiness, which became more and more easily excited, until, finally, the writing of a letter, or the reading of a newspaper, sufficed to convert my head into a kind of electric battery, from which thrills were sent to my fingers' ends. I had more than once been compelled to pause in directing a note; fearful lest the effort required to complete the address should produce some terrible catastrophe in my brain.

A week's excursion to Killarney proved beneficial, but not permanent in its effects. I longed for the air of the Swiss mountains. In 1859, I thought I had bidden them for a time farewell, purposing in future to steep my thoughts in the tranquillity of English valleys, and confine my mountain-work to occasional excursions in the Scotch Highlands, or amid the Welsh and Cumbrian hills. But in my weariness I felt as if the icy air of the Alps seemed essential to my restoration: the very thought of the snow-peaks and glaciers was a tonic; and to the Alps, therefore, I resolved once more to go. I wrote to my former guide, Christian Lauener, desiring him to meet me at Thun on Saturday the 4th of August; and on my way thither, I fortunately fell in with Mr. Hawkins. A brief conversation caused us to close like a pair of atoms possessing mutual affinities. We agreed to work together as a binary human compound, sharing for a time the same food and shelter, the same pleasures, and the same toils.

Arrived at Thun, Lauener was not to be found. Hawkins halted here, promising to join me next day at Grindelwald, and I crossed the lake alone. In driving from Neuhaus to Interlaken, a chaise met us, and swiftly passed; within it I could discern the brown visage of my guide. We pulled up and shouted,—the other vehicle stopped, Lauener leaped from it, and came bounding towards me with admirable energy, through the deep and splashing mud. "*Gott! wie der Kerl springt!*" was the admiring exclamation of my coachman. Lauener is more than six feet high, but mainly a mass of bone; his legs are out of proportion, longer than his trunk; and he wears a short-tail coat, which augments the apparent discrepancy. Those massive levers were now plied with extraordinary vigour to project his body through space; and it was gratifying to be thus assured that the man was in first-rate condition, and fully up to the hardest work.

On Sunday, the 5th of August, for the sake of a little training, I ascended the Faulhorn alone. The morning was splendid, but as the day advanced, heavy cloud-wreaths swathed the mountains. This attained a maximum about two, P.M., and afterwards the overladen air cleared itself by intermittent jerks,—revealing at times the blue of heaven, and the peaks of the mountains; then closing up again, and hiding in its dismal folds the very posts which stood at a distance of ten paces from the hotel door. The effects soon became exceedingly striking, the mutations were so quick and so forcibly antithetical. I lay down upon a seat, and watched the intermittent extinction and generation of the clouds, and the alternate appearance and disappearance of the mountains. More and more the sun swept off the sweltering haze, and the blue sky bent over us in domes of ampler span. At four, P.M., no trace of cloud was visible, and a panorama of the Oberland, such I had no idea that the Faulhorn could command, unfolded itself. There was the grand barrier which separated us from the Valais; there were the Jungfrau, Monk and Eiger, the Finsteraarhorn, the Schreckhorn, and the Wetterhorn, lifting their snowy and cloudless crests to heaven, and all so sharp and wildly precipitous, that the bare thought of standing on any one of them made me shudder. London was still in my brain, and the vice of Primrose Hill in my muscles.

I disliked the ascent of the Faulhorn exceedingly, having followed a monotonous pony-track up the ugliest of mountains. Once, indeed, I deviated from the road out of pure disgust, and taking a jumping torrent for my guide and colloquist, was led astray. I now resolved to return to Grindelwald by another route. My host at first threw cold water on my desires, but he afterwards relaxed and admitted that the village might be attained in a more direct way than that in which I had ascended. He pointed to some rocks, eminences, and trees, which were to serve as landmarks; and stretching his arm in the direction of Grindelwald, I took the bearing of the place, and scampered over slopes of snow to the sunny alp beyond them. To my left was a mountain stream making soft music by the explosion of its bubbles.* I was once tempted aside to climb an eminence, which had been sculptured to a

* When the smoke of a cigar is projected from the lips, each puff is usually accompanied by a little explosion, arising chiefly from the sudden bursting of a film which unites both lips. If an inflated bladder be jumped upon it will emit a sound as loud as a pistol shot, owing to the sudden liberation of the compressed air. To a similar cause the sound of breakers and of rippling streams appears to be almost and wholly due; wherever a ripple is heard, bubbles are sure to be in a state of formation and explosion. The impact of water against water is a comparatively subordinate source of sound, and does not produce the murmur of a brook or the musical roar of the ocean. (See a short paper on this subject in the *Philosophical Magazine* for February, 1851.)

dome by an ancient glacier, and where I lay for an hour watching the augmenting glory of the mountains. The scene at hand was perfectly pastoral; green sunny pastures, dotted with chalets, and covered with cows, which filled the air with the incessant tinkle of their bells. Beyond was the majestic architecture of the Alps, with capitals and western bastions flushed with the warm light of the lowering sun. A milder radiance fell upon the eastern wings, while the shaded corridors assumed a depth through which the vision seemed to plunge into the very heart of the Oberland. I do not think I ever enjoyed an hour more. There was health in the air and hope in the mountains. The jelly of my brain was consolidating, and with the consciousness of augmenting vigour I quitted my station, and galloped down the alp. I was soon amid the pinewoods which overhang the valley of Grindelwald, with no guidance save the slope of the mountain, which, at times, was precipitous; but the roots of the pines grasping the rocks afforded hand and foot such hold as to render the steepest places the pleasantest of all. I often emerged from the gloom of the trees upon lovely bits of pasture—bright emerald gems set in the bosom of the woods—from which glimpses of indescribable beauty were obtained. It appeared to me surprising that nobody had constructed a resting place on this fine slope. With a fraction of the time necessary to reach the top of the Faulhorn, a position might be secured, from which the prospect would vie in point of grandeur with almost any in the Alps; while the ascent from Grindelwald, amid the shade of the festooned trees, would itself be delightful.

Hawkins had arrived; our guide had prepared a number of stakes, and on Monday morning we mounted our theodolite and proceeded to the Lower Glacier. With some difficulty we established the instrument upon a site whence the glacier could be seen from edge to edge; and across it was fixed in a straight line a series of twelve stakes. We afterwards ascended the glacier till we touched the avalanche-debris of the Heisse Platte. We wandered amid the moulins and crevasses until evening approached, and thus gradually prepared our muscles for more arduous work. On Tuesday a sleety rain filled the entire air, and the glacier was so laden with fog that there was no possibility of our being able to see across it. On Wednesday, happily, the weather brightened, and we executed our measurements; finding, as in all other cases, that the glacier was retarded by its bounding walls; its motion varying from a minimum of thirteen and a half inches to a maximum of twenty-two inches a day. To Hawkins I am indebted both for the fixing of the stakes, and the reduction of the measurements to their diurnal rate.

Previous to leaving England I had agreed to join a party of friends at the Æggisch-horn, on Thursday the 9th of August. My plan was, first to measure the motion of the Grindelwald Glacier, and afterwards to cross the mountain-wall which separates the Canton of Berne from that of Valais, so as to pass from Lauterbrunnen to the Æggisch-horn in a single day. How this formidable barrier was to be crossed I knew not, but I did not doubt being able to get over it somehow. On mentioning my wish to Lauener, he agreed to try, and proposed attacking it through the Roth-thal. In company with his brother Ulrich, he had already spent some time in the Roth-thal, seeking to scale the Jungfrau from that side. Previous to either Lauener or myself, Hawkins had, I believe, entertained the thought of assailing the same barrier at the very same place. Having completed our measurements on Wednesday, we descended to Grindelwald and discharged our bill. We desired to obtain the services of Christian Kaufmann, a guide well acquainted with both the Wetterhorn and the Jungfrau; but on learning our intentions he expressed fears regarding his lungs, and recommended to us his brother, a powerful young man, who had also undergone the discipline of the Wetterhorn. Him we accordingly engaged. We arranged with the landlord of the Bear to have the main mass of our luggage sent to the Æggisch-horn by a more easy route. I was loth to part with my theodolite, but Lauener at first grumbled hard against taking it. It was proposed, however, to confine his load to the head of the instrument, while Kaufmann should carry the legs, and I should bear my own knapsack. He yielded. Ulrich Lauener was at Grindelwald when we started for Lauterbrunnen, and on bidding us good-bye, he remarked that we were going to attempt an impossibility. He had examined the place which we proposed to assail, and emphatically affirmed that it could not be surmounted. We were both a little chagrined by this gratuitous announcement, and answered him somewhat warmly; for we knew the moral, or rather immoral effect of such an opinion upon the spirits of our men.

The weather became more serene as we approached Lauterbrunnen. We had a brief evening stroll, but retired to bed before day had quite forsaken the mountains. At two A.M., the candle of Lauener gleams into our bedrooms, and he pronounces the weather fair. We are up at once, dress, despatch our hasty breakfast, strap our things into the smallest possible volume, and between three and four A.M., are on our way. The hidden sun crimsons faintly the eastern sky, but the valleys are all in peaceful shadow. To our right the Staub-bach dangles its hazy veil, while other *Bachs* of minor note also hang from the beetling rocks, but fall to earth too lightly to produce the faintest murmur. After an hour's march we deviate to the left, and wind upward through the woods which here cover the slope of the hill. The air is fresh and pleasant, and the dawn cheerfully unlocks the recesses of the mountains. In front of us the outlines of some of the Oberland giants are drawn against a cloudless sky. We quit the woods and emerge upon a green Alp, which we breast, regardless of the path, until we reach the chalets of the Roth-thal. We do not yet see the particular staircase up which Lauener proposes to lead us, but we inspect minutely the battlements to our right, marking places for future attack in case our present attempt should not be successful. The elastic grass disappears, and rough crag and shingle form alternately our floor. We reach the base of a ridge of debris, and mount it.

At our right is the glacier of the Roth-thal, along whose lateral moraine our way now lies. We are soon near the snow, which the morning sunbeams have already reached, and caused to glisten with innumerable reflections. Just as we touch the snow, a spring bubbles from the rocks at our left, spurting its fused crystal over stalagmites of ice. We turn towards it, and have each a refreshing draught. Lauener points out to us the remains of the hut erected by him and his brother when they wished to attempt the Jungfrau, and from which they were driven by adverse weather. We enter an amphitheatre, grand and beautiful this splendid morning, but doubtless in times of tempest a fit residence for the devils whom popular belief has banished to its crags. The snow for a space is as level as a prairie, but in front of us rise the mighty bulwarks which separate us from the neighbouring Canton. To our right are the crags of the Breithorn, to our left the buttresses of the Jungfrau, while between both is an indentation in the mountain-wall, on which all eyes are now fixed. From it downwards hangs a thread of snow, which is to be our leading-string to the top. Though very steep, the aspect of the place is by no means terrible: comparing with it my memory of other gulleys in the Chamouni mountains, I imagine that three hours will place us at the top. In the flush of pleasure which this belief excites, it is proposed that on reaching the top we shall turn to the left, and walk straight to the summit of the Jungfrau. Lauener is hopeful, but not sanguine. We are soon at the foot of the barrier, clambering over mounds of snow. Huge consolidated lumps emerge from the general mass; the snow is evidently that of avalanches which had been shot down the couloir, kneading themselves into vast balls, and piling themselves in heaps upon the plain. The gradient steepens, the snow is hard, and the axe comes immediately into play. Straight up the couloir seems the most promising route, and we pursue it for an hour, the impression gradually gaining ground that the work will prove heavier than we had anticipated. We turn our eyes on the rocks to our right,—they seem practicable, though very steep; we swerve towards them, and work upwards among them for three quarters of an hour. It is very laborious. Hawkins and the guides turn again to the left and regain the snow, leaving me among the crags. They have steps to cut, while I need none, and, consequently, I get considerably above them. The work becomes harder, and real rest is unattainable. I look upwards at the brow of the crag, to the base of which I cling, and feel sure that once the brow is attained, a ledge will appear on which I can sit down and take breath at my ease. I reach the brow; it rounds off a little to the base of the next cliff, and no sitting-room exists. This occurs half-a-dozen times. At every brow I pause,—legs, abdomen, and breast, are laid against the rough rock, so as to lessen by their friction the strain upon the arms, which are stretched to grasp some protuberance above. Thus I rest, and there I learn that three days' training is not sufficient to dislodge London from one's lungs. As I lie against the rock after each fit of exertion, I pant violently; the action, however, soon subsides, and I am off again. Meanwhile, my companions are mounting monotonously along the snow. Lauener looks up at me at intervals, and I can clearly mark the expression of his countenance; it is quite spiritless, while that of his companion bears the print of absolute dismay. Three hours have passed and the summit is not sensibly nearer. The men halt and converse together. Lauener at length calls out to me, "I think it is impossible." The effect of Ulrich's prediction appears to be cropping out; we expostulate, however, and they move on. After some time they halt again, and reiterate their opinion that the thing cannot be done. They direct our attention to the top of the barrier; light clouds scud swiftly over it, and snow-dust is scattered at intervals in the air. There is storm on the heights, which our guides affirm has turned the day against us. I cast about in my mind to meet the difficulty, and inquire whether we might not send one of them back with the theodolite, and thus so lighten our burdens as to enable us to proceed. Kaufmann volunteers to take back the theodolite; but this does not seem to please Lauener. There is a pause; suddenly Hawkins raises an animating cry of "forward!" Lauener doggedly strikes his axe into the snow, and resumes the ascent. I continue among the rocks, though with less and less confidence in the wisdom of my choice. My knapsack annoys me excessively; the straps fray my shoulders, and tie up half my muscles. Once or twice I have to get round a protruding face of rock, and then find my bonds very grievous. At length I come to a peculiar piece of cliff; near its base is an *arête* of snow, and at a height of about five feet above the latter the rock bulges out, so that a stone dropped from its protuberance falls beyond the *arête*. The snow is the only thing I have to stand upon. I work cautiously along it, squatting down so as to get under the rock, but soon find myself in difficulty. Had I a fair ledge beneath my feet I should have felt perfectly at ease, but I stood upon a snow-wedge, on the stability of which I dare not calculate. To retreat is dangerous, to advance useless; for right in front of me is a sheer precipice which completely extinguishes the thought of further rock-work. I examine the place below me, and if my footing yields I see no way of escaping a smash. To loose myself from the crag and attach myself to the snow is so perilous an operation that I do not attempt it; and, at length, I ignobly call to Lauener to lend me a hand. A gleam of satisfaction crosses his features as he eyes me on my perch. He manifestly enjoys being called to the rescue, but exhorts me to keep quite still. He works up towards me, and in less than half an hour has hold of one of my legs. "The place is not so bad, after all," he remarks, evidently glad to take me down, in more senses than one. I descend in his steps, and rejoin Hawkins upon the snow. From that moment Lauener is a regenerate man; he is not high-minded, but he does not fear: the despair of his visage vanishes, and I firmly believe that the triumph he enjoyed, by augmenting his self-respect, was the proximate cause of our subsequent success.

The couloir is a most singular one; it is extremely steep,

and along it are two great scars, resembling the deep cut channels of a mountain stream. They are, indeed, channels cut by the snow-torrents which rush occasionally from the heights. We scan those heights. The view is bounded by a massive cornice, from which the avalanches are periodically let loose.* The cornice seems firm to-day, still we cast about for some piece of rock which might shelter us from the destroyer should he leap from his lair. Apart from the labour of the ascent, which is enormous, the frequency of avalanches will always render this pass a dangerous one. Two P.M. arrives, and the air becomes intensely cold. Hawkins had wisely pocketed a pair of socks, which he now draws over his gloves, and finds them comforting. My leather gloves, being saturated with wet, are very much the reverse. We look aloft at intervals. The wind is high, and as it passes the crest of the Breithorn its moisture is precipitated and afterwards carried away. The clouds thus generated are moulded to the shape of the summit on which they form, and they shine for a time with the lustre of pearls. As they approach the sun they are suddenly flooded with the most splendid dyes. Those chromatic effects of interference to which I have so often referred,† exhibit themselves so finely as to make us forget, in our admiration of them, the storm which wafts them across the sky. At our right is now a vertical wall of brown rock, along the base of which we advance. At times we are sheltered by it, but not always; for the wind is as fitful as a maniac, and eddying round the corners sometimes shakes us forcibly, chills us to the marrow, and spits frozen dust in our faces. The rock, moreover, has absorbed the solar heat, and melted the mass adjacent, which is refrozen to a steep slope of compact ice. The steps are more than ever difficult, and the footing more insecure. And here I have occasion to admire that coolness of head and firmness of foot which afterwards give me confidence in my

* Hence the name which, with the consent of Hawkins, if not at his suggestion, I have given to the pass.

† In "The Glaciers of the Alps."

comrade on the cliffs of the Matterhorn. We swerve towards the centre of the couloir, and reach some roughly rounded rocks, which show their surfaces through the snow. Over these we must contrive to pass; they are encrusted with ice, and a rope is exhibited so as to afford assistance to a slipping man. We try at each step to fix the Alpenstock, but mine is coated with an enamel of ice by my wet gloves, and slips through my hands. This startles me, for my staff is my sole trust under such circumstances. The crossing of those rocks is a most awkward piece of work; a slip is imminent, and the effects of the consequent glissade not to be calculated. We clear them, however, and now observe the gray haze creeping down from the peak of the Breithorn to the point at which we are aiming. This, however, is visibly nearer; for the first time since we commenced to climb Lauener declares that he has good hopes—"Jetzt habe ich gute Hoffnung." Another hour brings us to a place where the gradient slackens suddenly. The real work is done, and ten minutes further wading through the deep snow places us fairly on the summit of the Col.

Looked at from the top the pass will seem very formidable to the best of climbers; to an ordinary eye it would appear simply terrific. We reached the base of the barrier at nine A. M.; it is now four P. M., and we have consequently spent seven hours upon that tremendous wall. From our present position the view is limited; clouds are on all the mountains, and the great Aletsch Glacier is hidden by dense fog. With long swinging strides we go down the slope. The snow is deep, and I again complain of the annoyance of my knapsack. Hawkins counsels me to give it to Kaufmann, who has very little to carry, but this I decline doing for some time. At length I halt, disengage myself from the rope, and transfer my burden to the shoulders of the guide. While we are thus engaged our two companions go forward, without being aware that we have seceded. Lauener marches first, holding the rope in his hand. Suddenly the snow yields under the feet of Hawkins, and he drops between the jaws of a crevasse. He sees the rope slip through Lauener's hand, but his Alpenstock which he holds transverse to the fissure, checks his descent and probably saves his life. Comment is needless as to this mode of holding the rope. We reattach ourselves and push forward; several times during our descent the snow coating is perforated, and hidden crevasses are revealed. At length we reach the glacier, and plod along it through the dreary fog. We clear the ice just at nightfall; pass the Märjalin See, and soon find ourselves in utter darkness on the spurs of the Æggisch-horn. We lose the track and wander for a time bewildered. We sit down to rest, and then learn that Lauener is extremely ill. To quell the pangs of toothache he has chewed a cigar, which after his day's exertion is too much for him. He soon recovers, and we endeavour to regain the track. In vain. The guides shout, and after many repetitions we hear a shout in reply. A herdsman approaches, and conducts us to some neighbouring chalets, whence he undertakes the office of guide. After a time he also finds himself in difficulty. We see distant lights, and Lauener once more pierces the air with his tremendous whoop. We are heard. Lights are sent towards us, and an additional half hour places under the roof of Herr Wellig, the active proprietor of the Jungfrau hotel.

After this day's journey, which was a very hard one, the tide of health set steadily in the right direction. I have no remembrance of any further exhibition of the symptoms which had driven me to Switzerland. Each day's subsequent exercise made both brain and muscles firmer. We remained at the Æggisch-horn for several days, occupying ourselves principally with observations and measurements on the Aletsch Glacier, and joined afterwards in that day's excursion—unparalleled in my experience—which has found in my companion a narrator worthy of its glories. And as we stood upon the savage ledges of the Matterhorn, with the utmost penalty which the laws of falling bodies could inflict at hand, I felt that there were perils at home greater even than those which then surrounded us. Foes, moreover, which inspire no manhood by their attacks, but shatter alike the architect and his house by the same mean process of disintegration. After the discipline of the Matterhorn, the fatal slope of the Col du Géant, which I visited soon afterwards, looked less formidable than it otherwise might have done. From Courmayeur I worked round to Chamouni by Chapieu and the Col de Bonhomme. I attempted to get up Mont Blanc to visit the instruments which had been planted on the summit a year previously; and succeeded during a brief interval of fair weather in reaching the Grands Mulets. But the gleam which tempted me thus far proved but a temporary truce to the war of elements, and after remaining twenty hours at the Mulets, I was obliged to beat an inglorious retreat. The main object of my Swiss expedition was however secured; I returned to England with a stock of health, which five months constant work of the most trying character has not sensibly affected. For benefits such as this it is natural that I should feel grateful to the Alps.*

* As this is partly a medical paper I may be permitted to refer to the question of diet at the higher Alpine hotels. If the authorities of the Alpine Club could be induced to take up this question, they might confer an inestimable benefit upon climbers. Through the lack of wholesome nutriment, the noblest stations in the Alps are sometimes converted into dens of dyspepsia, which even the mountain air cannot abolish. The Riffel and the Æggisch-horn, for example, are unrivalled positions, and the proprietors of the hotels on both are, as far as I know them, intelligent and obliging men. Let them aim, in all earnestness, at the substitution of wholesome, tender mutton for the wicked tissue which, under this name, is frequently presented to travellers, and they will double the attractiveness of their respective houses. This question touches both physics and morals. A man cannot climb as he ought to do upon woody fibre; nor can he adore aright, or lift his soul in any becoming way to those regions towards which his beloved mountains aspire, if the coats of his stomach are in a state of irritation.

10. *JOURNAL OF A YACHT VOYAGE TO THE FAROE ISLANDS AND ICELAND.*

BY J. W. CLARK, M.A.

In the following pages I have confined myself strictly to the record of the observations I myself made in Iceland. It would have been easy to have written a more entertaining account by reference to other works, and by noting the conclusions which men of science have arrived at respecting the natural phenomena of Iceland. I determined, however, to be as brief as possible, and to state the facts, as nearly as I could, in the words of the journal I kept on the spot.

August 3d. We sailed from Stromness the day before yesterday, and to-day the Faroes (Faröerne, the sheep Islands) were in sight early. We saw their lofty precipices looming hazily through the heat all day, but the wind was so light that we were still ten miles distant from them at sundown. Passed through a shoal of several hundred small whales.

August 4th. Anchored early at Thorshaven (the capital), in Stromöe, the largest of the seventeen islands, and found the "Fox" in harbour getting up her steam. Later in the day she started for Westmanshaven.

The anchorage is a good one, and well protected from easterly gales by the Island of Naalsöe, which forms a natural break-water. A heavy swell from the N.E. sets in, however, occasionally through the channel north of Naalsöe. The French have surveyed the harbour and islands, and published a chart; but the surveyors on board the "Fox" told me that they had discovered numerous errors in their

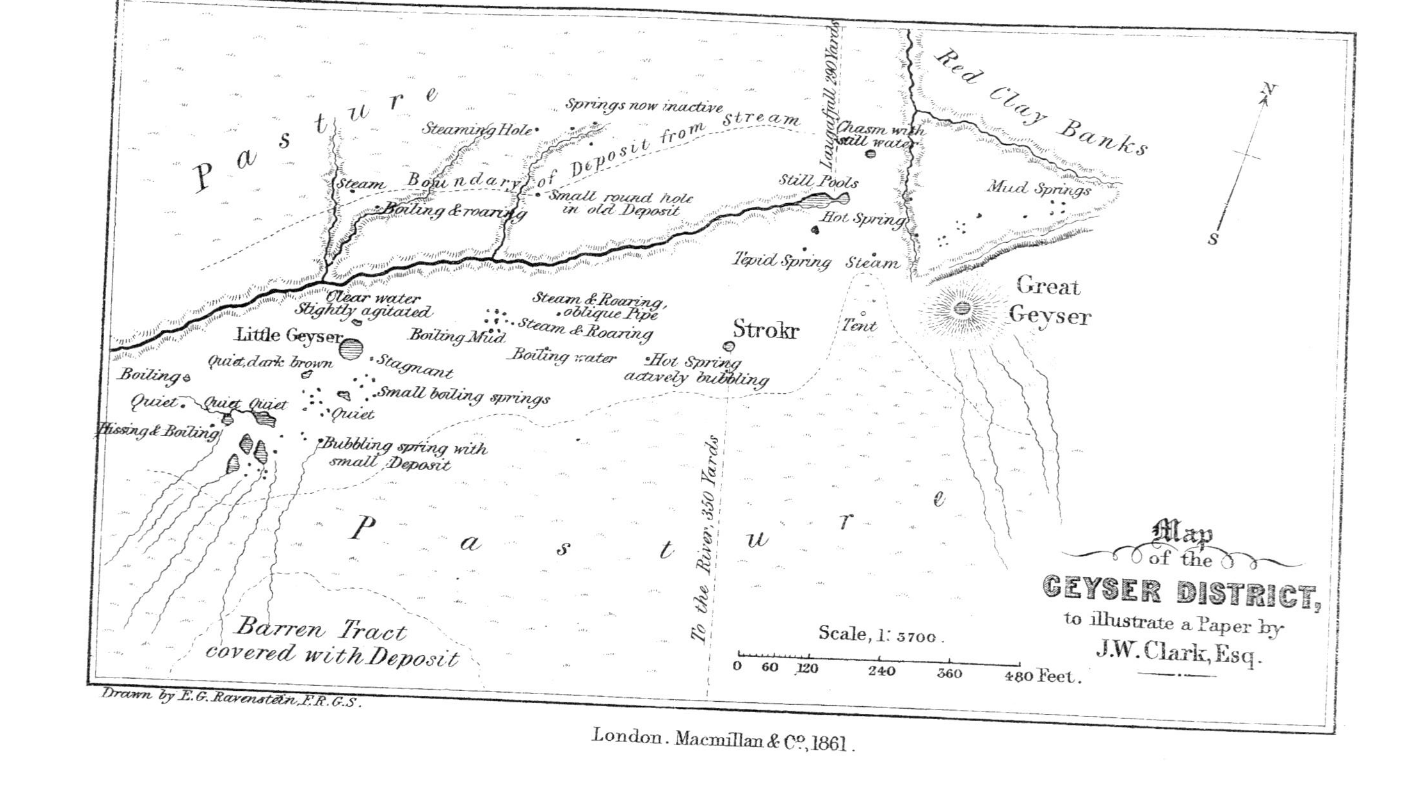

London. Macmillan & Co., 1861.

measurement; and indeed, when on the spot, one need only look at the place to see that they have studied neatness rather than accuracy. The only other chart, or rather map, of the Islands is one surveyed by order of the Danish Admiralty in 1806, and published in London at the Admiralty's Office, with corrections to 1858. It does little more than mark the anchorages, with few or no soundings. A good chart is greatly needed, as the Islands are much frequented by fishermen, and are exceedingly dangerous from the strong tides and races which run in their narrow fiords and over their lofty headlands.

The town, or rather village, is at the bottom of the large and shallow bay forming the harbour; built round a creek, and the spit which incloses it to the south. It is the queerest, quaintest place imaginable. The houses are built one above the other, regardless of order, up the steep hill side, which is so steep in some places, that the rock has been hewn, step-wise, to allow of building at all; and before the door of one house there frequently rises, fully as high as its roof, the substruction of natural rocks which are to support its opposite neighbour. Narrow lanes, thick with black mud, divide them from each other; now climbing, now descending the hill. These houses are all of wood brought from Norway, roofed with birch bark, above which is a layer of turf about six inches in thickness, with grass growing on it, whereon in many instances, sheep are browsing, carefully tethered lest they should miss their footing. Everybody lands at the end of the spit aforesaid, where the rock has been worn by long usage into something like a landing-pier. Here are a few posts, apparently for mooring ships, and generally occupied early by two or three Terns, so tame that they will let you come within a yard of them. Fishing boats fill the creek; you land among fish; fish guts lie all about in the rock crevices, to the great delight of huge starfishes; everywhere in the streets fish is laying out to dry; and south of the spit, where the ground is less abrupt, there is a boiler for the manufacture of fish-oil. It is needless to say that a fishy smell prevails everywhere. Notwithstanding, the people are clean, and their houses remarkably so, even in the case of the poorest. The larger ones are arranged after the German type, with a German love for polished furniture and floors, small light-coloured prints, white window curtains, and flower-pots. Some have a strip of garden, about as large as an ordinary drawing-room table, with a tame gull sulking in one corner of it.

The common people talk a dialect of their own, but the more educated merchants speak Danish.

The vast precipices of these islands are their most striking features. For miles and miles, in and out of the long fiords, they form the coast line, now descending gently, so as to be accessible, and to admit in some cases of cultivation; now so steep as scarce to afford footing to a climber. Here and there at their feet are narrow strips of pasture and corn land, with prosperous well-to-do farms; but generally a few cabins, tenanted by fishermen, are the only dwellings to be seen. In some places magnificent waterfalls, fed by the streams above, descend over the rocky cornice seven or eight hundred feet to the sea. This is especially the case in the narrow channel between Stromöe and Osteröe, where five or six enormous cataracts descend close together over the steep cliffs of the latter island. The channel is marked "Navigable," and was once passed through by a yacht; but subsequently, a brig attempting to do so for a wager, went ashore. The table-land above is an undulating, marshy moor, very like Shetland, but with fewer peat bogs. No attempt is made to cultivate it, but sheep and cattle find pasturage there.

The Danish Governor resides at Thorshaven. He spends three months only in the year there; the rest he passes at Copenhagen, where he has a seat in the parliament. We found him a pleasant, middle-aged man, talking a polyglot of English, French, and Danish. He seemed sadly oppressed with ennui, and to be looking anxiously for the arrival of the steamer which was to take him to Copenhagen and his wife.

There is little trade, except in fish. English and Scotch

vessels frequent the islands in great numbers for the fisheries, which this year have been unusually productive. The chief retail business in Thorshaven is conducted by a Hamburg merchant. His store, close to the landing place, was always crowded.

There are no roads. All journeys are performed on foot; horses being little used, except for burdens.

The religion is Lutheran. Two Roman Catholic missionaries have resided for the last three years at Thorshaven without making a single convert.

August 5th.—Sailed over to Naalsöe, distant about two and a half miles. We had been told by Mr. Müller, who is an Amptmand, or magistrate, of Thorshaven, and therefore a person of some consequence, and who, moreover, is very affable, and speaks English perfectly, that the Storm Petrel bred there. We searched for its nests without success. The cliffs of Naalsöe to seaward are splendid, with deep caves in them, where the sea birds breed. They are all carefully preserved by the government, as their down is collected yearly by the peasants, but I did not learn that it is kept as a Crown monopoly.

August 6th.—Weighed anchor early, and stood into the Kalbaksfiord, the first northward from Thorshaven. At its western end is a tract of marshy meadow land, shut in by an amphitheatre of hills, where we were told good shooting might be had. On our way up the fiord, the possessor of a substantial farm came on board with his wife and friends. We conversed through the medium of our pilot. Our visitors were greatly astonished at our yacht, the like of which they had never seen before. There seems to be no national costume. The men all wear suits of plain grey woollen; and the lady was not more old-fashioned in her dress than many an inhabitant of an English country town. Some of them offered blue woollen stockings for sale, so closely knitted as scarcely to be distinguishable from fine cloth.

The men are very ingenious in the manufacture of whale knives. They seem of excellent temper, and the cases are beautiful specimens of inlaying in wood.

August 8*th*.—At Thorshaven again. Yesterday morning we left our anchorage early, and sailed into the Kingsfiord in Osteröe. Its banks are rather more thickly inhabited than those of the Kalbaksfiord, bnt otherwise it resembles it exactly.

The wind being unfavourable for Iceland, I made an excursion to the Sudspitz of the island, where the governor had told us we should find at Kirkeböe, a "ruine superbe" of an old church. We struck across the island in a westerly direction, following the small river which falls into the sea a little south of Thorshaven. From the "col" we got a capital view over the sea, and the strangely shaped islands which rejoice in the names of the Horse, the Kolter, and the Shoe. Northwards we could see that the grand basaltic gorge leading up to Westmanshaven, was well worthy of its fame. Thence after about four miles' walking, we came to Kirkeböe and its church, at the foot of the cliffs at the south-west corner of the island. A handsome young farmer received us with great hospitality, and his only servant, a spruce little old woman, with long mittens reaching to her elbow, brought us coffee. The church is interesting, as showing that Gothic architecture, such as we find in the rest of Europe, prevailed in so remote a spot. It measures about twenty-five feet in breadth by eighty-seven in length: consisting of a long nave of six bays, lighted by large lancet windows on the south side only. At the east end there remains a wide arch, which seems once to have held a three-light window. The roof is gone, but the shafts which once supported its groining, still remain, with rather finely cut corbels. The walls are of very rough masonry, immensely thick. At present it is utterly desecrated.

August 9*th*.—By far the most common bird here is the Oyster Catcher. It abounds everywhere. You cannot walk a short distance in any direction without putting up three or four, who fly round and round, uttering their loud disagreeable cry. I am told that they arrive on March 12th, and depart about September 1st. Next in frequency of occurrence is the Whimbrel, but it is much more shy and difficult to get near. We have seen a good many specimens of the Skua Gull; the peasants shoot and eat them. Richardson's Skua is extremely common, in every variety of plumage, hovering near the large flocks of Arctic Terns, ready to chase and rob any that have caught fish. Buffon's Skua [Lestris parasitica] has been seen this year in great numbers at sea between the Faroes and the east coast of Iceland; but its breeding-places here are not known. The Pied Raven is often shot here. I saw one myself, at a distance, in my walk to Kirkeböe. (I was told subsequently by Dr. Edmonston of Shetland, that it is found in the nests of the common raven, while others of the same brood are wholly black. Thus it would appear to be merely a variety, and not a distinct species.)

The Eider Duck abounds here, and is strictly preserved, under a penalty of a dollar per bird, on account of its down. Besides these we have seen Snipe, Golden Plover, and most of the ordinary sea birds; many, however, have gone south already, while those that winter here have not yet arrived. At all seasons, however, I should think that these islands were too inaccessible for bird collecting with any success. Some fishermen caught a Hallibut this morning, measuring six feet three inches in length.

August 14*th*.—In sight of Iceland. A fair breeze took us on the morning of the 10th from Thorshaven as far as Skaapensfiord, and there left us, with full leisure to admire the wonderful caves that run far into the cliffs of Sand Island and Horse Island, and the gorgeous tints produced upon the cliffs themselves by the grass and lichens growing there. In the evening, however, it sprang up again, and having brought us within four or five miles of Cape Reykjanes, left us a second time. There we lay in a dead calm, "rolled to starboard, rolled to larboard," in the long heavy swell, without advancing half a mile all day. The coast, I confess, disappointed me. There is no grandeur about it: no rugged cliffs backed by a snowy range of volcanoes; instead, it presents a line of barren red rocks without a green speck anywhere to break the uniformity.

Near Cape Reykjanes it is low; but further east are some chains of abrupt serrated peaks, with a lofty table land beyond: behind which again, more peaks close in the far distance.

About seven P.M. a fair wind sprang up, and by nine we were abreast of the famous Fuglasker, where the Great Auk, the Geirfugl, used to build.

They are four rocks, lying south of Reykjanes, from which the largest, Eldey, is distant about three miles, and a low skerry, or drangr, about seven. Eldey is a precipitous, flat-topped mass of basalt, of no great height, but looks forbidding enough to justify the stories of its inaccessibility. Calm as it was, a heavy surge was beating up its sides. Another Geirfuglasker is marked on the map a few miles south of the Westmann Islands; and it is probable that among the numberless rocks in the great Breidifiord, on the west coast, there may be some on which the Great Auk still builds. The small north-west peninsula of Iceland, whose southern shore is washed by the Breidifiord, is more deeply indented with bays, more thinly inhabited, and less visited than any other part of the islands; and birds are said to be proportionately plentiful. There, if anywhere, the Great Auk may still be found.

August 15*th.*—Early this morning we tacked round the low and dangerous promontory of Skagi, with a fresh breeze, and entered Faxa-fiord. It is badly proportioned for picturesqueness, being forty miles across at its mouth, and about twenty deep. Nor, as you sail in, do the hills close round you: it keeps the same enormous width throughout, and it is only when you have made the entrance of one of its tributary fiords that you can see anything of its shores.

Far away to the north, forming its northern horn, we could see the snowy crown of Snæfell; a grand mountain, rising up, something like Etna, direct from the sea to a height of 8,000 feet. The southern coast, near to which we sailed, is low and brown, with here and there a green patch, with a few huts, and a church near them; and farther inland, some conical hills, in shape and hue much resembling dust-heaps.

Off Hafnfiord, a place of some trade, consisting of a row of houses rather better than the rest, a pilot came on board He was out fishing in a small boat, like those the Shetlanders and Faro-islanders get from Norway, whence these also are mostly imported, and had caught a great load of dog-fish. He told us they were excellent eating.

About two P.M. we anchored in Reykjavik harbour. It is well sheltered to the west by a long ridge of rocks, uncovered at low water, which connect a small island to the mainland. Farther out to sea are three or four other islets, low and grass-covered, inhabited, it seemed as we passed, by nothing but quantities of Kittiwakes and Puffins. Across the narrow arm of the fiord is the mountain of Esja, its sides furrowed by streams, and its lofty peaks rising to a great height.

In the afternoon we went ashore. The town stands along a straight, steep beach, about two hundred yards in length, and is slowly—at the rate of four or five houses a year—mounting the hills at either end of it. We landed at one of the slippery little jetties, which run down it, *à choix*, built in a rude way, partly of wood, partly of lava. Between them are piles of timber, fish, and other goods, waiting to be stowed or taken on board ship. These past, you are in the main street of the capital, a row of warehouses and shops, where all business is transacted. The houses are wholly of wood, of one story, with steeply sloping roofs, to throw off the winter snow, and warm and comfortable enough inside. Now they are beginning to build with stone, the frames only being of wood. The only stone to be had is a trap rock, very difficult to cut, but still cheaper and more durable than wood, which has to be brought from Norway. Behind are a few other streets, of minor importance, consisting generally of dwelling-houses, and a green space whereon stands the cathedral; and, at a respectful distance, some of the larger mansions, each in its garden. On the eastern hill is the college, a large white building, the governor's house, and the windmill. In fact, it is clearly the correct and fashionable thing to live at least 300 yards from the beach, if possible. Most of the houses face the north, the prospect, I suppose, being gayer than towards the south, where further progress is soon stopped by a large reedy lake.

There is a great air of comfort, and also a strong smell pervading the place. In about an hour all idea that we were in a strange town had worn off: everybody gave us so warm a welcome. First, we called on Count Trampe, the Governor, but he was absent in Copenhagen, having gone thither to resign office, so that at present there is no governor, but a deputy, Herr Jonassen, an Icelander, "pur sang." Then we visited the Rector of the College, a portly personage, speaking good English, as most people of any education here do; Herr Randrop, the apothecary, Doctor Hjaltalin, the medical officer of this division of Iceland, and many others. Isolated as these people are from all civilisation, a traveller is a person to be welcomed with all honour. If he does not die under his entertainer's kindness, it is not from want of murderous treatment on their part. Seven or eight times this day were we imperatively called upon to drink coffee, or chocolate, or beer, or wine, or brandy, or all five at once. Then it was equally imperative that we should return to supper, and go through it all again.

August 16*th.*—Determined to lose no more time, but to start to-morrow on our journey inland.

Went out in an Icelandic boat to look for sea-birds. Saw nothing but the most common kinds.

Landed at Vidöe, an island about a mile off, famous as the breeding-place of the Eider Ducks. It is farmed by an old Icelander, Stephenson by name, who lives on the island, in a large, feudal-looking farm-house, surrounded by his dependants. There is also a small Church hard by. Notwithstanding the near vicinity of so many people, the Eiders breed here in vast numbers, making their nests in the ground all up the grassy slopes, close to the farm buildings. They stay from the middle of May to the middle of June, leaving the young birds to shift for themselves. Mr. Stephenson's son assured me that this year they took more than one thousand eggs, and that, besides, each bird hatched two or three young ones.

August 17*th*.—A gloriously fine day, warm, with a bracing north wind, which promises us fine weather, they say. Started from Reykjavik, at eleven A.M. Our guide, Zoega, supposed by the Rector to be a descendant of him who wrote "De Obeliscis," speaks excellent English, which he has taught himself in the winter evenings, and improved by talking to Englishmen in the summer. Besides him, we have a subordinate guide, Johan, and a boy to look after the ponies. Of these there are twenty-six. Every rider has two, each of which is ridden for half a day. Meanwhile, the spare ones trot on in front, sometimes tied together, but generally loose, so as to be able, now and then, to get a mouthful of grass, if the incessant cries of the guides will let them. They are enduring little creatures, not so stout or so handsome as the Norwegian breed—with which, however, they seem to have been crossed—but sure-footed and docile. The baggage is packed very inconveniently—in wooden boxes slung across the pack-saddles. These last are primitive. A large piece of turf is laid on the pony's back; over it is strapped a stout wooden frame, furnished with pegs on either side, to which the boxes are hung. All would be very well if the ponies were warranted not to roll; but every two or three hours one is sure to lie down, and fling off his load, occasioning great delay while the complicated system of cords, &c., is replaced. Well if the catastrophe be not accompanied by the crash of breaking bottles, for the boxes offer but a slight defence.

We rode down the street, and past the windmill, and instantly found ourselves in the wild open country, where the only human beings we saw all day were a few peasants cutting turf, and loading it in crates slung on ponies, like our baggage. For a mile or so we had a decent road; then it ended abruptly and became a track, easy enough, however, to find. We rode along a branch of the fiord for four or five miles, getting glorious views, every now and then, down the little bays we crossed, of far-away Snæfell; and then, leaving the coast, struck inland. The country in general is a hilly, stony waste, strewn with large pieces of volcanic rock, flung about as pebbles lie at the bottom of a sea, with saxifrages and such-like plants growing among them. In the hollows between the low undulating hills there is plenty of bright green pasturage, but treacherous and marshy, as we found to our cost, by the horses sinking in up to their bellies, if they strayed to right or left of the track. There are plenty of lakes; we rode close to one, Hafravatn, and saw many in the distance.

In a few sheltered spots are small farms, with a little strip of garden before them, green with rape-tops and potatoes.

After riding thirteen miles or so, we came to Sele-dal, an upland pasture, with a clear stream brawling through it. Here we changed horses, and then climbed up a steep-path on to the high moorland, across whose dreary waste we rode, hour after hour, hoping every instant to come upon Thingvalla. To our left we got a good view of the peaks of Esja, and in front of the rounded mass of some great glacier. After ten miles of moor, the road made a rapid descent down a sandy hill, and on we went again on a lower level. We soon found we were on a lava bed, for wherever the sand was blown away, the black corrugated surface was laid bare, furrowed with huge concentric wrinkles, like the bubbles that form and burst on the slag of an iron furnace. The hills to our left became greener,—Iceland grass appears of a most intense green by contrast,—and to our right the lake of Thingvalla, a noble piece of water, about eight miles long, and from three to five broad, surrounded by grand mountains, came into view. At last, as suddenly as we had been led to expect, the ground fell away, and there was Thingvalla at our feet, three or four hundred feet beneath. Our expectations were great, but it surpassed them all. Imagine a vast deluge of lava, four miles wide, descending from between acute mountain peaks down to a blue lake, broken into every variety of fissure, and richly carpeted with lichens, mosses, and ferns; and beyond, a serrated ridge, dyed a bright scarlet by the setting sun, and you have some idea of this wonderful scene. A steep path leads down to the bottom of the precipice on which we stood. We then found ourselves in a deep ditch, as it were, some fifty feet wide, with the wall of basaltic columns, down which we had come, on one side, and on the other a great mass of lava, which seemingly had once fallen from above. The chasm they term Almanna-gia,—the way of all men. It runs for a great distance up into the mountains whence the lava flowed, and parallel to a similar one on the other side the stream, called Hrafna-gia. The two are the boundaries of the great settlement in the lava field which formed the valley and lake of Thingvalla—the Assembly in the Valley—where the ancient Icelandic parliament used to meet. It took us twelve hours to-day to travel twenty-six miles, including stoppages.

August 18*th*.—Spent the morning in examining Thingvalla. The Althing, or Parliament-house, is a narrow grassy ridge, between the two deepest chasms. It would hold, perhaps, a hundred people. It can be entered only at one point, by a natural bridge of extreme narrowness. Nothing can be lovelier than the blue water in the chasms, overhung with ferns and creepers. What a change from this to the rooms in the College of Reykjavik, where the deputies now sit on baize-covered seats instead of the greensward, and gaze on white-washed walls and a portrait of Christian VIII. instead of on mountains and the canopy of heaven!

I went down into a dry chasm, about one hundred feet deep, and examined the volcanic rock. Generally it is less honeycombed, as might be expected, at bottom than at top. Besides this, it is frequently composed of layers of large blocks, which severally are less honeycombed in the middle than at the edge, and are divided from each other by bands of excessively porous slags. The lava contains great quantities of feldspar.

Started at 1.30. The track runs parallel to Almanna-gia, along the bank of the Oxerá, for a short distance, and then strikes across Thingvalla. The lava here is less fissured, owing, I suppose, to its having descended a less steep declivity. Dwarf bushes, averaging two feet in height, grow all over this part of it,—they call it "the Forest,"—and extend up the valley and round the east shore of the lake. In one hour we reached Hrafna-gia, a chasm exactly like Almanna-gia, only less lofty and less steep, and then stretched over a wide moor, which, on coming to a deep chasm, we found to be lying over a stream of lava. We descended into the chasm: it appeared like a large bubble which had burst. It was of great extent, and full of ferns and mosses. Presently we came up with the Kalfstinder, the range of volcanic peaks which we had seen last night across Thingvalla. The one we passed nearest to, looked like an enormous heap of black dust, with rocks, charred and burnt, emerging from it here and there. A little south of it was an extinct crater, on a slight rise. It exactly resembled a large funnel, projecting about twenty feet above the surface, with rocks strangely twisted and contorted, and coloured of every shade of red and yellow. On looking down we could see a dark and apparently bottomless chasm, up which a cold blast blew. On descending the "col" on which this stood, we entered a wide grass plain, free from marsh. The soil was light and sandy, and probably formed, originally, of ashes ejected from the volcanoes. Behind us the peaks of the mountains rose clear and distinct, with horizontal beds of dark black deposit at their feet. After a ride of about thirteen miles from Thingvalla we pitched our tent on the banks of the Laugarvatn, near some noisy hot springs.

August 19th.—Spent at Laugarvatn. The largest hot springs are three in number; the water at more than 212° (we can boil our kettles by standing them in it). It bubbles and stirs in the centre of each basin, which is extremely shallow, and rises to a height of about two feet in intermittent eruptions. The soil around is sandy, with sulphurous incrustations on the surface. Near the largest spring the hissing from some concealed water is very loud. Some small apertures on the beach are continually fizzing. There are about twenty holes close together in the ground, clean as though drilled. In other places there are one or two together. There is another smaller spring close to our tent, which the peasants use for washing and cooking purposes. It is not so hot, nor does it bubble so vehemently. It is distant about one hundred yards from the large one. Beyond it also the ground smokes. Also out in the lake, about three hundred yards from the shore, a great steam rises. On the opposite shore, a mile off, a large body of steam is rising in two places. The smell of sulphur is very strong.

There is a good view from the hill behind, which is covered thickly with dwarf birch. We are in an enormous plain of marshy land, stretching away southward as far as one can see, broken only by some isolated hills. In the middle of it are two lakes, of which the Laugarvatn is the smallest. Seven rivers flow into them. The peasants just now are busy in cutting their crop of reedy hay all over the marsh, which gushes and oozes wherever you tread. How easily it might be drained, and become a valuable property! Large flocks of sheep, with wonderfully clear white fleeces, guarded by shaggy sheep-dogs, of a breed very like the Pomeranian, and as noisy and cowardly, and herds of oxen, up to their knees in water, are grazing on it. To the east, Hekla is seen in the distance.

August 20th.—We had a long and fruitless chase after a swan. A good many grebe persist in coming and feeding close to our tent, but of course vanish as soon as they find themselves observed. A great Northern Diver is fishing and cooing in the middle of the lake. Started at 10 A.M., and reached the Geysers at 5 P.M., riding very slowly. Distance sixteen miles. We had to make a detour in order to keep along the edge of the hills, and so avoid the marsh. Farms, in clusters of two or more, every few miles along the hill-side. After riding about eight miles, came to the Bruerá, a fine brawling stream, tumbling over shelf after shelf of volcanic rock to the plain. The main body of water roars down a deep chasm in the centre of its bed of lava, and over the flat shelves which extend on either side. Over these the ponies flounder as well as they can, while the central chasm is crossed by a bridge formed of planks laid across. Just below, the water tumbles over a semicircle of rock in a fine cascade. Then for three or four miles we rode among hills covered with the eternal dwarf birch, then descended into the plain, and turned northwards again, keeping along the low hills to our left. Very soon the Geysers became visible by their steam, situate on a rising ground, backed to the west by a detached hill, separated by a few hundred yards of level ground from the main chain.

Soon after our arrival, the Little Geyser threw up a cloud of steam about forty feet high; we then flung about two barrowfuls of earth into another spring, called Strokr, which caused him also to send up a series of columns of steam and water, mixed with clods, to a height of at least eighty feet. The Great Geyser gave hopes of an eruption; he rumbled with a noise like the distant discharges of ordnance, and the ground shook, but after all he only boiled over, like a gigantic tea-kettle.

August 21st.—The Great Geyser boiled over three or four times; and the last time, between 6 and 7 P.M., he threw up a column of water about three feet high. The Little Geyser went off shortly after. Strokr also erupted on compulsion in the afternoon.

August 22d.—The weather, which hitherto had been cloudless, changed last night, and we had heavy rain, with a south-west wind. The Great Geyser went off at 3.30 A.M., but the strong wind blew the clouds of steam so over our tent, that we could see but little. We all ran out, and getting round to windward, saw a large column of water rise three or four times, with a loud noise. The height might be eighty or a hundred feet. This was repeated at 7.45 A.M. At 11.45 he boiled over on all sides, with a great rush of water and effusion of steam, but no column rose. In the course of the afternoon he boiled over three or four times, and at 8 P.M. a column about six feet high rose.

August 23d.—The Great Geyser very quiet. He boiled

over twice in the night, and two or three times in the day. About nine P.M. this was repeated, with great effusion of steam, and surly, long-continued rumblings. The Little Geyser and Strokr very quiet.

August 24th and 25th.—The Great Geyser boiled over occasionally during these two days. The Little Geyser erupted two or three times, and Strokr whenever he was compelled to do so.

The springs, eighty in number, usually termed "the Geysers," are situate on a hill of no great elevation, but which rises gradually from south to north. It abuts upon Laugafjall, a detached hill, about 600 feet high, conspicuous for the twin peaks that crown its northern summit. It is precipitous and inaccessible to the west, but to the east slopes gradually down to the lower hill, in which the hot springs rise. It appears to consist of an igneous rock, similar to that which forms the main range a little beyond it; it splits easily into thin layers, which, at the summits, where they are exposed to view, are seen to have been upheaved into a vertical position.

Between Laugafjall and the hills is a strip of marshy meadow land, similar to that which extends on all sides of it to a greater or less distance. To the north it extends for a few miles to the foot of the hills which are the boundaries, as it were, of the great central wilderness. They are covered with short grass, heather, wortleberries, dwarf birch, and sallow, and afford pasturage to the few flocks belonging to Haukadalr, the last farm in this direction. The sheep are turned out to pasture on them in the morning, and fetched home in the evening, by some of the farming men, mounted on ponies. Beyond them you enter on a sandy desert, strewed with volcanic blocks, and frequently lumps of black slag; over which a glimpse is obtained of enormous glaciers, surrounded by a fringe of jagged, gloomy peaks, some black, some a lurid red; and nearer, of Bláfell, the Blue Mountain, conspicuous for its single, rounded peak. Beyond, to the east, extends a range of acutely-pointed peaks, with glaciers among them.

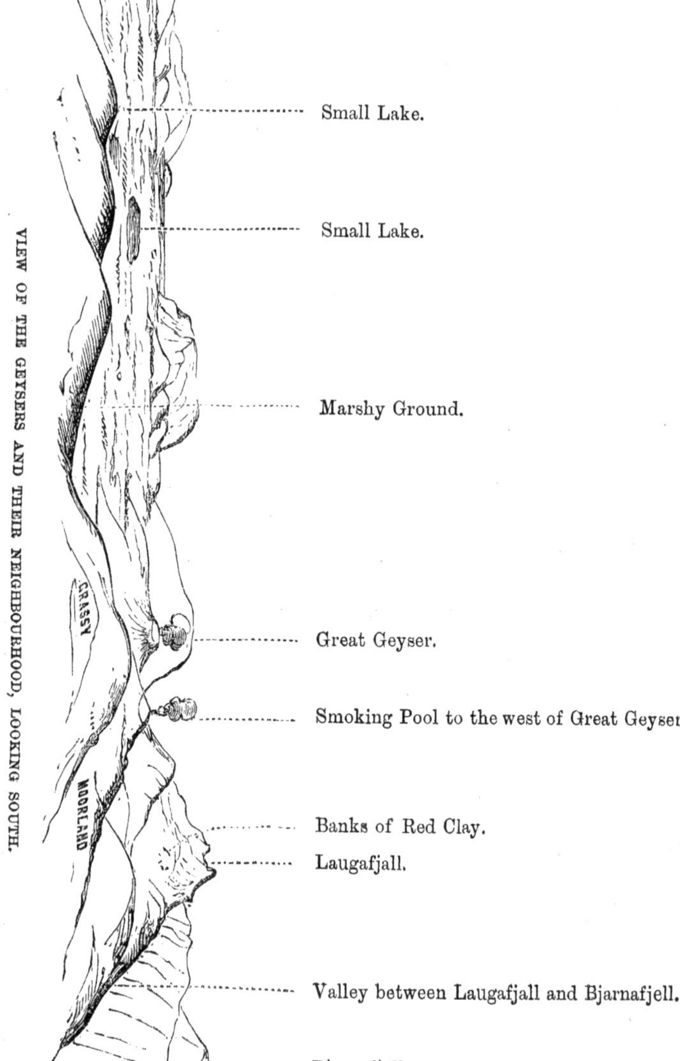

VIEW OF THE GEYSERS AND THEIR NEIGHBOURHOOD, LOOKING SOUTH.

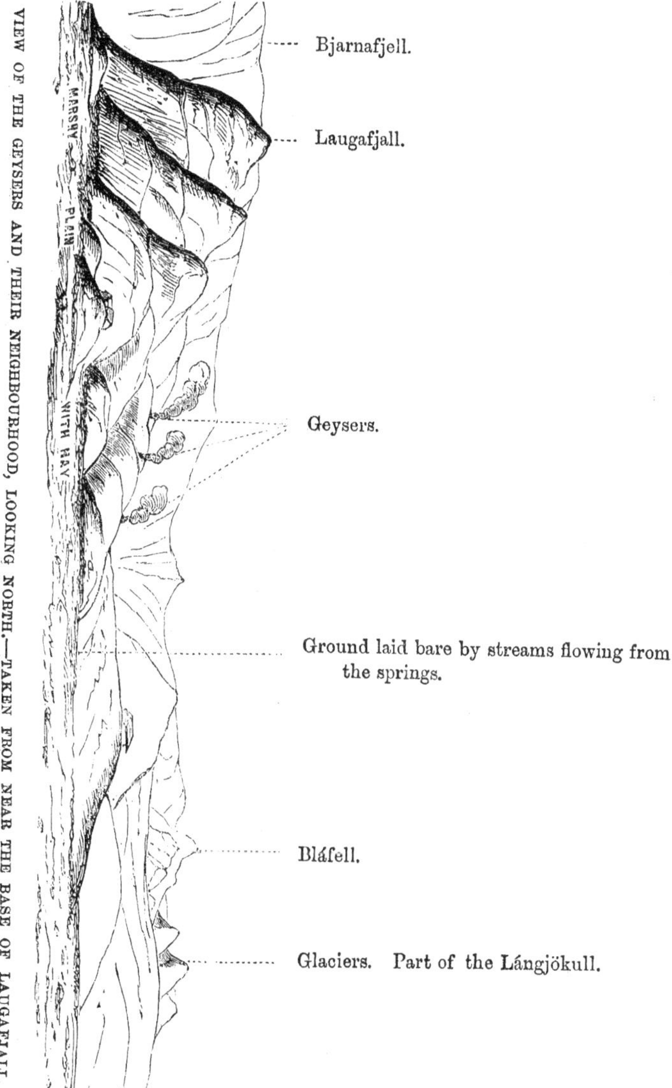

VIEW OF THE GEYSERS AND THEIR NEIGHBOURHOOD, LOOKING NORTH.—TAKEN FROM NEAR THE BASE OF LAUGAFJALL.

I only saw this from a distance, as I feared to leave Geyser for long; but two of our party, who penetrated as far as the Hagavatn, described the scene as wonderful. The great Lang-jökull descends to the water's edge, and makes a cliff of ice several hundred feet in height. To the east the plain extends about three miles beyond the Túngufljót, between which and the Hvitá, or White River, are several lofty ridges, over which we could see the peak of Hekla. To the south it may be said with accuracy to extend to the sea, for there is nothing, save a few isolated summits, to break its uniformity in that direction.

The position of the Geysers, and the neighbouring country, may perhaps be best understood by the accompanying outlines, taken from the north and south, respectively.

There are four kinds of springs :—

1. The Great Geyser, the Little Geyser, and Strokr, which throw up at intervals a column of steam and water to a great height, and with a loud report before, and during the eruption.

2. Springs continually boiling, with a loud hissing noise, but which never overflow their boundaries.

3. Pools of clear, smooth water, boiling hot. Their surface is never ruffled by any internal disturbance, but they continually overflow by some outlet.

4. Mud Springs.

The Great Geyser rises out of a low mount, gradually increasing in height as the deposit is formed, at the extreme north end of the hill. The ground falls away immediately behind it to the west and north, where a chasm, about forty feet in depth at its deepest part, hollowed out by a rivulet, runs down to join the river which flows past the hill to the east. The mount is entirely formed by, or coated with, the deposit of the spring. It lies in patches, like the head of a cauliflower, of a substance much resembling brain coral, in colour a dull grey, due probably to the great admixture of silica; or else, where water is continually flowing over it, in level plates. When the spring overflows, the water escapes down the chasm to the west, or else in several rivulets in an opposite direction, which finally fall into the river; wherever it flows, it destroys vegetation wholly. The grass, which comes close up to the foot of the Geyser on the north, is growing on older deposits which have gradually become coated with mould. On walking down the chasm aforesaid to its junction with the river, and along the banks of the latter, the mould, frequently reddish in colour, may be seen lying in layers, alternately with the deposit, to the depth of several feet, as though the latter had been intermittent. This is particularly noticeable where the brooks of Geyser water fall into the river. Its water is clear and cold, fed by several springs, which rise in the moorland beyond Haukadalr. The opposite bank is of black mould, low, and marshy. In the chasm to the west of the Geyser, the same formation may be seen, namely, layers of deposit alternating with sand and clay, on both sides, the chasm having been evidently formed subsequent to the deposit. On walking up the hill to the west, this old deposit may be traced for a short distance, where it joins the red clay-banks which at this point form the base of Laugafjall.

The basin of the Great Geyser measures forty-six feet by fifty-five feet eight inches. It was unfortunately always full while I was there, so that I had no opportunity of measuring the pipe, which descends vertically at the centre of the basin. The basin seemed to slope very gradually to the edge of the pipe. The mound is about thirty feet above the level of the spot on which we pitched our tent. The eruptions are quite irregular. It boils over eight or nine times in twenty-four hours. The Icelanders believe the eruptions to be more frequent in wet than in fine weather. The only eruption I saw was in a heavy rain, which had then lasted about six hours One of our party afterwards saw a very lofty column thrown up in fine weather.

The Little Geyser is surrounded by a circular mass of deposit, nineteen feet in diameter, like that of the Great Geyser, only flattened. It appears to rest on older deposit, but as the whole hill, for a quarter of a mile southwards from the Great

Geyser consists of nothing but deposits of various ages, perforated by springs which seem to change their position not unfrequently, it becomes extremely difficult to determine the age of any one portion. The mouth of the Little Geyser is two feet in diameter, becoming narrower as it deepens. Its sides are coated with deposit. The pipe is twelve feet two inches in depth, and one foot from the surface of the ground to the water. The eruptions seem more frequent than those of the Great Geyser, are not announced by any previous rumbling, and throw up a very small volume of water compared with the great quantity of steam.

Strokr—(the Churn)—is at the bottom of a shallow saucer with a radius of thirty feet, roughly speaking. It is coated with deposit lying in a direction parallel to the inclination of the saucer. Close round the pipe, extending to a distance of four feet ten inches from it, are five rings of a different deposit, lying vertically. On one side the innermost of these is about one foot high, surrounding the pipe balustrade fashion, and seems to have been once much higher. The pipe, eight feet in diameter, and forty-three feet three inches in depth, is a roaring gullet, coated with red incrustations. On looking in, the water can just be seen, boiling and spluttering. It erupts occasionally, and may be made to do so in three or four minutes at pleasure, by throwing in a sufficient quantity of clods of earth.

Of the second class of springs there are several. I have marked them on the map as "boiling water," "steam and roaring," "bubbling spring," "hissing spring," to denote the slight variations in their phenomena. In some the boiling water is visible in a shallow saucer; in others it can only be heard down a deep pipe; in others again it makes its presence known by a continuous effusion of steam; while in others there is a continuous hissing, but no steam or water visible.

We now come to the still pools. The one near the Great Geyser is by far the most beautiful of all the springs. It is in two divisions, which apparently join beneath, under a natural bridge, and is brimful of very hot water, of the loveliest blue imaginable, through which one sees the incrustations down its sides, to a great depth. Its depth is seventeen feet six inches at the northern end, and twenty-three feet seven inches at the southern. From it descends a copious stream, which deposits as it flows level layers of an orange-coloured incrustation, worn as smooth as polished marble by the action of the water. There are five more pools close together, beyond the Little Geyser: but they are by no means so beautiful. Their water is dirty and muddy, and between them is soft marshy ground, offering a treacherous footing. They overflow constantly in numerous streams, which run down the hill towards the river; but lose themselves among the grass before reaching it. Among them are some bubbling fountains, which go up every now and then with a spirt, but do not eject water beyond their margin. The arrangement of the deposit of these pools varies; in most of them it is smooth or only slightly arched; but in one near the Little Geyser, it is ribbed, so that a horizontal section would present a series of points, like the teeth of a saw.

The mud springs are very few. There are some in the cluster marked (A) between Strokr and the Little Geyser, and two or three on the bank above the Great Geyser. The mud always preserves the same level. Moss and grass grow at their edge.

There are everywhere copious evidences of changes that have taken place in the springs; some have ceased to be so active as heretofore; some, at present, emit only steam; and lastly, some have become wholly inactive, and their holes are fast filling up. South-west from Strokr is a fountain, always actively bubbling, Its deposit is formed in domical masses above and beneath the water, which always stands at about five feet from the surface. It has a shallow basin of four feet radius, on the outermost edge of which are some cauliflower incrustations, as though its operations had once resembled those of the Great Geyser. North of the Still Pools, near the Great Geyser, there is a deep, irregular chasm, about thirty feet in diameter at its widest part; the water is twelve feet from the surface, at boiling heat. The sides are much broken, and the total absence of all eruptions at present is attested by the fact that violets are growing nearly down to the water. The deposit consists of layers of silica and red earth. Similar chasms exist below the muddy pools beyond the Little Geyser, and near Strokr.

On descending from the Little Geyser to the stream which trickles down from the Still Pools, its right bank is found to be formed of old deposit to the height of about four feet, seemingly of the same character with that which the stream now carries in its bed, only much decomposed. Above the deposit lies a layer of soil about four feet thick. These beds extend for at least a hundred and fifty feet towards Laugafjall, even beyond the small gully, down which a stream trickles, and falls into the main one opposite the Little Geyser. On its banks are three small springs. Near this is a very small, but actively bubbling spring, which has forced its way through the old deposit. The banks above these springs are strewed with fragments of the volcanic rock fallen from above, intermingled with pieces of a sort of tufa, yellowish in colour, very vesicular, and light. A little further to the north east the whole of Laugafjall is strewn with fragments of a deposit similar to that now found only on the banks of the stream, intermingled with pieces of a tufa-like substance; showing that once there must either have been a spring here, or that this portion of the hill has been upheaved in comparatively later times. I think the former theory the most probable, as, when we ascend from the Great Geyser towards the double peak on the north end of Laugafjall, we find close under it evidences of an ancient spring in a bank of reddened soil, in which are numerous orifices, all hissing. The soil round them is hot, and encrusted with sulphur, notwithstanding which, grass and moss grow in the middle, favoured by the damp heat. They are at the bottom of a hollow basin, seven yards in diameter, which must have been formed by some more active spring. Below them begin the banks of soil and clay, strewn with fragments of an old deposit, which stretch down to the Great Geyser. They form a sort of *step*, rounded at the edge, and flat at top; and seem to have been thrown up subsequently to Laugafjall itself. They consist of grey clay, which in many places is coloured red by the admixture of iron; the presence of which may also be observed in the thin film of red colour coating most of the fragments of rock which lie upon them. Lower down, these banks are furrowed by several streams, and pierced by springs, of which in the chasm west of the Great Geyser there are six.

The smaller springs, indicated by black dots upon the map, are orifices of no great size, either emitting steam, or full of boiling water.

Down the stream, close to the farm, are several small hot springs close to the water's edge; and one large chasm, filled with warm stagnant water.

Near Haukadalr, about a mile from the Geysir, is a spring just tepid; near to it there is said to be another, actively boiling, but I could not find it. Haukadalr, in addition to its one farm, boasts a Church. It is small, and of wood. It was rebuilt a few years ago by the Danish Government, as were most of the churches of Iceland, to replace the turf structures of an earlier period. Externally it is very like a barn, with a sloping roof. It is entered by a door at the west end—speaking according to the usual way of placing churches, for it stands north and south—and is lighted by five sash windows, three on the south and two on the north sides. It would hold about fifty people, seated on open benches of wood. The chancel is separated from the nave by a plain screen, on the south side of which is the pulpit, entered from the inside only. The altar is a plain wooden table, with a cupboard under it for the vestments, which are the same as those used by the Lutheran Church in Germany. It has a railing round it equal in breadth to the table. One person only could stand inside it. The pulpit, and church generally, is painted red and blue. A loft is contrived in the roof by planks laid across the tie-beams, in which all the spare household stuff—the best clothes and saddles, and the Saga library of the neighbouring farm is stowed away. Two small bells hang on a frame above the westernmost beam; one is inscribed, "Copenhagen, anno 1762."

Time passed very heavily at the Geyser. One hardly dared to let him out of sight, lest there should be an eruption; and the heat of the weather, and the strong sulphureous smell pervading the whole place, made his neighbourhood anything but pleasant. Numerous ravens flew about Laugafjall, where they probably build, and sometimes came close to our tent in the early morning to look for pickings; but they were almost the only birds to be seen in any number. A few golden plovers, a snipe or two, and a small species of thrush were the only others. We saw traces of ptarmigan, but none of the birds themselves. Now and then, a few peasants would pass on their way to cut hay, and stop and stare at us, or sometimes bring a sick person to be physicked. They always assumed that we must be all doctors. Once, a book-hawker gave us a call. He was going to pass the night at Haukadalr, and thence journey to Reykjavik, taking the different farms on his way. His stock was tolerably plentiful, but not varied. It consisted of a hymn-book, King Magnus's "Collection of Laws," and two Sagas. The latter seemed the most popular. Zœga bought a copy, and sat all day reading them aloud to his subordinates under the shade of the saddles. The neighbouring farm supplied us with milk, skier, (a sort of curd, eaten with whortleberries and cream, and very nice when you are used to it,) and fresh meat. The only vegetables to be got were rape tops, potatoes not being ripe. After living for a week on bread and meat, we fell on them ravenously, after they had been boiled in the Geyser. We used to boil our kettle by standing it in the Still Pool, choosing a place where the deposit came up close to the surface, so that the water was only four or five inches deep. In about twenty minutes the kettle would boil.

Aug. 26th.—Started at noon for Hekla, with one of the party, who was as tired as I was of the tedious delay. Rode across the plain to the Túngufljót, which was easily crossed, and then came among parallel ridges of a columnar structure, running east and west, of no great height, separated by grass and marshy land. Thence came to the Hvitá—the White River, a wide stream of glacier water, flowing from the Langjökull—down whose right bank we had to ride some time in search of a ford. At last we got to a place where it was broad and shallow, and we got over without casualty. It was a long business, as the river was at least half a mile in breadth. A very short ride thence brought us to Reykjadalr, a substantial farm, where there was quite a concourse of people, in their holyday-dress, refreshing themselves with coffee and talk after church. Among the guests was a Norwegian veterinary surgeon, sent by the Government to investigate, and cure, if possible, the sheep-disease, which of late years has done fearful damage in Iceland. He had travelled for two years, and was of course well acquainted with the country. He said that it was best to buy horses, if wanted for a month, or more. They cost from 2*l.* to 5*l.* An hour's more riding brought us to Hruni, twelve miles from Geyser in a direct line, but as we went about sixteen miles;—a collection of two or three farms, prettily situated, a parsonage, and a church. We had heard how cordially Pastor Briem would welcome us; and as soon as we rode up to the door, he advanced and bade us enter. The house seemed neither better nor cleaner than the more substantial farms; but the owner is a man of education, who lives in this solitude with a large collection of books about him, in which he takes great delight. He conversed most intelligently and agreeably, as far as our limited Danish, and his limited Latin, would allow; affording a very pleasant contrast to the boorish clergyman of Thingvalla, who seemed little superior to the lowest peasant.

He gave us a capital supper of salmon, bread, butter, and cheese, with a bottle of claret, which was drunk with much formality,—he bowing to us whenever he emptied his glass, as a sign to us to do the same, after which he replenished all three glasses. Supper was served by his wife, but she did not partake of it with us. We talked about obsidian, and where it was to be found. He answered, quite surprised, "ubicumque;" and calling in his son, a boy of about six years old, bade him fetch some pieces out of the garden. He quickly returned with several, from two to four inches square. I next morning found a good many more lying about. Immediately above the house, is a hill, of a kind of soft muddy conglomerate, stuck full of fragments of various rocks, out of which I believe these pieces might have fallen. The clergyman told us there was a stream of it among the hills to the east, a few miles off, and offered to conduct us to it; but, as he described it to be a "rivus parvulus et interdum intermissus," and we knew we had a long ride before us, we declined his kind offer.

Aug. 27.—A cloudy morning, which alarmed us for the success of our projected ascent of Hekla. Through country resembling that of yesterday. The cliffs still in detached masses, east and west, of columnar structure. Forded the Laxá (Salmon River) without difficulty. A splendid gorge up the stream, just above where we crossed it. Thence four miles through a plain of ups and downs, overgrown with tussocks, and with here and there a deep marsh, to Thjórsárholt, where we were to cross the Thiorsá. It is a deep and wide river, with a strong stream. The horses had to swim. They were driven in with loud shouts, and pelted with stones till they took the water. Then Johann the guide, kneeling in the stern of the ferry-boat, held them all by their halters till more than half over, when they were let go, and, wisely choosing the least of two evils, all landed in safety on the further bank. We crossed in a boat. The whole business took about one hour.

Both banks of the river are thickly strewn with blocks of lava, containing great quantities of feldspar, and in some cases olivin also.

After rounding some low hills—the Skardsfjall—to our left, we came full in view of the chain of Hekla, seen at a distance of about ten miles, across the perfectly level plain which extends from its base to the Thiorsá. It looked awfully gloomy and uninviting, under a lowering sky, whose heavy clouds deepened the natural blackness of the lava.

We soon came on some of the old lava, which has flowed in all directions over the plain, though evidently from some other source than Hekla, as the streams in general run parallel to that mountain. It is much decomposed, and forms an excellent soil, to judge by the quality of the fine short grass which grows among the blocks, and between the streams, in long level fields which it was quite a pleasure to canter over. The plain is dotted with farms, and here and there a church.

After we had travelled about ten miles from the Thiorsá, the ground became more broken, and presently we entered a "forest," where the trees were not quite so stunted as usual; and then after three hours' riding from the river, reached Hals, a wretched little farm close under one of the spurs of Hekla.

These farms, one and all, are built upon the same model. A wall of stone and sods is raised to a height of three feet or so, upon which is placed a wooden frame. This is planked over, one small aperture being left for a window to each of the principal rooms. The roof is of wooden beams, overlaid with turf. Sometimes they are of one story; but the poorer ones, such as Hals, have only the ground-floor. Each of the outlying buildings, and the other farm-houses, if there be more than one, communicate by means of passages through the party walls. The whole is roofed with turf, so that at a distance they resemble a cluster of green hillocks more than a village. The rooms are small, damp, and dark. Most derive all the light they get from the door, or a hole in the roof. In the better farms, one apartment is floored, and set apart for strangers: this luxury is omitted in the poorer ones. The whole family sleep together in one room, along each side of which are built bed places of wood, something like ships' berths, and strewn with carpets and sheepskins. At Hals there must have been a dozen persons sleeping in a room measuring twelve feet by eight feet. They were certainly very poor people. We heard they had had great losses by the disease in sheep. All we could get from them was milk. They had only one pot for cooking in, and that had a hole in it. There being no room in which we could possibly sleep, they sent to a farm at some distance for a tent. Each farmer keeps one of these for use on his journeys. It was merely a large piece of canvas laid across a pole supported on two uprights, at a height of about three feet from the ground We shook down plenty of hay, and, crawling in, managed to pass a very comfortable night.

August 28th. To our great delight the bad weather of last night was succeeded by a cloudless morning. Started at nine A. M., with the farmer, an active little man, for our guide. The volcanic region which we were now entering is about twenty-five miles long, and sixteen broad at its widest part. It lies between two small rivers, the Vestri and Eystri Rángá, which fall into the broad Markarfljót, a few miles below the mountain. Hekla is the name given to the central and loftiest of several parallel ridges. It is twelve miles in length by three or four in width. The subordinate ridges lie along its sides like gigantic steps. Many of these seem once to have been active volcanoes, and stand to Hekla in the same relation as the Monti Rossi to Etna. All have steep smooth sides, formed of loose sand and decomposed rock, like those of a sifted ash-heap. Several streams of lava, of different ages, flow down among them from craters in the sides of the mountains. We rode for an hour and a half between these ridges, getting gradually higher and higher, till we came up with the lava of 1845, beyond which there was nothing but the central ridge, Hekla itself, to be climbed. We crossed a portion of the lava, a very distressing, but fortunately short piece of work, and then keeping near to its main stream, struck obliquely up the side of the mountain. The ascent offered no difficulty, but was very tiring on account of the steepness and the heat. The snow was in excellent condition for walking on; we wished that there had been more of it. About four hundred yards from the top we came to the crater whence the lava of 1845 issued. It was still smoking. Thence the stream descended in a vast volume down the steep mountain side to the plain, taking a westernly direction till it reached the level ground a little east of Hals. Then it stopped, before coming to the Rángá. It seemed to be a mass nearly equalling that which descended from the Val del Bove, in 1851. The top, which we reached at one P. M., is a ridge about half a mile long, depressed in the centre, with a crater at each end. Its direction is east and west. The westernmost of the two craters is broken down on its western side, and partially filled up with debris. The bottom is filled to a great depth with snow, melted into caverns by the hot vapours which rise from the bottom and from various small orifices in the sides. Moss grows on the side opposite the opening, despite the extensive incrustations of sulphur. On the middle of the ridge is a hot spring; the ground about it wet, with steam rising from it. The easternmost crater is the most picturesque, from the bright red colour of the rocks. Numerous jets of steam issue from its sides. Snow lies here in great quantities. A great deluge of lava blocks has been ejected from this crater in a southernly direction.

The few clouds which hovered over the mountain in the early morning, had quite cleared off, and the view was splendid. It must be one of the most extraordinary to be seen in any part of the world. To the east and south you look over a waste of glaciers, snow-fields, and lava, silent and lifeless. The ridges are generally flattened, and at this season had but little snow upon them. The glaciers also are flat and dirty, with little beauty of colour. I could see no moraines. This, I suppose, is due to the fact, that these Jökulls are not glaciers, properly so called, but fields of snow and ice. The term "Jökull" is applied very loosely to any tract where there is snow. There was little to be seen of the great Skapta Jökull, owing to clouds. Its highest peaks must be eighty or ninety miles from Hekla. To the north, the chief object was the muddy Thiorsá, fed by numerous tributaries; and beyond, the mountains and glaciers near the

Geyser. To the north-west and west stretched the plain over which we rode yesterday, green and fertile-looking, streaked with dark lava streams. Near the sea we could perceive that it became sandy, where the great rivers are bringing down yearly vast masses of deposit, and extending the coast-line. Out to sea, over a spur of the Eyafjalla Jökull, were the jagged peaks of the Westmann Islands. Nothing could exceed the beauty of the soft greys and blues in the shadows among the hills; a peculiar effect which we have already observed in other places. The height of Hekla is 5,000 Danish feet. Of the two summits, the easternmost is rather the highest.

On our way down, stopped to look for obsidian. At the upper part of the snow-slopes, near the crater of 1845, there are numerous rocks projecting through the snow, which have been reduced by the action of fire to something very nearly resembling obsidian. The great stream of it is on the south side of Hekla, near the Torfa Jökull; the Icelanders call it Hrafn-tinnah, and the stream of it the Hrafn-tinnah Hraun. To reach it requires a ride of twelve or thirteen hours from Hals, round the eastern end of Hekla. We reached Hals at six P.M., having descended very slowly.

Aug. 29th. Rode away early. The road the same as before as far as Thiórsárholt. Then we rode down the right bank of the Thiórsá for a long and weary way, over a great grassy plain. The view of Hekla rather obscured by clouds, but we could get a good idea of its grandeur, seen across so wide a level, with the detached glacier peaks, each higher than Hekla itself, between it and the sea. After riding near the river for several miles, we struck across the plain to the right, crossed an old lava stream—which, lying as it did far away from any rising ground, would seem to have been upheaved from beneath—and reached Hjálmholt, a substantial farm standing on a rising ground, at nine P.M. Our distance to-day must have been at least thirty miles. Hjálmholt is the largest and richest farm we have yet met with. It is furnished in the style of a merchant's house in Reykjavik, and the room allotted to us boasts of a sofa, clock, and other luxuries. From the farmer's cast of countenance, we suspect him to be a Jew, which will, of course, account for his affluence.

Aug. 30*th.* These hospitable Israelites gave us a breakfast of hot roast lamb, after which we started, and, descending into the plain, rode seven miles across it to Laugardœlir, where we were again to cross the Hvitá. A very strong north-east wind was blowing, from which we luckily were a good deal sheltered by the low hills on our right. We could judge of its strength by the clouds of sand that rose from the dunes along the coast, and from the occasional glimpses we got of the foam-flecked sea. The ferryman at Laugardœlir objected to cross in such a gale. We said we would not be stopped, there being evidently no danger, as the wind was blowing down stream. Our stock of expostulations was scanty, but finally they took effect, and he consented to leave the matter to the decision of the ponies. If they would swim, then he would trust his boat. They trotted down to the water's edge, snuffed at it for a moment, and then quietly entered and swam across, with no other casualty than being carried a few hundred yards down stream. Then he of course had to launch his boat, much to the amusement of a little old farmer, with a nose like a parrot's beak, who must have been near eighty, but who sat in the bows all the while we were crossing, waving his hat at intervals over his head, and shouting, "I'm not old! I'm not old!"

From the other side we had a fearfully cold ride of seven miles to Reykir, the wind having increased greatly. We slept there most comfortably in the church. As usual it was used as a receptacle for all the clothes, saddles, horse-rugs, &c. belonging to the family; and of these we made a capital bed.

Aug. 31*st.*—Reykir stands prettily in an amphitheatre of hills. It possesses a number of hot springs, closely resembling the Geysir. One threw up a column of water, or steam, exactly as the Geyser does, but to no great height. As we rode away, we passed a very large pool of still water, similar to that near the Great Geyser, only larger and more beautiful.

Another long ride of thirty-two miles to Krisuvík. From Hjalli, a village seven miles from Reykir, we got a clear view of Hekla, though nearly forty miles off, as the day was very fine, with a north-east wind. For the first time there was not a cloud on any of the glaciers. Between us and them all seemed level ground, the various heights being destroyed by the distance. Nearest to the sea is a Jökull with a domical top, something like that of Monte Rosa, and as snowy; then comes a long level ridge, followed by several peaks, one very acute, snowy, and nearly as high as Hekla, probably the highest peak of the Tindfjalla Jökull; then another long ridge, and, finally, Hekla itself. The summit nearest to the sea must no doubt have been that of the Eyafjalla Jökull, 5,200 feet high, one of several peaks rising out of a large ice-field, of which the other summits, of inferior height, are the Myrdals Jökull, the Godalands Jökull, and the Kötlugjá Jökull. It was from this last that a violent eruption broke out in May, 1860, when a deluge of water, carrying along with it blocks of ice "as big as houses," to quote the Icelandic report of the event, descended a distance of twenty miles into the sea. From this point we could see the alluvial deposit of the great rivers stopped by the lava-stream which descends into the sea south-west of Hjalli. Hence the coast-line, formed by these deposits, and by the moraines of the great Vatna Jökull, extends eastward for more than 180 miles. It is tolerably even, and differs from nearly all the rest of the Iceland coast in being wholly unindented with fiords.

We rode over lava, close to the sea, for about seven miles, and then for an equal distance through the Selvogsheidi, a tract of wild moorland, with a good many flowers among the vegetation, which otherwise was identical with that of the country beyond the Geysir. Then came lava again till we reached Vogsovar, a farm beside a small tidal lake. At Straundar Kirkja, a mile or so nearer the sea, good sleeping quarters may be found in the church. Near Vogsovar it was a beautiful sight to see the innumerable sea-fowl, especially gannets, fishing. They seemed very tame, and were close in shore, flying up high into the air, and thence dashing down into the water whenever they spied a fish. After leaving Vogsovar, we had a most painful and extraordinary journey over lava. To our right, about half a mile from the sea, was a range of hills, the Kistufell, of no great height. Between them and the sea there had evidently once been a bed of lava, similar in character to so much of what we have crossed elsewhere. It had cooled in domical masses, and its surface was corrugated in a similar way to the lava near Thingvalla. Here and there the small convex surfaces had burst, and formed deep depressions, or caverns. Over it, from Kistufell, had streamed three cataracts of more recent lava, perfectly distinguishable at the points where they had fallen over the mountain side, where, indeed, they were of no great width, and also where they had spread over the older lava in a mass similar in form to that a glacier takes when it expands after long confinement in a ravine. The whole is now covered thickly with long grey moss and lichens.

In one of the above mentioned depressions we passed within forty yards of a pair of white-tailed eagles. They had just made their evening meal of fish, and were digesting, with drooping wings, and probably asleep. They did not move for some time, but at length sailed away, with a very slow flight, to Kistufell.

At last the lava ended, and was succeeded by a plain of sand, across which we proceeded rapidly to Krisuvík.

September 1*st.*—Spent the morning at Krisuvík. The sulphur mountains are a range of no great height, extending for eight or nine miles in a north-easterly direction, forming the western boundary of the plain of Krisuvík, as Kistufell forms the eastern. The view is pretty, over the dark purplish coloured plain, dotted here and there with green spots, and intersected with rivulets. A large lake, the Kleisavatn, occupies its northern end; nearer to the sea are two smaller ones. In the middle of its broadest part, where it is about five miles across, are two steep detached volcanic hills, on the westernmost of which is the village of Krisuvík, occupying its southern face. The plain terminates seaward in a low and steep cliff, called the Krisuvikrberg, in which the Fulmar Petrel breeds. The warm yellowish-brown of the sulphur mountains is very beautiful, mixed as it is in places with the bright green of the grass, which grows in tolerable profusion in patches here and there. At a short distance from the village is a deep valley, where the chief deposit of sulphur is to be seen. It is a strange scene, full of jets of steam and cauldrons of water, spirting, boiling, and spluttering with a loud noise, and great effusion of vapour. Round and among them are banks of soft clay, very dangerous to walk over, as in an instant you are liable to sink up to your knees in the burning marl. A steep ascent from these brings you to a great bare patch, covered with sulphureous incrustations, as are the clay banks below. But the greatest quantity of sulphur is to be found above, where it lies in bright yellow masses, extremely pure. Just over the "col" is a vast assemblage of springs in a space about one hundred yards by fifty in size. The clay is full of fissures, in which are countless spirts of boiling water and steam, and some small basins of mud, which spirt much more leisurely. A great cloud of steam rises from the spot. A good deal of gypsum is to be found near. In no place have we seen the volcanic agency so active. The steam, the strange combination of fire and water, the loud noise, and the treacherous nature of the soil, recalled the scene in Dante's Inferno, where he saw the damned standing in boiling mud, that seethed like the pitch in the Venetian arsenal.

Further east in the hills are some other jets of steam, but they are small and uninteresting. The sulphur has been worked by an Englishman, but hitherto without much profit.

Hence we rode back to Reykjavik, eighteen miles. The journey was very tedious, over lava, where we could not go out of a walk. It lies between two ranges of tufa hills, very fantastic in outline, up which in some places it seems to have been forced. We passed through Havnfiord, and reached Reykjavik about eight P.M.

Sept. 2d—Sept. 8th. Spent in Reykjavik and its neighbourhood.

There is not much to see in Reykjavik. The college, a large endowed school, transferred hither a few years ago from Bessestaol, a village four miles off to the south, is the only public building. There are fifty or so scholars, who go through a course of study extending over six years, and then, if they intend to be lawyers or physicians, are obliged to go to the University of Copenhagen. If they intend to be clergymen, they study theology, pass an examination, and are ordained by the Bishop of Reykjavik. The livings, with two exceptions, are all in his gift. The same building includes the room in which the Althing still meets, a museum, quite in its infancy, and a library for the use of the college. I am afraid scholarship is at a low ebb. One of the lines in an epitaph over a young student, considered a great achievement, ended with "torpore captus abit"!

There is a town library in the loft in the roof of the cathedral. Any one subscribing a dollar a year may have five volumes out at once. At present it is poorly furnished with books, and the ladies of Reykjavik complain of the paucity of novels; but it is on the increase; and when removed into a more commodious room, to build which an Englishman lately left 1,000*l.*, it will be more accessible, and probably more interest will be taken in it.

The cathedral was rebuilt in 1847. It is of stone, with a wooden roof. There is little to be said about it, except that it is large and commodious. It consists of a nave with aisles, and a small chancel, in which is placed its only ornament, a marble font carved by Thorwaldsen. In the vestry they show a cope of red velvet, sent by the Pope to the last Roman Catholic Bishop, who died in 1550. The embroidery has been good, but now is much worn and faded. There was a very thin congregation on the Sunday we went to the cathedral. Scandalous persons affirm that it is only in the winter, when there is nothing else to do, that people frequent the church. Certainly on September 2d there were not more than fifty people present. Two young ladies appeared in the national costume, which has lately been revived. It consists of a skirt of silk, fastened round the waist by a band of velvet clasped with silver; a tight-fitting silk boddice with long sleeves more or less embroidered; and on the head a sort of helmet, covered with a bright coloured silk, from which a long veil hangs down the wearer's back to the ground. Bracelets, necklaces, buttons, and clasp are all of silver, worked in a beautiful filagree, exactly such as were made by their ancestors a thousand years ago. The great glory of the farmers' wives is to possess some of these, and they will give great prices for them. Throughout the country there is little or no costume. The men are dressed like English labourers, in suits of coarse cloth, which their wives weave, and shirts of coarse homespun. In every cottage there is a loom and a spinning-wheel.

The shops are mere warehouses, with a counter, at which you can make purchases. The wares consist entirely of the commonest articles of clothing and grocery, and a few fox and sheep skins and eider-down. There is a printing-press here, and at Akreyri on the north coast. Here they publish a weekly newspaper.

There are 1,400 inhabitants in Reykjavik, 200 of whom are Danes, the remainder Icelanders. The minority has wealth on its side, and takes to itself the chief offices. The governor, the bishop, the rector of the college, are all Danes. Two or three Icelanders are rich merchants, but they have not much influence. Of course the two parties regard each other with a good deal of jealousy, but on the whole they agree very well. The Icelanders are not wanting in intelligence, and possess one gift, the power of acquiring languages, in rare perfection; but poverty and habitual indolence, which prevent their even feeling the want of change, paralyse them. Each family is content to possess as many sheep, cows, and ponies, and as large a stock of dried fish as is wanted for its own use, and no more. The only foreign products they need are corn and coffee, and the sale of the wool of their flocks enables them easily to procure these from the Danes at Reykjavik, whither they resort once a year, generally at Christmas. Of commerce for their own profit they have no idea. If the fishery be plentiful, they take no more than is necessary for themselves. After it is salted and dried, they eat it with no further cooking. You see the children toddling about, holding half a stockfish by the tail, and gnawing it for their breakfast. The fisheries, which are most productive, only serve to enrich strangers, especially the French. A few English vessels resort to the north coast. Danish merchants reside at the Westmann Islands, and make the natives catch and salt the fish for them, as the Norwegians act by the Lapps. The case is the same at Akreyri. At Berufiord, on the east coast, where the Iceland spar would form an important item of national wealth, a Hamburg merchant has purchased, for a small sum, the exclusive right of collecting it. No steps have been taken to examine the mineral wealth of the country, which some persons, able to judge, think will prove to be large. Plumbago has been found in the north near Mount Krabla. The sulphur of Krisuvik enriches private English enterprise.

The Danish Government—which is restrained, however, by an Iceland Althing—makes as much as it can out of the country with the least possible outlay. There are no roads; there is no drainage. Yet notwithstanding all this excessive poverty, and crowding in small houses, the peasants are moral and religious, and can even read and write in the absence of schools. The lamp of learning has been handed down from father to son, and they instruct each other in the long winter evenings. In every cottage you find a few books: a Bible, some hymn-books, and a Saga or two.

The rigour of the climate has been a good deal exaggerated. It is never very hot, though once at the Geyser the thermometer stood at 93°—and never very cold. From May to September, the weather is generally fine, though the latter month is sometimes rainy. Snow rarely lies in large quantities before

February. The spring is the stormiest part of the year. With care, trees might certainly be got to grow, and possibly corn in some sheltered valleys. The impediment to agriculture is not the climate so much as the intractable nature of the soil.

The Government has of late removed the prohibition which forbids the Icelanders to trade with any nation but the Danes. The removal has not yet had much effect; a small trade goes on with Scotland in ponies, but they are not in great repute there.

Two Roman Catholic missionaries—French Jesuits—have settled here, and bought a small estate. The Government will not allow them to build a chapel; a piece of persecution which causes popular feeling to set in their favour. They make no converts, however.

The immediate neighbourhood of the town is low and marshy, and the plains strewn with blocks of trap rock. Near Havnfiord there is a variety of this in great masses, which they call Havnfiordite. At Fossvogr, a small bay in the first fiord to the south from Reykjavik, there is a bed of palagonite tufa, about eighteen feet thick, containing a few shells.

Sept. 8th. Sailed into the Hvalfiord, the first fiord to the north. Its scenery is very pretty, the southern shore being formed by the cliffs of Esja; and the northern sloping more gradually to the water's edge, with several farms on it. There is capital anchorage in a secluded bay at the upper end, near a farm called Hvammr. Dr. Hjaltalin went with us to show us the place where he had found some specimens of Iceland spar on a former visit. He thinks that it may possibly turn out a profitable vein. At present, only a few pieces have been found among the pebbles on the beach, and, of course, a good deal worn. Still they are clear and good. We found but little, and that little of very indifferent quality. Near our anchorage was a fine range of basaltic columns, with a vein of green stone cutting them diagonally.

Sept. 9th. Examined the northern shore for minerals. Count Sartorius found copper here. We got some specimens of the greenish clay, which does contain copper, but in very small quantities. Plenty of crystals of carbonate of lime in the rock, and some stilbites. Got also some pretty pieces of chalcedony and malachite. Marble, too, is found both here and in Esja.

Back to Reykjavik at night. We spent two more very pleasant days there, and finally sailed on the morning of September 12th. We anchored in Lerwick harbour on the 19th.

I will now add a few particulars which may be useful to future travellers in Iceland.

The steamer "*Arcturus*" runs every month, from March to October, from Copenhagen to Iceland, touching at Leith, and at Thorshavn in the Faro Islands. The voyage from Leith to Reykjavik occupies about five days, one of which is spent at Thorshavn. The agents are Messrs. Turnbull and Salverson, Leith.

Iceland is rather larger than Ireland. In form it is an irregular ellipse, of which the greatest length is about 285 English miles, and the greatest breadth 190. On a rough computation it has an area of 37,000 square miles; but this it is very difficult to estimate accurately, owing to the great number of fiords which run up far into the land, and the long narrow peninsulas which in many parts of the coast extend for several miles into the sea. This applies especially to the northern, eastern, and western coasts. The southern presents a low level line, continually increasing, owing to the débris brought down by the great rivers, and by the icefields of Hekla, and of the Vatna Jökull.

Of this area, however, it is only a comparatively narrow strip round the coasts that is inhabited; and that only by peasants dwelling in small farms remote from each other. The entire centre of the island, for an area of about 12,000 square miles, is a desert, rarely visited by the inhabitants, and regarded by them with some degree of apprehension. It consists partly of glaciers, partly of extensive lava fields, and partly of scrubby moor. It nowhere attains to any great elevation; its highest glacier peaks, which are quite isolated, are not more than 4,400 feet high. It takes four days, our guide told us, to cross from Haukadalr to the first farm on the north side of the island, during which time not a human being is to be seen. This track is one frequently used, as being the nearest way between Reykjavik and Akreyri, the two capitals, so to speak. The scenery about the glaciers, judging from the glimpses I got of it beyond the Geyser, must be very splendid.

The grandest glacier, however, in Iceland, and one wholly unexplored, is the great Vatna Jökull, in the south-eastern angle of the island. The district so named occupies on the map an area of 3,500 square miles, 140 times as large as that of the Finster Aarhorn glacier; but this of course must not be understood to apply to one glacier only. As we sailed within sight of it on our return voyage—and this was in September, when the snow had disappeared in most parts of Iceland—it seemed a vast snow field, with many single snowy peaks rising from it. One of these, the Orœfa Jökull, attains to a height of 6,000 feet, and is the highest mountain in Iceland. Generally, the whole field is at least as high as Hekla: that is, about 5,000 feet.

Travelling in Iceland is slow, according to our modern ideas. Still, as the most *blasé* tourist would hardly go to Iceland for novelty, it may be fast enough for scientific men, the only ones who are likely to visit it. Thirty miles a day is the utmost that can be accomplished, on an average; and, four or five days' continuous travelling, even at that rate, will be found very wearisome. There is not the relief of boat journeys which you have in Norway. There are no boats large enough to ferry horses in; there is no system of relays by which you can hire ponies from point to point, and substitute water for land conveyance at pleasure; with the horses with which you started you must return; and so are obliged to go round fiords at a cost of days, perhaps, which might be crossed in as many hours, if boats were to be had. Still, with all this delay, the whole island might be visited after a fashion, "parcouru," as the French say, in a single summer, between May and October.

The cost is considerable. Our Reykjavik guide, who was certainly a first-rate fellow, probably the best in the island, charged three dollars, about 6*s.* 9*d.* a day, for his own services; and two dollars a day besides for those of a boy to look after the ponies, often a long business, as they stray during the night. For the horses, we agreed to pay ten dollars a horse for the *journey*, which we specified, irrespective of the *time*. We were out sixteen days, so that our horses cost us no more than about 1*s.* 6*d.* a day each. Certainly, if the journey was intended to be a long one, with frequent stoppages, it would be better to buy horses; as they can be got cheap, and can easily be sold when done with. Their keep is not costly, and they generally feed themselves on the neighbouring pastures. In cases where fodder has to be bought, one penny a day covers all charges. Several horses are required even by a single traveller, as he must carry a great deal of baggage. First, a tent and bedding is almost necessary everywhere, and absolutely so in the wilder regions. Every farmer possesses a small tent, which he will lend; but it is of a very primitive cut, about two feet high, and destitute of all comfort. With the exception of a few clergymen and farmers, no one in Iceland possesses a house where a decent lodging can be obtained. The poorest in Norway is better than the richest there. Secondly, provisions should be taken. Except in very rare instances, no meat is to be had, unless the party be large enough to consume a whole sheep. The only bread to be met with is that made with coarse rye flour, and even that but rarely. The natives seem to live principally on "skier," and dry salt fish. Gulls and seals are a delicacy with the fishermen. Biscuits, therefore, and preserved meats, become necessaries in Iceland. Very little can be got at the shops in Reykjavik: so that all that is likely to be wanted should be taken from England. If it be the traveller's object to collect birds, he should take an India-rubber boat, as many of the inland lakes have either no boats of any kind near them, or some crazy old thing which leaks so fast that half the time is spent in baling.

For birds, the best localities are the north and east coasts. It was on the latter, in the Breidifjörd, and about the numerous bays in the peninsula forming the north-west corner of the island, that Faber found the rarest birds. The lake Myvatn, near Mount Krabla, is stated by all to be the best place for ducks. A very good ornithologist assured me that he had found all the ducks there. At Grimsey, an island off the north-coast, all the varieties of guillemot breed, and so does the gerfalcon, I am told. The Hvitávatn, a great glacier lake north of the Geyser, is said to be full of swans. I myself saw six in one small pond near Hekla. The great northern diver breeds on the islands in the lake of Thingvalla. White-tailed eagles are common ; I saw several near the coast, and one used to come daily to an island close to our anchorage at Reykjavik to feed, but he was too wary to be shot. The Iceland falcons come close to Reykjavik in the winter, and several are shot yearly. They are not at all rare. Dr. Hjaltalin told us that this year the famous Great Auk Scar had been visited by some fishermen from Reykjanes. No birds, however, were found, nor any traces of them ; since 1844, none have been seen, and as their value is known, and a hundred dollars offered for a pair in Reykjavik, the bird has little chance of escape if he does make his appearance. Great quantities of the bones are said to exist still near Reykjanes, relics of the days when boat-loads of the birds used to be brought from the Scar. Probably, however, the quantity consumed has been greatly exaggerated ; the Scar never could have been easy of access, and now seven or eight weeks will pass without a boat being able to approach it.

Reindeer are said to exist in considerable numbers in the interior. It is not long since they were introduced from Norway, but no use has ever been made of them. Of course, they never leave their highlands, and the idea of shooting and eating them has never been yet entertained by an Icelander. Blue and white foxes are trapped in great numbers in winter.

An old horse is killed, and the hunters place themselves *en cache* in the neighbourhood, and shoot the foxes as they come down to feed. In summer they are rarely if ever seen, as they resort to the most unfrequented places.

There fortunately is a capital map, the survey made by order of the Danish Government, and published in 1844, at Copenhagen. It can be got in London from Messrs. Williams and Norgate, for about 30*s*., mounted, in a case. I found it in general very accurate in frequented places, but in unfrequented ones it was by no means so good. No trustworthy chart has been published either in England or Denmark. The best is a French one, to be procured through the English from the French Admiralty. The best chart of the anchorage at Reykjavik is one given in Sir James Mackenzie's "Travels in Iceland," in 1800; a book whose general excellence I had ample opportunities of admiring. I can recommend it as a useful guide-book; but I ought to say, that Henderson's Iceland is considered by educated Icelanders to be the best work on their country. This I have never seen.

11. *NORWAY.*

BY H. F. TOZER, M.A.

'HE that will visit Norway, must first pay a heavy toll.' This dismal thought was uppermost in our minds on the morning of the 8th of July, 1860, when, after forty hours' heavy rolling in the German Ocean, we at last approached the harbour of Christiansand. But it was soon dispelled; for as we drew near to the shore, we perceived that we were coming to a perfectly unique country. All along the coast were pine-covered mountains, with large bosses of rock projecting from their sides, and inlets of the sea running in amongst them. We had never seen anything like it before; and after trying various comparisons, we agreed that you would get the clearest idea of its appearance, by supposing the Saxon Switzerland transported to the sea. On landing, we made our way through the town; and having crossed a river of some size, which forms its boundary on the land side, mounted the hills, which rise behind, to get a view over the surrounding district. The town lay below us, and the well-sheltered bay beyond; at our feet the river which we had crossed, the Torrisdals Elv, flows into the sea; and the level country which intervenes between the river and the mountains, is occupied by prosperous-looking farms and green meadows, from which splendid crops of grass were being taken. Away to the north is a picturesque break in the hills, through which the eye can follow the river in many of its windings; while to the east the broad Topsdal Fiord runs in landwards. The houses of the town are all built of wood, with tiled roofs, high-pitched to throw off the snow; but they are low, having generally two, or at the most three stories. The streets are very regular, owing, probably, to frequent fires; for in wooden towns fire is the great sanitory reformer, just as Etna, by its frequent eruptions, has made Catania the best-built town in Sicily.

The next day we proceeded along the coast, with fine bright weather, and before long began to thread the numerous islands which fringe the shore. In many places the passage is very narrow; but the water is deep. These islands are all of the same bossy nature as what we had seen before; some are bare rocks, but generally they are covered with wood, and log-huts and wooden houses are seen here and there upon them. It gave me quite the idea of what a back settlement in Canada might be, as seen from the inlets of one of the great lakes; and very charming and Eden-like many of the stations appeared,—so compact they were, each with its little bay and sailing-boat, with a small bright-green meadow, flanked by rocks, which in their turn were crowned with trees, and in the midst a picturesque cottage in a sheltered spot, painted with bright colours, yellow, red, or rich brown, as if the art of polychrome had long been there. After penetrating some way amongst these, we found ourselves in a wide *sound*,* with fine arms reaching out among the islands; the mountains also became higher, the houses larger and more numerous, and before long we discovered that we were approaching the pretty town of Arendal, which is built in a steep gully, running down to the sea at the meeting of three creeks, and commands some singularly nice lake scenery. The sea in these parts looks blue, though it cannot boast of the rich blue of the south; the sky, too, is a light blue, but most transparent, and the air clear and invigorating. We wound our way out to the open sea again, but before evening penetrated once more into a wilder and less frequented nest of islands. The sunset was superb: I have rarely seen such

* A sound has been distinguished from a fiord, thus: a sound is a thoroughfare; a fiord, a *cul de sac*.

distinct and delicately pencilled furrows of gold, and the last bright hues had not disappeared at midnight. During the night we steamed up the Christiania Fiord, the scenery of which somewhat resembles that of the less interesting Swiss lakes; and in the morning arrived at the capital.

Christiania presents few objects of interest to detain the traveller. Its appearance is commonplace, reminding you of Mannheim, or some of the less striking German towns; and since it has been ordered by law that all the houses shall be built of stone, it wants the semi-barbarous picturesqueness of other Norwegian towns. Accordingly the day that we remained there was principally spent in purchasing *carrioles* (the Norwegian travelling carriage), one for my friend R—— and one for myself,—for the carriole is a solitary vehicle,—harness and maps, together with cayenne pepper, and a few other things, which have the power of making unpalatable food seem palatable. The route which we proposed to ourselves was to go up the Gulbrandsdal, the principal inland valley of Norway, to the foot of the Dovre Fjeld, and thence by way of the Romsdal to Molde, where we hoped to catch the steamer for Trondjem and Hammerfest, and then returning to Molde, to make our way to Bergen across the less frequented western fiords, and after a visit to the Hardanger Fiord, to return to Christiania over the Fille Fjeld.

On Wednesday, July 11, we started by railway for Eidsvold, at the foot of the Miösen lake, and on the way saw evident signs of the great inundation which had taken place in the river which flows out of the lake; for Norway, as well as England, had been deluged with rain during the spring. At Eidsvold the carrioles had to be taken off the train, and hoisted on board the steamer; so, while this operation is going forward, I will endeavour to describe them. The carriole is the nearest possible approach to a skeleton carriage; in few words, it is composed of two long shafts, two large wheels, a little seat, and a little splash-board. The shafts are the great feature, as they support the body of the carriage, and being made of very strong ash-wood, and thin in proportion to their length, they yield with the motion of the vehicle, and render springs unnecessary. The wheels are behind the

seat, and just behind them again is a board, on which the luggage is placed; on the top of which sits the boy, who looks after the horses, and takes them back at the end of the stage. The seat is extremely small—Falstaff could not possibly have ridden in a carriole—the sides are about nine inches high, the back about eighteen; between this and the splash-board is a narrow bottom, where a knapsack will conveniently stand; and attached to the splash-board is an apron, which, together with a mackintosh, will enable you almost to defy rain. There are no traces, but the horse draws by thongs attaching the collar to the fore-part of the shafts. Your feet rest on either side of the splash-board against a cross-bar, which supports the front of the carriage; and as the seat is very low, so that your legs are nearly at right angles to your body, and there is hardly any support for the back, it is hard to see on what principles, mechanical or anatomical, it can possibly be comfortable; but it is so, notwithstanding, and you may travel in this way for the greater part of a day without fatigue.

The mention of a knapsack reminds me to give two words of advice on this subject to future travellers. The first is, Take a knapsack to Norway; the second, Don't wear it unless you are obliged. In spite of all that has been stated on the other side, I do not hesitate to say, that Norway is not a country for a pedestrian tour. Its area is too large; and both the special objects of interest, and the more comfortable stations, lie at too great a distance from one another. No doubt, if a person goes abroad for the *purpose* of roughing it, that mode of travelling will give him ample opportunities of doing so in Norway; and most travellers will have enjoyed, for once in a way, the independence—some would even say the romance—of eating goats' flesh, and lying on hard boards; but when our first enthusiasm has passed away, it is as well, perhaps, to secure the ordinary comforts of life, when they do not prevent us from seeing all that is worth seeing; and this for the pedestrian tourist in Norway is impossible. Yet a knapsack will be found serviceable for carrying what is wanted for ordinary use, and may be required for occasional excursions. But the carrioles are on board, and the steamer is waiting for us. *Lad os gaae.*

The Miösen lake is a very long and narrow piece of water, being upwards of sixty miles in length, and rarely more than two or three broad. The scenery is not grand, but soft and pleasant, with sloping hills, which here and there rise to some height above the water. It might be compared to the lake of Zurich, or the lower end of that of Constance; and though the cultivation cannot vie with the smiling shores of those lakes, yet there is a good deal of fine vegetation and thriving farms at the sides. Whenever we approached the land, we were welcomed by the aromatic smell of the trees, which recalled the fragrance of the "sweet south," though it had not the richness of the southern scents. But the greatest charm of all, was in the feeling of the evening-time, which succeeded the almost overpowering heat of the day; to breathe the air was perfect enjoyment; it was fresh without chill, and soft without languor. At eleven, P.M., when we reached Lillehammer, at the head of the lake, it was still daylight, and you might have read a book with the smallest print all the night through.

The scenery of the Gulbrandsdal, which commences at this point, is apt to disappoint the traveller, for the descriptions, which represent it as rich and beautiful, give a false idea of the reality. Every thing about it is wild and dreary, though on a grand scale; here and there patches of cultivation are seen, and the firs spread themselves all over the mountains, but it impresses you everywhere with a sense of desolation. This appearance, together with the size and comparative calmness of the river, distinguish it from a commonplace Alpine valley; and in places, when the dull bluish green waters of the Logan expand into lakes of considerable extent, the views are often picturesque. I will describe one scene which may suggest a general idea of the features of the valley. It is at Elstad, the place where we dined on this first day of our carriole journey, and where the station, or post-house, is in a fine position on a hill. The broad river, here of a grey-green colour, lies below you, broken into several channels by large sand-banks, on some of which numerous willows grow; opposite you are bluffs of rock and pine-clad slopes, with pastures here and there, and *sæters* or mountain farms upon them, while the highest mountains, which rise behind, are bare of trees. There is a certain breadth and grandeur about it; but the outlines are poor, and the colours are all neutral tint and dark green, so that it affords no relief to the eye or the mind.

At Oien, where we supped that evening, while the post-horses, which had only just returned from another stage, were resting, we had a pretty little episode. We had extracted a promise of pancakes (*pandekager*) from the unwilling hostess, who was evidently tired with a long day's work, and on starting for a walk had bestowed sundry judicious caresses on her child, whom we met in the fields. When we returned, we found her in high good humour, and while we were at supper, the little damsel was introduced, with her face washed and a crown of roses round her hat: it is hardly needful to add, that the pancakes were superb. At eleven o'clock, after a delicious evening drive, we arrived at Viig, where we intended to pass the night; and I proceeded to investigate the station, leaving R—— to manage that difficult mental arithmetic, which is required before paying the *skydskarl* or postboy; for the Norwegian mile is equal to seven English miles, (seven-leagued boots are still in use in Norway), and consequently the stage is often an awkward fraction of a mile, which, together with variations in the payment and *extras*, cause endless confusion and trouble. There were no signs of life about the station: on entering, I found the entrance-hall nicely strewn with pine-twigs, and some old armour was hanging about the walls, but the rooms were untenanted; I went upstairs and explored the bedrooms—but there was no one there. "Servants is in the arms o' Porpus," thought I; so, with the charitable intention of rousing them from their slumbers, I ascended another flight of stairs; but with as little success, for I was met by a closed door, and no amount of kicking could elicit a responsive voice. In fact, the house was empty; so I descended to my companion, and our resolution was soon taken, to occupy it ourselves, which accordingly we did, and, having deposited our boxes in the hall, went to bed in the best room. About an hour afterwards another traveller arrived, who, being an *habitué*, managed to find the woman of the house: we had to exclude her forcibly from our apartment, for the Norwegian female is not particular as to the stage of your toilet in which she surprises you; a subject on which we heard many eloquent observations from a French gentleman, who had been travelling in Lapland. "At one place," he said, "the mistress of the inn brought me a cup of coffee before I got up in the morning, and placed it by my bedside. I drank the coffee, which was good, and intended to get up, but she did not go. I waited some time, and made a few remarks, but she would not go. I was at my wits' end, for," he added, with pleasing *naïveté*, "I did not like to get up while she was in the room; but at last a bright thought struck me, and I said, 'will you get me another cup of coffee?' and while she was away, I jumped out of bed, and dressed as quickly as I could. And it was well that I did so; for she soon came back with the second cup of coffee, and did not again leave the room."

The dwelling houses throughout Norway are built of wood,

and they manage to make them wonderfully warm and air-tight. In one place in the Gulbrandsdal we saw one in process of building, and the process is as follows. They lay trunks of trees, shaped and squared, on one another, and between them are stuffed layers of moss, which acts as a warm kind of cement: the walls are plaistered or in some way covered on the inside, and then painted. Thus they wisely make use of the materials which they have at hand. On the sloping roofs are laid clods of earth, to form a compact covering, on which grass, flowers, and heather grow abundantly, so that they are sometimes coloured purple, and from time to time the owners make hay on their house-tops. The churches in the country districts are also of wood, and often very picturesque. Their form is different in different parts of the country; but those in this valley are mostly in the shape of a Greek cross, having a porch at the west end, and sometimes a second in one of the transepts; while over the centre rises a small tower, surmounted by a narrow sharp spire. They are generally devoid of ornament, though now and then you see quaint metal crosses over the gables. The roofs are tiled or slated, and in one or two places where the soil was slaty, we saw the walls plated all over with enormous slates, or, more accurately speaking, pieces of schist. At Lillehove, and also at Veblungsnæsset, in the Romsdal, there are curious octagonal churches, each with a small central tower and lantern; at the former place the tower is painted green, and the church forms a striking object from a distance in the valley.

One of the first things that strikes a person on going into the interior of the country is the scattered nature of the population. The villages are scarcely worthy of the name, and a large number of the stations are merely single houses: even the number of houses does not fairly represent the inhabitants, as the mountain farms are only used during the summer, the cattle being driven down to the less exposed vallies before the approach of winter; and the amount of land which is under cultivation is infinitesimally small. The people seem for the most part prosperous and contented; but on the road from Viig to Dombaas, at the foot of the Dovre Fjeld, near Solheim, where a large tributary stream from the Justedal glaciers flows into the Logan, we saw what is seldom found in Norway, a considerable number of beggars; in fact, begging is prohibited by law, but such prohibitions have little effect in these remote districts. They seemed extremely poor, and probably belonged to a class of persons whom Laing mentions as being intermediate between the wandering Laplanders and the farmers, and getting a precarious livelihood by cutting wood and similar employments.

The vegetation gradually diminishes all the way up the Gulbrandsdal, until at last there are but few firs to be seen on the mountains. The flora is principally composed of common English flowers, but they are so numerous as sometimes quite to colour the fields; the harebell grows to a very great size, and the roses are unrivalled, both for number of blossoms and depth of colour. But two of the most conspicuous plants, which attract the eye with their bright patches of pink and purple, the *Lychnis viscaria* and *Lithospermum purpureo-cæruleum*, are among the less common English flowers; the monkshood too grows by the roadside; and about Dombaas we found other rare ones, such as *Trientalis Europæa*, *Linnæa borealis*, *Cornus Suecica*, and the charming *Pyrola uniflora*, quite a poet's plant, with its arched stem, and single white starry flower gazing pensively on the ground: together with these were growing the buckbean and the cranberry.

Before leaving England we had heard a great deal about the hardships of Norwegian travel, but I am bound to say that this was not confirmed by my experience. The beds at most of the principal stations are clean, and though the fare is not always as good as at Dombaas, where we had salmon for supper, and reindeer venison (*rendyrsteg*) for breakfast, yet if a person judiciously chooses the best halting places, and possesses a certain knowledge of the language, he will seldom be reduced to starvation. At many places you can get meat; where this is not procurable, there will probably be fish or eggs (and eggs *in esse* are pancakes *in posse*, for the art of making these is universal throughout the country), then *flöde gröd*, or oatmeal porridge mixed with cream, is no despicable dish, and the coffee can hardly be surpassed in Paris. If after all you are reduced to the common cheeses and black rye-bread or *flad bröd*, a kind of thin oatmeal cake, you will enjoy a light, but not unpalatable diet; timber-bread and saw-dust puddings, which we read of, that is, food prepared from the bark of trees, though they are eaten by the people in times of scarcity, do not often come in the way of travellers. Occasionally you meet with very peculiar dishes; one of them, called *rödgröd*, or red porridge, I will describe for the benefit of those who take an interest in such matters. It is thin water-arrowroot sweetened, and flavoured with red wine or cherry juice; this is served as soup, and when elaborately made has the further addition of cinnamon, almonds, and raisins; it is the custom to eat with it, on another plate, pickled fish and potatoes. But a certain knowledge of the language is serviceable in the highest degree, for the Norwegian innkeepers are singularly unsuggestive, always leaving the traveller to ask for what he thinks procurable, without mentioning what eatables they can provide; and to judge from appearances, their feeling toward you is rather one of compassion than of welcome. When you come to a station, no one comes out to meet you; you are forced to explore for yourself until you arrive at the kitchen, where the landlady will probably be standing with her back to you, watching something on the fire; and if you ask very civilly, and she has nothing better to do, she will probably turn round and attend to you. You must not be discouraged by these undemonstrative ways. It will not be amiss to shake her by the hand and call her *Gamle Mo'* (old mother), if she has attained the age at which ladies like that appellation; but under other circumstances I can safely recommend my friends to adopt the plan which we pursued at Oien, and which, according to a distinguished writer, had great weight in deciding the contested election for the ancient and patriotic borough of Eatanswill.*

At Dombaas we left the high road from Christiania to Trondjem, which here begins to ascend towards the plateau of the Dovre Fjeld, and followed a less direct route, in order to visit the magnificent scenery of the Romsdal. Before reaching the lake, which forms the watershed of this valley and the Gulbrandsdal, we saw large masses of granite lying about in various directions; and as the surrounding mountains appear to be of a different formation, one would be led to regard them as traces of the action of those former glaciers, which seem quite to have altered the appearance of some districts of Norway. The finest part of the valley begins at Nystuen; from that place it descends steeply, and the river, the Rauma, begins to break into glorious cascades. We walked this stage, leaving our carrioles to be driven on by a boy from Nystuen, that we might explore at our leisure the different waterfalls. The first that I will describe is about halfway between Nystuen and Ormen; for beauty it has few rivals in Europe, and the falls of this valley have one charm, which is wanting to those of Switzerland, namely, that their water is quite clear, so that the cascades themselves are pure white, while the water in the pools below is blue. In this part of the valley another river comes to join the Rauma; before their junction the ground becomes exceedingly steep and broken, and the second river divides into two parts, one of which runs obliquely towards the Rauma, and the two

* A few words about the language may not be unacceptable to some of my readers. It is the same as Danish, the old Norse having died out; but the people are not pleased at hearing it called anything but *Norsk*. It has four principal peculiarities:—1. The definite article is placed after the substantive, as *hest*, horse; *hesten*, the horse: this is also found in Wallachian and Syriac. 2. The passive voice is formed by inflection, as *jeg elsker*, I love; *jeg elskes*, I am loved. 3. There is no masculine or feminine, but a common gender, besides the neuter. 4. It has the same distinction between the demonstrative and reflective pronouns of the third person, as is found in Latin; *han*, ille; *hans*, illius; *sig*, se; *sin*, suus. An attempt is now being made to revive the archaic form of the language, and books have been printed in that idiom; but the movement does not meet with much support.

rivers meet with a double fall in the same basin. The Rauma after some picturesque rapids falls about sixty feet in a broad white dashing mass ; the other stream, much narrower, and yet a good sheet of water, first slides down a sidelong groove in the rocks, then suddenly turns and plunges down about one hundred feet, and being divided by a grand black rock, mixes its spray with that of the other fall. Such are the falls in themselves ; but this is only part of the scene, for they have all the benefit of a striking contrast. As you stand on the high rocks opposite, you see their waters sweep away into a deep-blue pool of considerable size, and beyond this is the long deep valley, with other shining pools lighted up, as we saw the scene, by the westering sun, while in the distance rise magnificent peaks which bound the view. The rocks which surround this pool, and those at the back of the falls, are grand, and the vegetation beautiful ; the pines and fir-trees perch themselves in the most picturesque spots, and bright shrubs and brushwood cover the ground. But the third stream has yet to come : if you mount to a point some way above where you have been standing before, you see not only this view, but also a fine series of cascades, and at last a superb fall, which this stream makes in joining the combined waters of the other two. At this point, also, a pine, such as an artist ought to fall in love with at first sight, is thrown out against the Rauma fall, and the mountains behind rise broad and wild, here and there flecked by the white lines of the upper waterfalls of these rivers. Yet this scene is so little known that the traveller has to explore for himself, and make his own path to see it. Shortly before reaching Ormen, we found another fall, where the water plunges down, a mass of foam, white as wool, into a deep and narrow gorge, spanned by a slight bridge of pine-trees, on which, unprotected as it is at the sides, and exposed to the rush of wind which follows with a cataract, it requires a good head to look over. The views of the gorge, fall, and bridge, with their setting of trees, from whatever side we looked at them, were as exquisite as could be. Again, nearly opposite the inn at Ormen is a fall on the mountain side, which would make the fortune of an hotel in any other country. Like the Giesbach in Switzerland, it is a succession of single falls, one following closely on the other; but before it reaches the Rauma, it breaks into three parts, which descend together amongst the rocks which divide them. The singularly blue water of the river is a great ornament to the whole valley. As you descend to Ormen, the cliffs increase in grandeur, and are not unworthy of the finest Swiss passes; below that place they are finer still; and in one part of the valley, within the distance of two miles, numerous waterfalls, each worthy of a separate description, tumble over the rocks from a height of from 500 to 1,000 feet. They are enchanting; every kind of fall is represented there. Some dash forward from the loftiest precipices to "blow their trumpets from the steep;" some glide like spun glass over the cliffs, which they have polished in their course; others drop from rock to rock, and play at hide-and-seek, now disappearing, now re-appearing among the ravines, while some, the most beautiful of all, let fall—

> "Their wreaths of dangling water-smoke,
> That like a broken purpose waste in air."

At the Horjem station, between Ormen and the sea, is a magnificent pass, the steep precipices of which greatly reminded me of those of the Styx, in Arcadia, which are among the finest in Europe; but here there are glaciers clinging to the mountain-sides, though they are not more than 2,000 feet above the sea. On the left are the *Troldtinder*, or witch-peaks, a strange and weird line of jagged crests, broken into a thousand splinters, like the varied outline of the ridges of the Pyrenees. On the right is the Romsdalshorn, a very remarkable mountain, which rises precipitously to a great height above the valley, and at last throws up a single conical peak, like a huge eye-tooth, which is conspicuous from every side. There is an admirable view of it some way further down the stream, where it stands up above a reach in the broad blue river.

When we reached Veblungsnæsset, at the head of the Romsdal Fiord, we hired a boat and four men to take us and the carrioles to Molde, which lies on an island near the mouth of the fiord. The distance is about sixteen miles, but the tide was against us (it has considerable force in some of these fiords), so that, though we started in the afternoon, we did not reach our destination until one in the morning; but we had little reason to complain, for the scenery of the upper part of the Romsdal Fiord is hardly surpassed by any lake-scenery in Europe, not even by that of the lake of Lucerne, which in many respects it resembles. The precipices, close under which we went, are stupendous, and in many places descend abruptly into the deep sea. Trees grow wherever they can find room, and the vegetation is splendid; the Scotch fir, the birch, the alder and other trees of the brightest green coming down close to the water. The nearer mountains, of which one sees a long succession in passing through the winding bays of the fiord, are all grand; some more rounded in their outlines, some rent and jagged. Between these, smiling basin-like valleys intervene, above which rise the distant peaks of deepest purple, exquisitely broken, with snow and glaciers hanging to their sides. I do not remember to have seen in any other views so great variety of form and colour; but the day was unusually favourable, for, instead of the clear sky and intense heat, which we had had in the interior of the country, it was cloudy and broken, deepening the purple shadows, and throwing bright streaks of light over the mountain-sides. During the night the clouds cleared away, but neither moon nor stars appeared; they were fairly overpowered by the daylight. The night before, which we spent at Ormen, I went out about midnight to see if any stars were visible; one planet was shining brightly, but it was with great difficulty that at last I discovered two of the largest fixed stars; these were the last that we were destined to see for nearly three weeks.

On arriving at Molde, we knocked up the people at the inn, and got to bed and to sleep notwithstanding the garish light. The next morning, ascending the hill above the town, we obtained a view which has few equals as a panorama of distant mountains. It reminded me of the famous view from the esplanade at Corfu, where you see the long line of Albanian heights rising above the sea, though there, perhaps, the mountains are higher and more distant; but it would be hard to find a lake which is surrounded by mountains such as these. All the Romsdal peaks, and many others not less fine, are seen extended in a semicircle; below you lie the various branches of the fiord, diversified by islands, the nearer of which, in the middle distance, are very long and narrow, and fringed with trees; while in the foreground are the picturesque roofs of the town. From the summit of the hill the view is said to be still finer; but we had not time to reach it, and the ascent must be arduous, from the account which we received from a distinguished Dutchman, at breakfast that morning. "The other day," he said, "I ascended to the top of the hill, and—it was *very* hot, you know; and—I had on my black trousers, for it was Sunday; and—they were very tight, you know; and I looked round, and saw there was no one near; and so I— I— in fact, I took them off, you know;" here he shrugged his shoulders apologetically, "and—and walked up the hill without them." How we envied his coolness both of mind and body!

While we were waiting for the steamer, the landlord's daughter, a young lady with her hair dressed *à l'Impératrice*, played us some German and Norwegian airs with delightful taste on the pianoforte. I mention this because the people generally are very unmusical, having harsh voices and no ear; and she may, perhaps, be regarded as the exception which proves the rule, as she had been educated in Paris, a fact which explained the fashion of her hair, and her habit of looking in the glass to see if we were attending. Some of the national airs are spirited, and some plaintive, but they want character; perhaps the best, though not the most popular in the country, is the well-known "Hardy Norseman," which we heard on one or two occasions. The Church music is simply execrable. The principal national amusement, we were told, is dancing, in winter time; but during the short summer they are too much occupied with the fisheries, with the two harvests, which follow within a few weeks—sometimes even a few days—of each other, and with tending the cows on the mountain pastures, to have any time for recreations.

The steamer bore us away along the coast and among the islands to Christiansund, a place of some importance, built on the sides of a number of islets which surround a little bay; and thence up the Trondjem Fiord to the ancient capital, where we arrived just a week from the day we had left Christiania.

The city of Trondjem, or Drontheim, lies on the shores of the wide fiord of the same name; on two sides of it, to the east and west, are hills of considerable height; but in one respect its position is very singular, for the river Nid, which flows down here, just where it is about to reach the sea, makes a great bend inland, and renders the site of the city almost insular. This may be seen by ascending the tower of the cathedral, or better still, from the castle, which is on a height to the east of the city across the river. From this point you see the river winding its serpent-like course round the town, and in the foreground the old gray cathedral surrounded by trees, with green slopes coming down to the water, so that it rises above the river in the same manner as the Cathedral of Spires overlooks the Rhine. Then on one side is the fiord, bounded by mountains, the most conspicuous feature in which is the fortress on the little island of Munkholm, which defends the harbour: on the other are green meadows and knolls covered with trees, interspersed with neat country seats and church spires. One can hardly fail to notice in this view the raised terraces and levels, which are supposed to have been originally sea-beaches; we afterwards observed similar ones on the shores of the Alten Fiord. The town is entirely built of wood, which gives it a quaint appearance; it is not irregular, like Constantinople and other Oriental wooden towns, but is laid out in straight rows of two-storied houses, in wide open regular streets, at the end of which views may generally be obtained of the country or the sea.

Trondjem is the most interesting place in Norway from being the centre of its historical associations: it was the seat of government in the palmy days of the Norwegian monarchy, before the country was made a province of Denmark in the fourteenth century, and in its cathedral the ancient kings were crowned. Accordingly, when we heard, on our arrival in Norway, that the coronation of the new king, Karl XV., would take place there while we were in the north, we caught at the idea of seeing the ceremony, as a thing which more than anything else would carry us back to the olden time, and help our imaginations to realize the former glories of the kingdom. When we succeeded in obtaining more precise information, we found that it would take place just two days after our return from Hammerfest, so that it would not interfere with any of our plans, excepting that of seeing the North Cape, which, as it is a low promontory, and situated on an island, is only interesting as being the northernmost point of Europe. But then came the question, how were we to gain admission? In order to discover how the land lay, we went, shortly after our arrival at Trondjem, to our kind-hearted and obliging Consul, M. Knudtsen, and consulted him on the subject. He promised to do what he could for us, but remarked that there would be very little room; that people were coming from all quarters to see it, &c. &c.: in fact, it was evident, that without some bold move on our part, our chance was exceedingly small. So I stated that we were members of the Senate of the University of Oxford; and that that University had just conferred its highest honours on the representative of Sweden;* leaving the Consul, and through him the Grand Chamberlain, to whom it was to be reported, to draw the only conclusion which could fairly be drawn from these premises, viz., that honour should be paid to us as representatives of our University. When requested to write this down on paper, I felt rather astonished at my own *sang*

* Count Platen received the degree of D.C.L. at the Commemoration in 1860.

froid; which was only surpassed by that of my companion on a later occasion, when being asked by a dignified British functionary (who shall be nameless) whether we had brought our "uniforms" for the Coronation, he replied, that our cassocks were in England, and we did not *usually* travel in cap and gown.

On the evening of the 18th we started on our expedition northward, on board a steamer bearing the ill-omened name of *Æger*, which, however, we found to be derived, not from sea-sickness, but from an ancient hero. During the first two days we saw few objects worthy of a careful description. We were, all along, threading our way between the coast and the small outlying islands, only here and there coming out into the open sea; in many places the passage between the rocks is extremely narrow, and here the skill and knowledge of the Norwegian pilots is seen, for one would almost fancy at first sight that the vessel would graze her paddle-boxes. At one point we had to go some distance inland to the mouth of the Namsen river, a great fishing station, in the neighbourhood of which the islands are clothed with the spruce and Scotch fir; and then, after passing Torghatten, a lofty conical mountain with a hole piercing it, so that you can see the light through, we came in sight of the Seven Sisters, a long, bare grey rock, from the top of which at different points rise seven sharp peaks, darker in colour than the rest of the mass. All about this part of the coast the rocks are rounded and polished, an effect which Forbes attributes to the action of former glaciers.* After this Domnæs stood out before us, a strange and solitary mountain, opposite which, upon the main land, is one of the largest icefields in Europe. The numerous sea-birds which throng these islands are quite a study: all kinds of gulls and divers may be seen; black ducks; great black geese, heavy in flight, which seldom rise

* Mehwald disputes all Forbes' statements on this point, and accuses him of *Glaciermania*, (*Nach Norwegen*, p. 15.) An interesting sketch of the physical geography of Norway, together with a geological map, will be found in a pamphlet, *Den Skandinaviske Halvö*, by Löffler: Copenhagen, 1860.

more than a few feet above the water; cormorants, grey and white eider ducks, elegant terns, and oyster-catchers with red legs and bills. Once we saw the skua, or robber gull: he is a dark-coloured bird, and lives by making other gulls drop what they have caught and seizing it as it falls. On this occasion it was satisfactory to see that he had found his match, for a number of gulls had got over him, and were bullying him.

Shortly after passing the Arctic Circle we arrived at the town of Bodö,* or rather a collection of houses dignified with that name, to raise it to the position of chief town in the province of Nordland. As the steamer stops here several hours we landed, and proceeded to collect flowers in an extensive peat-bog in the neighbourhood. In this were growing numerous plants of the Moltebeer or Cloudberry (*Rubus Chamæmorus)*, which, though it is found in the northern parts of Scotland and Ireland, may fairly be called the peculiar fruit of Norway. But beware of this deceitful plant, ye field botanists! for when his white petals fall off, he paints his calyx red, so as to resemble a gorgeous flower, and passes himself off as the *Rubus Arcticus*, for which many have mistaken him. Several other collectors besides ourselves were the victims of his trickery, until we found the rogue in the act of putting on his false colours, with half his calyx green; and we exposed him. But in the fruit you will not be deceived; it grows single on the stalk, in shape like a blackberry, but twice as large; its colour, when ripe, is pale yellow, and the taste is delicious, though slightly vapid; but, when eaten with cream

* The termination "ö," which will often recur, signifies *island*. It is the same word as -ey, the termination of Sheppey, and -y of Ely, &c. In the title "Sodor and Man," the first name is a corruption of *Syder öer*, or "Southern islands," as the Hebrides were called, when they and the groups of islands to the north of Scotland were attached to the See of Trondjem. The cognate Saxon word is "ea," as in Angles-ea: the later form of this is "i," which forms the first syllable of our word "island," the letter *s* having been inserted from Latin and French associations. At Wells, where the precincts of the Bishop's palace are surrounded by water, a visitor may be surprised at receiving the following direction: "Go into the Bishop's *Eye*, and turn to the right."

and sugar, it is a dish for a king. Among other plants, we found the Butterfly Orchis and Alpine Ladies' Mantle, *Drosera intermedia, Comarum palustre, Saxifraga aizoides, Saussurea alpina, Erigeron alpinum, Bartsia alpina, Gnaphalium dioicum, Galeopsis versicolor:* and on the rocky hills to the north grows the splendid *Saxifraga cotyledon.*

From these heights there is a fine view over glittering inlets, strange peaks, and the wide sea, and far away to the north-west is obtained the first sight of the distant Lafoden Islands. If the reader will take the trouble to look at the map, he will see that, while the whole coast of Norway is fringed with islands, the Lafodens are gathered into a more conspicuous group, from the south-west corner of which runs off a long line of rocks and islets, resembling the fossil tail of some gigantic reptile. It was this outlying chain that we saw from Bodö, where they may be fifty miles distant; and from this singularly varied and beautiful outline they are very striking objects on the horizon. The smaller lie, one after another, like loose beads on a string; others rise to a considerable height, sharply cut against the sky; while the appearance of the whole line has aptly been compared to a shark's jaw. In order to reach them we have to cross the intervening bay, which is called the Vest Fiord; but we must omit the description of them for the present, for the weather is unfavourable. It is tantalizing, I must confess, to pass such peaks and precipices, though their tops are shrouded in clouds; and the blue crevasses of the glaciers suggest delightful wonders to the imagination; but we may see them better on our return; so let us hasten on our northward course, and see if we can catch the midnight sun.

Meanwhile let me say a few words about the company whom we had on board, for from the variety of people who got in and out from time to time, we had excellent opportunities of observing various classes. First we had a member of the *Storthing* or Norwegian parliament, an inhabitant of the Lafodens, who was chosen to epresent the Northern

Districts of Norway at the coronation at Stockholm; he was a farmer, a man of small property, but a very intelligent person. Then there were three priests and two lawyers, an engineer, and several merchants and farmers; when we first saw these men sitting in a line at the table, we thought we had seldom seen a more striking set of intelligent faces. Great numbers of the lower classes crowd on board at all the stations, an evident proof of the advantage this line of steamers is to the inhabitants of these parts: some go to get work, others to visit relations, others again to see a doctor, for which they have sometimes to go fifty miles. The number of boxes and bales too that are taken out at each place is surprising, when one considers the thinness of the population. The equality of the people is evinced by the friendly and unconstrained recognitions that pass between persons of very different classes: having been so much kept down by the Danes before 1814, they seem, like the modern Greeks, to have only slightly developed the formal distinctions of society. In their general physiognomy they are far more like the English than any other European nation: in the southern half of the country they are perhaps still more like the lowland Scotch; but they have neither the full faces of the former, nor quite as high cheek-bones as the latter. The lower classes are light complexioned, while many of the upper have a darker and thicker hue, somewhat like the English middle classes. But in proportion as you get further north, the Scotch element in the face gradually dies out, and the likeness to the English becomes most striking; a large proportion of the people seemed to me quite undistinguishable from the English, so much so, that when a young Englishwoman, attached to a copper mine on the Kaa fiord, came on board, I had no suspicion that she was otherwise than a native. In complexion, in features, in the colour of the hair and in general expression they are quite similar. They are decidedly a pleasing people; the upper classes are most attentive and obliging; the lower classes do not at first sight appear so, for in them that independence, which is the chief national characteristic, degenerates into roughness; but in reality they are thoroughly kind-hearted and good-natured, and a very even-tempered people.

The two points in Norwegian politics which most forcibly strike an Englishman are their liking for England and their hatred of Sweden. "We love the English and drink tea; the Swedes love the French and drink coffee," as we saw it epigrammatically stated in a newspaper of the country; and even if this comparsion should not hold good in every point (for it is hardly reconcilable with the excellence of Norwegian coffee), yet on the whole it declares the truth. The feeling which they express towards our countrymen is exceedingly friendly; a great number of the upper classes speak English, and a knowledge of that language is required of their naval officers. It is the only foreign country where I have heard a Frenchman making himself understood through the medium of English, and one person of that nation who only knew his own language, and persisted in asking for *des œufs à la coq* at breakfast, would have come badly off without English intervention in his behalf. But the antagonism to Sweden is even more remarkable. Whether it proceeds from the lingering recollections of former hostilities, or from complete diversity of national sentiment and institutions, or from jealousy of suspected interference, it certainly exercises a great influence over their actions. But notwithstanding this, and though their union under the same crown is the only formal connecting link between the two nations, they remain and will remain united from motives of common interest; partly because the union gives both nations more importance in the eyes of Europe, and partly through fear of a too powerful neighbour. For while European politicians are watching the movements of Russia in the Baltic and Black Sea and on the coasts of Kamskatka, that many-handed power keeps a watchful and eager eye on Norwegian Lapland, on the border of which her territory approaches within twenty-five miles of the sea, in hopes of obtaining a port on the shores of the Atlantic, kept open for traffic by the warm gulf stream all the year round, and not exposed, like the Sound, to be blockaded by the navy of an inferior power.

Though the Norwegian constitution is as near an approach to a perfect democracy as a constitutional monarchy can be, yet the spirit of the people, like that of the English, is essentially conservative; a fact which is illustrated by the favourite title of *Gamle Norge*, or old Norway, which they use in the same way as we do, when we speak of Old England. For the northern nations, it would seem, in seeking for a term of endearment for their fatherland, have looked rather to its old associations and institutions; while those of the south, the inhabitants of *la belle France, la bella Italia*, &c., have been enamoured rather of its beauty. But the time may not be far distant, when the constitution of Norway, notwithstanding its theoretic perfection and admirable adaptation to the wants of the people, will have to sustain a trying strain; for neither the people themselves, nor their manner of life, nor their narrow system of political economy, appear likely to adapt themselves easily to a wider sphere of action; and yet the vast undeveloped resources of the country, and its important maritime position, would seem to point to a future of great influence.

One of the priests whom we had on board was an artist, and the incumbent of two churches in the Lafodens, which are fourteen miles apart. The system of pluralities is common throughout Norway: in the Romsdal we found that five churches were served by the same priest, so that each had a service once in five weeks; but this is not considered an abuse, because the clergy are resident in their respective districts, and they are almost universally well-educated and intelligent men. If their stipends were smaller, the character of the country clergy would probably be lowered; as it is, the priest's residence (*prestegaard*) is generally the nicest house in the neighbourhood, and the priest's daughters are the most eligible young ladies. It is surprising under these circumstances that dissent does not spring up throughout the country; but though dissenters are tolerated now, neither they nor the Roman-Catholics seem to make any progress. The probable reason is, that the Church suits the people, and still more, that it is *national* in the same sense, though not the same degree, as the Greek and Armenian Churches; that is, it is bound up with their national history and associations. The Norwegians are a religious people: they come from great distances to church, even as much as twenty miles, and both in and out of Church they seem devout in their feelings and behaviour; but they cannot be considered a highly moral people. This arises partly from the large consumption of corn-brandy, which causes, not so much actual drunkenness, as intemperance; partly from the numerous impediments in the way of marriage; and partly from other causes, such as the temporary migrations of portions of the population to the sea-coast during the fishing seasons, and the solitary life of the women in the mountain farms.

On leaving the Vest Fiord, we made our way northward through the Tjeldesund, the general character of the shores of which is much softer than what we had lately passed; they slope gently down to the water with a good deal of northern vegetation, and here and there cultivated land and villages are seen. But both in this sound and in the Ramsund, which we entered at Sandtorv, we found it difficult to persuade ourselves that we were on the sea; they are so narrow and so calm that, as your eye ranges over their long reaches, you would much rather fancy yourself on a broad river. The average breadth may be about half a mile, which is considerably narrower than that "ocean stream," the Bosphorus. From this part to Tromsö the scenery, though not striking, is very peculiar: there are generally low hills in the foreground, and behind these mountains of no great height, patched with snow, or bearing small glaciers; but every object is so pale in colour, both the sky, and the water, and the mountains, that there is an appearance of faintness, and one might easily fancy that sounds would be deadened, as the ancients supposed them to be amongst the shades, and I almost expected to hear my own voice "thin as voices from the grave;" and at last an indefinable idea crept over me, that I was coming to the end of the world. This was during the day; but by night the appearance of the scenery was stranger still. There was a sort of weird light over all things, neither day nor night; more like early morning than late evening, but yet unlike any other light I have ever seen. The night that we spent in the harbour of Tromsö I shall not easily forget: a small drizzling rain came on, and it is hard to express how ghastly, how grizzly the light appeared. We cannot wonder that the superstitions of the northern nations should have been so wild, or that their fancies should have taken so grotesque a form, when they have lived in the midst of these strange scenes, or the still more striking wonders of the long winter nights.

Tromsö is the capital of Finmark, and the principal place north of Trondjem. It has a classical school, and is an Episcopal see, but the bishopric was then vacant. It has really the appearance of a town; the villages on the sea-coast are merely collections of small houses, which stand apart at some distance from one another in a most unsociable way, without having any notion of forming a street; in the larger ones the most prominent objects are the warehouses, supported on piles, which project into the sea; but Tromsö has regular streets and a busier look about it, and there are numerous merchant vessels in the harbour. On starting for a botanical walk, we saw for the first time, hay hanging to dry on large hurdles strongly resembling a gigantic towel-horse; in this way they make the most of their brief summer, and we afterwards found that this custom is common in most parts of Norway. We found here *Viola palustris, Gnaphalium Norvegicum*, *Maianthemum bifolium*, *Pyrola rotundifolia* and *media*.

Four hours after leaving Tromsö we arrived at Karlsö, a small island on the 70th degree of north latitude, on which is a church, which serves as the Sunday rendezvous of all the surrounding islands. Just beyond this we got a view out into the open sea, and it was a real pleasure to see it once more, and even to feel its swell, after having been so long cooped up in narrow lifeless sounds and straits; with all its passions and caprices it is a living and half-human monster! No wonder misanthropes, like Byron, have rejoiced to find—

> "Society where none intrudes
> By the lone sea, and music in its roar!"

for it is the nearest approach to that human society, from which their morbid sentiments have cut them off. At this point we entered on a series of views, which are quite unrivalled in their way, and would in themselves repay a journey from England. On the side towards the sea a picturesque island with fine bluffs stands out beyond Karlsö; to the east at one point is seen a long line of exquisitely broken peaks, and in the midst of them a deep inlet between the islands, at the end of which in the distance stands up a high snowy summit, quite a northern Alp; and to the south the Ulfs fiord runs far, far in, surrounded by a girdle of mountains which form a view such as almost to rival that from Molde. Peak rises behind peak, and range beyond range, in shapes so manifold, so delicate, so harmonious as almost to recal the incomparable Greek mountains. Amongst these heights lie glaciers of different forms and sizes, one of which, a great distance off, was very like the Rhone glacier, and apparently not much inferior in size. The finest mountains are those which separate the Ulfs from the Lyngen fiord; and when we had rounded the promontory in which they terminate, we were astonished at finding that their appearance from this side, cast the former views quite into the shade. It is a hopeless task to picture the scenery of the Lyngen fiord. I will only describe it as simply as I can, for no epithets can convey any idea of its grandeur. The mountains here descend steeply into the sea; the loftiest summits, though few of them tower above the rest, are sufficiently varied in elevation to prevent monotony; the outlines of the lower ridges also are as fine and as well marked as the others, and, like those in the Pyrenees, are so steep as seldom to allow the snow to remain on their crests; in the gorges which intervene, grand glaciers flow down, eight of which can be seen together in one view: all of them are broken, clear, and blue; but there are four, which I must briefly describe. The first you come to lies like a great crawling creature on the top of a crust of rock, and breaking short off where the rock descends, pours forth from one point a stream, which falls in two cascades to the valley. Another, the most striking, runs in one stream of ice, narrow in proportion to its length, from the mountain ridge to within fifty feet of the sea; most elegant in form, and in several places compressed between the rocks and breaking into more marked crevasses. A third, of no great size, is remarkable for its position, hanging on the very summit of a peak, so that it is hard to see from what snows it can be fed. And last of all, far up on the side of one mountain is a great basin full of ice, like a bowl of cream brimming over, from which at one point a glacier-stream escapes for some distance towards the sea. What strikes one especially about the northern glaciers is that they lie at a very steep inclination, and are free from moraine, two features which add greatly to their beauty. Some have a moraine at their foot, but the ice itself is almost always free. And when one considers that these mountains are not more than 4,000 or 5,000 feet high, one learns that elevation is not the most important element in mountain grandeur.

At Havnœs we left the Lyngen fiord by a side channel, where there is more vegetation, and the hill-sides are covered with birch-trees. The birch and the willow are the only trees which can endure the severe climate of this arctic region. All along this part, for several hours, the views continued to be superb; piles of peaks appeared, with glaciers lying among them. Here was seen a ridge, throwing up strange fingers, like the dolomite peaks of the Tyrol; there a great crust of ice showed itself among the projecting mountains-tops; but when we came to Kaagö, just before emerging into the open sea, on our way to the outlying island of Loppen, a glacier appeared which surpassed all the others, and is really worthy of a place on the side of Mont Blanc. It descends in two parts at first, divided by rocks much resembling the *Grands Mulets*, below which the two streams meet in a narrow place with extraordinary crushing, and the whole is precipitated in one vast mass down a steep cliff, where it stands clear from the rocks which flank its sides. We touched at Oxfiord, an Oxford of the north, which lies in a remarkably pretty position, close to a bright green valley, enclosed by steep rocks, with a waterfall at the back, while on the opposite side of the water, are fine peaks and glaciers; it is a contrast to, though hardly a rival of, its greater namesake. At last, after coasting round the Alten fiord, which is famed for its salmon-fishing—its murderous mosquitoes, which bite through leather gloves and gaiters, and harass the soul of the fisherman—and its unusual vegetation, for here the spruce-fir and other trees re-appear; we arrived on the 7th day of our voyage at Hammerfest, the northernmost town in the world.

This place lies in a small but very safe harbour, in the recesses of a large bay. When seen from the heights above it has a pretty appearance, as opposite the town a long strip of land runs out, forming a breakwater, not unlike that sickle-shaped tongue of land which protects the harbour of Messina. The town, which is on the south side, lies compactly together, almost enclosing the numerous trading vessels which resort thither, and lie close under the warehouses. Most of the houses are roofed with red tiles, though a few are covered with the same kind of garden which I have described as existing in the interior of the country. The streets are fairly regular, but most of the houses are built singly, and only form a street by standing in the same line. The pleasing custom of having flowers in the windows of the houses, which is usual throughout Norway, prevails also here. The Hammerfestians do not boast of an hotel; but there is a house which answers the purpose of one, with a notice over it *for reisende, i.e.* "for travellers." The merchant vessels, some of which are Norwegian, some Russian traders from the White Sea, are of the strangest build, reminding one almost of the English ships of Queen Elizabeth's time; but their occupants, especially the Russians, are stranger still. One wonderful being, with flat, coarse features, who wore an old red cap, and was enveloped in an enormous light red beard, and whom we saw paddling a punt across the harbour, we at once surnamed Charon. But what forces itself upon your attention more irresistibly than anything else, is the smell of fish; in fact, Hammerfest may not unfairly be called a mausoleum of dead fish. Some are seen hanging to dry on frames in various parts of the town; others are being tossed in great quantities, with a dry sound, from vessels on to the wharves, while others are being stowed away in warehouses. But the smell is all-pervading; go where you will, you cannot escape from it. We went miles into the country among the mountains in search of flowers, but it followed us even there.

The day and half which we spent at Hammerfest were principally devoted to botanizing, and our labours were amply rewarded, for the flora of this part is extremely interesting, some of the plants being Alpine, some Arctic, and some common to various other European floras. Amongst others we found *Viola biflora*, the exquisite little yellow violet, and *Gentiana nivalis*, both of which I had before found on high passes in the Alps; *Trollius Europæus, Viola montana, Silene acaulis, Dryas octopetala, Rhodiola rosea, Diapensia Lapponica, Andromeda hypnoides and polifolia, Azalea procumbens, Menziesia cærulea, Melampyrum pratense, Pedicularis palustris* and *Lapponica, Habenaria viridis, Allium Schœnoprasum.** There are no trees in this district, though here and there stumps and rotten branches show that some have existed until lately: and the almost entire absence of birds serves to increase the solitude. When wandering in this stern, unfruitful region, where the hardy birch and willow can no longer grow, and where the pine and fir have been left far behind, it is quite

* An excellent account of the flora of Lapland will be found in Henfrey's *Vegetation of Europe*, p. 89, &c.

strange to turn one's thoughts southward, and think of the smiling pastures of England, or still more of the luxuriant vegetation and "riotous prodigality" of life which is characteristic of Italy, or the bursting of the spring in Greece, when every tint of green may be seen, from the lightest shade of the almond to the darkest and glossiest evergreen, and the mountain sides are brightened with golden and purple blossoms.

I had often in former years been filled with a longing to

> "See the midsummer, midnight Norway sun
> Set into sunrise,"

but I had hardly expected to accomplish my desire, and while I was in the country my hopes had almost vanished, because the weather was cloudy, and the last night of our stay at Hammerfest was to be "positively his last appearance" during the whole night above the horizon. However, as on this last night the sky looked more propitious, and the steamer did not leave till two A.M., we determined to make one final trial. We crossed the harbour, and made for a high hill about three miles off, which lay between us and the sun. As we mounted, our hopes rose, for though the great luminary himself was hidden from us, yet we could see his light on the hills and islands around. When we reached the top about eleven o'clock, he burst upon us round and ruddy, but glowing and free from mist, though a long dark bank of ominous cloud lay below him on the horizon, threatening to engulf him before he could rise again. The view from this point would at any time be a striking one. Bare craggy islands fling their long, wild arms over the sea, dividing it into straits and sounds, or rise to a considerable height in numerous ridges and undulations. But now what would otherwise have been rough and barren was glorified by the most gorgeous roseate sunset light, and softened by the evening shadows lying behind all the hills. To the south was Hammerfest in deep shadow, its harbour perfectly calm, with a few small vessels lying at anchor, and the steamer which was soon to carry us far away: the mountains above were patched with snow, and about half-way up were crossed by the line of shadow thrown by the hill on which we were standing. Beyond this was the sound by which we had arrived, and then the large island of Seyland, crowned with two snow-peaks, and bathed in the richest light. All along to the west reached the long, dark, varied outline of another island, which cast its shadows into the grey-purple sea; and between these two, to the south-west, at the end of a deep sound, far, far away, a fine line of mountains bearing a ridge of ice, which was brightly lighted by the sun. Between all these islands and the peak on which we stood lay a wide sheet of water, and to the north the open sea, with a superb trail of light reflected from the sun: beyond were two small islands, and to the east a high mountain excluding the rest of the view. The clouds were spread in thin banks over the sky, and flushed by the light of the sun, which was now below them. As we looked round on this exquisite sight in the marvellous and awe-inspiring silence of midnight, it was hard to say what could be added to make the scene more perfect; and yet this was not all. Suddenly there arose opposite the sun the brilliant limb of a magnificent rainbow, which reappeared at intervals with increasing splendour for more than an hour: a solar rainbow at midnight! But the sun—you will be anxious to hear wha was his fate all this time. We had carefully watched him as he partially sank behind the clouds, and continued to skim the horizon, but when at last three-fourths of his disk were obscured, he began to rise again, and at one, we saw him round and clear once more on his upward course. It struck us that there was a marked difference between the effects before and after midnight, corresponding to the general difference between sunset and sunrise, the former being richer, the latter harder and more distinct in its lights. Few scenes have ever impressed me more forcibly than this, for here besides those two grand features of nature, which symbolize two of the highest attributes of Him, whose "righteousness standeth like the strong mountains," and whose "judgments are like the great deep," there was the sun pursuing his majestic course, the emblem of eternity, and the whole scene brought before our minds that state of being in which "there shall be no night!"

We charged down the hills again, and reached the steamer as she was nearly ready to start. Before I went to bed, between two and three, the sun was high in the heavens.

One great source of amusement which we had found during our stay at Hammerfest, consisted in watching the Lapps, who form a considerable part of the population, and a family of whom lived just opposite our windows. This singular people is interesting, not only because of their strange appearance and habits, but also because they belong to the same branch of the human race which now occupies the northern half of Asia, and which in early times had spread itself over Europe, before the present occupants of that country and of India had left their common home in the highlands of Central Asia. These original inhabitants were driven by the conquering tribes into the extremities of the continent; and their only representatives besides the Lapps, and their neighbours the Finns, are the Basques in the Pyrenees, the Magyars in Hungary, and the Albanians. The Lapps and Finns, or Quains, as they are often called in the country, are distinct tribes, so that, though their languages are cognate, they cannot understand one another. In appearance they are still more different, for the Finns, having been long settled in the country, have approached nearer to the Norwegian type of face, while the Lapps, either being nomad still, or having only lately given up their roving habits, have retained their original appearance, which would betray their Turanian origin, if that was not sufficiently indicated by their language. The first of this race that I saw, made a great impression upon me. It was shortly before we reached Tromsö, on our northward voyage, and as I was walking one morning towards the bows of the vessel, my nostrils were suddenly assailed by a peculiar goaty smell. Led on rather by curiosity than pleasure, I discovered, to my great delight, on the further part of the deck a nomad Lapp, enveloped in untanned skins, from which the unamiable odour proceeded ; but thinking that, like the Nubian young ladies, who anoint their sweet selves with castor oil, he might be more agreeable if seen from the windward side, I took up a safe position in that quarter, and regarded him from thence. He was a very little man, not more than four feet high; his legs, which were short in proportion to his body, were very wide apart at the hips, and bowed outwards. His face was not less peculiar, the most marked points being the narrow slit of the eyes slanting downward towards the temples; the small pupils, the high cheekbones set very far apart in the head, a yellow beardless skin like parchment, and the falling in of the face towards the chin. Some of these particulars might remind one of the description of the Huns. His upper dress was a loose coat of reindeer-skin, fastened by a girdle, below which were leggings, and loose boots also of reindeer-skin, tied with bands round the ancle. A considerable number of this people, like those we saw at Hammerfest, are now engaged in trade, but they retain the form of the national dress, only adopting a woollen material, which is often braided and slashed with various colours, while the girdle is richly decorated with brass ornaments. The men wear a red cap, the women a variegated head-dress, which I will not attempt to describe. This picturesque costume adds greatly to the appearance of the towns in which they live. They are all Christians, and a highly moral people; we were assured that only one Lapp had been convicted of a crime during the past year. A few of them, we were told, are priests; even the nomad Lapps can read: it is a remarkable, if not singular, instance of a nomad Christian nation. They are by no means an unintelligent-looking people. When we went into the church at Hammerfest, we found that the provost of the district—an officer who answers to our archdeacon—was holding an examination previous to Confirmation; and of the candidates, who were about one hundred in number, at least one-third must have been Lapps. It was a pretty and interesting sight to see them in their gay costume, ranged on either side of the nave. There was one old Lapp amongst them who had a wild face, and long, dishevelled, black hair, which he scratched *ad libitum*, hanging over his shoulders; he looked a model pirate of ancient days, and would have made an admirable companion portrait to Charon.

We had an opportunity of visiting an encampment of nomad Lapps on our return, in a valley called Tromsdal, on the mainland, opposite Tromsö. A gentleman from that town, who had friends on board, kindly acted as our guide, and provided a little picnic for us in the valley, including some *Engelsk Porter*, an expensive luxury in those parts, as an especial compliment to us. Here we first saw the reindeer, which are the property, the companions, and the means of subsistence of the Lapps. Near the head of the valley the whole herd were collected, about 500 in number, having just been brought in to be milked, from the mountains, where they find the reindeer moss. They were confined in two circular enclosures, surrounded by a stockade; and the appearance of the moving mass and twinkling horns was at first quite bewildering. They are of a dun colour, and smaller than I expected, few being more than three feet high; the antlers of many were large, though the summer is an unfavourable time for them. They make a grunting noise like a pig; their milk is very rich, but they do not yield more than a goat. The Lapps were very expert in catching them round the neck with a lasso, and drawing them in, when they wanted to milk them. The huts of the Lapps are of the rudest kind, being formed of branches and logs set upright, and covered with turf, so that from outside they look like gigantic bee-hives; inside they are begrimed with smoke, and the chimney is formed by a hole in the top, over which is a trap-door, which can be shut when necessary. Under a shed near the huts were their implements, which were mostly composed of crates, churns, and similar things, among which there were hanging a few small, flat cheeses. It is curious to see that, when they could easily buy these things in Tromsö, they follow the traditions of their fathers, like the Arabs, and other nomad nations, and make them themselves of birchwood and reindeer-skin. We were introduced to the Paterfamilias, the ancestor of the community, a very old man, singularly like a goat; but one old lady, who was busy in milking, had a bright face, and with her hair drawn off her forehead, and twisted into a knot at the back, might have reminded a person, whose imagination could have taken such a leap from barbarism to civilization, of Marie Antoinette. Another woman carried her child in a wooden case, which served the purpose both of a cradle and of baby-linen, and was slung in front when she wanted to suckle the child, and behind on ordinary occasions. We made a subscription for them, and gave them some tobacco, and before we left them were gratified by the pretty sight of the herd of reindeer winding its way in a long line back to the mountains.

The evening after we left Hammerfest, when we emerged at Havnæs on the middle of the Lyrgen Fiord, a wondrous sight awaited us. It was midnight, and over the mouth of the fiord was the most gorgeous sunset I have ever seen: the northern sky was streaked with translucent bars of the clearest purple, green, and gold, while here and there lay thin lines of delicate cloud, edged with a fretwork of the most brilliant light; and all this was reflected in the sea. The sun had disappeared behind the island I have before described, which stood out dark and grand in contrast; but he had not set to the mountains, and thus we saw his light resting in rosiest hues on the upper glaciers of that sublimest of Arctic inlets. Rose-hues on glaciers at midnight!

"Match me such marvel, save in *Arctic* clime!"

There is an unspeakable charm in an Eastern sunset, when the sun descends clear and undimmed to the horizon, and after his disappearance a flush of pink, transparent light streams upward to the zenith: the sunsets of our own misty atmosphere are superb, when the clouds are painted every conceivable colour by the broken light; but none can vie with these brilliant tints and delicately-pencilled lines of the sunsets of the North.

As we had missed the Lafoden Islands in going northward, we were fortunate in seeing them on our return. The shores of Norway are for the most part composed of metamorphic rock, but these islands are of granite, and for marvellous peaks and picturesque rocks they are unequalled. Every form is represented there. Some rise like huge castles with broken battlements, some throw up lofty pinnacles, others take the shape of cones or triangles, or dart up into *aiguilles* like those of Mont Blanc. Some of the islands are of considerable extent, while others are single peaks rising out of the water; among them lie innumerable rocks of various sizes. Between two of the larger islands is a narrow strait, leading to the outlying Steilö, which is called the Raftesund. Here the cliffs on either side rise steeply to an immense height, though in places they leave room at their base for a slope of bright green vegetation; while above, fine, broken glaciers cling to the ravines. We followed the line of the islands as far south as Balstad, and, towards night, crossed the Vest Fiord, in the middle of which you find yourself encircled by a girdle of mountains, which is only slightly broken towards the north and south. The general outline is splendid, but, at the distance of fifteen miles, the want of great height diminishes their grandeur. If any one asks why I have not described the Mälstrom, I must answer, with sorrow, that though there is a dangerous current between two of the islands which bears that name, yet the real Mälstrom, the Mälstrom of our imagination—is no more!

The evening after we recrossed the Arctic Circle, I was quite startled by seeing in the Eastern sky, brightening the skirts of a dark cloud, the golden face of our long-lost friend, the moon. Two nights later, as we were approaching Trondjem, the stars were shining brilliantly, and she was casting a long trail of light over the waters. It seemed quite strange to have suddenly plunged, as it were, into darker regions.

We found the old place looking very gay; there were

picturesque crowds of people, and an abundance of Norwegian flags (crimson, with a white cross) to light it up, and several fine frigates were lying in the harbour. Nor were we displeased by the intelligence that we were to have tickets for the coronation, which was to take place on the Sunday following (August 5th). On Friday afternoon the King arrived by water from the camp, which was some distance up the fiord, where he had been reviewing the national troops. At his approach the vessels saluted, and, when he passed, the sailors manned the bulwarks and cheered, (they are not accustomed to man the yards); the steamer anchored near the pier, and, having landed in a boat, he passed on foot through the assembled crowd to a carriage which was waiting to convey him to the palace. The "hurrahs" sounded poor to an English ear, though a large number of people were collected there; they did not seem to have much enthusiasm in their natures. Both the King and his brothers, Prince Oscar and Prince Auguste, are fine-looking men; very tall, with long faces and Jewish features, and dark beards and complexions. Prince Oscar is the popular man in Norway; the King is too imperious and overbearing for this independent people. Later in the day the Queen arrived from Christiania.

On the evening before the ceremony we received our tickets, accompanied by a plan of the building and of the arrangements of the seats. From this it was evident that as the entire body of the cathedral was to be occupied by those who should take part in the procession, and only a few seats to the sides were appropriated to spectators, it would be no easy matter to get a good view. Accordingly, that the trouble we had taken might not be in vain, having discovered the side door by which we were to be admitted, we arrived there at an early hour, and by judicious management got in first, and secured the first seats. These were slightly elevated above the dignitaries, opposite the king's throne and close to the pulpit, and commanded views both up and down the building. But before proceeding further, I will briefly describe the church.

It is a grey and weather-beaten old place, and bears witness to the misfortunes as well as the former grandeur of its country. Though the stone of which it is built is hard, and much of the ornamental work retains the sharpness of its outlines, yet much is in ruins, much has been patched, and the foundations seem in many places to have given way. But all this is so much in keeping with its history, that one could hardly wish it to be otherwise. Of the nave only the walls remain; the oldest parts are the transepts, the central tower, and a small chapel on the north side, originally separate from the rest of the building, which now serves as a chapter-house. All these are in the Norman style, and in an architectural point of view, the great interest of this building consists in its proving the wide-spread influence of that style. The choir and the narrow aisles at the sides are of a later date, corresponding to the style of our earlier Edwards; but the greatest peculiarity of all is an octagonal chapel at the east end, with a corridor or aisle running round it. It is separated from the choir by light pillars and open tracery, which perfect the octagon without much impeding the view; in the centre of it stands the altar, and behind this a cast of the grand statue of Christ, by Thorwaldsen at Copenhagen. The ornamental work of this chapel inside is rich, but extremely peculiar; the ball-flower and other common ornaments are mixed with some, which one would expect to see in Lombardic or even Egyptian architecture rather than Gothic, and the stonework is twisted into all sorts of forms, in a way which would scandalize an advocate of pure principles of architecture. From outside, however, it looks still more strange, for it rises at last to a bulb-like cupola covered with copper, such as we are more accustomed to see represented in Russian and Indian buildings.*

* The *cultus* of the two Saints of Trondjem Cathedral has passed into England through the Scandinavian nations. One of them is St. Olaf or Olave, a monarch who propagated Christianity by the sword. A well under the octagon chapel, the water of which, according to the Sagas, issued forth when

The high pews and enormous galleries, with which the building was filled before the arrangements for the coronation, had now been swept away; a large organ and a singing gallery had been erected at the west end between the transepts, and the seats were placed as in a cathedral choir. All the decorations were in admirable taste; the side walls towards the east end of the choir were richly ornamented with arcades and hangings of crimson and gold, and beneath, two thrones were sat, opposite one another, for the king and queen. On the king's right hand were seats for the princes, near them were others for the court and the chief ministers; the rest of the building was allotted to the representatives of the Storthing, to the army and navy, foreign ambassadors, municipal authorities, &c. At ten o'clock the clergy, about fifty in number, dressed in surplices, and wearing ruffs, like those which Queen Elizabeth used to wear, began to assemble about and behind the altar; and amongst them were seen the Bishops of Christiania, Christiansand and Bergen, simply dressed in their cassocks. Our eyes had wandered to another part of the building, when suddenly they were recalled by a young Englishman behind us exclaiming, "Oh! I say, just look at the Bishops now." They had just reappeared from the sacristy, robed in the most gorgeous apparel, copes of amber-coloured brocade, covering the whole person, and bearing a red cross in front. After this the candles were lighted on the altar, and they advanced to meet the king and queen, who were now approaching: and then the whole procession moved slowly into church. It was a superb spectacle, though one rather missed the bright British uniform: the royal pair

St. Olave's body was removed from the spot, is still in some measure regarded as possessing healing powers; a fact, which corroborates Mr. Clark's remark, as true as it is beautiful, that "A tradition to be lasting, must be writ on water." (*Peloponnesus*, p. 286.) The other is St. Clement of Rome, the patron saint of the church of St. Clement Danes, which was the great burial-place of the Danes in England. He seems to have been adopted as the patron Saint of the Sea-Kings, in consequence of the legend, that he was thrown into the sea with an anchor round his neck, and that his body was miraculously preserved in a submarine tomb, to which pilgrimages were made. The emblem of the parish of St. Clement Danes is an anchor.

wore robes of crimson velvet, ermine and gold, with immense trains; but the greatest sight of all were the heralds, gigantic men, who were gorgeously dressed, and covered with lace and feathers, which seemed to stream from every part of them, so that they resembled beef-eaters raised to the highest power. The man who interested me most was Professor Munch, the most learned man in Norway, who unites in his own person the titles of geographer, historian, and poet, as he has compiled the government map of the country, is writing its history, and composed the verses (and excellent poetry they were) to which the music was set on this occasion. In his appearance the poetical element predominates, for he has a dreamy face and long hair.

While the dignitaries were taking their seats, the choir had been performing some fine music, in parts of which mention was made of Olaf, Hako, and other great men of the olden time; the service began with a hymn, sung to Luther's Hymn tune, and then the Bishop of Bergen ascended the pulpit. He is a fine-looking old man, venerable and benign, but with a great deal of humour in his countenance. The subject of his sermon was the blessing of God, with special application to the occasion. It was a written discourse, simple, and delivered with energy, but so slowly and distinctly that we could follow it all through. Its brevity also was remarkable; but the King's patience, we were told, had been so tried by an unusually long sermon at his former coronation at Stockholm that he had given peremptory orders that it should not exceed twenty minutes. This was followed by a short Litany, and then, after the performance of some more music, came the ceremony of coronation. The king moved up to a seat, which had been prepared for him in front of the altar, so that he sat with his back to the people, facing the clergy. His robe having been taken off, the Bishop of Christiania invested him with the royal robe; next he placed the magnificent crown of Norway on his head, and then presented him with the ball, the sceptre, and other insignia, accompanying each part of the ceremony with prayer. One of the heralds then proclaimed "Karl XV. King of Norway, him and none other," a salute thundered from the harbour, and the King of Norway, looking every inch a king, returned to his throne. The same ceremony was repeated in the person of the queen; and then, after another hymn and the performance of some more music, the procession was formed once more, and they left the cathedral as they entered. From time to time I recalled the former history of Norway, and pictured to my mind's eye the old building as it must have appeared on similar occasions in the grand old days of the Norwegian Kings. And if the remark is true, that Norway, from the simple, straightforward character of its people, and their manner of life, is the most *Idyllic* of the countries of Europe, there was nothing in this scene to dispel the idea. Even the king himself, though a great contrast to "the blameless King Arthur," with his haughty look and proud carriage, was no bad representative of the stern, hard-handed monarchs of mediæval times. We slipped out before the procession arrived at the palace, and having climbed to an elevated position, saw it move along, the king and queen walking under canopies; it was a pretty sight, as we looked over the gay crowd down the long street to the quiet fiord, where a ship of war was seen dressed in all her flags.

Early the next morning we were off again, rejoicing at being once more seated on our carrioles; the bright green meadows too, along which we passed, were a continual source of delight after the pale colours of the far north. Our object being to make our way to the coast near Molde, as the first step on our route to Bergen, we chose the inland road by the valley of the Gula, the Dovre Fjeld, and the Romsdal. As several of the stations in this district are *slow*, we were obliged to send *forbud;* but as these terms may perhaps be unintelligible, I will endeavour to explain the posting system of Norway, which is probably the most elaborate in all Europe. At some stations, which are called *fast*, horses are regularly provided by a contractor appointed by the government; but where no such person can be found, the station is called *slow*, and the horses are supplied by the neighbouring farmers. If you give no warning, you always have to wait a considerable time before they arrive; but if you send *forbud* or "notice," stating the time of your coming, they are bound to be there. It is really a lordly way of doing things. You drive to a station, and there is your relay of horses with their owners waiting your pleasure; you come to a lake, and a boat with the required number of men is in readiness to take you over: and this the population are required to do by law at a certain rate of payment, for the traveller's benefit.

There are plenty of objects besides the scenery to attract our attention in this part of our route. The pole and bucket, which are used for drawing water out of the wells, are almost identically the same as the *shadóof*, which was and is still in use in Egypt. Here and there are huts closely resembling the original Greek temple, the temple *in antis*, the form of which was probably derived from huts of this character: those of the Turks in Asia Minor are the same at the present day.* Then about the farm-buildings we see numbers of magpies, which are the sacred bird of this country, as storks are in Holland and Turkey, together with the large grey-and-black crow, which always reminded me of a clergyman in weekday-clothes: they are the commonest birds of the interior. But here we are at Soknæs; and our old friend A——, who rents the fishing here, brings us to his comfortable room, where we are regaled with fresh butter, port wine, and—hear me patiently, Odin and Thor—the last number of the *Saturday Review*. The port, which had been bought of a *Landhandler*, or country merchant, would not have disgraced the table of "a fine old English gentleman;" but the greatest treat was the fresh butter, for the Norwegians (to their shame be it said), though they have the finest dairies in Europe, and abundance of unrivalled milk and cream, make nothing but salt butter, unless an Englishman steps in as the pioneer of

* See Fellowes' Lycia, abridged edition, p. 313, and compare Wordsworth's Greece, pp. 5, and 153–4.

civilization. We pocketed our literary *pièce de resistance,* and, as the *forbud* admits of no delay, were soon cracking our whips again *en route* for the Dovre Fjeld.

Before reaching that famous tract of country, we were destined to meet with an accident. I had just passed a Norwegian, who was quietly jogging along in his carriole, and my companion was following, when suddenly the Norwegian's horse swerved, the carrioles met with a crash, and their occupants were ejected, one into the ditch, the other into the road. I saw no more, for my horse became restive, and his state of mind was not improved, when R——'s horse came careering by, whirling along the overturned chariot. The boy, who rode behind me, at last secured the fugitive; and I was thankful to find, on reaching my friend, that we had no further injury to complain of than two broken shafts. These we patched up with pieces of wood and cord, which held them together until we reached the next station.

The Dovre Fjeld is a moor, just like Dartmoor, only on a larger scale, with large rolling hills, unbroken by projecting rocks, but here and there backed by higher mountains, the principal of which is Sneehatten. A few trees grow in the more sheltered parts, but, as you ascend higher, these also disappear; first you lose the alder and pine, next the birch, and last of all the willow. But its most distinguishing feature is the reindeer moss, which lies in great patches of a pale canary colour over the mountain sides, and is more peculiar than beautiful. At Dombaas we rejoined our former route, and, after driving once more down the magnificent Romsdal, took a boat to Vestnæs, on the southern shore of the fiord. The roses were now past, but the valley was adorned with bright bushes of the rosebay willowherb. The change that had taken place in the vegetation was very striking; and on our return to Trondjem, we had remarked the rapid advance of the harvest during our short visit to the north. In one part of the Romsdal a dog, which we had been asked to take to his home some distance down the valley, killed for us several lemmings, an animal which we desired to possess. It is of the mouse tribe, about five inches long, of a brown colour, with beautiful black spots on the head and neck; but its interest arises from its migrating in swarms from the Russian borders at intervals of about ten years, when the district which they traverse is covered by their hosts, and every trace of vegetation destroyed. When, at last, they reach the sea, some swim across to the outlying islands, but the greater part of them perish. They are regarded by naturalists as a sort of *ver sacrum*, a colony from an overstocked nation, which are forced to emigrate in search of food.

The part of Norway between Molde and Bergen is more deeply intersected by fiords than any other district, and though it is not much travelled, contains a greater succession of fine views than can be found elsewhere. From Vestnæs we crossed a tract of moorland, near which we found the *Arnica montana*, a flower of central Europe, resembling a large marigold, and which in Norway is called the "Erl King," and before long descended to Söholdt on a branch of of the Star Fiord. This place appeared to us the most delightful we had seen. It lies near a fine piece of water, and the mountains around are of some height; but the village itself stands in the midst of charming trees and meadows, which remind you of Scotland rather than Norway, and have an appearance of thoroughly home scenery: add to which, the inn can boast of English neatness and comfort, and there were ripe currants hanging in the garden. The following day was spent on the Stor Fiord, which runs in to this place from Aalesund, the principal town of these parts after Molde; but just before reaching Söholdt the fiord turns sharp round at right angles to its previous course, and as our route lay towards its head, we had to bid farewell to the numerous headlands which are seen on both sides as it runs out towards the sea, and follow this branch. It may be on an average a mile in width, but from the high rocks at its sides, it looks a very narrow piece of water. The nearer mountains, which are somewhat rounded in outline, descend in steep precipices to the fiord, or where they retire a little from the water are broken into picturesque ledges, about which grows the most luxuriant vegetation, Scotch fir, birch, hazel, mountain ash, and other trees. The Scotch fir, as it grows in this country, is an exquisite tree; and when it stands, as it often does, on the rocky promontories, close under which you pass, it might almost rival the Italian pine. The birch tree, though elegant, is formal in its shape, and a number of them never can mass themselves, or give breadth to a landscape; but their bright foliage admirably relieves the pines when interspersed among them, just as the beeches relieve the sombre firs in the Pyrenees. The little bights and bays that you pass as you coast along, are exceedingly pretty; and here and there a bright bit of meadow-land, with its attendant cottage, is seen on the hill-side, or projecting into the water. The rocks at the water's edge are in many places thickly lined with a crust of mussel shells, which, when washed by the tide, look almost like steel. But perhaps the most striking sight of all is the numerous waterfalls, which tumble from the heights in a succession of cascades, and not unfrequently fall sheer into the sea. When we had rowed about half way, a fine arm branched off on our left, and from hence to the head of the fiord the mountains became still higher and wilder, and many of the rocks were tinged with an iron hue.

In the evening we reached Hellesylt, which lies at the head of the fiord. We had not gone more than ten miles in the day, but the wind was unfavourable, and Norwegian boatmen are somewhat lazy. They are a good-humoured and amusing set, and chatter all the time they row. They are perfectly honest, too, except in the matter of brandy; but we could not too much admire their friendliness and unselfishness, for while some of them "shuffled" and "shirked their stroke" woefully, the rest seemed perfectly contented with doing the work of all. On these occasions R—— used frequently to take an oar, and I used to steer; and neither was light work, for the oars are of gigantic size, with a place for the fingers when they cannot be grasped; while the rudder is so managed that the whole weight falls on the steerer's arms, so that a day's steering is enough to weary the wrist of a Hardicanute.

Close to Hellesylt is a very striking fall, which comes down in broken cascades like Lodore on a large scale, over great masses of rock into the sea; the village at the side, and a wooden bridge above it, surmounted by rocks and trees, form a picturesque accompaniment. We passed over this the next morning, and after ascending steeply through a fine gorge, found ourselves in a green upland valley, through which we drove for several stages, and then descended to Grodaas, which lies on one arm of a lovely lake called Horningdals Vand. By a steep road we ascended along the rocks which flank one side of it, and crossing a promontory, descended again to the other arm. The views over the lower part of the lake, as seen from these parts, with projecting headlands and small islands quite covered with trees, are exquisite, and reminded us of some of the best parts of Loch Lomond. We followed the narrow arm to its head, then for a long time wound about through upland forest ground, interspersed with small dark lakes, and at last descended by an excessively steep and bad road to the waters of the Nord Fiord. The evening was now fast closing in, so we had to drive down as hard as we could tear; but it was with many regrets, for the water was of the softest tint of green, and had that solid look which Swiss lakes assume when seen from a height; and through the trees, among which our road ran, appeared a vessel with one large white sail reflected in the motionless water. A boat was here awaiting us, and late at night we arrived at Taaning, a very comfortable station, where, however, we should have been but poorly treated, had it not been for the kindness of an English gentleman, who rented the fishing: by his intervention we obtained everything we could desire.

From Taaning, we crossed the fiord to another of the bays which run in among the lofty mountains that surround its head, and landed at Oldören, from which place we intended to make an expedition to the Justedal glaciers, the largest ice-fields in Europe. Our object was to ascend to the plateau fo the ice, for these glaciers are level on the top; but though we were disappointed in this, as we found it could not be scaled from this point, yet the result proved that our time was not wasted. We started at once, accompanied by the landlord of the inn and the postmaster, and ascended the valley until we came to the Olden Vand, a narrow piece of water winding among huge mountains. When we had rowed some miles, there suddenly opened upon us a long valley, about half-a-mile in width, flanked by mountain walls, which, at its eastern end, runs up into what, in the Pyrenees, would be called a *cirque,* a semi-circular *cul-de-sac,* in the middle of which lies, or rather hangs, the magnificent Brixdal glacier, one of those which descend from the Justedal. On landing, we bent our steps towards this, over rough ground and piles of *débris,* and arrived at its foot after about two hours' walking. It descends in two great falls, one below the other, and all the lower part is jammed in between two huge peaks, which stand up like pillars of Hercules. No foot of a glacier that I have seen— not even that of Rosenlaui, is equal to this: the ice is clear and bright blue in colour, and its masses are most beautifully broken: as we saw it, a large piece had been pushed forward and was joined to the rest by an arch. You pass two other glaciers of great size on your left as you ascend from the lake. One of these is a huge basin of ice, which has the appearance of being enclosed in forests; as we saw it in coming down, its upper ridge was all gilded by the setting sun. The whole valley is full of waterfalls, which plunge down the mountain sides: one comes careering down within 200 yards of the Brixdal glacier, while another, a little lower down, on your right hand as you ascend, falls with a large body of water over the edge of a steep precipice, divided in two by a rock at the top; and in this manner it descends to a great depth in a double fall, the two streams of which are yet near enough to mingle their spray. It is surpassingly beautiful! Again, as we looked towards the west, we could see the calm lake lying in shadow in its cradle of enormous cliffs, and over all was spread the rosy flush of a magnificent sunset. So much for the pleasant part of our expedition; now for the disagreeables. As it was too late to return to Oldören that night, we had arranged to remain at one of the farms in the valley. Being of a suspicious nature, I had intended to sleep on a box or bench, but in an unwary moment we were persuaded by our conductor, who vividly depicted the cleanliness of the natives, to lie down on a bed. Alas! it was not to sleep, but to be crawled over, so terrible was the abundance of insect life! Between three and four in the morning I got up and washed my fevered face and hands in the icy stream hard by, and used my toothbrush too, though that proceeding would seem to be open to misrepresentation, if a story that we heard is true, that an Englishman under similar circumstances was reported to the family with whom he lodged, as having been seen by the river side, *sharpening his teeth for breakfast.*

We escaped as soon as possible, and returned to Oldören, from whence in the afternoon we were rowed down the Nord Fiord to Utvik, another delightful station. The shores of this fiord are more inhabited, and its scenery is softer than the others which we had seen; the sloping hill-sides which enclose one bay, from their smiling farms, well-cultivated fields, and numerous trees, reminded us of the valley of Schwytz, as seen from the lake of Lucerne. During the whole of the next day, we were passing through very fine country. After mounting the long hill behind Utvik, which commands grand views over the reaches of the Nord Fiord, we descended again amongst wild, rude mountains, in the midst of which you look down on a valley full of bright vegetation, ornamented with several small green lakes, and a long winding green river. Following the course of this stream, we arrived at a lake called the Breum Vand, about which the scenery reaches its greatest sublimity: along its nearer arm there is vegetation similar to that which had charmed us on the Stor Fiord; while about the further part rise magnificent masses of rock, which stand out with more character than is usually found in the mountains which surround these fiords. It is not a large piece of water; and when we had crossed it, we passed through another fine valley to the Jölster Vand, along the shores of which we drove for some fifteen miles. The road here was new and good, with the exception of excessively steep and stony bits in places ; indeed, though this is often described as a rough excursion, yet both the roads and inns of this part of Norway are decidedly above the average.

We had at one time intended to walk through this district, and were only prevented by the crowded state of the steamers at the time of the coronation, which rendered it impossible to send the carrioles by water to Bergen. They are a great source of trouble, wherever, as in this part, there are numerous water-stages, for the wheels have to be taken off each time, in order that they may be stowed away in the boats. But we never regretted having brought them, for the objections to a pedestrian tour, which I have already stated, apply here with especial force ; and, besides, we had become thoroughly enamoured of carriole travelling. It gives you full enjoyment of the air and sun, and at the same time sufficient occupation for your thoughts, together with an occasional appearance of danger in going fast down steep places, which combines a gentle excitement with perfect safety. The Norwegian ponies are very sure-footed, especially in rough and loose ground ; they go admirably at a moderate pace, and with a light carriole behind them, do not require to walk up any but very steep hills. Their appearance is very peculiar ; they have a round body, and their limbs are so round, that at first sight you would suppose them to be very fat, which is seldom the case. They are mostly creams, with a dark line running down the back ; their manes are hogged, and in many respects they are so like what the ancient Greek horses must have been, that the traveller might easily fancy he had a piece of the Elgin marbles before him.

From the Jölster Vand we descended through rich and beautiful country to Moe, where we stopped to see the Moe Fos, the largest waterfall in these parts. It looks about 400 feet high, and the river which forms it is of considerable size. There are two falls, the upper of which plunges almost unbroken into a dark basin, while the lower, emerging from this, throws itself in steep cataracts to the bottom. At last we arrived at Förde, near the head of the fiord of the same name, where there is an excellent hotel. It lies in the midst of a delicious valley of unusual width, flat and rich, with a river running through it, and abundant cultivation, such as only those can appreciate who have long been wandering in a rocky land. As we ascended again the next morning among pines, green turf, and heather, it was charming to look through the trees over this bright region, encircled by its girdle of mountains. When we had reached the top of the ascent, we drove for several hours by the side of bright gleaming lakes, and through upland valleys, partly meadow, partly forest land, until we descended through a narrow gorge to Vadheim, a station on a beautiful creek of the Sogne Fiord. From hence the steamer carried us to Bergen.

Both from its situation, and from its curious streets and buildings, Bergen has a right to be called the most picturesque town in Norway, and might almost take its rank with Nuremberg, Verona, and Granada. To understand its position, the reader must picture to himself a narrow bay, flanked by mountains, from one side of which runs out a piece of land in the form of the letter T, connected by a bridge with the opposite shore. On this piece of land and the mountain-slopes from which it runs out, the greater part of the town lies, and the water between these forms the main harbour; but numbers of suburbs and country houses fringe the water's edge in different directions. From the heights on the landward side of the place, where the eye is attracted by the numerous trees which are interspersed among the red-tiled roofs of the houses, and where the shipping are seen moored close under the buildings, the bird's-eye view is very striking, and the contrast is especially remarkable between the bright busy town, with its green gardens and fields, and the setting of barren heights and rocky islands which encases it, together with the grey unfriendly sea. Many of the streets are very irregular, and the wooden houses are quite charming from their quaintness, the most marked feature being a kind of large dormer window, which rises from the middle of the roof in front. The costumes of the peasants, too, which are singularly picturesque in this part of Norway, are nowhere better seen than in the market-place of Bergen ; one of the prettiest is that worn by unmarried women, consisting of a red boddice, and a double red snood round the head. In history Bergen is known as one of the great trading-stations of the Hanse towns, whose monopolies for a long time materially injured the commerce of Norway.

After a stay of two days we left the town by the southern road, casting frequent glances of admiration backwards, and not neglecting to notice the tasteful villas along the roadside. At Garnæs we came to a piece of water, which runs in from the sea near Bergen, and penetrates a long way inland with many windings : in this part it is called the Dale Fiord. The electric telegraph, which runs from Christiania to all the principal towns in Norway, is carried along one side of it ; and in some places where the cliffs overhang, it has to be supported on iron bars projecting from the rock. It is strange to see it in these unfrequented places, and it often recalled to my mind, by a curious association of ideas, the great arches of the aqueducts which stretch across the Campagna of Rome, like Civilization stalking over a waste of desolation. The station Dale lies near the head of a small branch which runs up transversely from the fiord ; and this bay is very striking, from its narrowness, the steepness of the cliffs, and the elegant trees. We drove across for a few miles, and descended again to the same piece of water, which doubles round, after making a circuit, and here is called the Bolstad Fiord ; such is the winding nature of these pieces of water. The precipices here are magnificent—as near an approach to perpendicular rocks as you will almost ever see; they are beautifully marked with purple stripes, and in places the lines of the strata are curiously traced by trees, which fix themselves in the ledges of the rocks. We found the harvest general in this part, and the corn fields added greatly to the look of the country; the sheaves were fastened to high poles instead of being piled on the ground. There were one or two charming little bits of cultivation about these bays of the fiord, which would have made perfect *vignettes.* One was a *sæter* or mountain farm, perched high up amongst the cliffs, with an emerald meadow, and the cottage roof so green from the bright grass growing on it, that you might have supposed it to be freshly painted. Another was a farm on a slope between the mountains and the sea, where the ground was divided up into patches of grass, golden corn land, and dark green potatoes; beside the farm-house a fine waterfall was dashing into the fiord.

These small allotments of land, devoted to different kinds of produce, denote the great subdivision of property among small landholders, which is the peculiarity of the tenure of land in Norway. It seems to conduce to the comfort and prosperity of the people, (though the Norwegians themselves will tell you that Mr. Laing's account of the life of the peasants is too highly coloured;) and it suits their simple and unambitious habits; but it prevents the development of the resources of the country, for they have no capital, by means of which to reclaim their immense tracts of uncultivated land. At Bolstadören, which lies at the head of the fiord, we landed, and again drove a few miles to the Evanger Vand, a freshwater lake of great beauty, cradled in the midst of superb mountains. We had been delayed by these water-stages, and at half-past eight, when we arrived at Evanger, the night was fast coming on—so little remained to us of our long protracted daylight! However, the inevitable *forbud* called us on to Vossevangen, two hours further; and having driven a long distance in the dark with a lame horse and an uncivil man, who possessed the voice of a raven, and a notion of using it, I at last arrived at my destination. On awaking in the morning I found Vossevangen a very pretty place; the fertile mountain-sides slope gradually down to a small lake, and are covered partly with forests, partly with smiling farms; while the village itself, at a little distance from our inn, formed a nice object with its cluster of white houses and a church with a dark wooden spire.

This is the point of departure for the Vöring Fos, the greatest waterfall in Europe. We started and drove for three hours through pretty forest scenery, and passing a fine waterfall, descended to the little lake of Graven. It is one of the great charms of the whole of this west part of Norway, that *all* the scenery is so good; not only are there occasional views of great magnificence, but all the ordinary scenery is pleasing and far from commonplace, whereas in most mountainous districts you meet from time to time with tracts of uninteresting country. At this point we had to leave the carrioles, as the road came to an end. After skirting the head of the lake under the rocks, we ascended the other side by a very steep path, from which the views over the dark still water increased in beauty in proportion as we ascended, and when we reached the ridge among the pine trees, we caught an exquisite peep of the Graven Fiord, a narrow piece of water, with headlands projecting into it, and beyond it a reach of the great Hardanger Fiord, of which it is a branch, while a falling shower glittered over all. The piece of ground which we were now traversing, has features characteristic of the mountain masses, which intervene between fiords, being steep on both sides and more or less level on the top; and so, when we had proceeded some distance along it, we descended again by a slanting path down the mountain side. Charming it was—a perfect shrubbery on either side of us—and when we could look below we caught sight of an exquisite circular lake (it proved to be the head of the Ulvik Fiord), embedded in sloping hills, with a pretty island on one side, in shape and position like the Isola San Giulio on the lake of Orta, and in front a little promontory, on which stood the white church of Ulvik, and one red-tiled house by its side. It is pleasant to find that there *are* circumstances under which whitewash conduces to the picturesque. At Ulvik, we got a boat to take us to Vik, at the head of the Eid Fiord, which is the highest point of the Hardanger; but in accordance with our almost universal ill-luck on the water, we had a head wind and heavy sea, and did not arrive until late at night.

Early the next morning we started on foot for the Vöring Fos. The scenery on the way thither is rude, grey, and gloomy. We soon came to a small lake, over which we were ferried by our guide, and then ascended a valley, in the midst of which was the white rushing river which forms the falls, until we came to a place where the path is carried in steep zigzags up the side of a mountain. After mounting this we crossed a piece of moorland, and made for a point, from which a great roar proceeded, and over which a wreath of spray was hanging. When we again saw the river, it was hurrying along, as if from a presentiment of its destiny, and shortly after this the Fos appeared before us. It is indeed worthy of its fame, and its beauty surprised me, for I expected it to be strange and grand, but hardly beautiful. It is a clear fall of 900 feet, and the body of water is very large; it descends into a narrow bare chasm, the sides of which are as nearly as possible perpendicular—a dizzy thing it was to look down from the edge of the precipice to the boiling surge beneath—and the spray dashes up from below with such force, that another waterfall, which descends on the opposite side of the chasm, is actually stopped by it and dispersed, before it can reach the bottom. Its chief beauty consists in its pure whiteness, and the fleecy, yet distinct and well-marked masses in which it descends, while a sufficient number of trees and shrubs grow on the heights around to prevent the scene from appearing savage. We returned to Vik, and then rowed down the Hardanger Fiord to Utne, a village at the extremity of the glacier-bearing promontory of the Folgefond, whence we made our way by the Graven Fiord back of Vossevangen.

Shortly after commencing our homeward journey to Christiania, we stopped at the little wooden church of Vinge, a building of great antiquity, on the walls of the interior of which are some paintings, a very rare thing in this country

They are on panel, in a hard style, representing for the most part figures of our Lord and saints, but in one place there is a picture of the scourging. Though they cannot be said to belong to a high style of art, yet there is considerable expression in the faces, and grace in the flowing lines of the drapery. They are evidently of some antiquity, but what may be their exact date, or whence they came, it would be hard to say. On the next stage, the man who accompanied my carriole, having walked up a hill, was jumping on behind, as usual, while the vehicle was in motion, when to my dismay he sprang too far, tumbled forward and fell flat on the ground, and in an instant the wheel went over him. I thought his legs must have been broken; but my faith in the lightness of carrioles and the toughness of the natives was not a little increased, when he got up, perfectly unhurt. We descended at last by a very steep and well-engineered zigzag into the magnificent Nærödal, a valley like the Romsdal, though not quite equal to it in grandeur. At Gudvangen, which lies at the head of the Næröens Fiord, we took a boat to Leirdalsören, the highest point of the great Sogne Fiord, which is seventy miles from the sea. The scenery of this fiord passes all description; it is far finer than the Romsdal Fiord, and quite outrivals any European lake scenery. It is narrow, and divided into a succession of bays by projecting headlands; the surrounding mountains are extremely steep, and rise in many places 5,000 feet above the water: and that which is generally the weak point of Norwegian mountains, want of character, is certainly not to be complained of here. Many of the precipices are of a sheeny silver-grey: other mountain tops are white, scaly, and almost leprous in their appearance; and I have never seen the birch trees,—small as they seem, and showing by their minuteness the height of the mountain sides on which they grow—so effective in ornamenting the lofty cliffs. Each bay, as it succeeds the other, appears the most sublime, until at last you open out into a wider fiord, and look back on another branch, almost as grand as that which you have left, running up into the far distant mountains, on the sides of which the patches of corn land are seen like mosaic work through the clear atmosphere.

The Sogne Fiord has an especial interest attaching to it, because most striking historical recollections still linger about its shores: the peasants still remember the part their forefathers took in the second crusade under King Sigurd I. It is one of the few points in which Norwegian history comes in contact with that of Europe at large; and few episodes can be found, which give such ample materials for picturesque description: the wild children of the North visiting the court of our second Henry, contending with the Moors by sea, entertained with splendid hospitality by their brethren the Norman princes, under the sunny sky of Sicily, and at last arriving at Jerusalem and fighting for the Cross. The want is here supplied, which the traveller cannot help feeling in other parts of the country, even in the midst of the most sublime scenery—the want of local historical associations. Greece and Norway, lying at the opposite extremities of Europe, may both be truly called "a land of mountains;" but the contrast between them is complete. The one is a land of "poetic mountains," a land where

> "The sense aches with gazing to behold
> The scenes our earliest dreams have dwelt upon"—

the other, though the spirit of the old mythology may still appear to rest upon it, and though many events in its annals are most striking in their details, fails for the most part to make its grandest features the exponents of its history.

About twenty miles from Leirdalsören, and not far from the road, is the wooden church of Borgund, a building of great antiquity, dating, probably, from the eleventh or twelfth century, and certainly one of the greatest curiosities in Christian architecture. The first view makes you think more of a Chinese pagoda than anything else: it rises story above story, roof above roof, gable above gable, until at last, by means of narrowing gables, one surmounting the other, it loses itself in a sort of spire. There are few windows, but each of those that there are, is surmounted by a gable, and all the gables have wooden crosses. The ridges of the roofs are ornamented, and at the end are long projecting finials of

the most grotesque description. All round the outside a low cloister runs, having a lean-to roof resting against the church, and an open arcade without, with semicircular arches and small pillars. There are three porches, answering to three doors on the north, south, and west sides; over the apse is a cupola, not altogether unlike that at Trondjem. The whole is covered with wooden tiles resembling scales, fastened together with nails, which are mostly of wood: it is entirely built of firwood, and covered with thick coats of tar, which give it a picturesque colour of dark sepia. The jambs of the doorways, and the semicircular arches above are elaborately decorated in a quaint style, with interlaced dragons and other ornaments. Inside there are large fir-poles standing up within the walls on all four sides of the nave, which act as pillars to support a clerestory: in this way something like aisles are formed; and cross-bars of wood, which run from one of these poles to another about half-way up, produce the effect of a triforium; but the whole building is so abnormal, that one is obliged to torture architectural words from their original meaning in order to describe it. The arches are everywhere round, as also is the vaulted roof, the supports of which rest on corbels shaped like barrels and carved. At the west end is a gallery. The wood inside is in most parts stained red, but the walls and roof are painted with strange designs of flowers and other objects. At first sight this nave, from its shape, its dull colours and general effect, reminded me forcibly of the *Narthekes*, or ante-chapels of the monasteries of Mount Athos. The nave is thirty-nine feet long, the chancel about fifteen; they are divided by a screen. The chancel has a flat roof within, and in the apse is a quaint altar-piece of later date than the building; but the font may be of any antiquity—a square stone basin, resting on a rude block. Not the least wonder about the place is that it has no foundations, being supported by stones, which rest on the earth. I examined this point carefully, and it was confirmed by the old man who opened the doors for us; but the poles which support the clerestory seem to run into the ground; and this would account for that part of the building standing quite upright while the rest has sunk in many parts: but it is a wonder that the whole structure has not been blown away. A little way from the church is the belfry, a building of the same date and character. The walls incline inwards, as they rise, for two-thirds of its height; then comes an open arcade, and above this is the high-pitched roof. It is supported by poles and cross-beams inside.

The question naturally arises, whence came this style of architecture? for a style there seems to have been, since other churches in various parts of Norway bear more or less resemblance to that of Borgund. The ornamental work, both of the exterior and interior, is evidently Celtic,* which will be

* This will be plain to any one who will compare the plates in Dahl's *Denkmale einer sehr ausgebildeten Holzbaukunst*, with Plates 63, 64, of Owen Jones' *Grammar of Ornament.*

sufficiently explained by the connexion which existed between the churches in Norway and the British Isles.* But for the plan, arrangement, and form of these buildings, a more distant origin is to be sought. Professor Dahl, who has made this subject his own, maintains their close affinity to the Byzantine style, and finds the connecting link in the migrations of the Varangians. This name was applied to the original Russians, who were Scandinavian conquerors: after establishing a dynasty in Russia in the ninth century, the great body of the invading tribe passed on to Constantinople, where they became the body-guard of the Byzantine emperors.† As the Byzantine style of architecture spread itself through Russia, it was not unlikely that it should penetrate to the original home of the Varangians. There are other traces of a connexion between this country and Constantinople: there is a Byzantine painting in the Museum at Bergen, and churches at Constantinople were dedicated to St. Olave; in several places in the Sagas also, mention is made of communication both with Russia and Constantinople: perhaps the bulb-like cupola of Trondjem Cathedral may be traced to a Russian model, and the form of the Greek cross, which is so common in the churches of the Gulbrandsdal, may have been introduced in the same way. If this theory is true, it serves as an additional proof of the wide-spread influence of that which is historically the most interesting of all the styles of architecture, the Byzantine, the traces of which are found in the west of France, in the north of Russia, in Spain, Africa, and India, and wherever Mahometanism has penetrated.‡

Between the head of the Sogne Fiord and Christiania the

* Neander, v. p. 403. Mosheim, ii. p. 247. Scotland, Ireland, and the Hebrides, were often visited by the Northmen in their piratical expeditions, and the Orkneys were for some time subject to the kings of Norway. See Laing's *Translation* of Snoiro Sturleson's *Heimskringla, passim.*

† Smith's Gibbon, vii. pp. 80—83, and notes. Geyer's *Histoire de la Suède*, p. 17. Laing's Heimskringla, iii. pp. 4, 296.

‡ Those who take an interest in wooden architecture may like to know, that the church of Little Greenstead in Essex, is the one ancient wooden church which exists in England.

country is pleasing, but not worth speaking of after what we had lately seen. It is very much the sort of scenery which, before starting, I had expected to find throughout Norway: deep valleys, with rushing rivers and high fir-clad mountain sides; occasional lakes, and sweeps of moorland. During the latter part of this route, however, we passed through the most cultivated country we had seen, the inclosures being often large, and the corn-fields running far up the mountains. For ten days before we started there had been torrents of rain, the effects of which were visible in many parts of our route; bridges were broken, and we had often to cross the streams by temporary bridges or ferries; the road in many parts was washed away, or covered with a mass of slush and soil, so that we had to make our way by circuitous paths through the fields. In one place, at the head of the Rans Fiord, a whole valley was laid under water, and only farm-buildings and trees could be seen standing out of it. On this journey we learnt more than ever how truly the carriole is the proper conveyance for Norway, for no other kind of carriage could have gone over such rough and broken ground.

On the third day of our journey we came in sight of the Miösen lake, and the next evening arrived at the capital, after an absence of nearly two months.

12. *A VISIT TO NORTH SPAIN AT THE TIME OF THE ECLIPSE.*

BY FRANCIS GALTON, F.R.S.

A DIRECTION was given to my summer rambles by the desire of witnessing the solar eclipse of last June, and by the fact that the path of its totality, where nearest to England, lay across a country which I ardently longed to visit. The result was, that I applied for permission, and obtained it, to form one of the party of astronomers who, under the leadership of the Astronomer-Royal, were taken by H.M.S. *Himalaya* to Spain.

The *Himalaya* is truly a noble vessel, and we were right imperially treated. Those whose experience has been drawn from coasting passenger-steamers, in English or Mediterranean waters, would hardly credit that anything floated comparable in spaciousness and luxury to this magnificent ship. And she is as fast and as easy, excepting a tendency to roll, as she is spacious and comfortable ; for we steamed out of Plymouth Sound on a Saturday forenoon, so steadily, that I hardly knew we were moving ; and on the Sunday night we were going at half-power, because we were too near the Spanish coast, whose bold outlines lay in full view on the early Monday morning.

It was therefore with one of those feelings of contrast so often enjoyed by travellers, that I, with my eyes still toned to that dim English daylight in which we had just bade farewell to our shores, found myself paddling up the Bilbao river in a small shore-going craft, under a full flood of southern sunshine, by the side of suburbs and quays crowded with people—where every incident, shape, colour, and sound, assured me that I was in a new country, and amidst a civilization that was neither English, French, nor Italian, nor resembling that of any other country I knew, but something wholly peculiar.

At Bilbao, the plans of that section of the *Himalaya* party, which had there been landed, were discussed and arranged. Different groups, of two, or three, or four persons, undertook to occupy different stations, with the purpose of scattering the observing power of our party as widely as possible over the path of totality. I joined myself to two friends—Mr. Atwood and Mr. Charles Gray—and we accepted one of the more distant positions, near Logroño. My friends were prepared to observe the "Red Protuberances," and I, for my part, had hoped to make some experiments on the heat radiated by the Corona, though, afterwards, an accident to my instrument compelled me to alter my plans.

The thoughtful arrangements for our comfort on landing, and the energy with which Mr. Vignolles fulfilled the self-imposed duty of host and guardian to our large party, were such as made us feel an almost painful debt of gratitude. I and my friends were billeted as guests in a capital house, belonging to a Spanish merchant, who tended us like infants. Even a packet of tea, provided by Mr. Vignolles, was in readiness for our use. Our luggage was looked after, our money was changed, our plans were settled, introductions to the authorities at Logroño were given to us, and every difficulty was smoothed away as soon as it was discovered. Not less do we owe to the leadership of the Astronomer-Royal, and to the trouble he took in originally organizing the expedition. It is a matter of congratulation that he has undertaken the part of historian to the eclipse, and that we shall soon learn the whole value of the results that have accrued from it, by means of a comparative analysis of the numerous observations that were made upon each separate phenomenon of that strange and magnificent meteor.

For my part, I do not profess to do more in this place than to give a brief account of two or three appearances which made considerable impression on me at the time, and which do not seem to have been so fully, if at all, observed by others, either in the present eclipse or in previous ones, and which I am glad of an opportunity of putting upon record. To these I will recur. At present, I will endeavour to describe a few of my general recollections of that rapidly improving part of Spain which I had the opportunity of seeing. I think I may be excused for doing so, although my stay was a very short one, because I have not found any book that gives a recent, and at the same time what appears to me to be a fair account of this portion of the Basque provinces. They are usually described as different from Spain only in being less Spanish, and by having a strong infusion of the Basque mountaineer element; yet I found it, as the Germans would say, thoroughly "selbst-standig," and with none of the airs of an outlying province of a larger and vivifying central kingdom. Bilbao is becoming exceedingly wealthy; the provinces to which it and Santander are the outlets, are being cut into by railways. There is every sign of abundant local activity; no beggary, or apparent poverty, or listless indolence: added to all this, there is a remarkable picturesqueness in its social life. In short, this portion of the Basque provinces did not appear to me as I had been led to expect.

Almost the first thing that arrested my attention on Spanish land was the chiaro-oscuro tint of everything I saw. It was especially remarkable in the soil and in the buildings. There was an abundance of bright colour, but it seemed to have none of that garish effect which is so remarkable under a French sky. The exquisite mellowness and depths of shading surpassed anything I had previously seen, and explained at once the possibility and the truthfulness of Murillo's treatment. It also showed me that the universal black dresses of the upper class of either sex were in no way incongruous or dismal when seen through a Spanish atmosphere, and with Spanish surroundings. The eye soon becomes used to a new influence, and while I always recognised its effect, I afterwards tried in vain to recall the vividness of that first impression of novelty. However, the converse effect struck me forcibly when I left Spain for France, and found myself at Bordeaux. There is a well known and strongly contrasting influence of this nature to be seen when crossing the hills above Villafranca, which separate Mentone from Nice; the east side of this very natural, though not the actual, frontier between two great kingdoms being thenceforth wholly Italian in its colours and its aspect, and the west side as French as it is possible to conceive.

It is evidently the lowermost stratum of air that has the greater power in giving a mellowness of light, or an apparent depth of blueness, to the sky. One sees this unmistakeably in those Italian valleys that lie south of the Alps, where a blue, low-lying haze, which a little hill-climbing surmounts, floods the strath and mellows the view. So, again, a man standing at Chamouni and looking south over Mont Blanc, proclaims that the sky is decidedly Swiss, that it is hard and pale blue; while another man, who is stationed on the opposite side of the mountain, at Cormayeur, and looks north, asserts that the sky is soft, and deep blue, and eminently Italian; yet, in each case, whatever sky the observer sees above the mountain's crest, is on the opposite side of it. The Swiss man sees an Italian firmament, and the Italian man a Swiss one. Hence it is manifest that the characters of these aërial tints do not reside in the stratum that lies above the level of high mountains. The peculiarity of the Chamouni, or Cormayeur sky, is caused by the quality of the atmosphere that dwells in the Chamouni, or Cormayeur valleys, and in no way by that which spreads aloft in the higher regions.

It was a great delight to me to find that the Spanish ways of life appeared thoroughly characteristic, and wholly uncopied from other nations of modern Europe. There is a common cant phrase used sometimes in respect to France, and sometimes to England, of "advancing in the van of European civilization." Yet, however flattering to our vanities, it would be a matter of deep regret if European civilization should ever become so far one and indivisible, that nations, whose instincts and geographical conditions of life are different, should make it a point of fashion or of education to live on the same model. One longs to see a freer development than exists at present, of the immense variety of aptitudes and peculiarities that are found in the human race, and are fostered by different geographical circumstances. Let us, at least, hope that a united Italy may develop a vigorous and high-class, but an autogenous form of social life. If she did so, it would be as welcome to the majority of educated Europe, as a new face and a new mind to a small provincial society. Yet an exception to this statement must be made on behalf of the French, to whom any hope of the kind would be wholly unintelligible. They are strangely unconscious of their own monotony, and seem honestly convinced of the doctrine they subscribe,—that all which is not Frenchified is pagan, that there is but one path of perfection, and that the panacea for afflicted aliens is French influence and the Code Napoleon.

With feelings very different from theirs, it was an inexpressible pleasure to me to witness a busy, thriving nationality, utterly distinct, as I have already said, from any I had seen before, and, moreover, of a character which strangely fitted into my peculiar tastes. Every wheel of life in these northern parts of Spain, so far as a stranger can judge by what goes on in the streets before his eyes, appears to move freely, while the whole forms a machine absolutely different from any other in Europe. Nothing in common use seemed borrowed from other countries. The dresses of the men, women, priests, porters, and muleteers, were peculiar and not ineffective. The cattle were mules and oxen, and did their work excellently—better, I dare say, under a driver of Spanish temperament than a horse would. The animals and the men are notoriously well matched; indeed, the skill of the muleteers, the mastery they showed over their art, and the ingenuity and novelty of their harness and pack-saddle appliances, were an endless astonishment to me. The street architecture was peculiar and exceedingly imposing, with its large, square, well-glazed balconies and numerous awnings. Every act of the people was original—their gait, their implements, their way of setting to work. I looked into many shops—such as tinkers', blacksmiths', potters', and so forth—and came to the conclusion, speaking very broadly, that if any of their patterns were introduced into England, or that if any of ours were made to replace theirs, the change would involve decided incongruity, and lead to questionable improvement. Another subject which struck me at once, and with which, up to the last moment of my stay in Spain, I became no less charmed, was the graceful, supple, and decorous movement of every Spanish woman. It was as constant a pleasure to me to watch their walk, their dress, and their manner, as it is a constant jar to all my notions of beauty to see the vulgar gait, ugly outlines, mean faces, bad millinery, and ill-assorted colours of the vast majority of the female population that one passes in an English thoroughfare. The hideous bonnet is still wholly absent in these parts, and, in place of it, every Spanish woman, of every class, has her dense, black, uncovered hair divided with a straight, clean, white parting down to the forehead, and beautifully smoothed on either side.

Taking it all in all, I felt myself as one dropped in a thoroughly new land, with an infinity to learn and observe. Yet I did not feel any strangeness in its ways, but imagined I could accommodate myself with ease and pleasure to the every-day matters of Spanish life, so far as I could judge from what lay on the surface. The marked orientalism of the place captivated me. I enjoy oriental life, even under the drawback of knowing that the natives are ready to spit at me as an unclean dog of a Christian; how much more, then, should I be at ease where I was only liable to be cursed as a Protestant heretic. The nurses sing oriental airs to the children; the colours of the peasantry are Moorish in hue, pattern, and harmony, yet Spain is no mere Moslem country in its appearance. Among many others, there are two notable points of difference in its favour—the one, that unveiled women form more than half of the population in the streets; and the other, a consequence of non-seclusion of the sex, that the houses are enlivened, as I have already observed, by their large projecting windows and numerous balconies.

We were treated with marked courteousness wherever we were recognised; but another minor welcome delighted me the most, by its evident sincerity. It was this: I have always noticed that a stranger is soonest discovered and objected to by children and by dogs. Now, it was a fact, which I do not recollect to have experienced elsewhere, that although I was dressed like an Englishman—for instance, I usually wore a light-coloured shooting-coat, while all the Spaniard upper classes wear black, and the lower ones national costumes—yet, whenever I explored side streets and came unexpectedly upon groups of children or scattered curs, they one and all treated me as a fellow-countryman, and hardly ever raised a cry of terror or a bark of antipathy. I fairly fell in love with Spain at first sight, and have continued constant in my admiration ever since.

Let me devote a paragraph to the Public Promenade. I had never realized that truly Spanish institution until I saw it. A large half-deserted square, or suburban garden, fills towards night with a well-dressed swarming crowd, that hums with low conversation. All the spare population of the town takes part in it. They walk in ranks of three or four, the two sexes never intermingled in the same group, and they pace rank behind rank, on a broad gravelled path, under the warm starry sky, between low trees. The promenade leads down the walk, round at the end, and back again. The ascending and descending stream almost touch each other, that everybody may have one good view of everybody else in each round. Conversation seems to be carried on merrily, but in a well-bred, gentle tone of voice. All ranks except the lowest take part in it, and all have the air of ladies and gentlemen. It is a very pleasing exhibition to a stranger, the more so, as there is no gendarmerie or beadledom. These great crowds seem to keep order for themselves; there is no appearance of military or police.

I saw few beautiful faces in the north of Spain, but I rarely saw a mean one. The men were all moulded in a high type, especially the peasantry. It was an absolute grief to me, when I left Spain, by way of that fashionable watering-place, St. Sebastian, to see the inferiority of physique, manner, and address, of the upper classes of Madrid society, who congregate there, to those of the Basque peasantry I had so lately travelled amongst. How remarkable is this in many oriental —I do not mean Indian—and semi-oriental countries! With us, the higher classes, speaking generally, have the higher make of body and mind, and by far the nobler social tone; they form a true aristocracy in our land, to whom Scriptural depreciations of the Syrian wealthy in respect to the Syrian humble are singularly inapplicable.

I have no fault to find with the inns in the only three towns where I stayed—Bilbao, Vittoria, and Logroño. (I do not reckon St. Sebastian as a genuine north Spanish town.) The lodging and cooking were not only equal, but considerably superior to that in the large towns of France, not on any regular line of tourist traffic—superior, for instance, to that in Nantes. There was no disagreeable quantity of garlic, or of anything that was unusual, in the food; and much of the common wine was exceedingly good. Some of the eatables—for instance, the sugary biscuits, like hardened froth, or fine pumice stone, but white and soluble, which all the world consumes, dipping them into chocolate or water—are excellent. The chocolate is really good; far better—I wonder why—than what I can get elsewhere. As for the solid articles, I don't care to enter into details: suffice it, that I found them toothsome and digestible, which English inn dinners are not. If the inns were dirty, yet the bed linen was clean, and the towns, from end to end, were remarkably free from dirt and bad smells. It is not doing justice to these parts of Spain to talk of them as being extraordinarily backward; as for mendicancy, it does not seem to exist. I had with me a recently published number of the "Journal of the Statistical Society," —that for June, 1860—in which is an exceedingly interesting account of the recent progress of Spain. The conclusion of the writer is, that her exports and imports had doubled between 1850 and 1856, and were steadily increasing (the last published census being of 1857), and that whatever tests may be applied to the stated fact of her rapid advancement, the result is uniformly favourable. I would strongly recommend all who care to learn the actual state of modern Spain, to study this paper.

The road from Bilbao to Vittoria is full of interest. Besides the history of the great Peninsula struggle, which gives some memorial to nearly every village, brook, and road, there is abundant intrinsic charm of landscape and wayside incident. One interesting phenomenon of physical geography, on which, by the way, our eclipse prospects were intimately dependent, was a subject of continual inquiry and remark. It was the rapid change from a humid sea-coast climate at Bilbao, on the north face of the Pyrenees, to an arid soil and a clear blue sky on the south of them. It is the old story. The cold mountains condense a large part of the moisture in the Atlantic winds; therefore, whatever air has passed over the mountain-tops is comparatively dry and cloudless. The valley of the Ebro is literally parched, and would be utterly barren if it were not for an elaborate system of field irrigation—elaborate, I mean, in its extent and comprehensiveness, but simple enough in its details.

We had naturally sought information with eagerness, from the moment of our landing, about the relative sunniness of different places on the calculated path of total eclipse—it was an all-important question to us—and I heard that, as a rule, travellers to the interior left Bilbao under an overcast sky, that they ascended the mountains in fog and rain, that the clouds broke long before reaching Vittoria, and that from Logroño onwards the sky was cloudless. I do not know that anybody has examined into the proportionate effect of this nature produced by mountains, with reference not only to their height, but to other geographical conditions. There seems to be considerable variation that is difficult to account for; for instance, not to travel further than our own country, the west wind is far wetter than the east wind, but the district at the eastern foot of the Westmoreland hills is little, if at all, drier than that on their western, notwithstanding the enormous quantity of rain that falls upon the latter. I believe the average distribution of cloud and blue sky, as distinct from rain and drought, to be far less uniform over any given district than is commonly supposed. In a country like England, a difference of a few miles makes a considerable alteration in the average character of the sky. Clouds collect over clay soils, and are dispersed over chalk. In fact, I endeavoured once, but failed from an absence of anything like a sufficient number of recorded facts, to compile, for my amusement, a sun and cloud chart of England, the intensity of shading to represent the average amount of cloudiness. I, however, collected enough matter to make me believe that there was, as I have stated, great inequality in this element of climate. Thus, with all the faults of a London atmosphere, the clearness of its sky at a late hour of the night, or rather at a very early one of the morning, is probably unsurpassed in all England; but in this case Sir J. Herschel has well described the cause.*

Until our arrival at Vittoria, my two companions and myself were almost as helpless as babies in the art of expressing our wants. Spanish is so obviously a language that one ought to know, from its resemblance to Latin, &c. —the mere light of nature enabling one to read it with reasonable fluency, after the rudimentary matters of grammar

* See the invaluable article by Sir J. Herschel on *Meteorology*, in the late edition of the Encyclopædia Britannica. It is, so far as I know, the only worthy exposition of that science, as a whole. I have always wondered it has not already been re-printed in an easily accessible form, and that it does not become a text-book at our Universities, and other places of advanced education. Meteorology is a branch of physical science which seems peculiarly well fitted for a University subject, especially when treated in so condensed yet comprehensive a manner as it has been by Sir J. Herschel.

have been once mastered, and a few minor words learnt—that I felt quite ashamed of myself at my inability to frame an intelligible sentence. What made the matter worse was, that the Spaniards I accosted did not seem hopeful about the possibility of understanding me. The power of impressing on a foreigner, of whose language you know but little, that it is within his power to comprehend you if he only chooses to try, is a *sine quâ non* to success in conversation. With mutual faith, abundant interchange of ideas may be carried on through the medium of an abominably broken dialect; without it, a fairly good vocabulary may be absolutely useless. French was an unknown language to hotel servants, diligence-office keepers, and all that genus. I heard of exceptions to this rule, but saw only one or two instances myself. However, after our second day at Vittoria, the spell of dumbness was broken by the effective assistance of a railway inspecting engineer, whose invaluable services had been made available to us through the kindness of Mr. Vignolles, and he henceforth managed all our little difficulties and wants.

This gentleman was one of a class who form an influential element in the districts where railroad-making, under English superintendence, is being carried on. A line of railway is undertaken by a contractor, inspecting engineers are appointed, each to a particular section of the line, a few miles in length, to see that the contractor does his work fairly. They live in strange out-of-the-way Spanish villages, lodging with some Spanish family, and spending all the day in riding about the line. Now and then, it is possible for them to take a few days' holiday at Vittoria or Logroño, or at the reputed Paris of these parts, Bilbao. They have exacted fixed charges at the hotels, introduced some good dishes into the bills of fare, and in one case, at least, where accommodation was bad, had established a respectable person in a new inn to the convenience of the travelling public. They are all of the class of young rising engineers, receiving considerable salaries, and looking forward to some future time when they themselves shall be contractors and wealthy men, in Europe,

Australia, or America, or wherever a good opening may then happen to exist.

It is of course impossible for a Protestant to forget for one moment that he is a reputed Heretic, and that on however good terms he may be with a Spaniard, there is an essential difference between them, which any accident may unmask. I was curious to know how far this feeling would affect the somewhat intimate relationship which must necessarily spring up between a lodger and his hosts. I understood from our friend the engineer that, as a general rule, there was no appearance of meddling intolerance, the Englishman being considered as an unaccountable sort of animal, and allowed to go his own gait; the more so, as an Englishman's probity and energy has a name in these parts of Spain. Yet little circumstances constantly arose to show how easily this thin crust of forced indifference might be broken through. The death of a Protestant, and the question of his burial, is sure to create a difficulty. Our friend told us that he every now and then received a serious, but kindly lecture, from some elderly female, pointing out to him the danger of his heretical ways, and the certain future that threatened him, and far more frequently, that semi-serious allusions were thrown out to the same purport.

I made many inquiries about the honesty and the morality of the Spanish peasantry, and being assured from different sources that it is very high, much higher than in England, I believe it. However, the use of the knife is rather common.

We hired a carriage at Vittoria, and passed, by a little used mountain road, over the Sierra de Tolonio to Logroño, beyond which our proposed station was situated. The crest of the Sierra formed the northern boundary of the valley of the Ebro, and we felt much anxiety to witness the reputed blue sky of the new country, for hitherto the weather had been capricious and frequently overcast. When we attained the ridge, and had descended clear of the clouds that lay on it, the largeness and aridity of the view took me by surprise. The valley was almost as tawny as an African wady, and some forty miles in breadth, running in ample sweeps between lines and groups of mountains that towered in wild disorderly masses, flanked with some noble crags, and garnished with a few isolated peaks. It was a first-class view, deserving to rank among the best ten or twelve of those with which I am acquainted. There are three views, more or less, of this description, to which I habitually refer myself as convenient standards of comparison, and which I usually quote, as the finest that I know. Their similarity lies in the amplitude of the mountain shoulder whence the view is taken, in the vast unbroken sweep of rich country extending from its foot, and in the completeness of the picture, owing to its limits being framed with natural objects, and not passing out of sight in an untidy, indistinct haze. These views are—1. That from the hills above Trieste. 2. From below the cedars of Lebanon, over the plains of Tripoli; and 3. From our own Devil's dyke, near Brighton. The sweep of the valley of the Ebro is little inferior to any of these.

The Spaniards, at least in the northern provinces, seem mad upon road-making; here and there were pieces of our present way tended with incommensurate care. It debouched by no less than three roads down into the valley. One was a bad one; then came another, with grand zigzags and parapets, as good as could be desired: but, not contented with this, a third road, also with zigzags, cutting across the second one at many places, was newly constructed. The hill side looked a labyrinth of roads from their curious intercrossings. Our driver, as he spun down hill, was constantly puzzled which turn to take, and the mules were pulling in opposite directions, at many awkward corners. We saw some ascending waggons in similar indecision, passing up different ways. Everywhere the road-makers seemed to revel in funds, though they certainly do not apply them equally.

On reaching the plain, our way led us through a village, called La Guardia. It was perched up on the top of a detached conical hill, burrowed with wine-vaults, in a situation that dominated the plain. It was battlemented with ancient walls and towers, and suggested the very ideal of its name. Here we had to stop to bait—it was eleven miles short of Logroño—and our proposed station was twenty miles on the other side of that town, on the opposite boundary of the Ebro valley, on a broad hill-top, inaccessible to carriages on account of some broken bridges, and deficient in buildings where our instruments could be housed and got into order. But La Guardia was fully as well situated both as regards the path of the shadow, and the stations of the other observing parties. House room for our instruments was there, the view of the plain towards the south-east, along which the black skirt of the shadow of totality would sweep when the sun reappeared, was uninterruptedly visible; and, lastly, the clouds clung about the high hill-tops, while all the sky above us was bright and clear. A few words sufficed to show that we equally appreciated these advantages, and we sallied forth, up the principal church-tower, among the clock and bells, about the tumble-down ramparts, and everywhere where we could hope to select the best station, to the wonderment of the natives, who did not at first comprehend the object of our proceedings. The result was, that we ventured to transmit a civil message to the owner of a house that rose high, and had a flat top, used for clothes-drying, and partially roofed over. It proved to be tenanted jointly by a priest and doctor. They cordially and most courteously welcomed us. We clambered up the little stone staircase that led to its roof, knocking our heads and grating our elbows, and found the place exceedingly well fitted for our wants. Our hosts put it at once at our full disposal. They gave us tressels into which we could screw the telescope-stands, tables, and chairs. We then went to a carpenter, who took in hand some little matters that were wanted by us, and did them, as I find foreigners usually do on such occasions, with an intelligence and quickness of apprehension rarely seen in an English mechanic. Finally, we locked up our precious instruments, in an empty room, to await the day preceding the eclipse, when we were to return to mount them in readiness, and to make a few prefatory observations. La Guardia was not a place to stay at with comfort—it was a mere village; besides, we had letters of introduction to Logroño, so we went on there and established our quarters, taking Spanish lessons, bathing in the Ebro, buying trifles, and prying everywhere.

Logroño was the most thoroughly national town we saw, and I have carried away a great affection for it. The streets and arcades are busy in the morning; besides business, there is a good deal of church-going. I was vastly interested in the movements of the ladies' fans at church. All the world knows that Spanish fans are in perpetual motion, and betray each feeling, real or assumed, that passes through the mind of its bearer. I felt convinced I could guess the nature of the service at any particular moment by the way in which the fans were waving. The difference between a litany and a thanksgiving was unmistakeable; and I believed that far minuter shades of devotion were also discernible.

In the afternoon, the military were paraded, and the bands played in the square. Of course, all the spare population went to see them; but what amused us especially, was the part taken by the nurses and the children, both here and at Vittoria. They came in hundreds, scattered among the crowd. The instant the music began, every nurse elevated her charge, sitting on her hand, at half-arm's length into the air, and they all kept time to the music by tossing the babies in unison, and slowly rotating them, *in azimuth* (to speak astronomically), at each successive toss. The babies looked passive and rather bored, but the energy and enthusiasm of the nurses was glorious. At each great bang of the drummers a vast flight of babies was simultaneously projected to the utmost arms' length. It was ludicrous beyond expression.

The environs of Logroño greatly pleased my particular taste. The land is utterly arid when in a state of nature, but wherever a runnel of water can be led, pumped up from the Ebro, there is fertility; consequently, the charms of an oasis are always present: there is the air of the desert, with abundance of neighbouring verdure to cheer the eye. I could not understand how it was, that not a single country residence had been anywhere seen since Bilbao. The landscape was exceedingly varied, and in all cases exhibited the appearance of a most liveable country. I had been everywhere looking for "gentlemen's seats," like the Yorkshire servant of Eothen's companion, when riding across the Balkan; yet I saw nothing but peasantry—hard-working men, who seemed only to want a good pattern of agricultural implements, and modern agricultural knowledge, to become first-rate small farmers—or else muleteers and others riding on gaudy saddle-cloths, so gaudy, that one which I bought at Logroño, of the common pattern and material, is now amongst the most showy pieces of drapery in my drawing-room. It is woollen, woven in bands of colours, and absolutely Moorish-looking.

The day before the eclipse, we drove to La Guardia, to arrange our instruments. It was there I discovered a disaster which had befallen mine. I had taken an actinometer (Herschel's), and on exposing it to the sun, found something had gone wrong. It proved that the enclosed thermometer-stem had broken. I candidly confess that a rising feeling of exultation accompanied this discovery; I was not now necessarily obliged to spend the precious three minutes of the eclipse in poring on an ascending column of blue fluid in a graduated stem, and noting down the results by a feeble lamp-light, but I was free to enjoy in full the whole glory of the eclipse. I should here say, that there is something very faulty in the mechanical arrangement of these very important instruments. Negretti and Zambra, who are the makers of them, tell me, that in no instance have they ever sold one that was not, sooner or later, returned for repair, the enclosed thermometer being broken.

It now became necessary to fix on some other limited class of observations; and I decided upon sketching the Corona, and also on endeavouring to determine the exact colour of the eclipse light, about which there had been discrepancy of opinion. For the first, I required merely my naked eye, pencil, paper, and a lantern. I happened, however, to possess a small theodolite telescope of the lowest power, very conveniently mounted, that would enable me to isolate any portion of the Corona I chose, and thus to guard against the possibility of optical illusion from adjacent appearances. For experimenting on the eclipse light, I happened also to have with me a tiny box of twelve colours, which I had selected some years ago, after numerous trials, as being those which were most distinct each from the other, that I could obtain. Whenever I wanted to paint upon a map different marks, meaning different physical features, or travellers' tracks, I used these colours. I accordingly painted a sheet of paper in squares, numbered very legibly, and proposed observing them from time to time during the eclipse, and to note whenever any of the twelve became mutually indistinguishable; then it would always be in my power, as I supposed, to reproduce this effect by light passing through glass, of a colour to be determined by after trials. After I had found a piece of glass that produced the required effect, its colour, when looked through, would be the average of that thrown down by the sky at the time of the eclipse. My colours were as follows—I especially mention their names, because I can recommend the selection to any person who wants a box for purposes similar to those for which I originally procured mine, and about which I took a good deal of trouble:—Violet carmine, Vandyke brown, Prussian green, Hooker's green, Emerald green, Orange chrome, Cobalt, Vermilion, Crimson lake, Olive green, Burnt sienna, Indian yellow. Nine of these, including most of the greens, strangely enough, are very distinguishable by candle-light.

Mr. Atwood and Mr. Gray had large telescopes, and chiefly devoted themselves, as I have said, to the Red Protuberances. We arranged our lanterns and watches in convenient positions, and rehearsed the proceedings of the morrow. The weather was far from being as satisfactory as we had expected. The clouds hung about the mountains, while La Guardia was comparatively free; so we felt reassured as to the wisdom of our choice, although exceedingly anxious as to the prospect of the precious three minutes of the eclipse, next afternoon, finding us under a favourable sky. The wretched weather of this summer has afflicted even Spain, but we returned to Logroño in hope.

The morning of the eventful day broke grey and unpromising—wind north, and therefore over the Sierra de Tolonio—drifting clouds from its summit, where an abundant reservoir of them lay piled. The drifted clouds were low cumuli, with few indications of blue between them; however, the sky improved as the day advanced, and when we had reached La Guardia, the clouds were settled into rounded forms, with large blue spaces in their intervals. The wind gradually died away, and our massive enemies moved very slowly and undecidedly, sometimes in one direction, sometimes in another. We had a good view of the beginning of the eclipse; after that, a succession of clouds passed before the sun, hiding it from time to time, and making us sorely anxious; but about twenty-five minutes before totality they gave place to our wishes, and the welcome crescentic sun shone perfectly clear from out of a good English blue sky—perfectly clear, I say, but not so deep a blue as we had previously seen in the magnificent atmosphere of the Ebro valley. There was, doubtless, vapour in the air, which the chill of the eclipse might possibly convert into a thwarting haze, or a source of accidental and puzzling appearances; nevertheless, from this time onwards, we had no trouble, the blue space above head enlarged rapidly and continuously, and the evening closed with a constant sunshine.

Crowds of people were clustered at the foot of our tower, and about a dozen spectators were on the roof-top by our side. They carefully and courteously respected the portion we occupied, and added to our pleasure by their shrewd remarks and manifest interest in our proceedings. My notes were as follows:—Eclipse commenced at 1h. 50m. by my watch. 2h. 15m. Light sensibly diminished. 2h. 22m. No apparent difference; my colours unchanged. B—— thinks the landscape is becoming fainter. 2h. 35m. Light still more peculiar; the colours as before. The people on the roof remark the colour of the sky to be darker. I doubt it. The spots on the sun, as seen through a telescope, appear decidedly darker. We all agree in this. 45m. The light certainly appears more yellow, but the country is yellow, and is now everywhere in full sunlight. My colours just as distinguishable as ever. 50m. Indian yellow, cobalt, and emerald green are lower in tone. I can distinguish all twelve colours perfectly. Light much fainter. 55m. Light far fainter. I made a hole in a paper screen, and watched the crescentic image of the speck of sun-light that shone through it on the floor. The shadows were very dark and sharp. Air cold. 58m. The numerous pigeons of the place began to fly home, fluttering about hurriedly, taking shelter wherever they could. There was something of a hush in the crowd.

At *about* 3h.—I forgot to note the exact watch time, I am sorry to say—totality came on in great beauty. The Corona very rapidly formed itself into all its perfectness. It did not appear to me to *grow*, but to stand out ready formed, as the brilliant edge of the sun became masked. I do not know to what I can justly compare it, on account of the peculiar whiteness of its light, and of the definition of its shape as combined with a remarkable tenderness of outline. There was firmness but not hardness. In its general form, it was well balanced, not larger on one side than the other. It reminded me of some brilliant decoration or order, made of diamonds and exquisitely designed. There was nothing to impress terror in the sight of the blotted-out sun; on the contrary, the general effect of the spectacle on my mind was one of unmixed wonder and delight. A low buzz of voices arose among the crowd at the foot of the tower, like what is heard when an exceedingly beautiful firework is displayed at a *fête*. The Corona-light sufficed abundantly for writing rough notes and for seeing my colours. Oddly enough, the *burnt sienna* and the *vermilion* alone ceased to be distinguishable from each other. Indian yellow had greatly lost brilliancy. I made a rough sketch of the Corona—it was too manifold in its details and too beautiful in its proportions for me, bad artist as I am, to do justice to it in the short time the spectacle lasted—yet the drawing which I made, and which is given here, is to my mind a fair diagram of this splendid meteor. I drew it without taking any measurements to guide me, but simply

Fig. 1

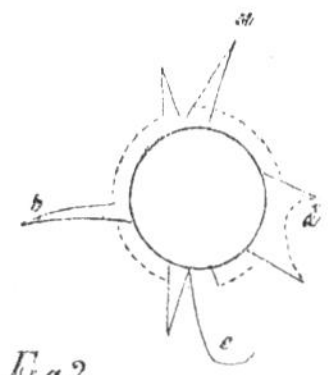

Fig. 2

as I would sketch any ordinary object. The uppermost part is that which was uppermost when I drew it. I used no lantern, and required none; there was a sufficiency of light. The principal facts were, firstly, that the long arms of the Corona, fig. 2, do not radiate strictly from the centre, neither are they always bounded by straight lines. The upper edge of *a* was truly tangential, that of *d* and of others, nearly so; *c* was remarkably curved, and so was the lower edge of *b*, though less abruptly; it was like a finch's beak, and remarkably defined. Secondly, the shape of the Corona was not absolutely constant; speaking generally, it was so; but in small details, it appeared to vary continually, by a slow diorama-like change. There was no pulsation or variation of intensity, visible in its light: I was particularly impressed by its solemn steadiness.

It seemed scarcely possible to believe that the light of the Corona was other than the rays from the sun, made visible in some incomprehensible manner round the edge of the moon, the appearance being eminently suggestive of a brilliant glistering body, hidden behind a screen. The nearest resemblance I can think of, to express my meaning (not that I am to be understood as supposing the remotest analogy between the causes of the two appearances), is the effect of a jet of water, playing from behind against some obstacle, and throwing an irregular halo of spray around it, on all sides. That a reasonable foundation may exist for ascribing the Corona to some diversion of the ordinary rays of the sun, however unintelligible the cause of this diversion may be, and not to a luminous atmosphere surrounding the sun, was powerfully impressed on me by certain appearances that were observed when totality had passed: they were these. Four or five minutes after the reappearance of the sun, Mr. Atwood called attention to remarkable luminous radiations, like sunbeams slanting through a cloud, and proceeding in narrow but long brushes from the cusps of the sun. They changed their angular directions, and even their shapes with such rapidity, that I was almost bewildered in a first attempt to draw them. If I looked down on my paper to draw a few strokes, the appearances had become changed when I again raised my head. Nevertheless, between 3h. 11m. and 3h. 13m. I managed to make three sketches; the two that were most characteristic are here very fairly represented. After 3h. 13m.

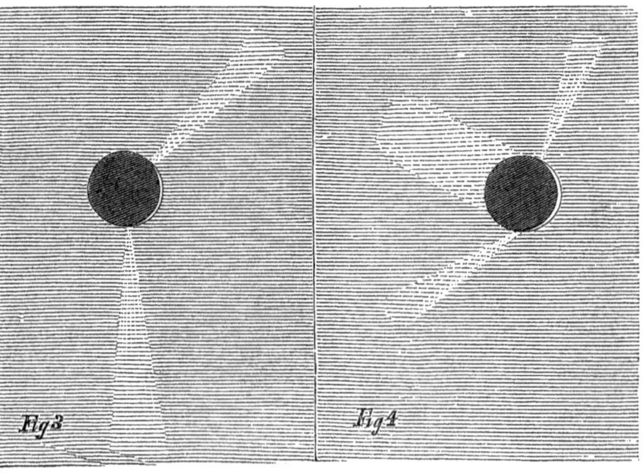

the light of the emerging sun was too strong to admit of further observation. The brushes were perfectly distinct and unmistakeable, they were best seen by holding up the hand so as to mask the sun, and they were perfectly visible through the telescope when it was so turned as to exclude the sun.

There was no mistake whatever about their existence. I trust the attention of observers of future eclipses will be directed to them, both before and after totality. Now, whatever may have been the cause of the brushes, would also, I should guess, be competent to create the greater part of the Corona: the two appearances being of identically the same genus. It will be observed that the brushes in Fig. 3 enclose an angle of about 130°, on the side of the emergent sun, and that this same angle had changed to about 195° in Fig. 4, to say nothing of the new appearance of a central bar of light. The angular change of the brushes was continuous, so long as I had an opportunity of looking continuously at them.

I have since often looked for, and have only just seen (Sunday, February 10th), an almost precise representation of these appearances, in the case of a small black snow-laden cloud sailing before the sun. When the clouds are in any way transparent, though some indications of these brushes may be observed, their effect is proportionately feeble, and if the sun be masked by an object at no great distance, the effect does not occur at all. The common artist representations of the sun about to rise over a distant hill, show that these appearances are generally recognised. Now I can hardly understand what I have described, on any other supposition than that of sunbeams being reflected from off the back of the cloud at a very acute angle athwart the line of sight. They would illuminate the haze of the atmosphere through which they passed, and being seen exceedingly foreshortened, would be the more apparent. But here I stop. I do not comprehend why the wisps of light should be projected from the cusps of the uncovering sun, and therefore have an apparent movement of revolution. Still less can I understand why the moon, which is presumed to have no atmosphere of any description, capable of being illuminated by passing rays, should exhibit this appearance so beautifully. When I shall have seen wisps of light, as in Figs. 3 or 4, coming from a cloud, but shaped in any way like those of Fig. 1—convergent and not divergent, curved and not straight—whether owing to irregular distribution of the adjacent haze or other less intelligible reason, I shall hardly resist feeling satisfied that the Corona is mainly due to the same description of cause that produces them, whatever that cause may really be. There may, in addition, be some luminous effect produced by an enveloping atmosphere of light round the sun, seen beyond the edges of the eclipsing moon.

The skirt of the shadow of totality sweeping over the country to the south-east, did not impress me as I had expected; there happened to be the shadow of a broad distant belt of clouds near the horizon, in which the eclipse-shade merged, and the skirt was never well defined. Our range of vision in that direction was immense. We could see but little, and I looked for nothing, towards the north-west.

The lightening of the landscape was rapid: even at 3h. 16m. everything looked to my eyes as almost natural. At the time of totality, the sky did not appear to me to descend. The sky was quite yellow near the horizon, but I remarked the absence of light, rather than the colour of the light; and a strangeness, rather than a mournfulness of effect. A couple of gusts of wind preceded totality.

As to my colours: after a good deal of trouble, I find I can reproduce the exact effect that I witnessed, by placing them in a closed box having a dark ceiling, and admitting a faint white light at a low angle. I then view the colours, also at a low angle, through a piece of dull yellow glass. All these details seem essential to effect: they are, in some sort, the equivalents to a yellow sky near the horizon, and gloom above head.

Thus was completed the object that had brought us to Spain, and we drove down the hill of La Guardia amid cries of "Viva Ynglaterra!" for we had become exceedingly popular in the town, thanks to the kind way in which our hosts had introduced us everywhere, and we increased the triumph of our departure by scattering coppers among the ragamuffins who had collected to see us go.

It was a marked instance of the local nature of sunny

weather, that the people at Logroño could not credit we had been so fortunate in our day. At that town, nothing of the eclipse had been seen; and a party from the *Himalaya*, Mr. Pole and Mr. Perry, who were stationed on a hill-top near it, and in full view of us, though some ten miles off, were greatly annoyed by clouds; they, too, could with difficulty understand our good fortune.

The instances are as many in this eclipse as in others, of discrepant observations and of important things forgotten. My fault was not noting the moment of totality. It would have been of service in calculating the extent to which the sun had emerged, and the exact position of its cusps at the time when Figs. 3 and 4 were drawn, in order to find out whether these brushes of light were exactly or not, in a line of prolongation of them. One very unlucky piece of forgetfulness is rumoured to have been made by an eminent photographer, not of the *Himalaya* party. He went, partly on commercial grounds, excellently provided with instruments, and all the way overland, on purpose to photograph the eclipse. Everything was prepared, the day was glorious, the totality came on, and the slide of the camera was carefully inserted. When all had passed, and the slide was opened in the dark chamber, alas! the operator had forgotten to put his *plate into the slide!*

Gray and myself did not return by the *Himalaya*, but went to St Sebastian, and ultimately spent a part of the summer together, in the Pyrenees—I having in the interim joined my wife at Bordeaux, and taken her with me.

The valley of the Ebro is separated from the Pyrenees by a belt of broken country, almost untraversed except by horse-roads, along some few of which, invalids are taken as they best can go, to the baths of Panticosa, &c. and occasionally across the Pyrenees, by one or other of the horse-passes, to the French watering-places of Eaux-bonnes, Luz, Cauterets, or Luchon. This belt I did not traverse. The northern part of it was very familiar to my eyes, owing to the numerous mountain-tops, beginning with the diligence-road by St. Sebastian, and ending with the Canigou, near the Mediterranean, whence I looked down upon it. The part adjacent to the main chain, including the small republic of Andorre, is very little traversed or known. On the French side, the plain is prolonged up the valleys, to the very bases of the mountains; but the Spanish side is far more tossed and tumbled.

Here that remarkable madness of mountain climbing, to which every healthy man is liable at some period of his life, and which I had always believed myself to have gone through once for all, in a mitigated form, began to attack me with extreme severity. I will spare the reader the details of the direction which my malady took, because none of the Pyreneean mountains are sufficiently high to afford a field for feats, though glorious for actual enjoyment. Yet they are of no despicable elevation or grandeur: there are plenty of 10,000 feet, and three of 11,000; while the ruggedness and steepness of their sides is fully equal to those of any other chain. I do not know where a worse piece of climbing is likely to be found than about those mountains, one of whose bases is well known as the "Grand Chaos," being crossed by the road from Luz to Gavarni; and there are few steeper hill-tops anywhere, than the Pie de la Pique, near Luchon, and the Fourcanade (which latter I had not an opportunity of attempting). I like, too, the absence of fir and pines, and the varied forest foliage that replaces them. The climate is more southern than that of Switzerland, being finer and gloriously hot. Again, when one is tired, a vast deal may be done on horseback along the numerous bridle-paths, that lead to many admirable points of view. One drawback is that the guides are rather a poor set, ignorant of the country, unable or unwilling to carry weights, and bad walkers. There are not half a dozen in all Luchon with whom I would care to be accompanied, yet Luchon is the destination of 2,000 yearly visitors.

The French give a bad name to the Spaniards of the Pyreneean chain; and as the accommodation of the country is, for the most part, villanous, and the language a *patois*, and there is nothing to do but to climb and shoot chamois, and explore the beauties of a new country, they do not care to penetrate there. There is no lack of chamois. Bears exist; in fact, I saw one just shot, but the brute had been tracked and mobbed. A single sportsman would have had small chance of finding him. There are abundance of eagles, and a few ptarmigan. The Spanish side is doubtless a wild land, and is not to be explored except by persons prepared to sleep in châlets or cabins, and to cook for themselves. It was always most annoying to me when I had clambered, for some hours, to a distant peak, that the absence of accommodation and means of bivouac drove me prematurely to return. I had long been convinced that the only way of exploring the interesting mountain tracts that still remain almost unknown in Europe, such as these Spanish Pyrenees, Dauphiné, the Savoy Alps, the Carpathians, the northern parts of Turkey and Greece, and so on, is for the traveller to take some means of making himself independent of beds, and, to a certain degree, even of a roof. But what those means should be, I could never determine. Alpine travellers seem wholly unversed in the art of comfortable bivouac. I hardly know a single instance when the nights spent by them on the hill-sides have not been recorded as nights of discomfort, and often of misery. Let those who doubt it refer to "Peaks and Passes." This is an old opinion of mine, and one which has set me widely to inquire about facts bearing on the subject. Saussure's experience is not much to the point, except in showing that a tent will stand in any weather; witness his hurricane on the Col du Géant. The brothers Schlagintweit also used tents, and they drove sheep for food. Dr. Rae's Arctic equipment is exceedingly interesting; he relied on snow houses, built with great neatness, for protection against the weather: so did Sir Leopold M'Clintock. I have, indeed, a selection of that energetic officer's travelling-gear; sledge, cook's apparatus, and tent-poles,—which he and Captain Allen Young used in their search after the fate of Sir John Franklin, and were afterwards so good as to give me. But none of these precisely meet the want I feel. The travelling-gear should be light and convenient for carrying on the back, and require no previous practice in its use. Each man should be independent of his neighbour; for the close proximity of snoring and flea-covered guides is a nuisance. Finally, the bedding must be capable of withstanding a night of severe weather,—wet, snow, and tempest.

These desiderata were well fulfilled by a contrivance I became acquainted with during the very close of my stay in the Pyrenees, when, I am sorry to say, it was hardly in my power to give it a fair trial. I must, therefore, speak from hearsay and the experience of others. I found a large class of men who were liable, at any hour, in any weather, to be ordered off to any place in the mountains, there to keep watch for two or three days; while everything was so systematized, that they simply had to take down a sort of large knapsack from their shelf, certain specified articles of dress, and a sufficiency of bread, meat, and wine, and were ready in a minute to be off to their post. These are the French douaniers, who go in twos, to watch any pass where a smuggling attempt may happen to be expected by their chief; and the contrivance which makes it possible to do so, is a sheepskin sleeping bag, of a kind I am about to describe, which folds up in the simplest manner possible, and is secured by five small straps. When so folded and secured, it shapes itself into a large, but military-looking knapsack, weighing seven pounds and a half. The bag is shown bottom upwards in Fig. 1. It is open from D to the end, and its coffin shape makes it fit a man without any superfluous space. Fig. 2 represents a gusset inserted between the top and bottom faces of the bag, of which the edge *c d* is sewn to the upper edge from C to D, and *c e* is sewn to the lower edge from C to E. This is very important, in order to give sufficient space to the breast and arms. The peculiar shape of the gusset gives an exceedingly cozy lay to the machine, about the back and sides. It is easy to spring in a moment out of a bag thus constructed, there being no embarrassment whatever at the sides or shoulders. In folding it up—the bag, of course, lying on the ground, with its upper side uppermost, and not as shown in the drawing—is folded

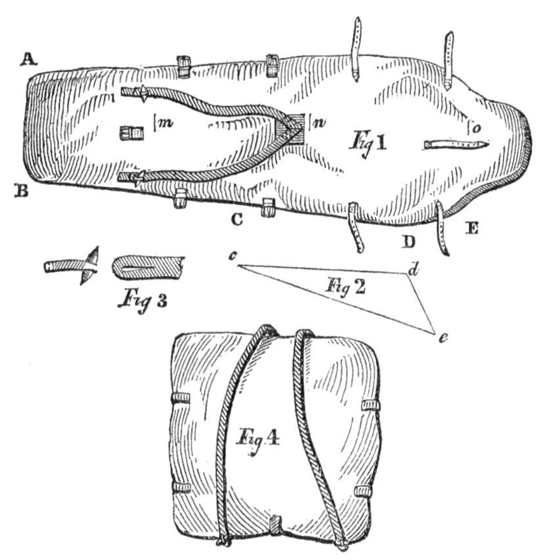

at *m* : again, first at *o*, and secondly, at *n*. Then it assumes the appearance of Fig. 4 (which, unluckily, has been drawn on rather too large a scale). Next, the straps are buckled to the corresponding buckles, the arms are slipped into the straps, and off walks the douanier, with his house on his back. Fig. 3 represents the fastening actually used for the knapsack straps, shown on a smaller scale in Fig. 1. I strongly suspect it is the best for these rude purposes. The left-hand part is a piece of wood, round which a thong is sewn. This makes the button. Two or three button-holes are cut in the corresponding knapsack strap. From the time when a man is lying fully dressed, shoes and all, inside one of these bags, to that when he has begun to march off with it, strapped upon his back, need not exceed ninety seconds. It is an invention, as I was informed, of about twenty-five years standing, and has, alone, rendered it possible to watch this mountain frontier with regularity and strictness. The Spaniard Customs' men, on their side, use cloaks, and cannot approach to the effectiveness of the French. The French douaniers seemed to speak with great fondness of their bags. They make them themselves, and they last many years. It is easy to buy one that has been more or less used, at a cost of about fifteen shillings. The average stature of a Frenchman is so much less than our own, that I did not meet with one large enough to shelter my shoulders and neck, and I did not care to make an imperfect experiment. For my own part, I abominate sheepskin, and bearskin, and buffalo robes, and carosses of all descriptions. They have great merits for rough work in a dry climate, but much wet reduces them to a miserably soppy state, and it is impossible to keep furs pure and moth-free without continued use. I much prefer some sort of waterproof, whether oiled linen or mackintosh, as an outside, and blanketing or home-spun cloth, within. It is heavier, and much more expensive, but I believe far the better of the two. I have had one made with a double blanket bag within ; this can be withdrawn, and simply laid on the waterproof for indoor use ; again, one can lie under one or two blankets at pleasure, according to the heat of the weather: from the slight trial I made, I should fear the heat of the sheepskin bags on a warm night. If I have another bag, I shall use *coarse* plaid, or home-made Welsh cloth instead of blanket. A soft weight strapped on the back is undoubtedly oppressive, and I think it is open to question, whether the bag would not be carried easier if it were attached to a wicker-work frame, placed between it and the back. Neither wind nor wet can hurt a sleeper inside his mackintosh cover. They are not oppressive to sleep in, as a slight half-unconscious fidgetting will pump out the used air, and re-supply it with fresh. Besides, the skin of a man who has been perspiring all day in a rare air, is incomparably more quiescent at night than that of a sedentary citizen. During the day-time the bags are of use, for the douaniers sit with them pulled up to their waist, when the weather is wet or cold. At night they take off their shoes, but nothing else, and wrap a small cloak round their heads and shoulders. The sheepskin is that of the beautiful merino sheep; it is double at the feet and legs, and also in the small of the back; those are the places where the cold is most felt.

Numerous travellers have used sleeping-bags, and there is no novelty in the fact of their rain-proof capabilities, but the way of folding them into a knapsack in place of carrying them in a cumbrous roll, is new and well worthy of record: so also is the fact that the high snow regions may be securely braved in one of them. Of course an Alpine man would prove his sleeping gear on low heights before risking himself on higher ones. The addition of a light tent, like an half-opened book, with one end closed by a triangular piece, and the other closeable with flaps, would give increased security against tempestuous weather. Such a tent, made of calico or holland, need not exceed six pounds in weight, and could be supported by aid of two alpen stocks.

Next, as to food. That usually taken by mountain climbers is assuredly far from the best. In the first place, the guides, the hotel-keepers, and, in part, the tourists themselves, think the occasion should be one of feasting. They take all kinds of absurdities. They also commit another mistake in the opposite direction by confining themselves to cold things, which agree with few stomachs: if they take warm things, it is chiefly tea or coffee. Now tea, hot or cold, is exceedingly refreshing in the middle of the day, and, to a certain degree, in the evening; but its influence in producing restlessness and sleepless nights, is powerfully increased by the conditions of an ordinary Alpine bivouac, viz. excitement, snoring guides, hard bed, pure air, and fleas. I believe all beyond a very small quantity of tea, coffee, and the rest of that genus, to be a mistake, in night bivouacs. This year, at first unknowingly, and afterwards experimentally, I made abundant experiments on this subject, making a good deal of coffee, chocolate, or tea habitually, in the middle of my longer walks, and in a couple of night bivouacs. I myself sleep through almost anything, but I felt its influence when I thought about it, and my companions complained of it.

I will venture to give two tables of rations, such as can be bought in any foreign market-place, calculated on Dr. Christison's principle, as containing 30 oz. of real nutriment per man, per day; of which 7½ oz. is nitrogenous, and 22½ carboniferous. When bread is mentioned, I should advise solid stuff, such as the peasantry use, not dinner rolls. (I say nothing about eggs, for I do not know their practical dietetic value.)

A.	Ounces.	Grammes.	B.	Ounces.	Grammes.
Bread	32	900	Bread	22	620
Cheese	6	170	Lean Meat	22	620
Butter	4	110	Butter	6	170
Sugar	2	60	Sugar	3	80
2 lbs. 12 oz. =	44		3 lbs. 5 oz. =	53	

Allow 4 oz. in addition, for pepper, salt, onion, tea, and a little milk.

The meat may be carried in either of three ways:—

1. Roasted or baked, but underdone; it may then be eaten without further cooking, or else it may be cut into slices, and *broiled* over the embers of a fire.

2. Ready cut into slices, to be *fried* in butter, in a frying-pan.

3. Ready chopped into lumps, the size of a walnut, to be thrown into boiling water, which must be removed in two minutes from off the fire, and afterwards be kept gently simmering, for half an hour. This makes broth and *boiled* meat, and is the most congenial sort of food to a man's stomach after hard work. The receipt is Liebig's.

A soup maigre, very good after much perspiration, is concocted in five minutes by boiling water, with slices of onions, and adding salt and pepper, and plenty of slices of bread, just before taking it off the fire: this is commonly used in the Pyrenees.

The frying-pan may be small, and like a very large soup-ladle, but is not wanted, except for No. 2, and for making omelets. The same vessels in which the meat, butter, &c. is packed (loaves of bread require no envelope), do well for fetching water, and for boiling purposes, while their lids serve as plates, or cups. They should be of thin tin, cylindrical, eleven inches high, and four and a half in diameter; they might be slipped, end to end, in a long woollen bag, and lie at the top of the knapsack. Their lids ought to be fitted much like the tops of pill-boxes, with rings, that shut flat, to take hold by. The handles of the vessels should be of wire, like bucket-handles, but two to each tin, for the convenience of holding them steady, when pouring out their contents. When not in use, they should fall closely back against the sides of the tin. A large spoon is almost necessary. For the convenient making of tea, place, before starting, a quantity of it, with its corresponding sugar, in a muslin bag; drop this, when you want to use it, in a tin of boiling hot water: let it stand the usual time, then pull out the bag, and the tea is made. Throw the bag away.

Finally, butter is carried conveniently in small tin or zinc boxes. Pepper and salt should be wrapped in rag, not only in paper, which always tears; it should also go in a small tin box. Milk, for tea, in a phial.

Now, as three days' rations of A. weigh about 8 lbs. and of B. 10 lbs., and reckoning 10 lbs. for the sleeping-bag, and 1 lb. for the tin vessels, or from 19 to 21 lbs. in all, it is evident that, allowing for wine carried in mackintosh or leather bags (which is an excellent way of carrying it, after the bags are once well seasoned for use), spare stockings, and a few fancy extras, 25 lbs. gross weight ought to suffice a man for three entire days. A practical English pedestrian would carry this up hill for half a day without suffering: a native porter would think nothing of it. I therefore conclude that a man with a couple of guides so equipped, and with the occasional help of a porter, might push his expeditions with ease and leisure to places he now can barely reach, even with severe exertion.

Also, that he can use the shelter of any cabin, or wretched inn, without fear of damp, and with the comfort of his own bedding. Perhaps some volunteers, mad upon bivouacking, may be inclined to try these bags. They would, I really believe, if carried in carts, or by an assistant peasantry, be no unimportant equipment for home campaigning against an invading army, and could be used with, or without, tents or house accommodation.

13. *SYRIAN TRAVEL, AND SYRIAN TRIBES.*

BY THE HON. RODEN NOEL.

MUCH attention having of late been directed to Syria, perhaps one or two rapid sketches of Syrian travel, with special reference to the inhabitants, may not prove uninteresting. After a protracted journey in Egypt, in company with Mr. Cyril Graham, I left Cairo for Syria, April 1, 1859, and continued in that country until 1860. Through the Delta of Egypt I passed into the Desert, which realizes the popular notion—not consisting, like many others, of hardened gravel powdered over with black scoriæ, but of deep, loose, yellow sand, in which a horse often finds much difficulty in walking, and where the camel, with his flat fleshy foot, is best adapted to the work. Extraordinary and not to be forgotten are these desert scenes. Breathless and cloudless is the blinding sky, as the traveller marches over sheets of deep loose sand, whose smooth mountain-mounds (for it is not always a plain) lie in the hollow blue crystal of the sky like cream-coloured snow; it and all things penetrated with that peculiar desert glare, or rather *unnatural light* (I know no other word), which in a picture would infallibly be called exaggerated. What makes it peculiarly trying to the eyes is, that while the forms of things are indistinct, and all the atmosphere seems vibrating, like the hot air over a lime-kiln (which produces mirage), yet all the colours are painfully vivid and hot; not toned down or softened in the dry atmosphere. A long file of camels comes silently over the brow of some sandy mound, looking gigantic and unearthly; their shadows cutting hard and black into the ground, their long heads and noses laid out flat upon the air, looking like strange visions of a dream; their bright head-geared and flowing-robed drivers seated upon them, and bending their bodies drowsily to the long swinging walk of the camel. Some few black sheep, driven by Bedawy over the desert, look like hard inky blots on the sand. The traveller plods on mechanically, not daring to look upward; as the author of Eôthen says, "feeling the sun his enemy," with its intolerable burn ever upon his head and back. Everything swims in the painful light. Dreamily he sees the camels and their drivers heaving forward through the dreary silence, relieved only by the occasional gurgle of half-emptied water in the barrels, which is like a refreshing hint to him of deep wells glimmering cool in the shadow, and plashing water drawn from them for drinking under the palms. Passing through the beautiful Philistia, I crossed the Judæan hills to Jerusalem. The hills, though barren, are covered with picturesque villages, with the house of the local chief, or Sheikh-el-Beled, in the midst; and he it is who administers justice, rather according to traditional usage than according to written law. He again is subject to the governor of the district, whose government consists (he having bought his office) in encouraging the rivalries of local chief families, and in appointing to the local headship the chief who can bribe highest. Thus Mr. Porter, whose handbook (*Murray*) contains the best general information on Syria, relates that a man was appointed to the governorship of a district in South Lebanon, by Mohammed Pasha, of Damascus. On his way to undertake his duties, a rival met him and killed him, and then wrote to the Pasha to inform him of this trifling occurrence. "No matter," replied the Pasha, "send me a hundred purses, and name what governor you please."

The Syrian peasantry, however, are a fine race, brave, shrewd, and industrious; they have great love for colour in dress, and display it very tastefully. They are handsome, tall, healthy, athletic; and wear endless daggers, dirks, and pistols, often handsomely mounted, in their broad red leather belts. A turban wound round a tarbûsh, or fez, is the usual headdress; whereas the Bedawy of the desert wear the kufiêh, a brilliant silk scarf, that hangs down behind, to protect the back of the neck, the part most susceptible of sunstroke, and the shoulders; and in order to save their mouths and faces from the fierce heat that radiates from the ground (which is as dangerous and disagreeable as the direct rays), they fold one end of the kufiêh so as to veil the whole of their faces, except the eyes. This also serves in the desert to conceal their faces in case they meet a foe. No Arab ever rides up to a strange encampment not thus concealed; nor is it etiquette for a host to bid him uncover.

The Moslems of the towns are a vicious, degraded set of men, whose religion has degenerated into a mere bigoted intolerance to all others, and a slavish observance of forms, which they believe will secure them immunity from the displeasure of Allah in the commission of any crime; and Allah is pleased rather than displeased with crimes committed against Nazarene dogs, in so far, at least, as the offence is committed cleanly—not in a bungling way, calculated to favour the chance of discovery and retaliation; even then, many sheikhs, dervîshes, and zealous Moslems assert that the punished man is a martyr. For why? Allah has a chosen people, the believers in Islâm. Infidel dogs are to burn for ever in the next world; but whatever the crimes of the faithful, *they* shall be finally restored. And the way to gain the favour of Allah is not so much by goodness, as by minute attention to religious ceremonies, enjoined in the Korân, and in the Sonnas or traditions. It is just the old Jewish spirit: "We are the children of Abraham, and wear broad our phylacteries; scouted be the impious notion that God can care for Gentiles." "Ye devour widows' houses, and for a pretence make long prayers."

The opinion of many Pagan races has been, and is, that if they neglect the rites enjoined on them by the Supreme Power, it must be *propitiated* even by the sacrifice of all that is dearest to them, a son or a daughter. However horrible this may be, we can believe that some have felt in doing so that they were right in thus giving up their own selves to the Supreme Will; but no such self-sacrifice can be implied in the mere washings and bowings which the Moslem thinks sufficient. The favouritism of his god makes it superfluous. While the heathen makes his deity unbending and revengeful, the Moslem makes his easy and indifferent in reference to those whom his caprice has favoured, and cruel to others. The Moslem faith has not always been so corrupt. There are drinking-fountains, and the remains both of Khans (vast inns, where poor travellers were lodged gratis), and of other charitable institutions, to attest the benevolence and generosity of Moslem princes and men of wealth in former days; but they are ruins. Mohammed and his legions conquered, strong in the faith and assertion of the supreme will of the one good God, who would have all men to be like him, by obeying his righteous precepts; alike strong against the empty formalism of the Jew, and the degrading idolatry of both Pagan and Christian. And so the old effeminate crumbling empires fell before the fierce warriors of the Crescent, simple in their habits and manner of life, brave, hardy, and inspired with religious zeal.

It is indeed impossible to read the Korân without perceiving how much that is true and excellent the prophet had imbibed both from Jew and Christian, while protesting against their formalism and idolatry. But this faith has degenerated into fatalism, for the most part the creed of those who have lost the healthy energy and strength of their own characters.

One is at first inclined to be pleased with the absence of false shame that characterises the Moslem in the regular performance of his devotions—so different to what is common among ourselves. When I landed at Alexandria, the first thing that struck me, was the sight of a camel, and his master kneeling on a prayer-carpet by him, sitting on his heels, as is the custom, telling his beads, bowing forward now and then, and touching the earth with his forehead. Striking also is the manner in which the Moslem never positively asserts that he will do a thing, but qualifies his expression by, "If God will." But one soon discovers that his devotion is too often a substitute for common honesty, and that the greater the saint the greater the sinner, contriving to be both at the same moment. Their dervishes and holy men, at whose tombs they pray, and who evidently hold the place that saints do, with the most ignorant and superstitious among Roman Catholics, have generally been greater rascals than the generality of their fellows while living. To illustrate this subject, I will relate something that I saw in Egypt. Our sailors asked permission to stop the vessel we had engaged to take us up the river, at a certain town, as they wished to pay their respects to a sheikh or dervîsh there. We gave it, and went ashore with them. Only a little way from the landing-place, and surrounded by a crowd of devotees, sate a hideous, wizened figure, that was so frightfully like a baboon, that one shuddered. He was old, shrivelled, and naked; he squatted by a fire, the embers of which he stirred with a stick; his filthy, grizzled beard, and matted hair, were covered with ashes; he had a low, cunning, brutal face, and small, leering eyes; he rocked himself and mumbled prayers, occasionally putting out a claw, which the infatuated bystanders kissed.

Returning to the ship, I asked his story. Our dragoman, an intelligent Moslem, replied, that he had been a robber, and had murdered two people barbarously.

"Then how did he escape justice?"

"By becoming a dervîsh," he answered. "The people then would not allow him to be touched."

"What good actions, then, has he done as a dervish?"

"Oh, none. But he is partly mad, and madness with us is sacred. Besides, he has supernatural powers. He puts his hand into the mouths of crocodiles, and they do not hurt him: and his touch can cure diseases. For his devotion is great."

Thus, a man stained with crime, by feigning semi-madness, and performing religious conjuring-tricks and antics, not only escapes punishment, but is venerated as a saint, gets his living, and is canonized when he dies.

This people have a uniform tendency to consecrate the deformed, the monstrous, and strange. It speaks to them of the supernatural; the mysterious supreme power or fate, which it is well to conciliate.

Though the Moslem fatalism may have been exaggerated as to its practical results, it does lead to deplorable consequences—very obvious to any intelligent visitor of these countries. The degradation of the national character has, doubtless, caused this degradation of the creed; but this again reacts on the character. You find that their professional men are, for the most, mere empirics, and seldom even intelligent empirics. There is little of native science, properly so called, among them. As to their arts, such of them as remain (and they are mostly decaying) are purely traditional. There is no belief that men, by reverent and patient study of natural laws, may adapt them to the improvement of their own condition, far less any interest in the study as such.

With us, the man who knows nothing of book-learning, at least becomes empirically wise respecting those natural phenomena that concern his profession. The sailor is weatherwise. But an Egyptian Nile sailor, though sharp and active enough in other respects, yet sees the same phenomena uniformly following one another, without ever perceiving their connexion: so that if you ask whether there are indications of wind in this quarter or in that, or any simple question concerning common river phenomena, he answers for ever, "God knows,"—never calculates on a probable occurrence, takes no measures to provide for it, and when he suffers loss in consequence, shrugs his shoulders with, "It was the will of God."

But of all Moslem races, probably the Turks are the most degraded. They have all the Oriental vices, their chief talent lying in cleverly simulating to be and to know all that they are not, and know not, which they often contrive by the expedient of looking wise, and preserving a dignified silence:

none greater adepts in the "Nil admirari," and in the noble art of affecting superiority to the vulgar necessity of learning. The indifferentism so much prized by some as a badge of "high breeding," is theirs to perfection. Their finesse, their tact in discovering and playing upon weaknesses, their assumed frankness and generosity, are marvellous. Well was it for us that we so long had at head-quarters a man who understood their character so thoroughly as Lord Stratford de Redclyffe. And I believe it will be proved that our present ambassador, Sir H. Bulwer, has acted with kindred intelligence, judgment, and vigour, in the present crisis. I must own, indeed, I found all those Turks in high office with whom I happened to come in contact, what the world calls courteous gentlemen. But Europeans living among these Moslem races are much discouraged. They do not keep faith with each other, much less with Christians. They seem, in most cases, insensible to kindness, and deficient in gratitude. They say that a Christian who does them kindnesses involving self-sacrifice, is but an instrument in the hand of Allah, to benefit his elect; and so it is to Allah, and not to the poor Giaour, the elect should be grateful.

The name of God is always upon their lips. The vendors of sherbet and fruits in the streets of Cairo and Damascus cry, "May God enable me to sell this well!" When friends meet, they utter a series of salutations, in which the name of God is always used. Also when a camel trips, they exhort him "to mind his steps, to go on, and put his trust in God." They will utter the most fearful imprecations, in which the name of God is also mixed, on man and beast. "Out of the same mouth truly proceed blessings and cursings." Yet the fact was once nobly significant, that the Arabic word, "I hope," "*Inshallah*," meant, "If God will," even as our own good-bye meant, "God be with you." Their compliments to one another, or to strangers, are astonishing. "All that I have is yours." "Whose is this house?" you ask the owner; "Yours," he insists. You admire this article, and however costly,—"It is yours, pray take it." Awkward strangers sometimes take them at their word, much to the disgust of the courteous Turk. However, they often do give handsome presents, but generally expect to gain some greater advantage by so doing, besides the present which etiquette obliges you to make in return.

It may be thought, perhaps, that I am unduly darkening this picture. I readily admit that the people in general have their virtues, especially some of the races, and there are noble exceptions in every race. The Nile sailors, for example, I had a great liking for. They are cheerful, hardy, and active, and kind to one another; and the poorest Moslem seldom passes a beggar in the street without relieving him. If he is unable he says, "May God relieve you." And in the recent massacres in Damascus, some of the more respectable Moslem inhabitants, it must be remembered, afforded protection to the Christians. The Emir Abd-el-Kader stands out, especially, as a noble instance. Now he is a decided Moslem. He is Professor in the Theological School of Damascus, and his opinion is much esteemed by large sections on theological matters. He is a rare specimen of those Mohammedans who lived before religion became a dead form; when salutations in the name of God had a real meaning; when men had faith in the living, good God. A man like Abd-el-Kader is worth a million of those Hindoo or Moslem gentlemen, such as Nana Sahib, who have been educated in European capitals, and received European instruction, without having imbibed the Spirit of Christianity. Our civilization has but torn from their souls the lingering faith that might have been sheltered under the creed of their race. That creed was so involved with physical problems or ceremonial observances, that we could not teach them our civilization without oversetting that. Do we think they acquired greater respect for us? What have they seen—what have we taught them—that we should suppose so? No! the bad is not eradicated as easily as the good. The old prejudices fostered by the old creed remained. They were not dispelled by the tone of society in Paris or London—strange, perhaps; yet, nevertheless, so it was—or by the conduct of Europeans with whom they came in contact abroad: for instance, by our policy and conduct toward them personally in India. They were, perhaps, fostered by familiarity with vice under novel, and to an Oriental, stimulating forms; for fellowship in evil does not really draw men together, but insensibly separates them. They lost all faith in God, and all regard for man.

It may be better to leave them without what we are pleased to term "civilization," if we shrink from showing to them that Saviour and Regenerator of the world for whom all humanity is panting. Let Nana Sahib be a specimen of the civilized enlightened Moslem. Let Abd-el-Kader be a specimen of the good uncivilized Moslem who retains his faith. I had the pleasure of seeing him at Damascus, and was much struck both with his appearance and conversation. His face and bearing indicate that remarkable combination of the man of action and the man of thought which is characteristic of him. He looks born to command in war and in council. Perhaps his face betokens a thinker whose trenchant logic would no more brook a metaphysical or theological mystery than the sword of Alexander the intricacies of a Gordian knot. He is said to be a man of original thought and independent opinions

In point of externals, the manner of any Oriental of rank is on the whole superior to the European, being less stiff than the English, and more dignified than the French, while his *petite morale* (his etiquette) embodies far more delicacy of tact than does that of European society in general. I suspect that, like Hajji Baba, in Morier's clever Eastern tale, any one of these Orientals might pass with us for a prince, so far as manner goes, even imposing on better judges than Mrs. Hogg and her "two head of daughters."

Expedition to Palmyra.—Some English ladies and Mr. Carl Haag (who in his picture of the Temple of the Sun, exhibited last year, has so successfully given the burning of the sunset into that fine transparent limestone), were my companions on this expedition. It may be considered no slight feat for ladies to ride ten, twelve, and twenty-four hours on camel back at a stretch, but indomitable English pluck can accomplish much. Sheikh Mignel, of the Anazi Bedawy, accompanied us, and furnished us with an escort. His kindness and courtesy were unvarying. He guarantees you from robbery on the part of any divisions of his own great tribe, one of the most powerful, on the payment to him of a heavy tribute, though not, of course, from the attacks of tribes hostile to his. As Tadmor is the one watering place in that great desert for all the Arab tribes who are usually scouring about in search of plunder, the journey can never be made without some risk; but it is in every respect a most interesting one. Having traversed an arid desert during so many burning weary hours, it is on surmounting a ridge of hills that the ruins burst on you. Unrivalled is that view: a city of temples, palaces, arches, colonnades, with the stupendous pile of the Temple of the Sun in the midst. As you sweep down the hills in among these deserted streets of columns, where the wind of centuries has heaped the sand, and now wails mournfully where once Zenobia drove and rode in triumph; as your eye ranges over the trackless waste of desert, and looks back to the purple mountains of noble form, against which many a fair column of golden stain stands relieved; as you watch the weird figures of your mounted Arabs, like winds incarnate, galloping among the ruins, shouting wildly, and charging one another with quivering lance in mimic fight, turning it gracefully, and wheeling their steeds in circle—all weariness ceases. You feel not the burning sun; there is a glow within your spirit, which expands to overflowing with the mingled sense of such departed human glory—such wild lawlessness and desolation triumphant now—such calm everlasting grandeur of Nature—and you could not tell why you weep. Those desert scenes are not to be forgotten. Oft will they come before the inward eye. When wearied with the long day's ride, the sheikh gave the word to halt for a few hours' rest on the yet warm sand, the camels would kneel, a bivouac fire would be lighted, the Arabs dismount from their mares, and gather round the flame, with its ruddy glow on their swarthy features and gay coloured dress, their lances planted upright in the sand, black against the brilliant orange of the evening sky, into which distant mountains rose "wine-empurpled." The freshness of the air, the sense of freedom, on those limitless plains—especially if you happen to be mounted on a swift Arab mare! However, for a long desert ride, I think the camel less fatiguing than the horse; and contrary to the assertion of some, that its quick, swinging walk is very easy. You can change your position on the saddle. We did not much relish, indeed, having the driver on the camel's back immediately behind us, for no remonstrances could prevent him indulging in his favourite amusement of prolonging a monotonous note whenever the camel trotted, which quavered harshly in one's ears with the rough motion of the animal. But when the camels got tired, the drivers would dismount, and joining hands, walk by the side, singing in chorus, "Go on, good camel, and then the fairest maidens of the village shall make thee kneel, and give thee thy food:" at which the good patient beasts really pricked up their ears, and strode on lustily. We were six days at Palmyra—unusually long—and there being a great scarcity of food, our poor camels had little, so that day by day we saw their humps diminishing. In the absence of food, they feed on their own fat, even as they drink the water they have stored in their second stomach. Then the other Arabs got wind of us, and we had to leave. How luxurious were those nights, wrapt in our cloaks, and sleeping under the open clear starry sky of Syria. Tents are forbidden, as you must be prepared to be up and off at a moment's notice. We were often forced to travel in the moonless parts of the night only, and then forbidden to speak or light a pipe, constantly on the look out for the flicker of bivouac fires afar. When the moon did rise, then the shadows of camel and rider blent were suddenly thrown on the pale sand, moving on, swift, silent, ghostly, and soon we crouched into some depression or wady, fireless; or if a fire was for a few minutes allowed, the Arabs squatted round it, and covered it with their broad Abâyeh cloaks. But in spite of some pleasantly exciting alarms, we arrived at Damascus without attack. I was most kindly received and tended through a fever I caught there, in the house of Mr. Graham, the Missionary, who was murdered in the recent massacres, and whose loss all who knew him most deeply deplore. My excellent friend Mr. Robson, the Missionary, whose own conduct during the massacre was so firm and praiseworthy, wrote that he died a martyr. It was proposed to him by his murderers, as a condition of safety, that he should renounce Christianity; and when he refused, he was at once dispatched.

When you visit a Bedawy Sheikh, if he wishes to do you honour, he has a sheep immediately slaughtered, which you eat out of a huge bowl, together with pilaw of rice, with your fingers: afterwards, black slaves bring you water and wash your hands with an embroidered napkin. While it is preparing, they bring coffee and pipes, and the wife makes ready an unleavened thin cake, which is excellent hot. You get delicious camel's milk, Leban (sour milk), and sometimes cucumbers, and every kind of gourd. While you eat, the sheikh, as a point of etiquette, refuses to enter the tent. He watches you from outside. At night he gives you his own cloaks to cover you, often very magnificent, but always swarming with vermin. The sheikh usually wears a crimson pelisse, edged with fur, and high red leather boots. But his tent does not differ from those of other Arabs. It is of black goat's hair, open one side. In many encampments, a curtain is hung up to divide the harîm from the tent of the men; and I have seen women sitting working tapestries or spinning, in the tent of the men, and joining in the conversation. They are far more virtuous than other Moslem women, and far less frivolous. They are not so strictly kept separate; and the laws that punish immorality are stern and stringently enforced. It shows a slight knowledge of human nature to suppose that any class of Moslem women are mere mindless playthings, in the sense of being without influence. But their false social position makes their influence too often *bad.* To some extent the

Bedawy occupy the position of the early Mohammedan conquerors, having many of their virtues and habits of life. They are simple, brave, patriarchal, hospitable. But they are false, often cruel, childishly covetous. It should be remembered, however, that there have always been two distinct Arab races, the dwellers in towns, and the wandering Bedawy. Now people talked at the time of the Syrian massacre of a new invasion of Barbarians, and of Damascus being at the mercy of the Arabs. So it has been for many years past; but the truth is, nothing would induce them as a body to avail themselves of their power to occupy this city or any other. They might plunder,—as they did. They have long overrun the plains, and the Turks have less weight in their eyes than the passing traveller. But see an Arab in a town, and in his native desert. You would not know him for the same man. Can yonder slouching, humble-looking creature, be one with that proud, fierce, erect, and dignified chief, sniffing the air like the impatient wide-nostrilled mare he bestrides?

He abhors the confinement of a house, and all the luxuries appertaining thereunto. His wealth consists of herds of camels, and mares, or flocks of goats and sheep. The Patriarchs were a sort of Bedawy; and the account of Oreb and Zeeb, Princes of Midian, whom Gideon defeated at the fountain of Jezreel, reads like a description of the hordes that range over the plain of Esdraelon to this day. They refuse to cultivate the rich land they roam over, and they drive away the diligent tiller, oppressing and living upon him. A voyage I made through the Arab tents by a very unfrequented path from Cæsarea to Nazareth, made the Old Testament accounts of the thickness of the population more intelligible to me. The site of a town or village unidentified presented itself within incredibly short distances—likewise in an unexplored part of Phœnicia, where the remains of Phœnician buildings, of so-called Cyclopean masonry, were very remarkable.

Of these interesting localities I will just say a few words. We crossed the Nahr Turka (Crocodile River of Strabo). I could get but the vaguest tradition about the crocodiles from any Arabs on the spot. "Have you seen them?" "No." "But my father"—"Has seen them?" "No. But he was told by a man that"—"He had seen them?" "No; but that watering his flocks on a certain day near here (we were at a woody place called Miemes), several sheep were drawn under, no doubt by the Timsäh (Crocodile)." In this stream there can scarcely have ever been anything but large water-lizards.

We came, at length, to Tell Kisah, where there are hewn cisterns, many rock tombs, and extensive mounds. The place, an important one, seems not to have been identified. Was it Kishion (or Kedesh) of Issachar? (See Josh. xxi. 28; I Chron. vi. 72). Having mentioned Kedesh, may I be permitted to say a word on the Ruins at Kedesh Naphteli (Cæsarea Philippi) beyond Nazareth, between Safed and Banias? This, the holy place of Naphtali was the birthplace of Barak, and near here Sisera was slain. (Judg. iv.) The ruins are interesting. It has been disputed whether they are Jewish, or Roman. There are fine old stone sarcophagi, some of them double. I believe Dr. Robinson inclines to think them Jewish. On the other hand, Mr. Porter asks—How, then, can we explain the "figures" (of gods or genii) sculptured on their sides? Now I looked for these figures, but *could not find them.* The sculpture is all much defaced, and in the elucidation of it much depends on the light, and time of day; I thought, however, I could make out the body of a bird; next, finding *an eagle sculptured with outspread wings* over one of the portals of the temple beyond, I returned to the sarcophagi, and distinctly traced the same device on them. The figures, then, are eagles. Now from the style of architecture there can be little doubt that this temple is Roman. Some friends and I subsequently discovered there a small bas-relief figure of a man wearing the toga; and made our servants dig out an old altar, on whose face there had been an inscription, now entirely illegible; but one or two letters left little doubt in my mind that it was in Greek. The eagle seems, then, to be the Roman eagle, and this goes far towards settling the question. The first ruin appears to have been a tomb, and may not be of the same date and origin.

As to Jewish Remains, there are few of importance in Palestine. The most perfect and interesting are at Kefr Birim, between Safed and Tyre. The front of an old synagogue is nearly perfect; the Jewish architecture is very peculiar; the treble column seems most characteristic of it. The capitals of each pillar are like the Torus and Plinth reversed. The mouldings are elaborate and fantastic, though poorly executed. One may be called the vertebrate style. I do not see any analogy between this building and those at Kedesh.

And now, a word respecting the Phœnician Remains of this district.

I was anxious to examine a rock tablet, which Mr. Porter speaks of as *Assyrian*, (on hearsay, I think,) near El Megrâh, a village near Cana, in the Mountain above Tyre. I found it to be *Egyptian*. It is much defaced. But the *Agathodæmon* over the whole group is unmistakeable; there is Disk, Uræus and wings. The king (or God) is seated on an Egyptian throne, and figures are presenting offerings; but they are nearly erased. Their slender Egyptian type and their head-dresses leave no doubt of their race.

The people here are Metawileh. Their Sheikh was profuse in his civilities, and gave me every assistance. With an Arab guide I explored the district around, and came upon numerous remains of old towns; the houses built of large, rough, irregular blocks, like the pedestal of the famous Sarcophagus of Hiram near Tyre. One could hardly make one's way through the dwarf oak that grew about the buildings. There were many gigantic portals, formed of two vertical blocks and another simply laid across them; the peculiar grooving of the jambs, together with the numerous millstones about, make it probable these may have been *olive-presses*, yet—curious fact—there are no olives in that country now.

In one case, a tree had rent the huge stone, and then died, leaving a fragment of itself between the lintel and jamb.

Meanwhile, a second old oak is luxuriating there and threatening to play the same prank. This impresses one with the idea of hoar antiquity. In one town I found a Jewish treble column among the older remains. Near it I visited a curious tomb, unlike any other rock-tombs I saw in Syria, though the variety of them is most remarkable. It is a chamber, small and square, hewn in the rock. On one wall was rudely scratched a disk, on another a character something like a capital Greek Gamma; on a third, a palm branch (the Phœnician emblem). How well would all this country repay exploration! It is very fine, the mountains are sublime, and the ravines are well wooded.*

I must not pause to describe Damascus, "the Queen of the East," of which so much has lately been said. On recovering from my illness in Beyrout, I rode by the magnificent ruins of Baalbek to Bludân, the Paradise of Anti-Lebanon, overlooking the fruitful Plain of Zebdary, where Mr. Brant, our consul, was staying, who was most kind to me, and whose energy and courage during the recent massacre at Damascus have been beyond all praise—demanding surely some substantial mark of appreciation from our Government. At Bludân there is a grove of prickly oak (Ballût) trees, a representation of one of those groves or high places so often mentioned in the Old Testament, as places of idolatrous worship. Astarte seems to have been the patroness of this one, for the people still follow the traditional usage of breaking a pitcher in honour of the "mother of the grove;" and they add that one man, who omitted to do this before starting for Damascus, was found strangled near the grove, doubtless by the mother herself. The superstitions of the Greek Christian peasantry are de-

* I got a sunstroke here that disabled me. I could scarcely ride so far as Tyre. Arrived there, a severe fever set in; but, by the kindness of our Vice-Consul at Tyre, I was placed in a felucca some days after, and then sailed in one night to Beyrout, where my life was saved by the care of friends, who (though strangers to me at that time) took me into their house. S. Broe, Esq. comptroller of the Ottoman Bank at that place, will, I trust, forgive my mentioning his name. His wife has proved a Miss Nightingale to many a traveller beside myself.

liberately encouraged by their priests, Astarte reappearing as Mary. On the eve of the fight at Beit Miri (August, 1859), there was an eclipse, and the people said the moon was "ominously struggling out of a nightmare of blood;" while at Bludân they were all shouting and striking pots and pans together, "to make the big fish disgorge her," which at last they succeeded in doing to their satisfaction.

The traveller, entering on the Lebanon from the plain of Bukâa, the ancient Cœlesyria, by Zahle, (the Christian town which has been lately decimated,) is much struck with the contrast between it and the Anti-Lebanon, which bounds the Bukâa on the east. That is rocky and desolate; but so soon as he enters on the Lebanon, he finds the mountains carefully terraced. Sometimes the soil is laid along the horizontal naked strata of limestone, sometimes along an artificial terrace of stones. Every inch of ground is made the most of; mulberries, for the sake of the silk crop, and vines, are universal. The latter are often trained along covered trellis-work, the rich luscious clusters depending from bowered sunny leaves. Figs are very frequent; so that the mountain combines excessive fertility, which pleasantly suggests the industry of the inhabitants, with unsurpassed sublimity. Those deep dark ravines over which the stone pines hang—those heights of grand wild form suggesting the landscapes of Salvator Rosa—with crests of rugged grey rocks, rising up height upon height to summits of perpetual snow! You ride along through groves of stone pine wherein the cicalas are ever shrill, over mere torrent-beds of paths as break-neck as can be; and beneath you are ledges of mountain, where gleaming villages and convents nestle in mulberries and vines. They stud every slope, every lower wooded crest, and the sweet convent chimes are ever floating over hill and valley. At every turn you meet gaily dressed peasants, Maronite or Druze, armed with a gun, or pistols and dirks in the folds of their sash, often driving mules with loads of cocoons. They wear full baggy trousers down to the knee, the leg bare, braided jackets with slashed sleeves, showing the bright coloured vestment beneath. The Druze women wear a silver horn on the head, called Tantûr; over this they throw a silk or linen veil which may cover them entirely, or be thrown back at pleasure. The Maronite women wear a silver head-dress, not unlike that of the Druzes, but less prominent: they wear very pretty ornaments. Beautiful from the mountain (from Beit Miri especially) is the view of Beyrout. It lies far below, on a tongue of rich cultivated land, washed by the far-smiling sapphire of the Mediterranean, its white clustered villas gleaming amid thick green-glowing orchards, and many scattered hamlets and convents on the plain and hill sides. Yet the view of it is perhaps more unique in loveliness from the sea approach, where it is backed by the plum-bloom piled mountains, and the snowy crests.

I will now give only a brief sketch of the Druzes and Maronites, confining myself chiefly to matters of personal observation.

It is not correct to say that the Druze religion is a secret, a full account of it having been published by M. De Sacy. There is much in it very mystical and metaphysical. Let me refer the reader to Lord Carnarvon's recent little book for a brief but excellent *resumé* of all the information we have on this subject and on the origin of the race. I will here state merely, that in A.D. 1017, Ben Ismail Ed-Derazz, a Persian, settled in Egypt, and became an adherent of Hakim, third Fatimiti Caliph, who, albeit a monster of iniquity, was proclaimed (and, perhaps, himself claimed to be) an Incarnation of the Deity. Derazz was driven out of Egypt, and took refuge in the neighbourhood of Mount Hermon, where he preached this doctrine among the people of the district. He thus gave his name to the Druzes; but yet, having subsequently proclaimed himself as a rival prophet, he is of the Druzes an object of execration. They regard the Persian Hamza as their true founder. He very much enlarged the system. They expect Hâkim, their Messiah, to come again to judgment, and reduce all to submission. It is with more reason alleged that their rites are secret. In company with a friend I visited the most celebrated of their chapels near Hasbeija, called Khulwât (solitudes). We found a council of Druze Okkâls sitting under some Ballûts (prickly oaks) on a stone divan. Their chief was a venerable man of ninety, with flowing white beard, but his bright blue eye told of unclouded intelligence. They were all patriarchs. They received us most courteously, and insisted on showing us over their chapel. It was spread with prayer-carpets. They next brought us in plates of raisins and pine-almonds, and begged us to be seated and partake of them, while a large congregation gathered round. On Thursday, when they assemble for worship in the early part of the evening, strangers are admitted, and partake of these eatables. Readers are squatted upon the floor, reading from the Korân, probably as a blind, to Moslems; but at a certain period strangers must retire, the Okkâls remaining alone. The question is, What do they do then? The sheikhs I have spoken to reply, "Nothing but pray, and read out of our own sacred books." It is commonly alleged that they worship a calf. Others say that the image of a calf enters into their rites, but that it is as a symbol of false religion, which they abhor; that it is a symbol of Iblis, the Evil Principle, or of Ed-Derazz. Others think that the calf story is a Maronite invention; for the direct evidence of the production of the image in worship seems to be furnished by Maronites, who are alleged to have gained access in disguise as Druzes to the Khulwât. On the face of it, this story is absurd to any one who knows the profound sagacity and caution of the Druzes. No Maronite would ever have got in, and if he had, he would never have got out to tell the tale. If we believe in the calf, we must believe more that comes from the same quarter. The Maronite Sheikh who told me about the calf said also that these disguised Christians saw a series of rude wooden images successively brought into the Okkâl assembly, flogged and spit upon with execrations, as representing the prophets of other religions. Among them were Mohammed, Moses, and Christ. Now Mohammed and Moses are regarded by the Druzes as prophets, while Christ and Hamza are incarnations of one of the five great celestial powers, who form a part of their system. (See De Sacy.) More than once have these Khulwât been plundered when the Druzes least expected it, and access obtained to their sacred books. But only sacred books were found; where then did they stow the calf and the images? In 1838, Ibrahim Pasha suddenly fell upon these very Khulwât near Hasbeiya, of which I have spoken above, and took away many Arabic MSS., but nothing else was found. Most important these MSS. proved; for in those which De Sacy had previously examined, there was a portion written in a species of cypher, containing, apparently, the innermost mysteries of the faith. To this cypher he had no clue; but the new MSS. contained its key in Arabic, and that accomplished oriental scholar, Dr. Van Dyck, has had access to them. I trust he will publish the results of his investigations ere long. He assured me he had found no trace of any idolatrous or impure rites, as among the Ismaeli and Ansayrii.

The Maronites, indeed, accuse them both of idolatry and atheism. Thus, the Sheikh I have mentioned above told me the learned Druzes assert that there was once a God, but he created a great wind, which carried him away; so he is for ever whirled round and round, powerless, in his own whirlwind. This is evidently the caricature of a myth. There is, indeed, a pantheistic element in their system, which, with some thinkers and teachers, may degenerate into atheism. It has been said, perhaps with some truth, that they are more a political than a religious body. Yet there is no reason to accuse them of atheism. They are a practical, energetic people; and the most remarkable and interesting feature of the race, is its perfect union and brotherhood. Every Druze is educated to feel himself the member of a body, and act as such, always making his private interest subordinate to that of the fraternity. He is trained in the most implicit obedience to his superiors; also to be silent or prevaricate when it is necessary. The Druzes are divided into Okkâl, initiated, and Juphal, ignorant. The former must profess to renounce all luxuries, even spirits and tobacco. They undergo a severe probation for two years, then assume the white turban. The Okkâls, on being initiated into Druze mysteries, are sworn not to reveal the Druze secrets. Towards each other, the Druzes practise the most generous virtues.

The body is governed by the Okkâls, they being the priest-governors who negotiate marriages, &c. The country is divided into districts, where a council of Okkâl assemble weekly. A delegate from each council is sent to each meeting of neighbouring councils. Thus, information and orders are transmitted in time of peace and war, with very great rapidity, from one spot to the other; and this enables the body to act in concert, and with all the effect of an union which constitutes strength, while the Maronites are singularly deficient in organization and discipline. These do not obey their chiefs, and are constantly quarrelling among themselves, even in the face of a common foe. This in great measure accounts for the easy victories of the Druzes over them last year, which is otherwise singular, seeing that they far outnumber the Druzes in Lebanon, the former being estimated at about 220,000 in the Pashalic of Sidon, and the latter at (Porter) only 60,000; especially as I do not believe the Christians to be deficient in physical courage. There are other things to be taken into account. There was a conviction (which the event justified) among the Christians, that the Moslems were everywhere about to act in concert with the Druzes, the Metawileh, and all other anti-Christian tribes, to exterminate them, which paralysed the Maronites. They believed (with perfect reason) that the Turks were aiding and abetting the designs of their foes; and yet, through a strange infatuation, partly to be explained by moral perplexity and fear, they trusted their lawful rulers so far, as on three successive occasions, at Hasbeiya, Rasheiya, and Deir-el-Kammar, to deliver up their arms to them, the Turks having solemnly promised them protection,—the Christians perhaps hoping that the fear of France would stay the Turks from any gross acts of treachery toward them. The result is known. History furnishes few parallels to the atrocious treachery in these three instances, practised by a government on the subjects who had obeyed and trusted it,—when the Christians were massacred in cold blood in the courts of the governor's castle, while Turkish soldiers guarded the gates. It is a notable fact, perhaps not very generally known, that when all of us in Syria were in momentary expectation of this war (in May last), the troops were sent out of Syria by the Pashas, on the plea of certain disturbances in Bosnia, so that the Turkish Minister in London could assure Lord J. Russell, that unfortunately there were no troops to act with.

The weak element in the Druzes is their *exclusiveness.* It is a *principle* with them to deceive those out of their own pale, for the advancement of the Druze interest. They do not seek converts—only to make the Druze race dominant. Towards enemies they have proved cruel and implacable. But, indeed, they are not the only mountain tribe who are guilty of this, though hospitable, generous, and virtuous in time of peace. This they are in a high degree. And former travellers speak of the good terms on which Maronite and Druze lived. They may probably share the same blood.

In the Pashalic of Damascus there are about 18,000 Druzes. There are great numbers in the Hawrân, the ancient Bashan, east of Damascus. Of these Mr. Porter says, "We are among a people of patriarchal manners, and patriarchal hospitality. Strangers cannot pass without being constrained to accept proffered hospitality: 'Will not my lord descend, while his servants prepare a little food?' is the urgent language of every village sheikh. The coffee (which is roasted, pounded, and boiled in the presence of the visitor) is always on the fire: a kid or lamb, representation of the old fatted calf, is soon got ready. One fancies himself carried back to the days of Abraham, when the good patriarch sat in his tent-door, ready to welcome every visitor, and hail every passer by." In fact, Eastern manners are everywhere permanent.

I shall not attempt to enter into the history of the Maronites (Mardaites), which may be found elsewhere; merely observing that their faith and rites agree pretty nearly with those of the rest of the Eastern Church, though in the twelfth century they submitted to the authority of the Pope. Their patriarch, who receives his Bull of Confirmation from Rome, resides in the convent of Canobûr, in the glen of the Kadîsha.

Many Maronite families have retained Frank names, which makes it probable that some of the Crusaders may have taken refuge and settled among them. They have long been under French protection; and French missionaries have done something toward their enlightenment.

I must own that, during my residence among them, though I respected the zealous and kindly labours of the Lazariste missionaries (at Ehden there were four or five), and admired their Roman Catholic Institutions, backed as they are by the powerful influence of their Government, yet I did not think the half-Frenchifying process had done much good to their manners; while it is to be feared that the Jesuits have fanned the flame of religious bigotry and fanaticism amongst them (as the emissaries of Russia have done for the Greeks), till they have been led to rely on the support of France, in case of a collision with their enemies.

We found the people unpleasantly curious and familiar, nor are they so energetic as the Druzes. Yet they are honest and brave, with fine frames and independent bearing. Our tents were always open, yet we never lost anything out of them.

We visited the largest of their convents, that of St. Antoine, situated, as most of them are, in a romantic glen (below Ehden), built into the clefts and sides of the rock, like the better-known Greek convent of Mar Saba, near the Dead Sea. The chapel, refectory, and cloisters were very venerable-looking and picturesque. Here there is a curious old printing-press, where some aged monks were engaged printing and binding some Syriac ecclesiastical MSS. (their ecclesiastical language being Syriac). Close to the convent is a gloomy old cavern, full of dark recesses, used as a madhouse, where they confine the insane and beat them into sanity—or, if Providence be merciful, as it more often is, to death. The shrieks of these poor maniacs, chained to the rock, echoing through these fearful twilight dungeons, are said to be terrible. If they can of themselves unhook the great chain that binds them, it is supposed to be a proof of their recovery. In some of the convents the chambers were subterranean, equally gloomy. The monks were for the most part dirty-looking *bon vivants*, of the order of St. Anthony. I visited, near St. Antoine, in the sides of the rock, the cells of two very old anchorites, but did not find their conversation specially edifying, and the caress one of them gave me with his blessing, in return for a silver coin, I did not duly appreciate, for the good fathers reeked of garlic.

At the village of Ehden, beautifully situated high in the Lebanon, near the celebrated Brotherhood of Cedars, where we spent some time, lives one of their principal Emirs, Yusuf Bey, of whom we saw much. I liked him greatly. He most kindly pressed us to stay in his castle, but we preferred our tents under the walnuts. His castle was conspicuous among the houses of the village—a strong baronial building, made for standing a siege, with small, deep sunk windows, double-arched, with a little pillar dividing the lights. He is much beloved by his people. He is famed for his oratory, and much deference is paid to his opinion, in these parts, both in political and social matters. He speaks French and Italian well. In many respects, you have among this people a living example of what society was among us in feudal times. The Emir is quite the old lord, or "*laford*," "loaf-giver" of ancient time. Yusuf keeps open house; his halls are crowded with the poorer mountaineers, who come nightly to partake of his bounty, and his table is spread for vast numbers. It is remarkable, that Yusuf Bey, so far back as August last year, prophesied exactly what has taken place in the mountain. The special design of the Turks in Lebanon, he said, was forcibly to overset the existing state of things, expressly guaranteed by treaty, between the Porte and the Western Powers: namely, that the Christians and Druze Sheikhs should govern their respective people independently; that Christians and Druzes respectively should be governed by their own Kaimakâns, or governors. The Pashas were always intriguing in the mountain, in order to depose the Christian Sheikhs, and appoint Turkish officials instead, even when they were not inciting the Druzes to violence. The Christian Kaimakân appointed by the Porte was in reality a Druze, though a pretended convert to Christianity; and his conduct plainly showed that he was the creature of Kurschid, the Pasha at Beyrout. On one occasion, when he had urged the expediency of Yusuf's resignation, on the plea that it would put a stop to local feuds, and give general satisfaction to that part of Lebanon, Yusuf *did* resign: but soon the mountaineers of all the district gathered round his palace, entreating him not to give them up to the tender mercies of the Turks. "What could I do?" he said to me. And so he resumed his hereditary position.

In conclusion, I will give a brief sketch of the affair at Beit Miri, 1859, which I witnessed, and which formed the commencement of these sad disturbances. I have already spoken of its romantic situation. The Europeans of Beyrout go there during the heat of summer. I took four bare walls, and furnished them from Beyrout. Some friends of mine, English ladies, were staying in the village, and had the best house. Mine belonged to a Greek priest, whose chapel my servants were fortunately able to save from plunder. The poor native women brought me their jewels and property to keep. I had a Maltese servant who was most kind in taking good care of it for them, and he devoted himself to ministering to their wants. (His name is G. Zarb. I can conscientiously recommend him as an excellent Dragoman and servant. He was with me a long time. He resides at Valetta.)

It was very difficult to get a correct version of the beginning of the affair, even though I was in the village, and as in the case of the massacres of 1860, it is impossible to say who fired the first shot, or gave the most immediate provocation; but so far as I can gather, it appears that two muleteers had a quarrel near Beit Miri, a Druze and a Maronite—and that the Druze got the worst of it. The Druzes of the place, therefore, insisted that the Christian should be given up to them to be punished. This the Christians would not consent to: so on Sunday, Aug. 7, 1859, they began firing on one another in the streets. After some time we could see Druze chiefs, with flowing white abbas (cloaks), riding among the pines below with a flag of truce, and Christian chiefs riding to meet them. But their parley came to nothing. The Bishop had before endeavoured to mediate, in vain. Then the Christians, being the most numerous, retired to their houses, chiefly to the flat-roofs, and the Druzes went down among the mulberry terraces below the hill on which the village stands, and a regular fight began. With these tribes, it is chiefly guerilla warfare, wherein man picks off his man. The firing lasted four hours. It was sharp and incessant. The Druzes were firing from behind mulberries and vines, whence every now and then a white puff of smoke issued. Their women stood by them with pitchers of water, giving them drink, and encouraging them. So, also, did the Christian women on the roofs of the houses, to their men, shrieking and waving their veils. The guns mostly in use were long Turkish ones, with gleaming brass-encircled barrels, and as I watched the Christians firing, from a ruined house near, I could see that the guns generally snapped four times for each shot that was fired. Some better guns (distributed by us, probably, in the time of Ibrahim Pasha) were, however, in use amongst them. It was a picturesque scene, but it became a sad one. You could see every now and then a man fall, and a wounded or dying man carried by. Altogether, on both sides, there were thirty killed and many wounded. The Druzes slowly crept up the terraces; at last the Christians gave way, and fled down the mountain in a body. They had no succours in view; while the Druzes were gathering from other villages, and the Christians feared they would be hemmed in if they remained. The Druzes celebrated their victory by sacking the Christian houses, in which they were joined by a handful of irregular soldiers whom the Pasha had sent up to stop the fighting (having well ascertained that it was all over), who took care to get their share of the plunder; and that night the Druzes sang their wild war-pæan, the burden of which we have since learned is—

"How sweet to shed the blood of Christians."

The contending parties were most anxious to make my house a place to fire from, and to take my powder, of which they knew I had a store; but being resolved to remain quite neutral, I could not accede to the wishes of either party; and when I intimated that their persistence would involve an act of personal hostility toward myself, they retired at length with many protestations of friendship; especially on being informed that they might send such of their women and wounded as the house would contain. Neither my friends nor myself suffered any discourtesy or molestation.

Some of the scenes I thus witnessed, were very heartrending, for the Eastern women are demonstrative in their grief. They sat on my open terrace, rocking themselves backward and forward, and moaning, having deposited their children within the house. The village surgeon had fled at the beginning of the affray, and there was no one to extract the bullets from the wounded. Several of these unfortunate creatures were brought to my house. One could only be saved by the amputation of an arm, and there was no one to afford him relief. One incident I may briefly mention. After the capture of the village, some Druzes made their way into a Christian house, and ordered a little boy, who was then alone with his mother, to sling some pitchers upon a donkey, and guide them to the fountain. The mother prayed in vain that they would not take him, as she knew that the Druzes are in the habit of killing the male Christian children in time of war. But they protested that he should return safe. On arriving at the fountain, the Druzes ordered the boy to give them the donkey, and to go back. The brave little fellow refused, saying his mother had nothing but this donkey left. Upon which one of the Druzes put a pistol to the boy's back, and shot him in cold blood. It was evening—his mother waited for him in vain. They left him under the cold open night, his wound stiffening in the mist. It was not till next day they brought him to me, with the bullet still in at his waist. I knew him well. He had been playing about my house with other children a few mornings before.

I have since heard that the Sardinian Consul was very kind in taking sufferers into his house, and relieving their wants. I did not personally know him.

But with respect to the Druzes, against whom there has been much fair, and some unfair indignation of late, let us in justice remember one thing. The Druzes, neither then, nor more recently, ever touched or insulted a woman. They never have. Their enemies confess this to be a fine trait in them. Woman has her place even in their Okkâl assemblies. A very bright spot in the character of an eastern race, is this almost solitary recognition of the social position of woman. In the triumphs of Christians—aye! even of the most civilized and enlightened—have women been thus respected by stern vindictive men flushed with victory? Doubtless we were right in insisting, conjointly with the French, that the chief actors in these cold-blooded massacres should be delivered up to take their trial—that they might never again be so deluded as to think that England's Protestant and peculiar interests would lead her to wink at their iniquity. But are the actors so much worse than the instigators? Turkey having used the Druzes to crush the Christians, would now gladly avail herself of the indignation of European Christians to aid her in humbling the Druzes. That policy of a corrupt and enfeebled state has long been hers. But the Druzes have a claim on England. They have shown unvarying gratitude for our goodness to them in saving many of their race in the time of Ibrahim Pasha. Their services in return have not been slight, and every English traveller testifies to their kindness and generous hospitality.

Whatever may be the interests of France, it would be

directly opposed to the interests of England to permit the weakening of this strong and healthy Druze nationality in Syria. Yet this is evidently what France and Turkey, for different reasons, would both view with complacency. It seems certain that a system of flagrant persecution was at one time adopted by the authorities towards the Druzes. They look to us as their protectors; but I fear that England has of late lost much of her ancient prestige in the eyes of these Eastern races. Why should these things be?

THE END.

R. CLAY, SON, AND TAYLOR, PRINTERS, LONDON.

13.4.61.
3,000 dy. 8vo.

POPULAR WORKS FOR THE YOUNG.

PRICE FIVE SHILLINGS EACH.

Tom Brown's School-Days. By AN OLD BOY.

With a new Preface. Seventh Edition. Fcap. 8vo. 5*s.*

"*Those manly, honest thoughts, expressed in plain words, will, we trust, long find an echo in thousands of English hearts.*"—QUARTERLY REVIEW.

Our Year. A Child's Book in Prose and Rhyme.

By the Author of "John Halifax." With numerous Illustrations by CLARENCE DOBELL. Royal 16mo. cloth, gilt leaves, 5*s.*

"*Just the book we could wish to see in the hands of every child . . . . written in such an easy, chatty, kindly manner.*"—ENGLISH CHURCHMAN.

Professor Kingsley's Heroes, or Greek Fairy Tales.

New Edition, with Illustrations.
Royal 16mo. cloth, gilt leaves, 5*s.*

"*A welcome and delightful volume, for the stories are prose poems both as to matter and manner.*"—ECLECTIC REVIEW.

Ruth and Her Friends. A Story for Girls.

With Frontispiece. Third Edition.
Royal 16mo. cloth, gilt leaves, 5*s.*

"*The tone is so thoroughly healthy, that we augur the happiest results from its wide diffusion.*"—THE FREEMAN.

POPULAR WORKS FOR THE YOUNG—*Continued.*

Days of Old: Stories from Old English History.

By the Author of "RUTH AND HER FRIENDS." With Frontispiece. Royal 16mo. cloth, gilt leaves, 5*s.*

"*A delightful little book, full of interest and instruction . . . fine feeling, dramatic weight, and descriptive power in the stories.*"—LITERARY GAZETTE.

Agnes Hopetoun's Schools and Holidays.

By Mrs. OLIPHANT (Author of "Margaret Maitland"). With Frontispiece. Royal 16mo. cloth, gilt leaves, 5*s.*

"*One of Mrs. Oliphant's gentle, thoughtful stories. . . . described with exquisite reality . . . teaching the young pure and good lessons.*"—JOHN BULL.

Little Estella, and other Tales.

With Frontispiece. Royal 16mo. cloth, gilt leaves, 5*s.*

"*Very pretty, pure in conception, and simply, gracefully related . . . genuine story telling.*"—DAILY NEWS.

David, King of Israel.

By JOSIAH WRIGHT, M.A. Head Master of Sutton Coldfield Grammar School. With Illustrations after SCHNORR.

Royal 16mo. cloth, gilt leaves, 5*s.*

"*An excellent book . . . well conceived, and well worked out.*"—LITERARY CHURCHMAN.

My First Journal.

By GEORGIANA M. CRAIK, Author of "Lost and Won." With Frontispiece. Royal 16mo. cloth, gilt leaves. 4*s.* 6*d.*

"*True to Nature and to a fine kind of nature . . . the style is simple and graceful . . . a work of Art, clever and healthy toned.*"—GLOBE.

THE RECOLLECTIONS OF GEOFFRY HAMLYN.

By HENRY KINGSLEY, Esq.

Second Edition. Crown 8vo. cloth, 6*s.*

"*Mr. Henry Kingsley has written a work that keeps up its interest from the first page to the last,—it is full of vigorous stirring life, and though an eager reader may be prompted to skip intervening digressions and details, hurrying on to see what comes of it all, he will, nevertheless, be pretty sure to return and read dutifully all the skipped passages after his main anxiety has been allayed. The descriptions of Australian life in the early colonial days are marked by an unmistakeable touch of reality and personal experience . . . . . Mr. Henry Kingsley has written a book which the public will be more inclined to read than to criticise, and we commend them to each other.*"—ATHENÆUM.

THE ITALIAN WAR OF 1848-9,

And the Last Italian Poet. By the late HENRY LUSHINGTON, Chief Secretary to the Government of Malta. With a Biographical Preface by G. STOVIN VENABLES.

Crown 8vo. cloth, 6*s.* 6*d.*

"*As the writer warms with his subject, he reaches a very uncommon and characteristic degree of excellence. The narrative becomes lively and graphic, and the language is full of eloquence. Perhaps the most difficult of all literary tasks —the task of giving historical unity, dignity, and interest, to events so recent as to be still encumbered with all the details with which newspapers invest them—has never been more successfully discharged. . . . Mr. Lushington, in a very short compass, shows the true nature and sequence of the event, and gives to the whole story of the struggle and defeat of Italy a degree of unity and dramatic interest which not one newspaper reader in ten thousand ever supposed it to possess.*"—SATURDAY REVIEW.

SCOURING OF THE WHITE HORSE.

By the Author of "TOM BROWN'S SCHOOL DAYS." With numerous Illustrations by RICHARD DOYLE. Eighth Thousand. Imp. 16mo. printed on toned paper, gilt leaves. 8*s.* 6*d.*

The execution is excellent. . . . Like Tom Brown's School Days, the White Horse gives the reader a feeling of gratitude and personal esteem towards the author. The author could not have a better style, nor a better temper, nor a more excellent artist than Mr. Doyle to adorn his book."—SATURDAY REVIEW.

EDITED BY W. G. CLARK, M.A.

Public Orator in the University of Cambridge.

George Brimley's Essays. With Portrait.

Second Edition. Fcap. 8vo. cloth. 5*s.*

"*One of the most delightful and precious volumes of criticism that has appeared in these days. . . . To every cultivated reader they will disclose the wonderful clearness of perception, the delicacy of feeling, the pure taste, and the remarkably firm and decisive judgment which are the characteristics of all Mr. Brimley's writings on subjects that really penetrated and fully possessed his nature.*"—NONCONFORMIST.

Cambridge Scrap-Book. Containing in a Pictorial Form a Report on the Manners, Customs, Humours, and Pastimes of the University of Cambridge. Containing nearly 300 Illustrations. Second Edition. Crown 4to. half-bound, 7*s*. 6*d*.

Volunteer's Scrap-Book. A Series of Humorous Sketches Illustrative of the Volunteer Movement. By the Author of the "CAMBRIDGE SCRAP-BOOK." Fancy boards, half-bound, 7*s*. 6*d*.

Yes and No; or Glimpses of the Great Conflict. 3 Vols. 1*l*. 11*s*. 6*d*.

"*The best work of its class we have met with for a long time.*"—PATRIOT.

"*Has the stamp of all the higher attributes of authorship.*"—MORNING ADVERTISER.

"*Of singular power.*"—BELL'S MESSENGER.

BY ALEXANDER SMITH,

Author of a "Life Drama, and other Poems."

City Poems. Fcap. 8vo. cloth, 5*s*.

"*He has attained at times to a quiet continuity of thought, and sustained strength of coherent utterance . . . he gives us many passages that sound the deeps of feeling, and leave us satisfied with their sweetness.*"—NORTH BRITISH REVIEW.

A Life Drama and other Poems. Fcap. 8vo. cloth, 2*s*. 6*d*.

BY JOHN MALCOLM LUDLOW,

Barrister-at-Law.

British India, its Races, and its History, down to the Mutinies of 1857. 2 vols. fcap. 8vo. cloth, 9*s*.

"*The best historical Indian manual existing, one that ought to be in the hands of every man who writes, speaks, or votes on the Indian question.*"—EXAMINER.

"*The best elementary work on the History of India.*"—HOMEWARD MAIL.

MR. CORNWALL SIMEON'S

Stray Notes on Fishing and Natural History. With Illustrations. 7*s*. 6*d*.

"*If this remarkably agreeable work does not rival in popularity the celebrated 'White's Selborne,' it will not be because it does not deserve it . . . the mind is almost satiated with a repletion of strange facts and good things.*"—FIELD, July 28, 1860.

Life on the Earth: Its Origin and Succession.

By JOHN PHILLIPS, M.A. LL.D. F.R.S. Professor of Geology in the University of Oxford. With Illustrations. 6*s*. 6*d*.

"*We cannot praise too highly the calm and scientific spirit by which* PROFESSOR PHILLIP'S *work is pervaded throughout.*"—LITERARY GAZETTE.

MR. WESTLAND MARSTON'S NOVEL.

"A Lady in Her Own Right." 10*s*. 6*d*.

"*A perfect masterpiece of chaste and delicate conception, couched in spirited and eloquent language, abounding in poetical fancies. . . . Seldom have we met with anything more beautiful, perfect, or fascinating than the heroine of this work.*" LEADER.

Artist and Craftsman. A Novel. 10*s*. 6*d*.

"*Its power is unquestionable, its felicity of expression great, its plot fresh, and its characters very natural. Wherever read, it will be enthusiastically admired and cherished.*"—MORNING HERALD.

Blanche Lisle, and other Poems. By CECIL HOME. 4*s*. 6*d*.

"*The writer has music and meaning in his lines and stanzas, which, in the selection of diction and gracefulness of cadence, have seldom been excelled.*"—LEADER, June 2, 1860.

"*Far above most of the fugitive poetry which it is our lot to review . . . full of a true poet's imagination.*"—JOHN BULL.

BY W. WHEWELL, D.D.

Master of Trinity College, Cambridge.

The Platonic Dialogues for English Readers.

Volume I. Second Edition, containing the SOCRATIC DIALOGUES. Fcap. 8vo. cloth, 7*s.* 6*d.*

Volume II. containing the ANTISOPHIST DIALOGUES. Fcap. 8vo. cloth, 6*s.* 6*d.*

So readable is this book that no young lady need be deterred from undertaking it: and we are much mistaken if there be not fair readers who will think, as Lady Jane Grey did, that hunting or other female sport is but a shadow compared with the pleasure there is to be found in Plato. The main questions which the Greek master and his disciples discuss are not simply for these in Moral Philosophy schools; they are questions real and practical, which concern Englishmen in public and private life, or their sisters or wives who are busy in lowly and aristocratic households."—ATHENÆUM.

THE REPUBLIC OF PLATO.

A New Translation into English. With an Analysis and Notes. By J. LL. DAVIES, M.A., and D. J. VAUGHAN, M.A., Fellows of Trinity College, Cambridge. SECOND EDITION. 8vo. cloth, 10*s.* 6*d.*

"*So eloquent and correct a version will, we trust, induce many to become students of the Republic. . . The whole book is scholarlike and able.*"—GUARDIAN.

"*Free, nervous, idiomatic English, such as will fascinate the reader.*"—NONCONFORMIST.

Memoir of George Wilson, M.D. F.R.S.E. late Regius Professor of Technology in the University of Edinburgh. By his SISTER. 8vo. cloth, with Portrait, 14*s.*

The Five Gateways of Knowledge. A Popular Work on the Five Senses. By GEORGE WILSON, M.D.

In fcap. 8vo. cloth, with gilt leaves, 2*s.* 6*d.*

PEOPLE'S EDITION, in ornamental stiff covers, 1*s.*

"*Dr. Wilson unites poetic with scientific faculty, and this union gives a charm to all he writes. In the little volume before us he has described the Five Senses in language so popular that a child may comprehend the meaning, so suggestive that philosophers will read it with pleasure.*"—LEADER.

The Progress of the Telegraph. By GEORGE WILSON, M.D. Fcap. 8vo. 1*s.*

"*Most interesting and instructive . . . at once scientific and popular, religious and technical; a worthy companion to the 'Gateways of Knowledge.'*"—LITERARY CHURCHMAN.

MEMOIR OF THE REV. GEORGE WAGNER,

Late of St. Stephen's, Brighton.

By J. N. Simpkinson, M.A., Rector of Brington, Northampton. Second Edition. Crown 8vo. cloth, 9*s*.

"*A deeply interesting picture of the life of one of a class of men who are indeed the salt of this land.*"—Morning Herald.

BY FRANCIS MORSE, M.A.

Incumbent of St. John's, Ladywood, Birmingham.

Working for God. And other Practical Sermons. Second Edition. Fcap. 8vo. 5*s*.

"*For soundness of doctrine, lucidity of style, and above all for their practical teaching, these sermons will commend themselves.*"—John Bull.

"*There is much earnest, practical teaching in this volume.*"—English Churchman.

BY THE REV. J. LLEWELYN DAVIES, M.A.

Rector of Christ Church, St. Marylebone, late Fellow of Trinity College, Cambridge.

The Work of Christ; or the World reconciled to God. Sermons Preached at Christ Church, St. Marylebone. With a Preface on the Atonement Controversy. Fcap. 8vo. cloth, 6*s*.

BY THE REV. D. J. VAUGHAN, M.A.,

Vicar of St. Martin's, Leicester, late Fellow of Trinity College, Cambridge.

Sermons on the Resurrection. With a Preface. Fcap. 8vo. cloth, price 3*s*.

BY THE REV. J. F. THRUPP, M.A.

Late Fellow of Trinity College, Cambridge.

Introduction to the Study and Use of the Psalms. Two Vols. 8vo. 21*s*.

"*What Mr. Thrupp has attempted he has for the most part done well. The plan, considering that the author appeals to the great body of English readers, is admirable. The result is a volume as interestingly readable as it is critically valuable. We commend these volumes with peculiar satisfaction and confidence to the earnest attention of all students of sacred Scripture.*"—Freeman.

THE WORKS OF

WILLIAM ARCHER BUTLER, M.A.,

Late Professor of Moral Philosophy in the University of Dublin.

FIVE VOLUMES 8vo. UNIFORMLY PRINTED AND BOUND.

"*A man of glowing genius and diversified accomplishments, whose remains fill these five brilliant volumes.*"—EDINBURGH REVIEW.

SOLD SEPARATELY AS FOLLOWS.

1. Sermons, Doctrinal and Practical. FIRST SERIES. Edited by the Very Rev. THOS. WOODWARD, M.A., Dean of Down. With a Memoir and Portrait. Fifth Edition. 8vo. cloth, 12*s.*

"*Present a richer combination of the qualities for Sermons of the first class than any we have met with in any living writer.*"—BRITISH QUARTERLY REVIEW.

2. Sermons, Doctrinal and Practical. SECOND SERIES. Edited by J. A. JEREMIE, D.D., Regius Professor of Divinity in the University of Cambridge. Third Edition. 8vo. cloth, 10*s.* 6*d.*

"*They are marked by the same originality and vigour of expression, the same richness of imagery and illustration, the same large views and catholic spirit, and the same depth and fervour of devotional feeling, which so remarkably distinguished the preceding Series, and which rendered it a most valuable accession to our theological literature.*"—From DR. JEREMIE'S PREFACE.

3. Letters on Romanism, in Reply to DR. NEWMAN'S Essay on Development. Edited by the Very Rev. THOMAS WOODWARD, M.A., Dean of Down. SECOND EDITION. Revised by the Ven. ARCHDEACON HARDWICK. 8vo. cloth, 10*s.* 6*d.*

"*Deserve to be considered the most remarkable proofs of the Author's indomitable energy and power of concentration.*"—EDINBURGH REVIEW.

4. Lectures on the History of Ancient Philosophy. Edited from the Author's MSS., with Notes, by WILLIAM HEPWORTH THOMPSON, M.A., Regius Professor of Greek in the University of Cambridge. 2 vols. 8vo., £1 5*s.*

"*Of the dialectic and physics of Plato they are the only exposition at once full, accurate, and popular, with which I am acquainted: being far more accurate than the French, and incomparably more popular than the German treatises on these departments of the Platonic philosophy.*"—From PROF. THOMPSON'S PREFACE.

THE WORKS OF

JULIUS CHARLES HARE, M.A.,

Sometime Archdeacon of Lewes, Rector of Herstmonceux, Chaplain in Ordinary to the Queen, and formerly Fellow and Tutor of Trinity College, Cambridge.

NINE VOLS. 8vo. UNIFORMLY PRINTED AND BOUND.

1. Charges to the Clergy of the Archdeaconry of Lewes. During 1840 to 1854, with Notes on the Principal Events affecting the Church during that period. And an Introduction, explanatory of his position in the Church, with reference to the Parties which divide it.
   3 vols. 8vo. cloth, £1 11*s*. 6*d*.

2. Miscellaneous Pamphlets on some of the Leading Questions agitated in the Church during the years 1845 to 1851.
   8vo. cloth, 12*s*.

3. Vindication of Luther against his recent English Assailants. Second Edition. 8vo. cloth, 7*s*.

4. The Mission of the Comforter. With Notes. Second Edition. 8vo. cloth, 12*s*.

5. The Victory of Faith. Second Edition. 8vo. cloth, 5*s*.

6. Parish Sermons. Second Series. 8vo. cloth, 12*s*.

7. Sermons preacht on Particular Occasions. 8vo. 12*s*.

The two following books are included among the collected Charges, but are published separately for purchasers of the rest.

Charges to the Clergy of the Archdeaconry of Lewes. Delivered in the years 1843, 1845, 1846. Never before published. With an Introduction, explanatory of his position in the Church, with reference to the Parties that divide it. 8vo. cloth, 6*s*. 6*d*.

The Contest with Rome. A Charge, delivered in 1851. With Notes, especially in answer to Dr. Newman on the Position of Catholics in England. Second Edition. 8vo. cloth, 10*s*. 6*d*.

THE WORKS OF

CHARLES KINGSLEY, M.A.

Chaplain in Ordinary to the Queen, Rector of Eversley, and Regius Professor of Modern History in the University of Cambridge.

1. The Limits of Exact Science as Applied to History. An Inaugural Lecture, delivered before the University of Cambridge. Crown 8vo. 2*s*.

2. Two Years Ago. Third Edition. Crown 8vo. cloth, 6*s*.

"*Genial, large hearted, humorous, with a quick eye and a keen relish alike for what is beautiful in nature and for what is genuine, strong, and earnest in man.*"—GUARDIAN.

3. "Westward Ho!" or the Voyages and Adventures of Sir Amyas Leigh, Knight, of Borrough, in the County of Devon, in the reign of Her most Glorious Majesty Queen Elizabeth. New Edition. Crown 8vo. cloth, 6*s*.

"*Almost the best historical novel to our mind of the day.*"—FRAZER'S MAGAZINE.

4. The Heroes: Greek Fairy Tales for my Children. New and Cheaper Edition, with Eight Illustrations. Royal 16mo. beautifully printed on toned paper, gilt edges, 5*s*.

"*We doubt not they will be read by many a youth with an enchained interest almost as strong as the links which bound Andromeda to her rock.*"—BRITISH QUARTERLY.

5. Glaucus; or, the Wonders of the Shore. A Companion for the Sea-side. Containing Coloured Illustrations of the Objects mentioned in the Work. Fourth Edition. Beautifully printed and bound in cloth, gilt leaves. 7*s*. 6*d*.

"*Its pages sparkle with life, they open up a thousand sources of unanticipated pleasure, and combine amusement with instruction in a very happy and unwonted degree.*"—ECLECTIC REVIEW.

6. Phaethon; or, Loose Thoughts for Loose Thinkers. Third Edition. Crown 8vo. boards, 2*s*.

7. Alexandria and Her Schools. Four Lectures delivered at the Philosophical Institution, Edinburgh. With a Preface Crown 8vo. cloth, 5*s*.

WORKS

BY C. J. VAUGHAN, D.D.

Chaplain in Ordinary to the Queen, Vicar of Doncaster, and Chancellor of York Cathedral.

1. **Notes for Lectures on Confirmation.** With Suitable Prayers. Third Edition. Fcap. 8vo. limp cloth, red leaves, 1*s.* 6*d.*

2. **St. Paul's Epistle to the Romans.** The Greek Text with English Notes. 8vo. cloth, 7*s.* 6*d.*

"*For educated young men this commentary seems to fill a gap hitherto unfilled. We find in it a careful elucidation of the meaning of phrases by parallel passages from St. Paul himself, with a nearly continuous paraphrase and explanation by which the very difficult connexion of the argument of the Epistle, with its countless digressions and ellipses and abrupt breaks, is pointedly brought out. An educated lad, who thought for himself, would learn more of the real meaning of St. Paul's words by thoroughly thinking out the suggestive exposition of them here supplied, than by any amount of study bestowed upon more elaborate and erudite works. . . As a whole, Dr. Vaughan appears to us to have given to the world a valuable book of original and careful and earnest thought bestowed on the accomplishment of a work which will be of much service, and which is much needed.*"—GUARDIAN.

3. **Memorials of Harrow Sundays.** A Selection of Sermons preached in the School Chapel. With a View of the Interior of the Chapel.
Second Edition. Crown 8vo. cloth, red leaves, 10*s.* 6*d.*

4. **Epiphany, Lent, and Easter.** A Selection of Expository Sermons. Crown 8vo. cloth, red leaves. 7*s.* 6*d.*

"*Each exposition has been prepared upon a careful revision of the whole passage . . . and the extreme reverence and care with which the author handles Holy Writ, are the highest guarantees of success. Replete with thought, scholarship, earnestness, and all the elements of usefulness.*"—LITERARY GAZETTE.

5. **Revision of the Liturgy.** Five Discourses. With an Introduction. I. Absolution. II. Regeneration. III. The Athanasian Creed. IV. Burial Service. V. Holy Orders.
Second Edition. Cr. 8vo. cloth, red leaves (1860), 117 pp. 4*s.* 6*d.*

"*The large-hearted and philosophical spirit in which Dr. Vaughan has handled the specific doctrines of controversy point him out as eminently fitted to deal with the first principles of the question.*"—JOHN BULL.

6. **Rays of Sunlight for Dark Days.** A Book of Select Readings for the Suffering. With a Preface by C. J. Vaughan, D.D. Royal 16mo. Elegantly printed with red lines, and handsomely bound, red edges, 4*s.* 6*d.*

"*Among the many books of comfort for the sorrowful and afflicted . . . scarcely has there been one that had the fitness to its end that we find in this little book. The spiritual wisdom and healthy feeling with which the contents have been selected, equally appear in their character, their suitable brevity, and their catholic union. We find thoughtfulness, tenderness, devoutness, strength in these well-chosen extracts.*"—NONCONFORMIST.

BY JOHN McLEOD CAMPBELL,

Formerly Minister of Row.

The Nature of the Atonement, and its Relation to Remission of Sins and Eternal Life.

8vo. cloth, 10*s*. 6*d*.

"*This is a remarkable book, as indicating the mode in which a devout and intellectual mind has found its way, almost unassisted, out of the extreme Lutheran and Calvinistic views of the Atonement into a healthier atmosphere of doctrine. . . . We cannot assent to all the positions laid down by this writer, but he is entitled to be spoken respectfully of, both because of his evident earnestness and reality, and the tender mode in which he deals with the opinions of others from whom he feels compelled to differ.*"—LITERARY CHURCHMAN.

BY THE RIGHT REV. G. E. LYNCH COTTON, D.D.,

Lord Bishop of Calcutta and Metropolitan of India.

Sermons and Addresses delivered in Marlborough College, during Six Years.

Crown 8vo. cloth, price 10*s*. 6*d*.

"*We can heartily recommend this volume as a most suitable present for a youth, or for family reading; wherever there are young persons, the teaching of these discourses will be admirable.*"—LITERARY CHURCHMAN.

Sermons: Chiefly connected with Public Events in 1854.

Fcap. 8vo. cloth, 3*s*.

"*A volume of which we can speak with high admiration.*"
CHRISTIAN REMEMBRANCER.

Charge delivered to the Clergy of Calcutta at his Primary Visitation in September, 1859. 8vo. 2*s*. 6*d*.

THE ORE-SEEKER.

A Tale of the Hartz Mountains. By A. S. M.

Illustrated by L. C. H. Printed on toned paper, with elaborate full-page Illustrations and Initial Letters, and bound in elegant cloth with gilt leaves, 15*s*.

This work is most elaborately illustrated, and is published as a Christmas present. The OBSERVER of Nov. 18, 1860, says of it:—

"*One of the most beautiful of the illustrated volumes published in the present season, and one pre-eminently fitted for a Christmas present. . . . Love and truth beautify the story, and render it delightful to all persons. . . . The illustrations are many of the finest specimens extant.*"

BY THE VENBLE. ARCHDEACON HARDWICK.

Christ and other Masters: A Historical Inquiry into some of the chief Parallelisms and Contrasts between Christianity and the Religious Systems of the Ancient World.

Religions of China, America, and Oceanica. In one volume.
Religions of Egypt and Medo-Persia. In one volume.

8vo. cloth, *7s. 6d.* each.

"*Never was so difficult and complicated a subject as the history of Pagan religion handled so ably, and at the same time rendered so lucid and attractive.*" —COLONIAL CHURCH CHRONICLE.

BY THOMAS RAWSON BIRKS, M.A.,

Rector of Kelshall, Examining Chaplain to the Lord Bishop of Carlisle; Author of "The Life of the Rev. E. Bickersteth."

The Difficulties of Belief, in connexion with the Creation and the Fall. Crown 8vo. cloth, *4s. 6d.*

"*A profound and masterly essay.*"—ECLECTIC.

"*His arguments are original, and carefully and logically elaborated. We may add that they are distinguished by a marked sobriety and reverence for the Word of God.*"—RECORD.

BY THE VERY REV. R. C. TRENCH, D.D.,

Dean of Westminster.

1. **Synonyms of the New Testament.**
Fourth Edition. Fcap. 8vo. cloth, *5s.*

2. **Hulsean Lectures for 1845—46.**
CONTENTS. 1.—The Fitness of Holy Scripture for unfolding the Spiritual Life of Man. 2.—Christ the Desire of all Nations; or the Unconscious Prophecies of Heathendom.
Fourth Edition. Fcap. 8vo. cloth, *5s.*

3. **Sermons Preached before the University of Cambridge.** Fcap. 8vo. cloth, *2s. 6d.*

BY DAVID MASSON, M.A.,

Professor of English Literature in University College, London.

1. Life of John Milton, narrated in connexion with the Political, Ecclesiastical, and Literary History of his Time. VOL. I. 8vo. With Portraits. 18*s.*

"*Mr. Masson's Life of Milton has many sterling merits . . . his industry is immense; his zeal unflagging; his special knowledge of Milton's life and times extraordinary . . . . with a zeal and industry which we cannot sufficiently commend, he has not only availed himself of the biographical stores collected by his predecessors, but imparted to them an aspect of novelty by his skilful re-arrangement.*"—EDINBURGH REVIEW. *April,* 1860.

2. British Novelists and their Styles: Being a Critical Sketch of the History of British Prose Fiction. Crown 8vo. cloth, 7*s.* 6*d.*

"*A work eminently calculated to win popularity, both by the soundness of its doctrine and the skill of its art.*"—THE PRESS.

3. Essays, Biographical and Critical: chiefly on English Poets. 8vo. cloth, 12*s.* 6*d.*

CONTENTS.

I. Shakespeare and Goethe.—II. Milton's Youth.—III. The Three Devils: Luther's, Milton's, and Goethe's.—IV. Dryden, and the Literature of the Restoration.—V. Dean Swift.—VI. Chatterton: a Story of the Year 1770.—VII. Wordsworth.—VIII. Scottish Influence on British Literature.—IX. Theories of Poetry.—X. Prose and Verse: De Quincey.

"*Distinguished by a remarkable power of analysis, a clear statement of the actual facts on which speculation is based, and an appropriate beauty of language. These Essays should be popular with serious men.*"—THE ATHENÆUM.

THE ILIAD OF HOMER.

TRANSLATED INTO ENGLISH VERSE.

By I. C. WRIGHT, M.A., Translator of "Dante," late Fellow of Magdalen College, Oxford. Books I.—VI. Crown 8vo. 5*s.*

"*We know of no edition of the 'sovran poet' from which an English reader can derive on the whole so complete an impression of the immortal Epos.*"—DAILY NEWS.

THE WORKS OF THE REV.

FREDERICK DENISON MAURICE, M.A.,

Incumbent of St. Peter's, Vere Street, St. Marylebone.

Lectures on the Apocalypse, or Book of the Revelation of St. John the Divine. Crown 8vo. cloth, 10*s*. 6*d*.

What is Revelation? With Letters on Mr. Mansel's Bampton Lectures. 10*s*. 6*d*.

Sequel to the Inquiry, "What is Revelation?" With Letters on Mr. Mansel's Strictures. 6*s*.

Exposition of the Holy Scriptures:
- (1.) The Patriarchs and Lawgivers. 6*s*.
- (2.) The Prophets and Kings. 10*s*. 6*d*.
- (3.) The Gospel of St. John. 10*s*. 6*d*.
- (4.) The Epistles of St. John. 7*s*. 6*d*.

Exposition of the Ordinary Services of the Prayer Book: 5*s*. 6*d*.

Ecclesiastical History. 10*s*. 6*d*.

The Doctrine of Sacrifice. 7*s*. 6*d*.

Theological Essays. Second Edition. 10*s*. 6*d*.

The Religions of the World. Third Edition. 5*s*.

Learning and Working. 5*s*.

The Indian Crisis. Five Sermons. 2*s*. 6*d*.

The Sabbath, and other Sermons. 2*s*. 6*d*.

Law on the Fable of the Bees. 4*s*. 6*d*.

The Worship of the Church. A Witness for the Redemption of the World. 1*s*.

The Name Protestant, and the English Bishopric at Jerusalem. Second Edition. 3*s*.

The Duty of a Protestant in the Oxford Election. 1847. 1*s*.

The Case of Queen's College, London. 1*s*. 6*d*.

Death and Life. In Memoriam C.B.M. 1*s*.

Administrative Reform. 3*d*

MANUALS FOR THEOLOGICAL STUDENTS,

UNIFORMLY PRINTED AND BOUND.

This Series of Theological Manuals has been published with the aim of supplying books concise, comprehensive, and accurate, convenient for the Student and yet interesting to the general reader.

I.

Introduction to the Study of the Gospels. By BROOKE FOSS WESTCOTT, M.A. formerly Fellow of Trinity College, Cambridge. Crown 8vo. cloth, 10*s*. 6*d*.

"*The worth of Mr. Westcott's volume for the spiritual interpretation of the Gospels is greater than we can readily express even by the most grateful and approving words. It presents with an unparalleled completeness—the characteristic of the book everywhere being this completeness—wholeness of view, comprehensiveness of representation, the fruits of sacred learning.*"—NONCONFORMIST.

II.

A General View of the History of the Canon of the New Testament during the FIRST FOUR CENTURIES. By BROOKE FOSS WESTCOTT, M.A.

Crown 8vo. cloth, 12*s*. 6*d*.

"*The Author is one of those who are teaching us that it is possible to rifle the storehouses of German theology, without bearing away the taint of their atmosphere: and to recognise the value of their accumulated treasures, and even track the vagaries of their theoretic ingenuity, without abandoning in the pursuit the clear sight and sound feeling of English common sense .... It is by far the best and most complete book of the kind; and we should be glad to see it well placed on the lists of our examining chaplains.*"—GUARDIAN.

"*Learned, dispassionate, discriminating, worthy of his subject, and the present state of Christian Literature in relation to it.*"—BRITISH QUARTERLY.

"*To the student in Theology it will prove an admirable Text-Book: and to all others who have any curiosity on the subject it will be satisfactory as one of the most useful and instructive pieces of history which the records of the Church supply.*"—LONDON QUARTERLY.

THEOLOGICAL MANUALS—continued.

III.

History of the Christian Church, during the Middle Ages and the Reformation (A.D. 590–1600).

By the Venerable CHARLES HARDWICK, Archdeacon of Ely.

2 vols. crown 8vo. 10*s.* 6*d.* each.

Vol. I. History of the Church to the Excommunication of Luther. With Four Maps.

Vol. II. History of the Reformation.

Each Volume may be had separately.

"*Full in references and authority, systematic and formal in division, with enough of life in the style to counteract the dryness inseparable from its brevity, and exhibiting the results rather than the principles of investigation.* MR. HARDWICK *is to be congratulated on the successful achievement of a difficult task.*" —CHRISTIAN REMEMBRANCER.

"*He has bestowed patient and extensive reading on the collection of his materials; he has selected them with judgment; and he presents them in an equable and compact style.*"—SPECTATOR.

"*To a good method and good materials* MR. HARDWICK *adds that great virtue, a perfectly transparent style. We did not expect to find great literary qualities in such a manual, but we* have *found them; we should be satisfied in this respect with conciseness and intelligibility; but while this book has both, it is also elegant, highly finished, and highly interesting.*"—NONCONFORMIST.

IV.

History of the Book of Common Prayer,

together with a Rationale of the several Offices. By FRANCIS PROCTER, M.A., Vicar of Witton, Norfolk, formerly Fellow of St. Catharine's College, Cambridge. Fourth Edition, revised and enlarged. Crown 8vo. cloth, 10*s.* 6*d.*

"MR. PROCTER'S 'History of the Book of Common Prayer' *is by far the best commentary extant . . . . . . Not only do the present illustrations embrace the whole range of original sources indicated by* MR. PALMER, *but* MR. PROCTER *compares the present Book of Common Prayer with the Scotch and American forms; and he frequently sets out in full the Sarum Offices. As a manual of extensive information, historical and ritual, imbued with sound Church principles, we are entirely satisfied with* MR. PROCTER'S *important volume.*"

CHRISTIAN REMEMBRANCER.

"*It is indeed a complete and fairly-written history of the Liturgy; and from the dispassionate way in which disputed points are touched on, will prove to many troubled consciences what ought to be known to them, viz.:—that they may, without fear of compromising the principles of evangelical truth, give their assent and consent to the contents of the Book of Common Prayer.* MR. PROCTER *has done a great service to the Church by this admirable digest.*"

CHURCH OF ENGLAND QUARTERLY.

MACMILLAN AND CO.'S

Class Books for Colleges and Schools.

I. ARITHMETIC AND ALGEBRA.

Arithmetic. For the use of Schools. By BARNARD SMITH, M.A.
New Edition (1860). 348 pp. Answers to all the Questions. Crown 8vo. *4s. 6d.*

Key to the above. Second Edition, thoroughly Revised (1860).
382 pp. Crown 8vo. *8s. 6d.*

Arithmetic and Algebra in their Principles and Applications.
With numerous Examples, systematically arranged. By BARNARD SMITH, M.A. Seventh Edition (1860), 696 pp. Crown 8vo. *10s. 6d.*

Exercises in Arithmetic. By BARNARD SMITH, M.A. Part I.
48 pp. (1860). Crown 8vo. *1s.* Part II. 56 pp. (1860). Crown 8vo. *1s.* Answers, *6d.* The Two Parts bound together *2s.*; or with Answers, *2s. 6d.*

Arithmetic in Theory and Practice. For Advanced Pupils. By
J. BROOK SMITH, M.A. Part First. 164 pp. (1860). Crown 8vo. *3s. 6d.*

A Short Manual of Arithmetic. By C. W. UNDERWOOD, M.A.
96 pp. (1860). Fcp. 8vo. *2s. 6d.*

Algebra. For the use of Colleges and Schools. By I. TODHUNTER,
M.A. Second Edition. Crown 8vo. 516 pp. (1860). *7s. 6d.*

II. TRIGONOMETRY.

Introduction to Plane Trigonometry. For the use of Schools.
By J. C. SNOWBALL, M.A. Second Edition (1847). 8vo. *5s.*

Plane Trigonometry. For Schools and Colleges. By I. TODHUNTER,
M.A. Second Edition, 279 pp. (1860). Crown 8vo. *5s.*

Spherical Trigonometry. For Colleges and Schools. By I.
TODHUNTER, M.A. 112 pp. (1859). Crown 8vo. *4s. 6d.*

Plane Trigonometry. With a numerous Collection of Examples.
By R. D. BEASLEY, M.A. 106 pp. (1858). Crown 8vo. *3s. 6d.*

Plane and Spherical Trigonometry. With the Construction and
Use of Tables of Logarithms. By J. C. SNOWBALL, M.A. Ninth Edition, 240 pp. (1857). Crown 8vo. *7s. 6d.*

III. MECHANICS AND HYDROSTATICS.

Elementary Treatise on Mechanics. With a Collection of
Examples. By S. PARKINSON, B.D. Second Edition, 345 pp. (1860). Cr. 8vo. *9s. 6d.*

Elementary Course of Mechanics and Hydrostatics. By J. C.
SNOWBALL, M.A. Fourth Edition. 110 pp. (1851). Crown 8vo. *5s.*

MECHANICS AND HYDROSTATICS—*continued.*

Elementary Hydrostatics. With numerous Examples and Solutions. By J. B. PHEAR, M.A. Second Edition. 156 pp. (1857). Crown 8vo. 5*s.* 6*d.*

Analytical Statics. With numerous Examples. By I. TODHUNTER, M.A. Second Edition. 330 pp. (1858). Crown 8vo. 10*s.* 6*d.*

Dynamics of a Particle. With numerous Examples. By P. G. TAIT, M.A. and W. J. STEELE, M.A. 304 pp. (1856). Crown 8vo. 10*s.* 6*d.*

A Treatise on Dynamics. By W. P. WILSON, M.A. 176 pp. (1850). 8vo. 9*s.* 6*d.*

Dynamics of a System of Rigid Bodies. With numerous Examples. By E. J. ROUTH, M.A. 336 pp. (1860). Crown 8vo. 10*s.* 6*d.*

IV. ASTRONOMY AND OPTICS.

Plane Astronomy. Including Explanations of Celestial Phenomena and Instruments. By A. R. GRANT, M.A. 128 pp. (1850). 8vo. 6*s.*

Elementary Treatise on the Lunar Theory. By H. GODFRAY, M.A. Second Edition. 119 pp. (1859). Crown 8vo. 5*s.* 6*d.*

A Treatise on Optics. By S. PARKINSON, B.D. 304 pp. (1859). Crown 8vo. 10*s.* 6*d.*

V. GEOMETRY AND CONIC SECTIONS.

Geometrical Treatise on Conic Sections. With a Collection of Examples. By W. H. DREW, M.A. 121 pp. (1857). 4*s.* 6*d.*

Plane Co-ordinate Geometry as applied to the Straight Line and the Conic Sections. By I. TODHUNTER, M.A. Second Edition. 316 pp. (1858). Crown 8vo. 10*s.* 6*d.*

Elementary Treatise on Conic Sections and Algebraic Geometry. By G. H. PUCKLE, M.A. Second Edition. 264 pp. (1856). Crown 8vo. 7*s.* 6*d.*

Examples of Analytical Geometry of Three Dimensions. With the Results. Collected by I. TODHUNTÈR, M.A. 76 pp. (1858). Crown 8vo. 4*s.*

VI. DIFFERENTIAL AND INTEGRAL CALCULUS.

The Differential Calculus. With numerous Examples. By I. TODHUNTER, M.A. Third Edition. 404 pp. (1860). Crown 8vo. 10*s.* 6*d.*

The Integral Calculus, and its Applications. With numerous Examples. By I. TODHUNTER, M.A. 268 pp. (1857). Crown 8vo. 10*s.* 6*d.*

A Treatise on Differential Equations. By GEORGE BOOLE, D.C.L. 486 pp. (1859). Crown 8vo. 14*s.*

A Treatise on the Calculus of Finite Differences. By GEORGE BOOLE, D.C.L. 248 pp. (1840). Crown 8vo. 10*s.* 6*d.*

VII. PROBLEMS AND EXAMPLES.

A Collection of Mathematical Problems and Examples. With Answers By H. A. Morgan, M.A. 190 pp. (1858). Crown 8vo. 6*s*. 6*d*.

Senate-House Mathematical Problems. With Solutions—

1848-51. By FERRERS and JACKSON. 8vo. 15*s*. 6*d*.
1848-51. (Riders.) By JAMESON. 8vo. 7*s*. 6*d*.
1854. By WALTON and MACKENZIE. 8vo. 10*s*. 6*d*.
1857. By CAMPION and WALTON. 8vo. 8*s*. 6*d*.
1860. By ROUTH and WATSON. Crown 8vo. 7*s*. 6*d*.

VIII. LATIN.

Help to Latin Grammar; or, the Form and Use of Words in Latin. With Progressive Exercises. By Josiah Wright. M.A. 175 pp. (1855). Crown 8vo. 4*s*. 6*d*.

The Seven Kings of Rome. A First Latin Reading Book. By Josiah Wright, M.A. Second Edition. 138 pp. (1857). Fcap. 8vo. 3*s*.

Vocabulary and Exercises on "The Seven Kings." By Josiah Wright, M.A. 94 pp. (1857). Fcap. 8vo. 2*s*. 6*d*.

A First Latin Construing Book. By E. Thring, M.A. 104 pp. (1855). Fcap. 8vo. 2*s*. 6*d*.

Rules for the Quantity of Syllables in Latin. 10 pp. (1858). Crown 8vo. 1*s*.

Theory of Conditional Sentences in Latin and Greek. By R. Horton Smith, M.A. 30 pp. (1859). 8vo. 2*s*. 6*d*.

Sallust.—Catilina and Jugurtha. With English Notes. For Schools. By Charles Merivale, B.D. Second Edition, 172 pp. (1858). Fcap. 8vo. 4*s*. 6*d*.

Catilina and Jugurtha may be had separately, price 2*s*. 6*d*. each.

Juvenal. For Schools. With English Notes and an Index. By J. E. Mayor, M.A. 464 pp. (1853). Crown 8vo. 10*s*. 6*d*.

IX. GREEK.

Hellenica; a First Greek Reading Book. Being a History of Greece, taken from Diodorus and Thucydides. By Josiah Wright, M.A. Second Edition. 150 pp. (1857). Fcap. 8vo. 3*s*. 6*d*.

Demosthenes on the Crown. With English Notes. By B. Drake, M.A. Second Edition, to which is prefixed Æschines against Ctesiphon. With English Notes. (1860). Fcap. 8vo 5*s*.

Demosthenes on the Crown. Translated by J. P. Norris, M.A. (1850). Crown 8vo. 3*s*.

GREEK—*continued.*

Thucydides. Book VI. With English Notes and an Index. By P. FROST, Jun. M.A. 110 pp. (1854). 8vo. *7s. 6d.*

Æschylus. The Eumenides. With English Notes and Translation. By B. DRAKE, M.A. 144 pp. (1853). 8vo. *7s. 6d.*

St. Paul's Epistle to the Romans: With Notes. By CHARLES JOHN VAUGHAN, D.D. 157 pp. (1859). 8vo. *7s. 6d.*

X. ENGLISH GRAMMAR.

The Child's English Grammar. By E. THRING, M.A. Demy 18mo. New Edition. (1857). *1s.*

Elements of Grammar taught in English. By E. THRING, M.A. Third Edition. 136 pp. (1860). Demy 18mo. *2s.*

Materials for a Grammar of the Modern English Language. By G. H. PARMINTER, M.A. 220 pp. (1856). Fcap. 8vo. *3s. 6d.*

XI. RELIGIOUS.

History of the Christian Church during the Middle Ages. By ARCHDEACON HARDWICK. 482 pp. (1853). With Maps. Crown 8vo. cloth. *10s. 6d.*

History of the Christian Church during the Reformation. By ARCHDEACON HARDWICK. 459 pp. (1850). Crown 8vo. cloth. *10s. 6d.*

History of the Book of Common Prayer. By FRANCIS PROCTER, M.A. 464 pp. (1860). Fourth Edition. Crown 8vo. cloth. *10s. 6d.*

History of the Canon of the New Testament during the First Four Centuries. By BROOK FOSS WESTCOTT, M.A. 594 pp. (1855). Crown 8vo. cloth. *12s. 6d.*

Introduction to the Study of the Gospels. By BROOKE FOSS WESTCOTT, M.A. (1860). Crown 8vo. cloth. *10s. 6d.*

The Church Catechism Illustrated and Explained. By ARTHUR RAMSAY, M.A. 204 pp. (1854). 18mo. cloth. *3s. 6d.*

Notes for Lectures on Confirmation: With Suitable Prayers. By C. J. VAUGHAN, D.D. Third Edition. 70 pp. (1859). Fcap. 8vo. *1s. 6d.*

Hand-Book to Butler's Analogy. By C. A. SWAINSON, M.A. 55 pp. (1856). Crown 8vo. *1s. 6d.*

History of the Christian Church during the First Three Centuries, and the Reformation in England. By WILLIAM SIMPSON, M.A. 307 pp. (1857). Fcap. 8vo. cloth. *5s.*

Analysis of Paley's Evidences of Christianity. By CHARLES H. CROSSE, M.A. 115 pp. (1855). 18mo. *3s. 6d.*

FORTHCOMING BOOKS.

I.

Life and Correspondence of M. de Tocqueville. By G. DE BEAUMONT. Translated from the Original with the Author's Sanction. Two vols. 8vo.

II.

Memoir of the Rev. John Clay, late Chaplain of Preston Gaol. With Selections from his Writings and Correspondence, and a Sketch of the Progress of Prison Discipline in England. Edited by his SON. 8vo. with Portrait.

III.

The Moor Cottage: A Tale of Home Life. Crown 8vo.

IV.

Life of Edward Forbes, THE NATURALIST. By GEORGE WILSON, M.D., late Professor of Technology in the University of Edinburgh, and ARCHIBALD GEIKIE, F.G.S., of the Geological Survey.

V.

Pictures of Old England. By DR. PAULI. Translated from the Original by E. C. OTTE.

VI.

Cicero's Second Philippic with Notes and Introduction. Translated from the German of KARL HALM. By JOHN E. B. MAYOR, M.A. Fellow and Classical Lecturer of St. John's College, Cambridge, Editor of "Juvenal," &c.

VII.

An Elementary Treatise on Quaternions. With numerous Examples. By P. G. TAIT, M.A., Professor of Natural Philosophy in the University of Edinburgh.

VIII.

A Treatise on Geometry of Three Dimensions. By PERCIVAL FROST, M.A., St. John's College, and JOSEPH WOLSTENHOLME, M.A., Christ's College, Cambridge.

IX.

A Treatise on Trilinear Co-ordinates. By N. M. FERRERS, M.A., Fellow and Mathematical Lecturer of Gonville and Caius College.

R. CLAY, SON, AND TAYLOR, PRINTERS,
BREAD STREET HILL.

www.ingramcontent.com/pod-product-compliance
Lightning Source LLC
LaVergne TN
LVHW021315110826
845150LV00003B/580

* 9 7 8 1 4 2 5 5 5 7 9 4 2 *